Canadian Securities Course
Volume 2

Prepared and published by

CSI

200 Wellington Street West, 15th Floor
Toronto, Ontario M5V 3C7

Telephone: 416.364.9130
Toll-free: 1.866.866.2601

Fax: 416.359.0486
Toll-free fax: 1.866.866.2660

www.csi.ca

Credentials that matter.

VOLUME 2

Contents

SECTION VI

PORTFOLIO ANALYSIS

SECTION VII

ANALYSIS OF MANAGED PRODUCTS

17 Fundamentals of Managed and Structured Products ....17•1

Investment Analysis

Chapter *13*

Fundamental and Technical Analysis

13

Fundamental and Technical Analysis

LEARNING OBJECTIVES

By the end of this chapter, you should be able to:

1. Compare and contrast fundamental and technical analysis, and evaluate the three market theories explaining stock market behaviour.

2. Describe how the four macroeconomic factors affect investor expectations and the price of securities.

3. Analyze how industries are classified and explain how industry classifications impact a company's stock valuation.

4. Calculate and interpret the intrinsic value of a stock using the dividend discount model (DDM).

5. Define technical analysis and describe the tools used in technical analysis.

THE ROLE OF INVESTMENT ANALYSIS

A great deal of information is available when making an investment decision. There is market and economic data, stock charts, industry and company characteristics, and a wealth of financial statistical data. The amount of this information can be overwhelming and, at the same time, can add clarity and perspective to the investment-making process.

Fortunately for investors and advisors, there are different branches of analysis which helps to organize the information. Some analysis focuses relatively narrowly on companies themselves, while some looks more broadly, using an international and market perspective. Our focus here is to gain a better understanding of how analysts use the information available to value a security and make a recommendation on its purchase or sale.

Although these fundamental and technical analysis techniques are widely used and reported in the financial press, their use and interpretation is often misunderstood. An advisor or investor considering an investment based on an analyst's interpretation of these techniques, or on their own analysis, must have a clear understanding of what the techniques measure, how they are determined, and how they are interpreted.

For example, suppose you are considering an investment in the stock of a cyclical company and there are reports that an economic slowdown is imminent. What does that mean for the industry, the economy and your investment? This chapter will give you the necessary tools to answer those questions and others.

🔑 KEY TERMS

Advance-decline line

Blue-chip

Continuation pattern

Contrarian investor

Cycle analysis

Cyclical industry

Cyclical stock

Defensive industry

Dividend Discount Model (DDM)

Economies of scale

Efficient Market Hypothesis

Elliott Wave Theory

Emerging growth industry

Fundamental analysis

Growth industry

Head-and-shoulders-formation

Industry rotation

Mature industry

Moving average

Moving Average Convergence-Divergence (MACD)

Neckline

Oscillator

Price-earnings ratio

Random Walk Theory

Rational Expectations Hypothesis

Resistance level

Return on equity (ROE)

Reversal pattern

Sentiment indicator

Speculative industry

Support level

WHAT ARE THE METHODS OF ANALYSIS?

Fundamental Analysis

Fundamental analysis involves assessing the short-, medium- and long-range prospects of different industries and companies. It involves studying capital market conditions and the outlook for the national economy and for the economies of countries with which Canada trades to shed light on securities' prices.

In fact, fundamental analysis means studying everything, other than the trading on the securities markets, which can have an affect on a security's value: macroeconomic factors, industry conditions, individual company financial conditions, and qualitative factors such as management performance.

By far the most important single factor affecting the price of a corporate security is *the actual or expected profitability of the issuer.* Are its profits sufficient to service its debt, to pay current dividends, or to pay larger dividends? Fundamental analysis pays attention to a company's:

• Debt-equity ratio, profit margins, dividend payout, earnings per share,

• Interest and asset coverage ratios,

• Sales penetration, market share, product or marketing innovation, and the quality of its management.

Technical Analysis

Technical analysis is the study of historical stock prices and stock market behaviour to identify recurring patterns in the data. Because the process requires large amounts of information, it is often ignored by fundamental analysts, who find the process too cumbersome and time-consuming, or believe that "history does not repeat itself".

Technical analysts study price movements, trading volumes, and data on the number of rising and falling stock issues over time looking for recurring patterns that will allow them to predict future stock price movements. Technical analysts believe that by studying the "price action" of the market, they will have better insights into the emotions and psychology of investors. They contend that because most investors fail to learn from their mistakes, identifiable patterns exist.

In times of uncertainty, other factors such as mass investor psychology and the influence of program trading (sophisticated computerized trading strategies) also affect market prices. This can make the technical analyst's job much more difficult. Mass investor psychology may cause investors to act irrationally. Greed can force prices to rise to a level far higher than warranted by anticipated earnings. Conversely, uncertainty can also cause investors to overreact to news and sell quickly, causing prices to drop suddenly.

> *Example:* In the 2008-2009 sub-prime crisis, extreme investor uncertainty resulted in healthy stocks with proven long-term track records collapsing along with weaker stocks, only to sharply rebound once investor confidence returned.

Program trading, as is found in the algorithmically driven type of activity normally referred to as high-frequency trading, can trigger mass selling of stocks in a way that is unrelated to the expected earnings of the stocks. The "flash crash" of May, 2010 is one example of this. The DJIA fell almost 600 points in less than 5 minutes precipitated by computerized high-frequency trading, only to rebound and erase this deficit within 20 minutes.

Complete the following Online Learning Activity

Fundamental and Technical Analysis Overview

There are different branches of analysis which can help investors organize the vast amount of information that is available when making investment decisions. Fundamental analysis and technical analysis have different ways to answer the question of how to examine the value of the stock.

 Complete the **Fundamental and Technical Analysis** overview.

Market Theories

Three theories have been developed to explain the behaviour of stock markets. Table 13.1 describes these theories and their unique assumptions and conclusions.

TABLE 13.1	STOCK MARKET THEORIES	
Theory	**Assumptions**	**Conclusions**
Efficient Market Hypothesis	Profit-seeking investors in the marketplace react quickly to the release of new information. As new information about a stock appears, investors reassess the intrinsic value of the stock and adjust their estimation of its price accordingly.	A stock's price fully reflects all available information and represents the best estimate of the stock's true value.
Random Walk Theory	New information concerning a stock is disseminated randomly over time. As a result, price changes are random and bear no relation to previous price.	Past price changes contains no useful information because any developments affecting the company have already been reflected in the current price of the stock.
Rational Expectations Hypothesis	People are rational and have access to all necessary information. People will use information intelligently in their own self-interests and will make intelligent decisions after weighing all available information.	Past mistakes can be avoided by using the information to anticipate change.

The efficient market hypothesis, the random walk theory and the rational expectations hypothesis all suggest that stock markets are efficient. This means that at any time, a stock's price is the best available estimate of its true value.

Many studies have been conducted to test these theories. Some evidence supports the theories, while other theories support market inefficiencies. For example, it seems unlikely that:

• New information is available to everyone at the same time

• All investors react immediately to all information in the same way

• All investors make accurate forecasts and correct decisions

If all investors reacted to new information in the same way and at the same time, no investor should be able to outperform others. However, there have been times when investors have been able to consistently outperform index averages like the S&P/TSX Composite Index. This evidence suggests that capital markets are not entirely efficiently priced.

For example, investors do not react in the same way to the same information. One investor may buy a security at a certain price hoping to receive income or make a capital gain. Another investor may sell the same security at the same price because that investor believes the security is overvalued. Also, not everyone can make accurate forecasts and correct valuation decisions. Finally, mass investor psychology and greed may also cause investors to act irrationally. Even when investors do act rationally, thorough stock valuation can be a complex task.

Since stock markets are often inefficient, a better understanding of how macroeconomic factors, industry factors, and company factors influence stock valuation should lead to better investment results. These three factors all help to determine changes in interest rates and in the actual or expected profitability of companies. In the following section we examine some pricing models based on these factors.

WHAT IS FUNDAMENTAL MACROECONOMIC ANALYSIS?

Many factors affect investor expectations and therefore play a part in determining the price of securities. These factors can be grouped under the following categories: fiscal policy, monetary policy, flow of funds and inflation.

Sudden unpredictable events can affect – favourably or unfavourably – the Canadian economy and the prices of Canadian securities. Such events include international crises such as war, unexpected election results, regulatory changes, technological innovation, debt defaults, and dramatic changes in the prices of important agricultural, metal and energy commodities. Many commodity price swings can be predicted by examining supply/demand conditions. Other price changes may not be easy to predict because they depend on price-setting agreements or on the action of cartels such as the Organization of the Petroleum Exporting Countries (OPEC), which sets oil prices.

The Fiscal Policy Impact

The two most important tools of fiscal policy are levels of government expenditures and taxation. They are important to market participants because they affect overall economic performance and influence the profitability of individual industries. They are usually disclosed in federal and provincial budgets.

TAX CHANGES

By changing tax levels, governments can alter the spending power of individuals and businesses. An increase in sales or personal income tax leaves individuals with less disposable income, which curtails their spending; a reduction in tax levels increases net personal income and allows them to spend more.

Corporations are similarly affected by tax changes. Higher taxes on profits, generally speaking, reduce the amount businesses can pay out in dividends or spend on expansion. On the other hand, a reduction in corporate taxes gives companies an incentive to expand.

Several factors limit the effectiveness of fiscal policy. One is the lengthy time lag required to get parliamentary approval for tax legislation. There is also a lag between the time fiscal action is taken and the time the action affects the economy.

GOVERNMENT SPENDING

Governments can affect aggregate spending in the economy by increasing or decreasing their own spending on goods, services and capital programs.

On the simplest level, an increase in government spending stimulates the economy in the short run, while a cutback in spending has the opposite effect. Conversely, tax increases lower consumer spending and business profitability, while tax cuts boost profits and common share prices and thereby spur the economy.

Some fiscal policy measures are intended to help certain sectors of the economy. For example, tax incentives have been used to stimulate the housing.

Fiscal policies can also be designed to achieve government policy goals. For example, the dividend tax credit and the exemption from tax of a portion of capital gains were designed to encourage greater share ownership of Canadian companies by Canadians.

Savings by individuals can be encouraged by measures such as Registered Retirement Savings Plans (RRSPs) and Tax Free Savings Accounts (TFSAs). Such policies increase the availability of cash for investments, thereby increasing the demand for securities.

GOVERNMENT DEBT

The main problem with a large government debt is that it restricts both fiscal and monetary policy options. Fiscal and monetary policy choices affect the general level of interest rates, the rate of economic growth and the rate of corporate profit growth, and all of them affect the valuation of stocks. With high levels of government and consumer indebtedness, the government's ability to reduce taxes or increase government spending is impaired.

The Monetary Policy Impact

It is the responsibility of the Bank of Canada to maintain the external value of the Canadian dollar and encourage real, sustainable economic growth by keeping inflation low, stable and predictable. The Bank of Canada will take corrective action if these goals are threatened, that is, it will change the rate of monetary growth and encourage interest rates to reflect the change. As we learned in Chapter 5:

- If, during a period of economic expansion, demand for credit grows and prices move upwards too quickly, the Bank of Canada will try to lessen the pressure by restraining the rate of growth of money and credit. This usually leads to higher short-term interest rates.

- On the other hand, if the economy appears to be slowing down, the Bank of Canada may pursue an easier monetary policy that increases the money supply and the availability of credit, leading to lower short-term interest rates.

Changes in monetary policy affect interest rates and corporate profits, the two most important factors affecting the prices of securities. Therefore, it is important to understand Bank of Canada policy and how successful it is in achieving its aims.

MONETARY POLICY AND THE BOND MARKET

When economic growth begins to accelerate bond yields tend to rise. If inflation begins to rise during an expansion the central bank will most often raise short-term interest rates to slow economic growth and contain inflationary pressures. This may lead to a more moderate economic growth rate or even a growth recession (a temporary slowdown in economic growth that does not lead to a full recession). If long-term rates fall while short-term rates rise, then the bond market temporarily signals its approval of the degree of economic slowing.

> **Example:** If the Federal Reserve raises short-term interest rates to slow economic growth and bond yields fall simultaneously, reflecting the perceived success of this policy, then the Federal Reserve has maintained the balance between economic growth and the needs of the bond market.

MONETARY POLICY AND THE YIELD CURVE

When long-term bond yields fall while short-term rates rise, this is called an inverting or a tilting of the yield curve. It suggests a temporary reprieve from short-term interest rate pressure and less competition for equities from the level of bond yields. The process is generally as follows:

- Rising bond yields cause a decline in bond prices. (Recall the inverse relationship between bond prices and yields.)

- As short-term interest rates rise, the rate at which bond yields increase slows down. Bond yields are still rising but at a slower pace.

- As this rise in short-term rates continues, the economy usually slows, bond prices begin to stabilize and briefly fall less than equities. This is due to the fact that a slowing of economic growth benefits bonds at the expense of stocks.

- Suddenly, with each short-term interest rate increase, long-term bond yields begin to fall. This is crucial evidence that the bond market is satisfied with the slowing of economic growth.

Strong evidence exists to show that the S&P/TSX Composite Index and S&P 500 are sensitive to the tilting of the yield curve. A decline in long-term rates reduces competition between equities and bonds.

On the other hand, higher real bond yields over time increase the degree of competition between bonds and equities and slowly undermine equity markets.

The Flow of Funds Impact

The flow of funds is important to stock valuation. When the relative valuation of stocks and bonds or stocks and T-bills changes, capital flows from one asset class to the other. These flows are determined largely by shifts in the demand for stocks and bonds on the part of Canadian retail and institutional investors and of foreign investors. These shifts are caused largely by changes in interest rate levels. However, understanding why these shifts occur can be important to determining if a rise or fall in stock market levels is sustainable.

NET PURCHASES OF CANADIAN EQUITY MUTUAL FUNDS

Net purchases of Canadian equity mutual funds influence the TSX. Since falling interest rates tend to improve the value of stocks relative to bonds, equity mutual fund purchases should rise as interest rates fall.

For the most part, this has generally proven to be true. However, between 2000 and 2002 and between 2008 and 2009, both T-bill yields and net purchases of mutual funds fell. The 2002-03 irregularity was attributed to the uncertainty caused by the prolonged bear market beginning in 2000 that drove retail investors out of the market, causing net purchases of Canadian equity mutual funds to fall despite the fall in T-bill yields. The net purchase of equity funds recovered in 2003 and was strong for a few years until turning negative again in 2008 during the most recent financial crisis.

NON-RESIDENT NET PURCHASES

Another factor that influences the direction of markets is new demand by foreign investors for Canada's stocks and bonds. Although this demand can help sustain a stock market rise or decline, it lags behind other changes. Non-resident net purchases tend to increase after a rise in the market and tend to persist even after it starts to fall.

Non-resident net purchases of stocks are largely determined by the currency trend and the market trend, which are, in turn, affected strongly by changes in interest rates and, therefore, by changes in monetary policy. However, foreign investors still tend to view a rising market and a strengthening currency as good reasons to buy that country's stocks.

The Inflation Impact

Inflation creates widespread uncertainty and lack of confidence in the future. These factors tend to result in higher interest rates, lower corporate profits, and lower price-earnings multiples. There is an inverse relationship between the rate of inflation and price-earnings multiples.

Inflation also means higher inventory and labour costs for manufacturers. These increases must be passed on to consumers in higher prices if manufacturers are to maintain their profitability. But higher costs cannot be passed on indefinitely; buyer resistance eventually develops. The resulting squeeze on corporate profits is reflected in lower common share prices.

Here is a historical look at inflation in North America over the past 60 years:

• In North America, from 1950 to 1970, the annual increase in the inflation rate, as measured by changes in the Consumer Price Index (CPI), was seldom regarded as a problem.

• The average annual increase in the two decades before the mid-1960s was less than 2.5%, with periodic fluctuations coinciding with variations in the business cycle.

• Between 1978 and 1982, inflation was higher than in any other period in history, averaging 10.3% a year.

• Inflation fell dramatically after 1982 and then again after 1992, both instances largely the result of monetary policy actions of the Bank of Canada.

• Over the last several years, inflation in Canada has remained within historically low levels.

WHAT IS FUNDAMENTAL INDUSTRY ANALYSIS?

It has often been suggested that industry and company profitability has more to do with industry structure than with the product that an industry sells. Industry structure results from the strategies that companies pursue relative to their competition. Companies pursue strategies that they feel will give them a sustainable competitive advantage and lead to long-term growth. Pricing strategies and company cost structures affect not just long-term growth, but the volatility of sales and earnings.

Therefore, industry structure affects a company's stock valuation. It is a framework that can easily be applied to virtually every industry. Many investors and IAs rely on research departments and other sources of information on industry structure.

Classifying Industries by Product or Service

Most industries are identified by the product or service they provide. For example, the S&P/TSX Composite Index classifies stocks into 10 major sectors based on the Global Industry Classification Standard (GICS). An astute investor can understand the competitive forces within an industry by classifying industries based on their prospects for growth and their degree of risk. These two factors help determine stock values.

ESTIMATING GROWTH

The initial approach is to study an industry's reported revenues and unit volume sales over the last several years, preferably over more than one business cycle. Three basic questions must be asked:

1. How does the growth in the industry's sales compare with the rate of growth in nominal Gross Domestic Product (GDP)?

2. How does the rate of change in *real* GDP compare with the industry's rate of change in unit volumes?

3. How does the industry's price index compare with the overall rate of inflation?

By extending this approach to all companies in the same industry, it is possible to assess how effectively any one company is competing. For example, is the company acquiring a growing share of a growing industry, a growing share of a stable industry, a growing share of a declining industry or a declining share of a declining industry?

Furthermore, a company's revenues result from a combination of the prices they charge and the volume of unit sales. Revenue growth may result from higher prices or increased sales volume. Is recent revenue growth improving? How stable are prices or volume? The degree of stability is important in understanding the degree of investment risk and the possible timing of the investment during a business cycle.

LAWS OF SURVIVORSHIP

In theory, all industries exhibit a life cycle characterized by emerging growth, growth, maturity and decline. However, the length of each stage varies from industry to industry and from company to company. For example, the entire railway industry life cycle from its beginnings to its present maturity or decline is more than 150 years. Some high-technology industries have gone through a complete life cycle in a few years.

Each stage in the industry life cycle affects the relationship between a firm's pricing strategies and its unit cost structure, as sales volume grows or declines. For example, the steel industry has been in operation for many years and is in the mature to declining stage of its life cycle. Growth has slowed and competition has forced prices down, to the point at which some competing steel companies have been forced out of business.

Often, as the size of a market increases, a decline in unit costs occurs due to **economies of scale**. These may result from experience gained in production or volume price discounts for raw materials used in production. A change in unit costs may affect pricing strategies aimed at gaining market share, which in turn determines profit margins, earnings and long-term growth. The lowest cost producer in an industry is best able to withstand intense price competition, either by pricing its product to maximize profits or setting prices at low levels to keep potential competitors from entering the business.

Since companies constantly strive to establish a sustainable competitive advantage, a firm usually becomes either:

- A low-cost producer capable of withstanding price competition and otherwise generating the highest possible profit margins; or

- A producer of a product that has real or perceived differences from existing products. These differences may make it possible to achieve higher profit margins while avoiding intense price competition.

Often some smaller market segments or niches are left unserviced by firms focusing on either of these strategies. These niches may be filled by smaller, specialized companies, known as niche players.

Classifying Industries by Stage of Growth

EMERGING GROWTH INDUSTRIES

New products or services are being developed at all times to meet society's needs and demands. Today, rapid innovation is particularly evident in software and hardware development in the computer industry.

Emerging growth industries may not always be directly accessible to equity investors if privately owned companies dominate the industry, or if the new product or service is only one activity of a diversified corporation.

Emerging industries usually demonstrate certain financial characteristics. For example, a new company or industry may be unprofitable at first, although future prospects may appear promising. Large start-up investments may even lead to negative cash flows. It may not be possible to predict which companies will ultimately survive in the new industry.

GROWTH INDUSTRIES

A **growth industry** is one in which sales and earnings are consistently expanding at a faster rate than most other industries. Companies in these industries are referred to as growth companies and their common shares as growth stocks. A growth company should have an above-average rate of earnings on invested capital over a period of several years. It should also be possible for the company to continue to achieve similar or better earnings on additional invested capital. The company should show increasing sales in terms of both dollars and units, coupled with a firm control of costs.

During the growth period, the companies that survive lower their prices as their cost of production declines and competition intensifies. This leads to growth in profits. Cash flow may or may not remain negative. Growth stocks typically maintain above-average growth over several years and growth is expected to continue.

Growth companies often finance much of their expansion using retained earnings. This means that they do not pay out large amounts in dividends. However, investors are willing to pay more for securities that promise growth of capital. In other words, growth securities are characterized by relatively high price-earnings ratios and low dividend yields. Growth companies also have an above average risk of a sharp price decline if the marketplace comes to believe that future growth will not meet expectations.

MATURE INDUSTRIES

Industry maturity is characterized by a dramatic slowing of growth to a rate that more closely matches the overall rate of economic growth. Both earnings and cash flow tend to be positive, but within the same industry, it is more difficult to identify differences in products between companies. Therefore, price competition increases, profit margins usually fall, and companies may expand into new businesses with better prospects for growth. Where consumer goods are concerned, product brand names, patents and copyrights become more important in reducing price competition.

Mature industries usually experience slower, more stable growth rates in sales and earnings. The reference to more stable growth does not suggest that they are immune from the effects of a recession. However, during recessions, stable growth companies usually demonstrate a decline in earnings that is less than that of the average company. Companies in the mature stage usually have sufficient financial resources to weather difficult economic conditions.

DECLINING INDUSTRIES

As industries move from the mature/stable to the declining stage, they tend to stop growing and begin to decline. **Declining industries** produce products for which demand has declined because of changes in technology, an inability to compete on price, or changes in consumer tastes. Cash flow may be large, because there is no need to invest in new plant and equipment. At the same time, profits may be low.

Classifying Industries by Competitive Forces

Michael Porter, in his book *Competitive Strategy: Techniques for Analyzing Industries and Competitors (Free Press, 1980)*, described five basic competitive forces that determine the attractiveness of an industry and the changes that can drastically alter the future growth and valuation of companies within the industry.

1. The ease of entry for new competitors to that industry: Companies choose to enter an industry depending on the amount of capital required, opportunities to achieve economies of scale, the existence of established distribution channels, regulatory factors and product differences.

2. The degree of competition between existing firms: This depends on the number of competitors, their relative strength, the rate of industry growth, and the extent to which products are unique (rather than simply ordinary commodities).

3. The potential for pressure from substitute products: Other industries may produce similar products that compete with the industry's products.

4. The extent to which buyers of the product or service can put pressure on the company to lower prices: This depends largely on buyers' sensitivity to price.

5. The extent to which suppliers of raw materials or inputs can put pressure on the company to pay more for these resources; these costs affect profit margins or product quality.

In the final analysis, companies can thrive only if they meet customers' needs. Therefore, profit margins can be large only if customers receive enough perceived value.

Classifying Industries by Stock Characteristics

Industries can be broadly classified as either **cyclical** or **defensive**. Few, if any, industries are immune from the adverse effects of an overall downturn in the business cycle, but the term *cyclical* applies to industries in which the effect on earnings is most pronounced.

CYCLICAL INDUSTRIES

Most cyclical S&P/TSX Composite Index companies are large international exporters of commodities such as lumber, base metals (such as nickel) or oil. These industries are sensitive to global economic conditions, swings in the prices of international commodities markets, and changes in the level of the Canadian dollar. When business conditions are improving, earnings tend to rise dramatically. In general, cyclical industries fall into three main groups:

- **commodity basic cyclical**, such as forest products, base metals, and chemicals
- **industrial cyclical**, such as transportation, capital goods, and basic industries (steel, building materials)
- **consumer cyclical**, such as merchandising companies and automobiles

The energy and gold industries are also cyclical, but tend to demonstrate slightly different cyclical patterns.

Most cyclical industries benefit from a declining Canadian dollar, since this makes their exportable products cheaper for international buyers. However, the rate of expansion or contraction in the U.S. business cycle is still the single greatest influence in determining the profitability of cyclical Canadian companies. The currency is an important secondary factor.

DEFENSIVE INDUSTRIES

These industries have relatively stable return on equity (ROE). Defensive industries tend to do relatively well during recessions. The term **blue-chip** denotes shares of top investment quality companies, which maintain earnings and dividends through good times and bad. This record usually reflects a dominant market position, strong internal financing and effective management.

In both the United States and Canada, some consumer stocks have generated such stable long-term growth that they are considered defensive. The utility industry would be considered an example of a defensive blue-chip industry.

Many investors consider shares of the major Canadian banks to be blue-chip industries. However, banks are also typically sensitive to interest rates. As interest rates rise, banks must raise the rate they pay on deposits to attract funds. At the same time, a large part of their revenue is derived from mortgages with fixed interest rates. The result is a profit squeeze when interest rates rise. Bank stock prices are therefore sensitive to changes in the level of interest rates and particularly the level of long bond yields. Utility industry stocks also tend to be sensitive to interest rates, because they tend to carry large amounts of debt.

SPECULATIVE INDUSTRIES

Although all investment in common shares involves some degree of risk because of ever-changing stock market values, the word *speculative* is usually applied to industries (or shares) in which the risk and uncertainty are unusually high due to a lack of definitive information.

Emerging industries are often considered speculative. The profit potential of a new product or service attracts many new companies and initial growth may be rapid. Inevitably, the industry consolidates, many of the original participants are forced out of business, and a few companies emerge as the leaders. The success of these leaders in weathering the developmental period may result from better management, financial planning, products or services, or marketing. Only an experienced analyst should try to select the companies that will emerge as dominant forces in an emerging industry.

The term speculative can also be used to describe any company, even a large one, if its shares are treated as speculative. For example, shares of growth companies can be bid up to high multiples of estimated earnings per share as investors anticipate continuing exceptional growth. If, for any reason, investors begin to doubt these expectations, the price of the stock will fall. In this case, investors are "speculating" on the likelihood of continued future growth which may, in fact, not materialize.

RETURN ON EQUITY (ROE)

To compare cyclical and defensive industries, it is important to understand the concept of **return on equity (ROE)**. This ratio is important to shareholders because it measures the profitability of the common shareholders' capital in the business.

Defensive industries tend to outperform cyclical industries during recessions. Because the ROE of a cyclical industry falls faster than the ROE of a defensive industry during recessions, cyclical stock prices also fall faster. Therefore, stocks with a stable ROE demonstrate defensive price characteristics. However, during periods of sustained economic growth, the superior growth in the ROE of cyclical industries tends to produce superior price performance in those industries. This is one of the basic factors influencing a pattern of alternating industry leadership during a business cycle. This pattern is referred to as sector rotation and the pattern is used by portfolio managers.

Complete the following Online Learning Activity

Fundamental Industry Analysis

The fundamental industry analysis involves analyzing the demand for competing products or services, the potential growth of the industry, the nature of the competitive environment and the characteristics of the stock is. How is fundamental industry analysis used to examine the value of the stock?

 Complete the **Fundamental Industry Analysis** activity.

WHAT ARE FUNDAMENTAL VALUATION MODELS?

Dividend Discount Model

The widely used **dividend discount model** (**DDM**) illustrates, in a simple way, how companies with stable growth are priced, at least in theory. The model relates a stock's current price to the present value of all expected future dividends into the indefinite future.

The dividend discount model assumes that there will be an indefinite stream of dividend payments, whose present values can be calculated. It also assumes that these dividends will grow at a constant rate (represented as g the growth rate in the formula).

The discount rate used is the market's required or expected rate of return for that type of investment. We can think of the required rate of return as the return that compensates investors for investing in that stock, given its perceived risk. The mathematical formula that represents this model is:

$$\text{Price} = \frac{Div_0\,(1+g)}{r-g} = \frac{Div_1}{r-g}$$

Where:

Price	is calculated as the current intrinsic value of the stock in question
Div_0	is the dividend paid out in the current year
Div_1	is the expected dividend paid out by the company in one year
r	is the required rate of return on the stock
g	is the assumed constant growth rate for dividends

Example: ABC Company will pay a dividend of $0.94 this year. If the company reports a constant long-term growth rate (g) of 6%, ABC will pay out an expected dividend in one year's time of $0.996 or $1.00 ($0.94 × 1.06).

It is technically incorrect to assume that r in the denominator is equal to the general level of interest rates or that g is simply equal to growth in corporate profits. However, these simplifying assumptions make it possible to illustrate how changes in interest rates and corporate profits affect stock price valuation during a business cycle. There are other, more complex formulas that accommodate changing dividends and changing growth rates.

Although the dividend discount model has many practical limitations, it is a useful way to think of stock valuation.

Example: ABC Company is expected to pay a $1 dividend next year. It has a constant long-term growth rate (g) of 6% and a required return (r) of 9%. Based on these inputs, the DDM will price ABC at a value of:

$$\text{Price} = \frac{Div_1}{r-g} = \frac{\$1}{0.09-0.06} = \$33.33$$

The DDM tells us that, based on the expected dividend, the required return and the growth rate of dividends, the stock has an intrinsic value of $33.33. We can interpret the DDM in the following way: If ABC is selling for $25 in the market, the stock is considered undervalued because it is selling below its intrinsic value. Alternatively, if ABC is selling for $40, the stock is considered overvalued because it is selling above its intrinsic value.

Using the Price-Earnings Ratio

The P/E ratio offers investors a way of comparing the prospects of a company. Generally it is assumed that when investor confidence is high, P/E ratios are also high, and when confidence is low, P/E ratios are low. However, P/E levels are strongly inversely related to the prevailing level of inflation and, therefore, to the prevailing level of interest rates.

The P/Es of individual stocks are even more variable and are affected by many factors specific to individual companies, such as comparative growth rates, earnings quality, and risk due to leverage or stock liquidity. Analysts consider individual company P/Es in relation to the relevant market index or average and compare that number with an average relative P/E over some prior time period, such as three years or five years.

Complete the following Online Learning Activity

Fundamental Valuation Models

The Dividend Discount Model (DDM) and the Price-to-Earning (P/E) ratios are two ways to value a stock.

 Complete the **Fundamental Valuation Models** activity.

WHAT IS TECHNICAL ANALYSIS?

Technical analysts view the range of data studied by fundamental analysts as too massive and unmanageable to pinpoint price movements with any real precision. Instead, they focus on the market itself, whether it is the commodity, equity, interest rate or foreign exchange market. They study, and plot on charts, the past and present movements of prices, the volume of trading, statistical indicators and, for example in the case of equity markets, the number of stocks advancing and declining. They try to identify recurrent and predictable patterns that can be used to predict future price moves.

In the course of their studies, technicians attempt to probe the psychology of investors collectively or, in other words, the "mood" of the market.

Technical analysis is the process of analyzing historical market action in an effort to determine probable future price trends. As mentioned, technical analysis can be applied to just about any market, although the focus of this section is on equity markets. Market action includes three primary sources of information – price, volume and time.

Technical analysis is based on three assumptions:

- All influences on market action are automatically accounted for or *discounted* in price activity. Technical analysts believe that all known market influences are fully reflected in market prices. They believe that there is little advantage to be gained by doing fundamental analysis. All that is required is to study the price action itself. By studying price action, the technician attempts to measure market sentiment and expectations. In effect, the technical analyst lets the market "do the talking," believing that the market will indicate the direction and the extent of its next price move.

- Prices move in trends and those trends tend to persist for relatively long periods of time. Given this assumption, the primary task of a technical analyst is to identify a trend in its early stages and carry positions in that direction until the trend reverses itself. This is not as easy as it may sound.

- The future repeats the past. Technical analysis is the process of analyzing an asset's historical prices in an effort to determine probable future prices. Technicians believe that markets essentially reflect investor psychology and that the behaviour of investors tends to repeat itself. Investors tend to fluctuate between pessimism, fear and panic on the one side, and optimism, greed and euphoria on the other side. By comparing current investor behaviour as reflected through market action with comparable historical market behaviour, the technical analyst attempts to make predictions. Even if history does not repeat itself exactly, technical analysts believe that they can learn a lot from the past.

Comparing Technical Analysis to Fundamental Analysis

In comparing technical analysis with fundamental analysis, remember that the demand and supply factors that technicians are trying to spot are the result of fundamental developments in company earnings. The main difference between technical and fundamental analysis is that the technician studies the effects of supply and demand (price and volume), while the fundamental analyst studies the causes of price movements. Where a fundamental analyst might suggest a bull market in equities will likely come to an end due to rising interest rates, a technical analyst would say that the appearance of a head-and-shoulder top formation indicates a major market top.

Studying fundamentals can give an investor a sense of the long-term price prospects for an asset. This might be the first step in investment decision-making. However, at the point of deciding when and at what level to enter or leave a market, technical analysis can serve a vital role, particularly when investing or trading investment products such as futures or options.

Commonly Used Tools in Technical Analysis

Mastering technical analysis takes years of study. It takes skill and experience to read price action and know which indicators work best in which markets. Even then, the success of most technical systems relies on expert money management rules and execution skills.

The four main methods used by a technical analyst to identify trends and possible trend turning points are chart analysis, quantitative analysis, analysis of sentiment indicators and cycle analysis. They are often used in conjunction with one another.

CHART ANALYSIS

Chart analysis is the use of graphic representations of relevant data. Charts offer a visual sense of where the market has been, which helps analysts project where it might be going. The most common type of chart is one that graphs either the hourly, daily, weekly, monthly, or even yearly high, low and close (or last trade) of a particular asset (stock, market average, commodity, etc.). This type of chart is referred to as a bar chart, and often includes the volume of trading at the bottom. Figure 13.1 is an example of a bar chart. Other price charts, not discussed here, include candlestick charts, line charts, and point and figure charts.

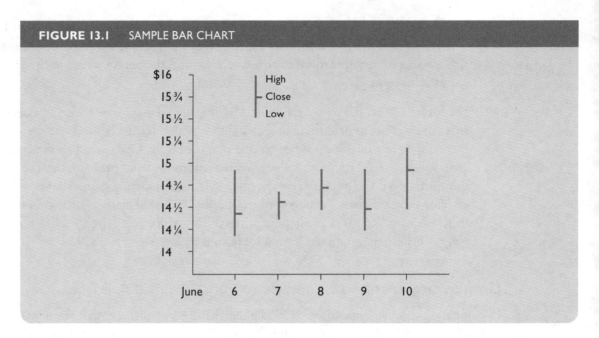

FIGURE 13.1   SAMPLE BAR CHART

Technical analysts use price charts to identify support and resistance levels and regular price patterns. Support and resistance levels are probably the most noticeable and recurring patterns on a price chart. The most common types are those that are the lows and highs of trading ranges.

- A **support level**, the low of the trading range, is the price at which the majority of investors start sensing value, and therefore are willing to buy (demand is strong), and the majority of existing holders (or potential short sellers) are not willing to sell (supply is low). As demand begins to exceed supply, prices tend to rise above support levels.

- A **resistance levels**, the high of the trading range, is the opposite. At this point, supply exceeds demand and prices tend to fall.

Chart formations reflect market participant behavioural patterns that tend to repeat themselves. They can indicate either a trend reversal (reversal pattern), or a pause in an existing trend (continuation pattern).

Reversal patterns are formations on charts that usually precede a sizeable advance or decline in stock prices. Although there are many types of reversal patterns, probably the most frequently observed pattern is the **head-and-shoulders formation**.

This formation can occur at either a market top, where it is referred to as a head-and-shoulders top formation, or at a market bottom, where it is called either an inverse head-and-shoulders or a head-and-shoulders bottom formation.

Figure 13.2 demonstrates a head-and-shoulders bottom formation.

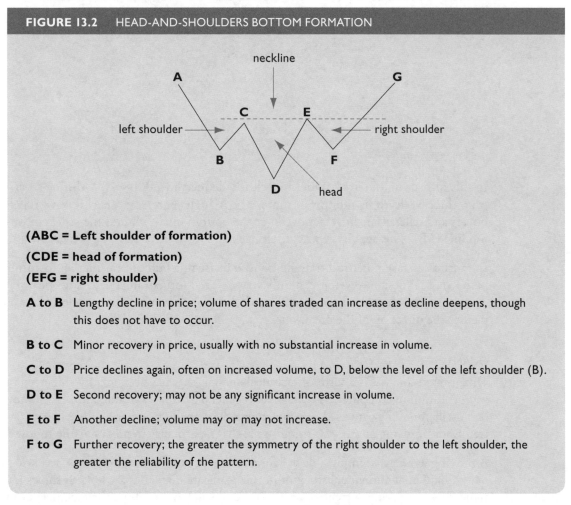

FIGURE 13.2   HEAD-AND-SHOULDERS BOTTOM FORMATION

(ABC = Left shoulder of formation)

(CDE = head of formation)

(EFG = right shoulder)

A to B   Lengthy decline in price; volume of shares traded can increase as decline deepens, though this does not have to occur.

B to C   Minor recovery in price, usually with no substantial increase in volume.

C to D   Price declines again, often on increased volume, to D, below the level of the left shoulder (B).

D to E   Second recovery; may not be any significant increase in volume.

E to F   Another decline; volume may or may not increase.

F to G   Further recovery; the greater the symmetry of the right shoulder to the left shoulder, the greater the reliability of the pattern.

Joining the two recovery points C to E (indicated by the broken line) produces the **neckline**, which can be extended out to the right of the chart pattern. The final step that confirms the reversal pattern is an advance that carries the stock above the neckline on increased volume. Then, an *upside break-out* has taken place.

Continuation patterns are pauses on price charts, typically in the form of sideways price movements, before the prevailing trend continues. These patterns are referred to as a consolidation of an existing trend. They are quite normal and healthy in a trending market.

One continuation pattern is called a symmetrical triangle, and is shown in Figure 13.3.

FIGURE 13.3   SYMMETRICAL TRIANGLE

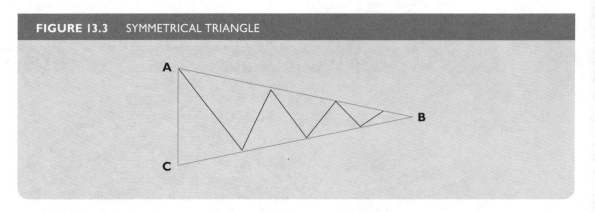

In this formation, the stock trades in a clearly defined area (CB – AB), during a period ranging from three weeks to six months or more. The triangle represents a fairly even struggle between buyers and sellers. The buyers move in at the bottom line (CB) and the sellers move out at the top line (AB). This activity repeats itself back and forth until one side proves stronger.

In most cases, a symmetrical triangle is just a pause in a bull or bear market (continuation pattern). At times, however, it can indicate a reversal formation. There is no clear method of distinguishing whether a triangle will be a continuation or a reversal, so close attention must be paid to the direction of the break-out.

QUANTITATIVE ANALYSIS

Quantitative analysis is a form of technical analysis that has been greatly enhanced by the growing sophistication of computers. There are two general categories of statistical tools: moving averages and oscillators. They are used to supplement chart analysis, either by identifying (or confirming) trends, or by giving an early warning signal that a particular trend is starting to lose momentum.

A **moving average** is simply a device for smoothing out fluctuating values (week-to-week or day-to-day) in an individual stock or in the aggregate market as a whole. It shows long-term trends. By comparing current prices with the moving average line, the technician can see whether a change is signalled.

A moving average is calculated by adding the closing prices for a stock (or market index) over a predetermined period of time and dividing the total by the time period selected (see Table 13.2).

TABLE 13.2	CALCULATION OF FIVE-WEEK MOVING AVERAGE FOR A PARTICULAR STOCK CLOSING PRICE
Week One	$17.50
Week Two	18.00
Week Three	18.75
Week Four	18.35
Week Five	19.25
Total	**91.85**
Average (divided by 5)	**$18.37**

An amount of $18.37 would be plotted on a chart at the end of Week Five. At the end of Week Six, a new five-week total would be calculated for Weeks Two to Six, dropping Week One. If Week Six's closing price was $19.50, the total would be $93.85 and the average would be $18.77, which would be plotted on the chart next to the previous week's $18.37.

Although we have shown a five-week average in the example for simplicity, a 40-week (or 200-day) moving average is a common longer-term moving average used by technical analysts.

If the overall trend has been down, the moving average line will generally be above the current individual prices, as shown in Figure 13.4.

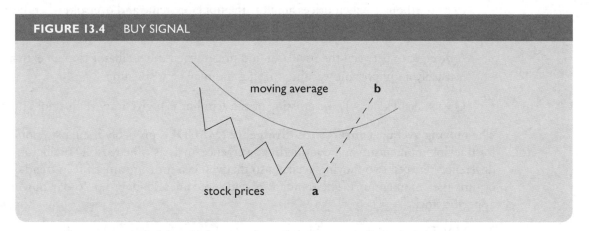

FIGURE 13.4   BUY SIGNAL

If the price breaks through the moving average line from below on heavy volume (line a–b) and the moving average line itself starts to move higher, a technician might speculate the declining trend has been reversed. In other words, it is a *buy signal*.

If the overall trend has been up, the moving average line will generally be below the current individual prices, as shown in Figure 13.5.

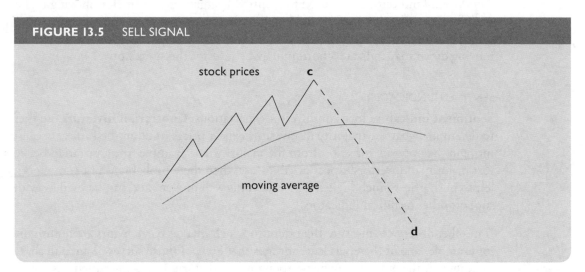

FIGURE 13.5   SELL SIGNAL

If the price breaks through the moving average line from above on heavy volume (line c–d) and the moving average line itself starts to fall, the upward trend is reversed. This is a *sell signal*.

Oscillators are indicators that are used when a stock's chart is not showing a definite trend in either direction. Oscillators are most beneficial when a stock is moving in either a horizontal or sideways trading pattern, or has not been able to establish a definite trend.

There are several different types of oscillator indicators. The readings from an oscillator will fluctuate either from 0 to 100 or -1 to +1. This indicator can be used in one of three ways:

- When the oscillator reading reaches an extreme value in either the upper (for example, closer to 100 on a scale of 0 to 100) or lower end (for example, closer to -1 on a scale of -1 to +1) of the band, this suggests that the current price move has gone too far. The market is said to be overbought when prices are near the upper extreme and oversold when near the lower extreme. This warns that the price move is overextended and vulnerable.

- A divergence between the oscillator and prices when the oscillator is in an extreme position is usually an important warning that a trend may be weakening.

- On a scale of -1 to +1, the crossing of the zero line can give important trading signals.

The **moving average convergence-divergence** (**MACD**) is probably the most popular indicator for tracking momentum and conducting divergence analysis. The MACD oscillator takes the difference between two moving averages so that you can measure any shift in trend over a period of time (i.e., momentum). The standard periods used are a 12-day and 26-day moving average of a specific stock.

The MACD is calculated by subtracting the 26-day moving average from the 12-day moving average. This creates our first line, the MACD. A 9-day moving average of the MACD is then created and this second line is called the signal line.

We have two lines: the MACD and the signal line. Signals are generated when the MACD crosses the signal line.

The MACD indicator is also used to identify divergences. If a stock is moving higher but the MACD is trending lower, this could be interpreted as a warning signal that the stock price is losing its upward momentum. Likewise, a series of higher MACD lows when the stock price is moving down may indicate a bottom may be near for the stock's price.

SENTIMENT INDICATORS

Sentiment indicators focus on investor expectations. **Contrarian investors** use these indicators to determine what the majority of investors expect prices to do in the future, because contrarians move in the opposite direction from the majority. For example, the contrarian believes that if the vast majority of investors expect prices to rise, then there probably is not enough buying power left to push prices much higher. The concept is well proven, and can be used as evidence to support other technical indicators.

A number of services measure the extent to which market participants are bullish or bearish. If, for example, one of these services indicates that 80% of those surveyed are bullish, this would indicate that the market may be overbought and that caution is warranted. As mentioned above, however, contrarian indicators should only be used as evidence to support other indicators.

CYCLE ANALYSIS

The tools described above help technical analysts forecast the market's most probable direction and the extent of the movement in that direction. **Cycle analysis** helps the analyst forecast when the market will start moving in a particular direction and when the ultimate peak or trough will be achieved.

Cycles can last for short periods of time, such as a few days, to decades. What makes cycle analysis complicated is that at any given point, a number of cycles may be operating.

There are at least four general categories of cycle lengths:

- Long-term (greater than two years)

- Seasonal (one year)

- Primary/intermediate (nine to 26 weeks)

- Trading (four weeks)

One of the better-known cycle theories is the Elliott Wave Theory.

The **Elliott Wave Theory** is a complicated theory based on rhythms found in nature. Elliott argued that there are repetitive, predictable sequences of numbers and cycles found in nature and similar predictable patterns in the movement of stock prices.

According to this theory, the stock market moves in huge waves and cycles. Superimposed on these waves are smaller waves, and superimposed on the smaller waves, even smaller waves, and so on. Elliott found that the market moves up in a series of five waves and down in a series of three waves. These larger waves may have smaller waves superimposed on them. In addition, there are various refinements. For example, when the market moves up, the third wave cannot be the shortest of waves one, three and five.

OTHER INDICATORS IN EQUITY MARKET ANALYSIS

In addition to the tools mentioned above, technical analysts look at other indicators to gauge the overall health of equity markets.

Volume changes: Although volume plays an important role in technical analysis, it is used mostly to confirm other indicators. In a bull market, volume should increase when prices rise. This tells investors that the weight of money is on the buying side of the market. When prices rise and volume does not increase, the market may be in the beginning stages of a potential bearish reversal. A bear market should see the opposite, namely, heavier volume on price declines and reduced volume on the subsequent corrective rallies.

Breadth of market: Breadth monitors the extent of the number of stocks participating in a market trend. For example, the larger the number of stocks participating in a market trend, the greater the breadth. If, in an uptrend in the stock market, breadth measurements are persistently weak, the trend has a higher probability of failing. If, in a downtrend in the stock market, breadth declines while the stock market continues to decline, it could be a significant indicator that the market is close to bottoming. There are several ways to measure breadth.

The cumulative **advance-decline line** is the most popular way of measuring breadth. It is a non price measure of the trend of the market. Starting with an arbitrary number such as 1,000, the analyst takes the difference between the number of issues advancing and the number of issues declining. If more issues advanced than declined, add this difference to the starting line. If more issues declined than advanced, subtract the difference from the starting line. Continue this procedure daily until an advancing or declining line has been plotted. Technical analysts compare advance-decline lines to the Dow Jones Industrial Average, to see if both are telling the same story.

Like the advance-decline line, the new highs and new lows indexes take into account the market as a whole and therefore measure its breadth. Daily or weekly, the number of stocks making new highs is divided by the number of issues traded to give the new highs index, and a similar calculation is done for new lows. Each index is then plotted separately.

The market is considered strong when new highs are increasing and weak when new lows are increasing. Technical analysts who use this index believe:

- The number of new lows reaches unprecedented peaks at the end of a bear market;

- The number of new highs begins to increase very early in a bull market; and

- The number of new highs begins to decline long before the advance-decline line or the Dow Jones Industrial Average reach their highest levels.

Complete the following Online Learning Activity

Technical Analysis

Technical analysts believe that all the information they need about a stock can be found in its price and volume charts. Technical analysis is the process that uses charts and other tools to identify patterns to predict price trends in the future.

 Complete the **Technical Analysis** activity.

SUMMARY

By the end of this chapter, you should be able to:

1. Compare and contrast fundamental and technical analysis, and evaluate the three market theories explaining stock market behaviour.

    -   Fundamental analysis focuses on assessing the short-, medium- and long-range prospects of different industries and companies to determine how the prices of securities will change.

    -   Technical analysis looks at historical stock prices and stock market behaviour to identify recurring and predictable price patterns that can be used to predict future price movements.

    -   The main difference between technical and fundamental analysis is that technicians study the effects of supply and demand (price and volume), while fundamental analysts study the causes of price movements.

    -   The Efficient Market Hypothesis states that at any given time a stock's price will fully reflect all available information and thus represents the best estimate of a stock's true value.

    -   The Random Walk Theory assumes that new information concerning a stock is disseminated randomly over time. Therefore, price changes are random and bear no relation to previous price changes.

    -   The Rational Expectations Hypothesis assumes that people are rational and make intelligent economic decisions after weighing all available information.

2. Describe how the four macroeconomic factors affect investor expectations and the price of securities.

    -   There are four categories of macroeconomic factors: fiscal policy, monetary policy, the flow of funds and inflation. A change in any one of these factors requires a re-thinking of current investment strategies.

3. Analyze how industries are classified and explain how industry classifications impact a company's stock valuation.

    -   Most industries are identified by the product or service they provide.

    -   Investors and advisors who understand the competitive forces in an industry can consider the prospects for growth and degree of risk, which are two factors that help determine stock values.

4.   Calculate and interpret the intrinsic value of a stock using the dividend discount model (DDM).

   •   The Dividend Discount Model is used to value a company so that a decision can be made on whether the company's stock is under- or overvalued relative to its current price.

5.   Define technical analysis and describe the tools used in technical analysis.

   •   Technical analysts study, and plot on charts, the past and present movements of security prices, the volume of trading and other statistical indicators.

   •   The analysis focuses on trying to identify recurrent and predictable patterns that can be used to predict future price movements.

   •   Three key assumptions underlie technical analysis: all market influences are automatically accounted for in price activity, prices move in trends and those trends tend to persist for relatively long periods of time, and the future repeats the past.

Online Frequently Asked Questions

CSI has answered many frequently asked questions about this Chapter. Read through online Module 13 FAQs.

Online Post-Module Assessment

Once you have completed the chapter, take the Module 13 Post-Test.

Chapter 14

Company Analysis

14

Company Analysis

CHAPTER OUTLINE

What is Company Analysis?
- Statement of Comprehensive Income Analysis
- Statement of Financial Position Analysis
- Other Features of Company Analysis

How are Financial Statements Interpreted?
- Trend Analysis
- External Comparisons

What is Financial Ratio Analysis?
- Liquidity Ratios
- Risk Analysis Ratios
- Operating Performance Ratios
- Value Ratios

How is Preferred Share Investment Quality Assessed?
- Investment Quality Assessment
- Selecting Preferreds

Summary

Appendix A – Company Financial Statements

LEARNING OBJECTIVES

By the end of this chapter, you should be able to:

1. Identify the factors involved in performing company analysis to determine whether a company represents a good investment.

2. Explain how to analyze a company's financial statements using trend analysis and external comparisons.

3. Describe the different types of liquidity ratios, risk analysis ratios, operating performance ratios and value ratios, and evaluate company performance using these ratios.

4. Evaluate the investment quality of preferred shares.

THE COMPONENTS OF COMPANY ANALYSIS

The decision to invest, or not invest, in the securities of a company is a conscious choice. In making that choice, an advisor or investor exercises independent judgment. As we learned in the previous chapter, advisors and investors generally perform some form of fundamental analysis of relevant factors in an effort to make successful, rather than unsuccessful, investment choices.

The reality of investing is that there are no guarantees; all investment has risk of one type or another. One of the goals of performing company analysis before investing in a company's securities is to help identify risks and opportunities, which can help reduce, although never eliminate, potential surprises regarding the investment decision.

Company analysis is used to look at company-specific factors that can affect investment decisions. The approach involves looking at a company and deciding: Is it a good investment? Does it fit into an investment strategy? How will changes in specific or general economic or market factors affect the company? Are there risk factors or strengths hidden in the financial statements not readily apparent after a quick review of the company? Is there more to the company than is reported in company press releases or news stories? In short, what do the financial numbers tell us about the company?

Being able to rigorously analyze the financial statements of a company is key to an advisor's or investor's ability to answer the above questions.

KEY TERMS

Asset coverage ratio

Capital structure

Cash flow

Cash flow/total debt outstanding ratio

Current ratio

Debt/equity ratio

Dividend payout ratio

Dividend yield

Earnings per common share (EPS)

Financial Ratio

Gross profit margin ratio

Interest coverage ratio

Inventory turnover ratio

Liquidity ratio

Net profit margin

Net tangible assets (NTA)

Operating performance ratio

Preferred dividend coverage ratio

Price-earnings ratio (P/E ratio)

Quick ratio

Return on common equity (ROE)

Risk analysis ratio

Trend ratio

Value ratio

Working capital

WHAT IS COMPANY ANALYSIS?

Fundamental industry analysis was the main subject of Chapter 13. The subject of this chapter is fundamental company analysis, which means looking at a company to determine whether it is a good investment. Company analysis uses the financial statements to determine the financial health and potential profitability of the company. You may want to review the accounting principles learned in Chapter 12 before proceeding through this chapter.

Statement of Comprehensive Income Analysis

The analysis of a company's profit tells the investor how well management is making use of the company's resources.

REVENUE

A company's ability to increase revenue is an important indicator of its investment quality. Clearly, revenue growth is desirable while flat or declining revenue trends are less favourable; high rates of growth are usually preferable to low or moderate rates of increase. The analyst will look for the reason for an increase, such as:

- An increase in product prices

- An increase in product volumes

- The introduction of new products

- Expansion into a new geographic market (such as the United States)

- The consolidation of a company acquired in a takeover

- The initial contribution from a new plant or diversification program

- A gain in market share at the expense of competitors

- A temporary increase in sales due to a strike at a major competitor

- Aggressive advertising and promotion

- The favourable impact of government legislation on the industry

- An upswing in the business cycle

With this knowledge, the analyst can isolate the main factors affecting revenue and evaluate developments for their positive or negative impact on future performance.

OPERATING COSTS

The next step is to look at cost of sales.

By calculating cost of sales as a percentage of revenue, it is possible to determine whether these costs are rising, stable, or falling in relation to sales. A rising trend over several years may indicate that a company is having difficulty keeping overall costs under control and is therefore losing potential profits. A falling trend suggests that a company is operating cost effectively and is likely to be more profitable.

The analyst should determine the main reasons for any changes in the gross profit margin. Although it may be difficult to identify the causes, they are important in understanding what affects the company's cost structure. For example:

- The cost at which a company obtains its raw materials has a major impact on its gross profit margin. Companies that rely on commodities such as copper or nickel, for example, may have to cope with wide swings in raw material costs from one year to another.

- The introduction of new products or services with wider profit margins can improve profitability.

DIVIDEND RECORD

The analyst will also want to look at a company's historical dividend record; for example, how much does the company generally pay out in the form of dividends to shareholders. An unusually high dividend payout rate (more than 65%, for example) may be the result of:

- Stable earnings that allow a high payout

- Declining earnings, which may indicate a future cut in the dividend

- Earnings based on resources that are being depleted, as in the case of some mining companies

Similarly, a low payout may reflect such factors as:

- Earnings reinvested back into a growth company's operations

- Growing earnings, which may indicate a future increase in the dividend

- Cyclical earnings at their peak and a company policy to maintain the same dividend in good and bad times

- A company policy of buying back shares rather than distributing earnings through higher dividend payouts

Statement of Financial Position Analysis

Fundamental analysts also pay attention to a company's overall financial position. A thorough analysis of the statement of financial position (previously the balance sheet) helps them understand other important aspects of a company's operations and can reveal factors that may affect earnings. For example, a company with low interest coverage will be limited in its dividend policy and financing options.

THE CAPITAL STRUCTURE

The analysis of a company's capital structure provides an overall picture of a company's financial soundness (that is, the amount of debt used in its operations). It may indicate the need for future financing and the type of security that might be used (such as common shares for a company with a heavy debt load). Analysts also look for:

- A large debt issue approaching maturity, which may have to be refinanced by a new securities issue or by other means

- Retractable securities, which may also have to be refinanced if investors choose to retract (a similar possibility exists for extendible bonds)

- Convertible securities, which represent a potential decrease in earnings per common share through dilution

- The presence of outstanding warrants and stock options, which represents a potential increase in common shares outstanding

THE EFFECT OF LEVERAGE

The earnings of a company are said to be *leveraged* if the capital structure contains debt and/or preferred shares. The presence of senior securities accelerates any cyclical rise or fall in earnings. The earnings of leveraged companies increase faster during an upswing in the business cycle than the earnings of companies without leverage. Conversely, the earnings of a leveraged company collapse more quickly in response to deteriorating economic conditions.

Table 14.1 illustrates the leverage effect of preferred shares on common share earnings. However, a similar effect will occur in a company that uses debt to finance its operations. In either case, a relatively small increase in revenue can produce a magnified increase in earnings per common share; the reverse is true when revenue declines. The market action of shares in leveraged companies shows considerable volatility.

TABLE 14.1	THE EFFECT OF LEVERAGE ON PER SHARE EARNINGS

Assume that two companies, A and B, each have a total capitalization of $1 million and each earned the following profit:

Year One – $ 50,000

Year Two – $100,000

Year Three – $ 25,000

Company A's capitalization consists of 100,000 common shares, no par value. Company A's common share capitalization is equal to it's total capitalization of $1 million.

Company B's capitalization consists of 50,000 5% preferred shares of $10 par value and 50,000 common shares of no par value. Company B's preferred share capitalization is $500,000 (calculated as 50,000 preferred shares multiplied by $10 par value) and Company B's common share capitalization is $500,000.

Note the effect of the variation in earnings on the earnings per common share for the two companies.

TABLE 14.1 THE EFFECT OF LEVERAGE ON PER SHARE EARNINGS – *Cont'd*			
	Year One	**Year Two**	**Year Three**
Company A (No Leverage)			
Earnings available for dividends	$ 50,000	$100,000	$25,000
Preferred dividends	Nil	Nil	Nil
Available for common	$ 50,000	$100,000	$25,000
Per common share	$ 0.50	$ 1.00	$ 0.25
% Return earned on common shares	5%	10%	2.5%
Company B (50% Leverage)			
Earnings available for dividends	$ 50,000	$100,000	$25,000
Preferred dividends	$25,000	$25,000	$25,000
Available for common	$25,000	$ 75,000	Nil
Per common share	$ 0.50	$ 1.50	Nil
% Return earned on common shares	5%	15%	0%

To calculate the % return on common shares in Year One for Company A, we divide the $50,000 available for common by the $1,000,000 common share capitalization to arrive at, in percentage terms, 5%.

To calculate the % return on common shares in Year One for Company B, we divided the $25,000 available for common by the $500,000 common share capitalization to arrive at, in percentage terms, 5%.

The stock of Company A is less risky than the stock of Company B, which must pay out interest on senior preferred capital before it can pay dividends to common shareholders. Stock A has more stable earnings, because it is less vulnerable to shrinkage in earnings, though it is also less sensitive to any increase in earnings.

Other Features of Company Analysis

Qualitative analysis: Qualitative analysis is used to assess management effectiveness and other intangibles that cannot be measured with concrete data. The quality of a company's management is unquestionably a key factor in its success. The ability to evaluate the quality of management comes from years of contact with industry and company executives, experience, judgment, and even intuition. It is not a topic that we can cover in this course.

Liquidity of common shares: Liquidity is a measure of how easy it is to sell or buy a security on a stock exchange without causing significant movement in its price. Trading should be sufficient to absorb transactions without undue distortion in the market price. Institutional investors dealing in large blocks of shares require a high degree of liquidity. Information on trading volume is readily available from most financial newspapers and stock exchange publications.

Continuous monitoring: When an investor decides to buy shares in a company, he or she should monitor the operations of the company for changes that might affect the price of the shares and the dividends that the company pays. Quarterly financial reports to shareholders are an especially important source of information and analysts scrutinize them in detail. Analysts also glean useful material from prospectuses, trade journals, and financial publications.

Complete the following Online Learning Activity

Company Analysis

Analyzing a company involves a detailed examination of financial statements to determine the company's financial health and potential profitability.

Read the company analysis overview to learn more about the key sources of information for company analysis.

 Complete the **Company Analysis** overview.

HOW ARE FINANCIAL STATEMENTS INTERPRETED?

Caution must be used when analyzing and interpreting financial statements. While there are a number of disclosure requirements and accounting rules that a company must adhere to, International Financial Reporting Standards provide flexibility. The management of the company may potentially select accounting practices that make the company look as healthy and prosperous and in as good a financial shape as possible, in order to attract investors or make management look successful.

Before delving into ratio analysis, it is also important to look over the statements in general first, and read the notes to the financial statements. There are often clues that the financial health of the company may be deteriorating, before financial ratios relay the same information.

An analyst reads the notes to the financial statements very carefully. A few of the most common warning signs are listed in Table 14.2.

TABLE 14.2	SOME WARNING SIGNS FOUND IN THE NOTES TO THE FINANCIAL STATEMENTS – *For information purposes only*

Changes in accounting practices or auditors

- Look for changes in accounting practices which increase revenue, or decrease expenses, when the actual operation of the company did not change. The company may be trying to appear more prosperous than it really is.

- Look for changes in accounting practices that decrease revenue, or increase expenses, when the actual operation of the company did not change. The company may be trying to deflate profit now, so that it appears to be growing in profitability in the next few years.

- A change in the auditors of a company may signal a fundamental disagreement between the auditors and company management concerning how certain transactions should be treated.

A series of mergers and takeovers

- Companies have been known to acquire a series of smaller companies to manipulate the consolidated statement of financial position in their favour, or to hide the unprofitability of the parent company.

Does this mean that if any of the above notes are present, the company is a bad investment? Not necessarily; the point is to be aware of these issues and research further for explanations. Companies often change accounting practices in response to new situations, changes in industry practice or directives from accounting boards.

Trend Analysis

Ratios calculated from a company's financial statements for only one year have limited value. They become meaningful, however, when compared with other ratios either *internally*, that is, with a series of similar ratios of the same company over a period, or *externally*, that is, with comparable ratios of similar companies or with industry averages.

Analysts identify trends by selecting a base date or period, treating the figure or ratio for that period as 100, and then dividing it into the comparable ratios for subsequent periods. Table 14.3 shows this calculation for a typical pulp and paper company:

TABLE 14.3	PULP AND PAPER COMPANY A – EARNINGS PER SHARE				
Year	**Year 1**	**Year 2**	**Year 3**	**Year 4**	**Year 5**
EPS	$1.18	$1.32	$1.73	$1.76	$1.99
	$\frac{1.18}{1.18}$	$\frac{1.32}{1.18}$	$\frac{1.73}{1.18}$	$\frac{1.76}{1.18}$	$\frac{1.99}{1.18}$
Trend	100	112	147	149	169

The above example uses Year 1 as the base year. The earnings per share for that year, $1.18, is treated as equivalent to 100. The **trend ratios** for subsequent years are easily calculated by dividing 1.18 into the earnings per share ratio for each subsequent year.

A similar trend line over the same period for Pulp and Paper Company B is shown in Table 14.4.

TABLE 14.4	PULP AND PAPER COMPANY B – EARNINGS PER SHARE				
Year	**Year 1**	**Year 2**	**Year 3**	**Year 4**	**Year 5**
EPS	$0.71	$0.80	$0.90	$0.84	$0.78
	$\dfrac{.71}{.71}$	$\dfrac{.80}{.71}$	$\dfrac{.90}{.71}$	$\dfrac{.84}{.71}$	$\dfrac{.78}{.71}$
Trend	100	113	127	118	110

The trend line of each of these two companies shows the characteristic fluctuations of pulp and paper company earnings. For example, adding new machinery often causes temporary over-capacity and reduces earnings until demand catches up with supply. The trend line for Company B suggests some over-capacity in recent years, as earnings show a decline.

Trend ratio calculations are useful because they clearly show changes. They are also simple to do and easier to interpret than the alternative, which is the two-step method of calculating percentage changes from year to year.

A trend line will be misleading if the base period is not truly representative. It is also impossible to apply the method if the base period figure is negative, that is, if a loss was sustained in the base year.

External Comparisons

Ratios are most useful when comparing financial results of companies in the same or similar industries (such as comparing a distiller with a brewer). Differences shown by the trend lines not only help to put the earnings per share of each company in historical perspective, but also show how each company has fared in relation to others. Different industries may have different industry standards for the same ratio. In fact, a range is often employed rather than a specific target number.

Industry standards are different from industry ratios in that the industry ratio, the average of the industry, will change each year depending on performance of the industry as a whole. Industry standards are relatively static, that is, they remain the same regardless of the performance of the industry or the economy. Standards provide a longer-term view of the industry. For example, a company being analyzed may have a ratio that is above all the others in the industry, but due to a recession, all companies within the industry may be below the industry standard. The company may be seen as a top performer; however, the industry itself is not performing. To be thorough, an analyst must compare the company to both the current average of the industry, as well as the historical industry standard.

To make it easier to follow and understand the method of calculating ratios, we have numbered the items used in the following examples to correspond to the relative items in the sample financial statements of Trans-Canada Retail Stores Ltd. These statements can be found in Appendix A.

WHAT IS FINANCIAL RATIO ANALYSIS?

Having learned what the financial statements reveal about the financial condition of a company, the next step is to put that knowledge to work by testing the investment merits of the company's bonds and stocks. The tool most commonly used to analyze financial statements is called a ratio, which shows the relationship between two numbers.

Four types of ratios are commonly used to analyze a company's financial statements:

1. **Liquidity ratios** are used to judge the company's ability to meet its short-term commitments. An example is the working capital ratio, which shows the relationship between current assets and current liabilities.

2. **Risk analysis ratios** show how well the company can deal with its debt obligations. For example, the debt/equity ratio shows the relationship between the company's borrowing and the capital invested in it by shareholders.

3. **Operating performance ratios** illustrate how well management is making use of the company's resources. For example, the net profit margin indicates how efficient the company is managed after taking both expenses and taxes into account. These ratios include profitability and efficiency measures.

4. **Value ratios** show the investor what the company's shares are worth, or the return on owning them. An example is the price-earnings ratio, which links the market price of a common share to earnings per common share, and thus allows investors to rate the shares of companies within the same industry.

Ratios must be used in context. One ratio alone does not tell an investor very much. Ratios are not proof of present or future profitability, only clues. An analyst who spots an unsatisfactory ratio may suspect unfavourable conditions. Conversely, analysts may conclude that a company is financially strong after compiling a series of ratios.

The significance of any ratio is not the same for all companies. In analyzing a manufacturing company, for example, analysts pay particular attention to the working capital ratio, which is a measure of the use of current assets. In an electric utility company, however, the working capital ratio is not as important, because electric power is not stored in inventory, but produced at the same time that it is used.

> **Study Tip:** For CSC exam 2, students will not be required to carry out calculations using the ratios presented in the following sections. However, students may be examined on interpreting ratio results, comparing the results between similar companies, and determining how a ratio could be impacted from changes in a key ratio component.

Liquidity Ratios

Liquidity ratios help investors evaluate the ability of a company to turn assets into cash to meet its short-term obligations. If a company is to remain solvent, it must be able to meet its current liabilities, and therefore it must have an adequate amount of working capital.

By subtracting total current liabilities from total current assets, we obtain the company's **working capital**, also referred to as *net current assets*.

WORKING CAPITAL RATIO OR CURRENT RATIO

The ability of a company to meet its obligations, expand its volume of business, and take advantage of financial opportunities as they arise is, to a large extent, determined by its working capital or **current ratio** position. Frequent causes of business failure are the lack of sufficient working capital and the inability to liquidate current assets readily.

The working capital for Trans-Canada Retail would be calculated as follows:

Current Assets (item 9)	$12,238,000
Less: Current Liabilities (item 22)	$4,313,000
Equals: Working Capital	$7,925,000

This relationship is often expressed in terms of a ratio. In this example, the working capital ratio would be expressed as:

$$\frac{\text{Current assets}}{\text{Current liabilities}} \text{ or } \frac{\text{Item 9}}{\text{Item 22}} = \frac{\$12,238,000}{\$4,313,000} = 2.84 : 1$$

Current assets are cash and other company possessions that can be readily turned into cash (and normally would be) within one year. Current liabilities are liabilities of the company that must be paid within the year. Trans-Canada Retail Stores Ltd. has $2.84 of cash and equivalents to pay for every $1 of its current liabilities.

The interpretation of the ratio depends on the type of business, the composition of current assets, inventory turnover rate, and credit terms. A current ratio of 2:1 is good but not exceptional, because it means the company has $2 cash and equivalents to pay for each $1 of its debt. However, if 50% of Company A's current assets were cash, whereas 90% of Company B's current assets were in inventory, but each had a current ratio of 2:1, Company A would be more liquid than B because it could pay its current debts more easily and quickly.

Also, if a current ratio of 2:1 is good, is 20:1 ten times as good? No. If a company's current ratio exceeds 5:1 and it consistently maintains such a high level, the company may have an unnecessary accumulation of funds which could indicate sales problems (too much inventory) or financial mismanagement.

Different businesses have different working capital requirements. In some businesses (such as distilleries), several years may elapse before the raw materials are processed and sold as finished products. Consequently, these businesses require a large amount of working capital to finance operations until they receive cash from the sale of finished products. In others (such as meat packers), the manufacturing process is much shorter. Cash from sales is received more quickly and is available to pay current debts. Such businesses can safely operate with less working capital.

QUICK RATIO (THE ACID TEST)

The second of the two most common corporate liquidity ratios, the **quick ratio**, is a more stringent test than the current ratio. In this calculation, inventories, which are generally not considered liquid assets, are subtracted from current assets. The quick ratio shows how well current liabilities are covered by cash and by items with a ready cash value.

$$\frac{\text{Current assets} - \text{Inventories}}{\text{Current liabilities}}$$

$$\frac{\text{Item 9} - \text{Item 5}}{\text{Item 22}} \text{ or } \frac{\$12,238,000 - \$9,035,000}{\$4,313,000} \text{ or } \frac{\$3,203,000}{\$4,313,000} = 0.74:1$$

Current assets include inventories that, at times, may be difficult to convert into cash. Therefore, the quick ratio offers a more conservative test of a company's ability to meet its current obligations. Quick assets are current assets less inventories. In this example, the ratio is 0.74 to 1, which means there are 74 cents of current assets, exclusive of inventories, to meet each $1 of current liabilities.

There is no absolute standard for this ratio, but if it is 1:1 or better, it suggests a good liquid position. However, companies with a quick ratio of less than 1 to 1 may be equally good if they have a high rate of inventory turnover, because inventory that is turned over quickly is the equivalent of cash. In our example, however, a quick ratio of 0.74:1 is probably satisfactory, since the company we are looking at is a retail store chain, an industry characterized by large inventories and a high turnover rate.

Risk Analysis Ratios

The analysis of a company's capital structure enables investors to judge how well the company can meet its financial obligations. Excessive borrowing increases the company's costs, because it must service its debt by paying interest on outstanding bank loans, notes payable, bonds or debentures.

If a company cannot generate enough cash to pay the interest on its outstanding debt, then its creditors could force it into bankruptcy. If the company must sell off its assets to meet its obligations, then investors who have purchased bonds, debentures, or stock in the company could lose some or all of their investment.

ASSET COVERAGE

This ratio shows a company's ability to cover its debt obligations with its assets after all non-debt liabilities have been satisfied. The ratio shows the **net tangible assets** of the company for each $1,000 of total debt outstanding. It enables the debtholder to measure the protection provided by the company's tangible assets (that is, assets other than goodwill and other intangibles assets) after all liabilities have been met.

Asset values are usually calculated over a number of years to identify a trend.

$$\frac{\text{Total assets} - \text{goodwill} - [\text{Current liabilities} - \text{short-term debt such as current portion of long-term debt and short-term borrowings}]}{\text{Total debt outstanding (i.e., short-term debt} + \text{long-term debt)} \div \$1,000}$$

$$\frac{\text{Item } 10 - \text{Item } 2 - [\text{Item } 22 - (\text{Item } 18 + \text{Item } 21)]}{(\text{Item } 18 + \text{Item } 21 + \text{Item } 15) \div \$1,000}$$

$$or \quad \frac{\$19,454,000 - \$150,000 - [\$4,313,000 - (\$120,000 + \$1,630,000)]}{(\$120,000 + \$1,630,000 + \$1,350,000) \div \$1,000}$$

$$= \quad \frac{\$16,741,000}{\$3,100} = \$5,400 \text{ per } \$1,000 \text{ total debt outstanding}$$

Debtholders need to know the asset value behind each $1,000 of total debt outstanding. Normally, debtholders have a claim against all the company's assets after providing for liability items, which rank ahead of their claims. To be conservative, goodwill and other intangible assets are first deducted from the total asset figure.

In our example, there is $5,400 of assets backing each $1,000 of total debt outstanding after providing for current liabilities, other than short-term borrowings and the current portion of long-term debt, both of which are included in total debt outstanding. For example, if the industry standard for this ratio is that retail companies should have at least $2,000 of net tangible assets for each $1,000 of total debt outstanding, Trans-Canada Retail Stores Ltd. meets, and in fact, exceeds this standard.

Industry standards for this ratio vary due, in part, to the stability of income provided by the company. Utilities, for example, have a fairly stable source of income. They are characterized by heavy investment in permanent property, which accounts for a large part of their total assets. They are also subject to regulation, which ensures the utility a fair return on its investment. Consequently, there is a greater degree of earnings' stability and continuity than for retail stores.

Trans-Canada Retail Stores Ltd. has only one issue of long-term debt outstanding (item 15). The calculation of net tangible assets (NTA) for each $1,000 of total debt outstanding is, accordingly, relatively straightforward. If more than one issue were outstanding, the NTA coverage calculation would include that debt figure as well, but of course the senior issue would be better covered than a junior issue, because of the senior issue's higher priority in interest and liquidation proceeds.

DEBT/EQUITY RATIO

The **debt/equity ratio** shows the proportion of borrowed funds used relative to the investments made by shareholders in the company. If the ratio is too high, it may indicate that a company has borrowed excessively, and this increases the financial risk of the company. If the debt burden is too large, it reduces the margin of safety protecting the debtholder's capital, increases the company's fixed charges, reduces earnings available for dividends, and in times of recession or high interest rates, could cause a financial crisis for the company.

$$\frac{\text{Total debt outstanding (i.e., short- and long-term)}}{\text{Equity}}$$

$$\frac{\text{Item } 21 + \text{Item } 18 + \text{Item } 15}{\text{Item } 14}$$

$$or \quad \frac{\$1,630,000 + \$120,000 + \$1,350,000}{\$13,306,000}$$

$$= \frac{\$3,100,000}{\$13,306,000} \times 100 = 23.30\% \ (0.23:1)$$

Thus, the debt/equity ratio for Trans-Canada Retail Stores Ltd. is 23.30% or 0.23:1, which is acceptable if it does not exceed the industry standard for retail stores.

Sometimes, analysts will make adjustments to this ratio by including total liabilities to the calculation. We have excluded other liabilities from the calculation to focus the ratio on a company's financial risk or leverage through the use of debt.

CASH FLOW/TOTAL DEBT OUTSTANDING

Cash flow from operating activities is a measure of a company's ability to generate funds internally. Other things being equal, a company with a large and increasing cash flow is better able to finance expansion using its own funds, without the need to issue new securities. The increased interest or dividend costs of new securities issues may reduce cash flow and earnings, while issuing convertibles and warrants may dilute the value of common stock.

The **cash flow/total debt outstanding ratio** gauges a company's ability to repay the funds it has borrowed. Short-term borrowings must normally be repaid or rolled over within a year. Corporate debt issues commonly have sinking funds requiring annual cash outlays. A company's cash flow from operating activities should therefore be adequate to meet these commitments.

Before calculating this ratio, it is important to recall, from CSC Volume 1, the concept of cash flow from operating activities and consider its significance.

Cash flow from operations is:

- A company's profit

- *Plus* all deductions not requiring a cash outlay, such as amortization.

- *Minus* all additions not received in cash, such as share of profit of associates

- *Plus* the change in net working capital

Because of the substantial size of non-cash items on a statement of comprehensive income (items which do not involve an actual outlay or receipt of funds), cash flow from operating activities frequently provides a broader picture of a company's earning power than profit alone. Consequently, cash flow from operating activities is considered by some analysts a better indicator of the ability to pay dividends and finance expansion. It is particularly useful in comparing companies within the same industry. It can reveal whether a company, even one that shows little or no profit after depreciation can meet its debts.

Proper use of cash flow means considering it in relation to a company's total financial requirements. In financial statements, the cash flow statement puts cash flow from operating activities into perspective as a source of funds available to meet financial requirements.

A relatively high ratio of cash flow to total debt outstanding is considered positive. Conversely, a low ratio is negative. Analysts use minimum standards to assess debt repayment capacity and provide another perspective on debt evaluation. For example, the industry standard for cash flow/total debt outstanding for retail stores might be that annual cash flow in each of the last fiscal five years should be at least 20% (0.20:1) of total debt outstanding.

$$\frac{\text{Cash flow from operating activities}}{\text{Total debt outstanding (i.e., short- and long-term)}} \times 100$$

$$\frac{\text{Item } 34 + \text{Item } 36 - \text{Item } 32 + \text{Item } 37}{\text{Item } 21 + \text{Item } 18 + \text{Item } 15} \times 100$$

$$or \quad \frac{\$1,298,000}{\$3,100,000} \times 100 = 41.87\% \ (0.42:1)$$

The preceding calculation shows that the cash flow/total debt outstanding ratio for Trans-Canada Retail Stores Ltd. is 0.42:1, which is acceptable, since it exceeds the 0.20:1 industry standard.

Analysts usually calculate the cash flow to total debt outstanding ratio for each of the last five fiscal years. An improving trend is desirable. A declining trend may indicate weakening financial strength, unless the individual ratios for each year are well above the minimum standards. For example, if the latest year's ratio was 0.61 (Year 5) and preceding years' ratios were 0.60 (Year 4), 0.63 (Year 3), 0.65 (Year 2), and 0.70 (Year 1), there would seem to be no cause for concern, because each year's ratio is so strong.

INTEREST COVERAGE

The **interest coverage ratio** reveals the ability of a company to pay the interest charges on its debt and indicates how well these charges are covered, based upon profit available to pay them. Interest coverage indicates a margin of safety, since a company's inability to meet its interest charges could result in bankruptcy.

It is essential to take into account *all* interest charges. Default on any one debt may impair the issuer's ability to meet its obligations to the others, and lead to default on other debts.

Interest coverage is generally considered to be the most important quantitative test of risk when considering a debt security. A level of profit well in excess of interest requirements is deemed necessary as a form of protection for possible adverse conditions in future years. Overall, the greater the coverage, the greater the margin of safety.

To assess the adequacy of the coverage, it is common to set criteria. For example, an analyst may decide that an industrial company's annual interest requirements in each of the last five years should be covered at least three times by profit available for interest payment in each year. At this level, the analyst would consider its debt securities to be of acceptable investment quality.

A company may fail to meet these coverage standards without ever experiencing difficulties in fulfilling its debt obligations. However, the securities of such a company are considered a much higher risk, because they lack an acceptable margin of safety. Thus, the interest coverage standards are only an indication of the *likelihood* that a company will be able to meet its interest obligations.

It is also important to study the year-to-year trend in the interest coverage calculation. Ideally, a company should not only meet the industry standards for coverage in each of the last five or more years but increase its coverage. A stable trend, which means that the company is meeting the minimum standards but not improving the ratio over the period, is also considered acceptable. However, a deteriorating trend suggests that further analysis is required to determine whether the company's financial position has seriously weakened.

Aberrations in the trend may occur, for example, as the result of a prolonged strike, which may cause earnings to drop within a single year, but which will probably not impair the company's basic financial soundness in succeeding years.

However, a steep decline in earnings, particularly if it is prolonged or caused by a fundamental deterioration in the company's financial position, should prompt a revaluation of the investment quality of a debt issue. A sudden reversal from a profit to a loss also merits close scrutiny. Other changes, such as a rapid build-up in short-term borrowings, could also reduce the investment quality of a company's debt securities. Thus, analysts must monitor companies to ensure that developments do not adversely affect its ability to fulfill its debt obligations.

$$\frac{\text{Profit before interest charges and taxes}}{\text{Interest charges}}$$

$$\frac{\text{Item } 34 + \text{Item } 31 + \text{Item } 33 - \text{Item } 32}{\text{Item } 31}$$

$$or \quad \frac{\$1,208,000 + \$289,000 + \$880,000 - \$5,000}{\$289,000}$$

$$= \quad \frac{\$2,372,000}{\$289,000} = 8.21 \text{ times}$$

The calculation shows that Trans-Canada Retail Stores Ltd.'s interest charges for the year were covered 8.21 times by profit available to pay them. Stated in another way, it had $8.21 of profit out of which to pay every $1.00 of interest.

Again, industry standards will vary from industry to industry. Standards vary, not only for companies in different industries, but also for companies in the same industry, depending upon their past earnings records and future prospects. The record of a company's interest coverage is particularly important, because a company must meet its fixed charges both in good times and bad. Unless it has already demonstrated its ability to do so, it cannot be said to have met the test.

In general, the lower the ratio the more a company is burdened by interest charges to cover its debt. For example, a ratio below one indicates a company's inability to generate enough revenue to cover its interest charges.

A high interest coverage ratio is not required for utility companies. They have a licence to operate in specific areas with little or no competition, and rate boards establish rates that enable them to earn a fair return on their capital investment. By contrast, the profit of retail companies are likely to be more volatile, so a higher coverage ratio is necessary to provide a greater margin of safety. In addition to meeting the minimum standards for each of the last five fiscal years, companies should show a steady or rising trend in their year-to-year profit available for interest charges and in their year-to-year interest coverage figures over the same period. A weakening or declining pattern is usually a danger signal.

Operating Performance Ratios

The analysis of a company's profitability and efficiency tells the investor how well management is making use of the company's resources.

GROSS PROFIT MARGIN

The **gross profit margin ratio** is useful both for calculating internal trend lines and for making comparisons with other companies, especially in industries such as food products and cosmetics, where turnover is high and competition is stiff. The gross margin is an indication of the efficiency of management in turning over the company's goods at a profit. It shows the company's rate of profit after allowing for the cost of sales.

$$\frac{\text{Revenue} - \text{Cost of sales}}{\text{Revenue}} \times 100$$

$$\frac{\text{Item 24} - \text{Item 25}}{\text{Item 24}} \times 100$$

$$or \quad \frac{\$43,800,000 - \$28,250,000}{\$43,800,000} \times 100$$

$$= \frac{\$15,550,000}{\$43,800,000} \times 100 = 35.50\%$$

NET PROFIT MARGIN

Net profit margin is an important indicator of how efficiently the company is managed after taking both expenses and taxes into account. Because this ratio is the result of the company's operations for the period, it effectively sums up management's ability to run the business in a single figure.

$$\frac{\text{Profit} - \text{share of profit of associates}}{\text{Revenue}} \times 100$$

$$\frac{\text{Item 34} - \text{Item 32}}{\text{Item 24}} \times 100$$

$$or \quad \frac{\$1,208,000 - \$5,000}{\$43,800,000} \times 100$$

$$= \frac{\$1,203,000}{\$43,800,000} \times 100 = 2.75\%$$

To make comparisons between companies or from one year to another, the profit must be shown before share of profit of associates is added in, since not all companies have this item.

NET (OR AFTER-TAX) RETURN ON COMMON EQUITY

The **return on common equity** (**ROE**) ratio shows the dollar amount of earnings that were produced for each dollar invested by the company's common shareholders. The trend in the ROE indicates management's effectiveness in maintaining or increasing profitability in relation to the common equity capital of the company. A declining trend suggests that operating efficiency is waning, although further quantitative analysis is needed to pinpoint the causes. For shareholders, a declining ratio shows that their investment is being employed less productively. This ratio is very important for common shareholders, since it reflects the profitability of their capital in the business.

$$\frac{\text{Profit}}{\text{Total Equity}} \times 100$$

$$\frac{\text{Item 34}}{\text{Item 14}} \times 100$$

$$\text{or} \quad \frac{\$1,208,000}{\$13,306,000} \times 100$$

$$= \quad 9.08\%$$

INVENTORY TURNOVER RATIO

The **inventory turnover ratio** measures the number of times a company's inventory is turned over in a year. It may also be expressed as a number of days required to achieve turnover, as shown in the example below. A high turnover ratio is considered good. A company with a high turnover requires a smaller investment in inventory than one producing the same revenue with a low turnover.

$$\frac{\text{Cost of sales}}{\text{Inventory}}$$

$$\frac{\text{Item 25}}{\text{Item 5}}$$

$$\text{or} \quad \frac{\$28,250,000}{\$9,035,000} = 3.13 \text{ times}$$

To calculate inventory turnover in days, divide 365 (days) by the inventory turnover ratio:

$$\frac{365}{3.13} = 116.61 \text{ days}$$

This ratio indicates the management's efficiency in turning over the company's inventory and can be used to compare one company with others in the same field. It also provides an indication of the adequacy of a company's inventory for the volume of business being handled.

Inventory turnover rates vary from industry to industry. For example, companies in the food industry turn over their inventory more rapidly than companies engaged in heavy manufacturing, because a longer period of time is required to process, manufacture, and sell finished products.

Examples of high-turnover industries: baking, cosmetics, dairy products, food chains, meat packing, industries dealing in perishable goods, quick-consumption low-cost item industries.

Examples of low-turnover industries: aircraft manufacturers, distillers, fur goods, heavy machinery manufacturers, steel, and wineries.

If a company has an inventory turnover rate that is above average for its industry, it generally indicates a better balance between inventory and sales volume. The company is unlikely to be caught with too much inventory if the price of raw materials drops or the market demand for its products falls. There should also be less wastage, because materials and products are not standing unused for long periods and deteriorating in quality and/or marketability. On the other hand, if inventory turnover is too high in relation to industry norms, the company may have problems with shortages of inventory, resulting in lost sales.

If a company has a low rate of inventory turnover, it may be because:

- The inventory contains an unusually large portion of unsaleable goods;

- The company has over-bought inventory; or

- The value of the inventory has been overstated.

Since a large part of a company's working capital is usually tied up in inventory, the way in which the inventory position is managed directly affects the company's earnings and the rate of return earned on the company's common equity.

Value Ratios

Ratios in this group – sometimes called market ratios – measure the way the stock market rates a company by comparing the market price of its shares to information in its financial statements. Price alone does not tell analysts much about a company unless there is a common way to relate the price to dividends and earnings. Value ratios do this.

PERCENTAGE DIVIDEND PAYOUT RATIOS

Dividend payout ratios indicate the amount or percentage of the company's profit that is paid out to shareholders in the form of dividends.

$$\frac{\text{Common share dividends}}{\text{Profit}} \times 100$$

$$\frac{\$387,500}{\$1,208,000} \times 100 = 32.08\%$$

Deducting the percentage of earnings being paid out as dividends from 100 gives the percentage of earnings remaining in the business to finance future operations. In our example, 32.08% of available earnings were paid out as dividends in the year, therefore 67.92% was reinvested in the business.

Dividend payout ratios are generally unstable since they are tied directly to the earnings of the company, which change from year to year. The directors of some companies try to maintain a steady dividend rate through good and poor times to preserve the credit rating and investment standing of the company's securities. If dividends are greater than earnings for the year, the payout ratio will exceed 100%. Dividends will then be taken out of retained earnings, a situation that erodes the value of the shareholders' equity.

EARNINGS PER COMMON SHARE

The **earnings per common share** (**EPS**) ratio shows the earnings available to each common share and is an important element in judging an appropriate market price for buying or selling common stock. A rising trend in EPS has favourable implications for the price of a stock.

In practice, a common stock's market price reflects the anticipated trend in EPS for the next 12 to 24 months, rather than the current EPS. Thus, it is common practice to estimate EPS for the next year or two. Accurate estimates for longer periods are difficult because of the many variables involved.

Along with dividend per share, this is one of the most widely used and well understood of all ratios. It is easy to calculate and is commonly reported in the financial press.

From the notes to the financial statements for Trans-Canada Retail Stores, the weighted-average number of common shares outstanding is 387,500.

$$\frac{\text{Profit}}{\text{Weighted-average number of common shares outstanding}}$$

$$\frac{\text{Item 34}}{\text{Weighted-average number of common shares outstanding}}$$

$$\frac{\$1,208,000}{387,500} = \$3.12 \text{ per share}$$

Because of the importance of EPS, analysts pay close attention to possible dilution of the stock's value caused by the conversion of outstanding convertible securities, the exercise of warrants, shares issued under employee stock options, and other changes.

Fully diluted earnings per share can be calculated on common stock outstanding plus common stock equivalents such as convertible preferred stock, convertible debentures, stock options (under employee stock-option plans), and warrants. This figure shows the dilution in earnings per share that would occur if all equivalent securities were converted into common shares. Since Trans-Canada Retail Stores Ltd. has no convertible securities, let us consider Company ABC, which had the following:

- 300,000 warrants converted on a 1-for-1 basis into common shares;

- Weighted-average number of common shares is 2,800,000 common shares; and

- Profit of $10,455,000.

$$\frac{\text{Profit}}{\text{Weighted-average number of common shares outstanding}}$$

$$\frac{\$10,455,000}{2,800,000} = \$3.73 \text{ per share}$$

Earnings per common share using the formula above would be calculated thus:

Fully diluted earnings per common share would require the following adjustments:

- The number of common shares would increase by 300,000, since 300,000 warrants would be converted on a 1-for-1 basis.

The formula is then:

$$\frac{\text{Adjusted profit}}{\text{Adjusted weighted-average number of common shares outstanding}}$$

$$= \frac{\$10,455,000}{2,800,000 + 300,000}$$

$$= \frac{\$10,455,000}{3,100,000} = \$3.37 \text{ fully diluted per share}$$

Profit after all prior claims have been met belongs to the common shareholders. The shareholders therefore will want to know how much has been earned on their shares. If profit is high, directors may declare and pay out a good portion as dividends. Even in growth companies, directors may decide to make at least a small dividend payment because they realize that shareholders like to receive income. On the other hand, if profit is low or the company has suffered a loss, they may not pay dividends on the common shares.

Describing earnings in terms of common shares shows shareholders the profitability of their ownership interest in the company and whether dividends are likely to be paid. In the Trans-Canada Retail Stores example, earnings are $3.12 for each common share. Since regular dividends of $1.00 per share per year are being paid on common shares, the calculation also indicates that the dividend is well protected by earnings. In other words, earnings per common share are $2.12 more than regular dividend payments.

Since common share dividends are declared and paid at the discretion of a company's board of directors, no rules can be laid down to judge the amount likely to be paid out at a given level of profit. Dividend policy varies from industry to industry and from company to company.

Estimating the dividend possibilities of a stock may take into account:

- The amount of profit for the current fiscal year

- The stability of profit over a period of years

- The amount of retained earnings and the rate of return on those earnings

- The company's working capital

- The policy of the board of directors

- Plans for expanding (or contracting) operations

- Government dividend restraints (if any)

Before a company can pay a dividend, it must have sufficient earnings and working capital. It is up to the directors to consider the other factors and reach a decision on whether to pay a dividend and how large the payment should be.

DIVIDEND YIELD

The **yield** on common stock is the annual dividend rate expressed as a percentage of the current market price of the stock. It represents the investor's return on the investment.

$$= \frac{\text{Indicated annual dividend per share}}{\text{Current market price}} \times 100$$

Assuming a current market price of $26.25 for the common shares of Trans-Canada Retail Stores, the yield is:

$$\text{Common: } \frac{\$1.00}{\$26.25} \times 100 = 3.81\%$$

Dividend yields allow analysts to make a quick comparison between the shares of different companies. However, to make a thorough comparison, the following factors must also be considered:

- The differences in the quality and record of each company's management

- The proportion of earnings re-invested in each company

- The equity behind each share

All these factors should be taken into account in addition to yield – preferably over several years. Only then can an analyst make an informed evaluation.

PRICE-EARNINGS RATIO OR P/E MULTIPLE

The **price-earnings ratio** or **P/E ratio** is probably the most widely used of all financial ratios because it combines all the other ratios into one figure. It represents the ultimate evaluation of a company and its shares by the investing public.

$$\text{Formula:} \quad \frac{\text{Current market price of common}}{\text{Earnings per share (in latest 12-month period)}}$$

Assuming that the current market price of Trans-Canada Retail Stores' common stock is $26.25 and that the company's earnings per common share is $3.12, the P/E ratio is:

$$\frac{\$26.25}{\$3.12} = 8.41 : 1 \text{ or } 8.41 \text{ times}$$

P/E ratios are calculated only for common stocks.

The main reason for calculating earnings per common share – apart from indicating dividend protection – is to make a comparison with the share's market price. The P/E ratio expresses this comparison in one convenient figure, showing that a share is selling at so many times its actual or anticipated annual earnings. P/E ratios enable the shares of one company to be compared with those of another.

Example: Company A – Earnings per share: $2; price: $20

Company B – Earnings per share: $1; price: $10

P/E ratio for Company A: $\dfrac{\$20}{\$2} = 10 : 1$

P/E ratio for Company B: $\dfrac{\$10}{\$1} = 10 : 1$

Though earnings per share of Company A ($2) are twice those of Company B ($1), the shares of each company represent equivalent *value* because A's shares, at $20 each, cost twice as much as B's. In other words, both companies are selling at 10 times earnings.

The elements that determine the quality of an issue – and therefore are represented in the P/E ratio – include:

- Tangible factors contained in financial data, which can be expressed in ratios relating to liquidity, earnings trends, profitability, dividend payout, and financial strength.

- Intangible factors, such as quality of management, nature and prospects for the industry in which the issuing company operates, its competitive position, and its individual prospects.

All these factors are taken into account when investors and speculators collectively decide what price a share is worth.

To compare the P/E ratio for one company's common shares with that of other companies, the companies should usually be in the same industry.

In the Trans-Canada Retail Stores example, we calculated the price-earnings ratio on the earnings of the company's latest fiscal year. In practice, however, most investment analysts and firms make their own projections of a company's earnings for the next twelve-month period and calculate P/E ratios on these projected figures in relation to the stock's current market price. Because of the many variables involved in forecasting earnings, the use of estimates in calculations should be approached with great caution.

The P/E ratio helps analysts determine a reasonable value for a common stock at any time in a market cycle. By calculating a company's P/E ratio over a number of years, the analyst will find considerable fluctuation, with high and low points. If the highs and lows of a particular stock's P/E ratio remain constant over several stock market cycles, they indicate selling and buying points for the stock. A study of the P/E ratios of competitor companies and that of the relevant market subgroup index also helps to provide a perspective.

The P/E ratio comparison assists in the selection process. For example, if two companies of equal stature in the same industry both have similar prospects, but different P/E ratios, the company with the lower P/E ratio is usually the better buy.

As a rule, P/E ratios increase in a rising stock market or with rising earnings. If earnings are increasing over time, this is a positive for the company and the company's stock price should rise over time. Investors would see rising earnings as a positive development and would be willing to pay a higher price for the stock. The increase in the stock price is usually greater than the increase in earnings. Therefore, the P/E ratio would increase. The reverse is true in a declining market or when earnings decline.

Since the P/E ratio is an indicator of investor confidence, its highs and lows may vary from market cycle to market cycle. Much depends on changes in investor enthusiasm for a company or an industry over several years.

EQUITY VALUE (OR BOOK VALUE) PER COMMON SHARE

The **equity value per common share** measures the asset coverage for each common share.

From the notes to the financial statements, we see that Trans-Canada has 400,000 common shares outstanding as at December 31, 20XX. Please note this is not the same number as the weighted-average number of common shares outstanding. The weighted-average number of common shares outstanding calculation takes into account the length of time the common shares were outstanding. The calculation of the weighted-average number of common shares is beyond the scope of this textbook.

$$\frac{\text{Equity}}{\text{Number of common shares outstanding}}$$

$$\frac{\text{Item 14}}{400,000}$$

$$or \quad \frac{\$13,306,000}{400,000} = \$33.27 \text{ per common share}$$

There is no simple answer as to what constitutes an adequate level of equity value per common share. Although a per-share equity (or book) value figure is sometimes used in appraising common shares, in actual practice the equity value per common share may be very different from the market value per common share. Equity per share is only one of many factors to be considered in appraising a given stock. Many shares sell for considerably less than their equity value, while others sell for far in excess of their equity value.

This disparity between equity and market values is usually accounted for by the actual or potential earning power of the company. The shares of a company with a high earning power will command a better price in the market than the shares of a company with little or no earning power, even though the shares of both companies may have the same equity value. Thus, we cannot quote a meaningful standard for an adequate book value per common share.

Complete the following Online Learning Activity

NFR Inc - Company Analysis

In this activity you will have an opportunity to practice using the formulas and calculating key ratios to analyze NFR, a fictitious Canadian company.

 Complete the **NFR Inc - Company Analysis** activity.

Complete the following Online Learning Activity

Comparing Performance

You have now had a chance to work through calculating financial ratios for NFR Inc. In this activity you will review and compare the ratios of NFR against another company in the same industry and determine which company offers the better investment.

 Complete the **Comparing Performance** activity.

HOW IS PREFERRED SHARE INVESTMENT QUALITY ASSESSED?

As discussed in CSC Volume 1, preferred shares have different characteristics than common shares. For example, preferred shareholders are entitled to a fixed dividend, they do not have the right to vote, and the prices of preferred shares act more like bonds than common stocks. For these reasons, preferred shares are evaluated differently than common shares.

Investment Quality Assessment

The investment quality assessment of preferred shares hinges on three critical questions:

• Do the company's earnings provide ample coverage for preferred dividends?

• For how many years has the company paid dividends without interruption?

• Is there an adequate cushion of equity behind each preferred share?

Analysts study a number of factors to answer these questions. The four key tests employed to finalize an assessment are:

• Preferred Dividend Coverage

• Equity (or Book Value) per Preferred Share

• Record of Continuous Dividend Payments

• An Independent Credit Assessment

PREFERRED DIVIDEND COVERAGE RATIO

Like interest coverage, the **preferred dividend coverage** ratio indicates the margin of safety for preferred dividends. It measures the amount of money a firm has to pay dividends to preferred shareholders. The higher the ratio the better, as it indicates the company has little difficulty in paying its preferred dividend requirements. Typically, preferred dividend coverage is calculated for the last five years, and a trend is plotted. Ideally a rising or stable trend is revealed. The calculation of this ratio is beyond the scope of this textbook.

EQUITY (OR BOOK VALUE) PER PREFERRED SHARE

Preferred share rank before common shares in any liquidation, winding up, or distribution of assets. When the preferred shareholders' claims have been met, the holders of common shares are entitled to what is left. Analysts like to see that the minimum equity value per preferred share in each of the last five fiscal years is at least two times the dollar value of assets that each preferred share would be entitled to receive in the event of liquidation. The calculation of equity per preferred share is beyond the scope of this textbook.

DIVIDEND PAYMENTS

Has the company established a record of continuous dividend payments to its preferred shareholders? This information can be obtained from individual company annual reports.

CREDIT ASSESSMENT

Just as with bonds, a company's preferred shares may be rated by one of the recognized bond rating services. If it is, what is the rating and is it high enough to merit investment?

In Canada, DBRS and Standard & Poor's assign ratings to a number of Canadian preferred shares.

To arrive at a preferred share rating, the rating services subject company reports to a rigorous evaluation.

An unexpected change in the rating of a preferred share issue will usually affect the shares' market price. An unexpected downgrading to a lower rating has negative implications. An upgrading to a higher rating is a favourable development.

Selecting Preferreds

In addition to the four key tests just covered, other factors should be investigated before a purchase decision is reached. When choosing any equity security, marketability, volume of trading and research coverage by investment firms should be investigated. Questions specific to preferreds include:

- What features (e.g., cumulative dividends, sinking funds) and protective provisions have been built into the issue?

- Is the yield from the preferred acceptable compared to yields from other, similar investments?

In addition to the checkpoints cited for selecting straight preferred shares, the following should be considered for convertible preferreds:

- Is the outlook for the common stock positive? A conversion privilege is valuable only if the market price of the common rises above the exercise price during the life of the conversion privilege.

- Is the life of the conversion privilege long enough? The longer the life of the conversion privilege, the greater the opportunity for the market price of the common and preferred to respond to favourable developments.

Complete the following Online Learning Activity

Financial Ratios Summary

This summary provides you with a review of all the financial ratios covered in this module.

   Complete the **Financial Ratios** summary.

SUMMARY

After reading this chapter, you should be able to:

1. Identify the factors involved in performing company analysis to determine whether a company represents a good investment.

   • Analysis of company earnings indicates how well management is making use of company resources (e.g., the trend in the net profit margin).

   • Analysis of the statement of financial position helps to better understand important aspects of company operations and can reveal factors that may affect earnings (e.g., the amount of debt currently reported).

2. Explain how to analyze a company's financial statements using trend analysis and external comparisons.

   • Financial ratios become meaningful when compared with other ratios over a period. A series of similar ratios for the same company can be compared; or the company's ratios can be compared to those of similar companies or industry averages.

   • Ratios are most useful when comparing financial results of companies in the same or similar industries. Trend lines help to put the ratios of each company in historical perspective and identify how each company has fared in relation to others.

3. Describe the different types of liquidity ratios, risk analysis ratios, operating performance ratios, and value ratios, and evaluate company performance using these ratios.

   • Liquidity ratios are used to evaluate a company's ability to meet its short-term commitments. Ratios in this category look at the relationship between current assets and current liabilities.

   • Risk analysis ratios show how well a company can deal with its debt obligations. Because financial risk can increase with higher levels of debt, these ratios help to show whether a company has sufficient earnings to repay the funds it has borrowed and its ability to make regular interest payments on its outstanding debt.

   • Operating performance ratios illustrate how well management is making use of company resources. These ratios focus on measuring the profitability and efficiency of operations. They look specifically at the company's ability to manage its resources by taking into account revenue and the costs and expenses incurred in producing earnings.

   • Value ratios show the investor what the company's shares are worth, or the return on owning them, by comparing the market price of the shares to information in the company's financial statements. For example, these ratios look at the earnings available to common shareholders, the dividend yield or return on company shares, and the ultimate valuation of a company through the price-earnings ratio.

4. Evaluate the investment quality of preferred shares.

    •   The investment quality assessment of preferred shares hinges on three critical questions: Does the company generate enough earnings to cover its preferred dividend obligations? How consistently has the company paid dividends without interruption? What is the equity cushion behind each preferred share?

    •   The preferred dividend coverage ratio, the equity (or book value) per preferred share, the record of continuous dividend payments, and independent credit assessments can be used to analyze the quality of a company's preferred shares.

    •   DBRS and Standard and Poor's assign ratings to a number of Canadian preferred shares.

Online Frequently Asked Questions

CSI has answered many frequently asked questions about this Chapter. Read through online Module 14 FAQs.

Online Post-Module Assessment

Once you have completed the chapter, take the Module 14 Post-Test.

APPENDIX A – COMPANY FINANCIAL STATEMENTS

The financial statements on the following pages should be referred to when reviewing this chapter. To make them easier to understand, these financial statements differ from real financial statements in the following ways:

1. Comparative (previous year's) figures are not shown.

2. *Notes to Financial Statements* are not included.

3. The consecutive numbers on the left hand side of the statements which are used in explaining ratio calculations do not appear in real reports.

Note: It is assumed that Trans-Canada Retail Stores Ltd. is a non-food retail chain.

Trans-Canada Retail Stores Ltd.
CONSOLIDATED STATEMENT OF FINANCIAL POSITION
as at December 31, 20XX

ASSETS

1.	Property, plant and equipment	$	6,149,000
2.	Goodwill		150,000
3.	Investments in associates		917,000
4.	TOTAL NON-CURRENT ASSETS		7,216,000
5.	Inventories		9,035,000
6.	Prepaid expenses		59,000
7.	Trade receivables		975,000
8.	Cash and cash equivalents		2,169,000
9.	TOTAL CURRENT ASSETS		12,238,000
10.	TOTAL ASSETS	$	19,454,000

EQUITY AND LIABILITIES

11.	Share capital	$	2,314,000
12.	Retained earnings		10,835,000
			13,149,000
13.	Non-controlling interest		157,000
14.	TOTAL EQUITY	$	13,306,000
15.	Long-term debt		1,350,000
16.	Deferred tax liabilities		485,000
17.	TOTAL NON-CURRENT LIABILITIES	$	1,835,000
18.	Current portion of long-term debt		120,000
19.	Taxes payable		398,000
20.	Trade payables		2,165,000
21.	Short-term borrowings		1,630,000
22.	TOTAL CURRENT LIABILITIES	$	4,313,000
23.	TOTAL EQUITY AND LIABILITIES	$	19,454,000

Approved on behalf of the Board:

[Signature], Director

[Signature], Director

Trans-Canada Retail Stores Ltd.
CONSOLIDATED STATEMENT OF COMPREHENSIVE INCOME
For the year ended December 31, 20XX

OPERATING SECTION

24.	Revenue	$ 43,800,000
25.	Cost of sales	(28,250,000)
26.	Gross Profit	15,550,000
27.	Other income	130,000
28.	Distribution costs	(7,984,800)
29.	Administration expenses	(4,657,800)
30.	Other expenses	(665,400)
31.	Finance costs	(289,000)
32.	Share of profit of associates	5,000
33.	Income tax expense	(880,000)
34.	Profit	1,208,000
	Other comprehensive income	0
35.	Total comprehensive income	$ 1,208,000

Trans-Canada Retail Stores Ltd.
CONSOLIDATED STATEMENT OF CHANGES IN EQUITY
For the year ended December 31, 20XX

	Share Capital	Retained Earnings	Total	Non-controlling interests	Total Equity
Balance at January 1, 20XX	1,564,000	10,026,500	11,590,500	145,000	11,735,500
Changes in equity for 20XX					
Issue of share capital	750,000		750,000		750,000
Dividends		(387,500)	(387,500)		(387,500)
Total comprehensive income		1,196,000	1,196,000	12,000	1,208,000
Balance at December 31, 20XX	2,314,000	10,835,000	13,149,000	157,000	13,306,000

Trans-Canada Retail Stores Ltd.
CONSOLIDATED STATEMENT OF CASH FLOWS
For the year ended December 31, 20XX

OPERATING ACTIVITIES

34.	Profit	$ 1,208,000
	Add or (subtract) items not involving cash	
36.	Depreciation	496,000
32.	Share of profit of associates	(5,000)
37.	Change in net working capital	(401,000)
	NET CASH FLOW PROVIDED BY OPERATING ACTIVITIES	$ 1,298,000

Trans-Canada Retail Stores Ltd.
CONSOLIDATED STATEMENT OF CASH FLOWS
For the year ended December 31, 20XX

FINANCING ACTIVITIES

38.	Proceeds from issue of share capital	$	750,000
39.	Repayment of long-term debt		(400,000)
40.	Proceeds from new long-term debt		50,000
41.	Dividends paid		(387,500)
	NET CASH PROVIDED BY FINANCING ACTIVITIES	$	12,500

INVESTING ACTIVITIES

42.	Acquisitions of capital assets	$	(900,000)
43.	Proceeds from disposal of capital assets		75,000
44.	Dividends received from associates		2,000
	NET CASH FLOW USED IN INVESTING ACTIVITIES	$	(823,000)
45.	INCREASE IN CASH AND CASH EQUIVALENTS		487,500
46.	CASH AND CASH EQUIVALENTS – YEAR END		2,169,000

AUDITORS' REPORT

To the Shareholders of Trans-Canada Retail Stores Ltd.

We have audited the statement of financial position of Trans-Canada Retail Stores Ltd. as at December 31, 20XX and the statement of comprehensive income, statement of changes in equity and statement of cash flows for the year then ended, and a summary of significant accounting policies and other explanatory information.

Management is responsible for the preparation and fair presentation of these consolidated financial statements in accordance with International Financial Reporting Standards.

Our responsibility is to express an opinion on these consolidated financial statements based on our audit. We conducted our audit in accordance with International Standards of Auditing. Those standards require that we comply with ethical requirements and plan and perform an audit to obtain reasonable assurance whether the consolidated financial statements are free of material misstatement.

An audit involves performing procedures to obtain audit evidence about the amounts and disclosures in the consolidated financial statements. The procedures selected depend on the auditor's judgement, including the assessment of the risk of material misstatement of the consolidated financial statements, whether due to fraud or error. In making those risk assessments, the auditor considers internal control relevant to the entity's preparation and fair presentation of the consolidated financial statements in order to design audit procedures that are appropriate in the circumstances, but not for the purpose of expressing an opinion on the effectiveness of the entity's internal control. An audit also includes assessing the appropriateness of accounting principles used and the reasonableness of accounting estimates made by management, as well as evaluating the overall financial statement presentation.

We believe that the audit evidence we have obtained is sufficient and appropriate to provide a basis for our audit opinion.

In our opinion, these financial statements give a true and fair view of the financial position of the company as at December 31, 20XX and of their financial performance and cash flows for the year then ended in accordance with International Financial Reporting Standards.

Toronto, Ontario

February 8, 20XX Signature of Auditors

Portfolio Analysis

Chapter *15*

Introduction to the Portfolio Approach

15

Introduction to the Portfolio Approach

LEARNING OBJECTIVES

By the end of this chapter, you should be able to:

1. Describe the relationship between risk and return, calculate rates of return of a single security, identify the different types and measures of risk, and evaluate the role of risk in asset selection.

2. Explain the relationship between risk and return of a portfolio of securities, calculate and interpret the expected return of a portfolio, and identify strategies for maximizing return while reducing risk.

3. List the steps in the portfolio management process.

4. Evaluate investment objectives and constraints and explain how to use them in creating an investment policy statement (IPS) for a client.

5. Describe the content of an investment policy statement and explain the purpose of an IPS.

PORTFOLIO ANALYSIS

No perfect security exists that meets all the needs of all investors. If such a security existed, there would be no need for investment and portfolio management, and no need to measure the return and risk of an investment. Advisors and portfolio managers spend a great deal of time selecting individual securities, allocating investment funds among security classes, and managing risks and returns.

Recognizing that there are no perfect securities, investors and advisors use measures and methods to estimate risk and predict return. Based on these results, they construct portfolios designed to fit the particular needs and circumstances of individual investors. Building portfolios that correlate to specific investor needs is key to being successful in the investment industry. Generating the highest returns is not enough; higher returns that require exposure to risky investments may not be appropriate for a particular investor.

In this chapter, we integrate information about individual securities, the markets, and the different analysis techniques to focus on developing securities portfolios designed to meet the specific needs of investors. There are many factors to consider, including developing a portfolio based on specific circumstances, justifying portfolio selections and estimating the risk and return for a portfolio. Effective portfolio management requires attention to varied information.

KEY TERMS

Alpha	Investment policy statement
Beta	Liquidity risk
Business risk	Non-systematic risk
Correlation	Political risk
Default risk	Rate of return
Diversification	Real rate of return
Ex-ante return	Risk-free rate
Ex-post return	Systematic risk
Foreign exchange risk	Time horizon
Holding period return	Variance
Inflation rate risk	Volatility
Interest rate risk	

WHAT IS RISK AND RETURN?

Risk and return are interrelated. To earn higher returns investors must usually choose investments with higher risk.

Given a choice between two investments with the same amount of risk, a rational investor would always take the security with the higher return. Given two investments with the same expected return, the investor would always choose the security with the lower risk.

Each investor has a different risk profile. This means that not all investors choose the same low-risk security. Some investors are willing to take on more risk than others are, if they believe there is a higher potential for returns.

In general, risk can have several different meanings. To some, risk is losing money on an investment. To others, it may be the prospect of losing purchasing power, if the return on the investments does not keep up with inflation.

Given that all investors do not have the same degree of risk tolerance, different securities and different funds have evolved to service each market niche. Guaranteed investment certificates (GICs) were developed for those seeking safety, fixed-income funds were developed for those seeking income, while equity funds were developed for those seeking growth or capital appreciation.

Few individuals would invest all of their funds in a single security. The creation of a portfolio allows the investor to diversify and reduce risk to a suitable level.

Consider the following possible investments and the types of return generated:

- An investor who buys Government of Canada bonds expects to earn interest income (cash flow).

- An investor in common shares expects to see the stock grow in value (capital gain) and may also be rewarded with dividends (cash flow).

Returns are rarely guaranteed and that is why returns are often called "expected returns."

While an investment may be purchased in anticipation of a rise in value, the reality is that values can decline. A decline in the value of a security is often referred to as a capital loss. Therefore, returns can be reduced to some sort of combination of: cash flows and capital gains or losses.

The following formula defines the expected return of a single security:

EXPECTED RETURN

Expected Return	=	Cash Flow + Capital Gain (or − Capital Loss)
Where:		
Cash Flow	=	Dividends, interest, or any other type of income
Capital Gain/Loss	=	Ending Value − Beginning Value
Beginning Value	=	The initial dollar amount invested by the investor
Ending Value	=	The dollar amount the investment is sold for

Rate of Return

Returns from an investment can be measured in absolute dollars. An investor may state that she made $100 or lost $20. Unfortunately, using absolute numbers obscures their significance. Was the $100 gain made on an investment of $1,000 or an investment of $100,000? In the first example the gain may be significant, while in the latter it could signal a poor investment choice.

The more common practice is to express returns as a percentage or as a rate of return or yield. Within the investment community it is more common to hear that "a fund earned 8%" or "a stock fell 2%." To convert a dollar amount to a percentage, the usual practice is to divide the total dollar returns by the amount invested.

$$\text{Return \%} = \frac{\text{Cash Flow} + (\text{Ending Value} - \text{Beginning Value})}{\text{Beginning Value}} \times 100$$

RATE OF RETURN ON AN INDIVIDUAL STOCK EXAMPLE

1. If you purchased a stock for $10 and sold it one year later for $12, what would be your rate of return?

$$\text{Rate of Return} = \frac{\text{Zero Cash Flow} + (\$12 - \$10)}{\$10} \times 100 = 20\%$$

2. If you purchased a stock for $20 and sold it one year later for $22, and during this period you received $1 in dividends, what would be your rate of return?

$$\text{Rate of Return} = \frac{\$1 + (\$22 - \$20)}{\$20} \times 100 = 15\%$$

3. If you purchased a stock for $10, received $2 in dividends, but sold it one year later for only $9, what would be your rate of return?

$$\text{Rate of Return} = \frac{\$2 + (\$9 - \$10)}{\$10} \times 100 = 10\%$$

The above examples illustrate that cash flow and capital gains or losses are used in calculating a rate of return. It should also be noted that all of the above trading periods were set for one year, and hence the percent return can also be called the annual rate of return. If the transaction period were for longer or shorter than a year, the return would be called the **holding period return**. The above generic formula will form the basis of yield calculations described later in this chapter.

Rates of return can be **ex-ante**, a projection of expected returns, or **ex-post**, meaning looking back at the actual returns previously earned (historical returns). Investors estimate future returns, i.e., ex-ante returns, to determine where funds should be invested. Ex-post returns are calculated in order to compare actual results against both anticipated results and market benchmarks.

The biggest problem with the rate of return measurement is that it does not take risk into account.

EX-ANTE AND EX-POST RATES OF RETURN EXAMPLE

An investor purchases an equity fund in the expectation that the unit value will rise from $10 per unit to $12 per unit by the end of the year. The investor's expected rate of return would be:

$$\text{Rate of Return}_{\text{ex-ante}} = \frac{\text{Zero Cash Flow} + \$2 \text{ Capital Gain}}{\$10} \times 100 = 20\%$$

At the end of the year the unit's value was actually $10.50. The investor's actual rate of return was:

$$\text{Rate of Return}_{\text{ex-post}} = \frac{\text{Zero Cash Flow} + \$0.50 \text{ Capital Gain}}{\$10} \times 100 = 5\%$$

Choosing a realistic expected rate of return can be a very difficult task. One common method is to expect the T-bill rate plus a certain performance percentage related to the risk assumed in the investment. Corporate bond issues with a higher risk profile would be expected to earn a higher rate of return than the more secure Government of Canada bond issues.

HISTORICAL RETURNS

An understanding of historical returns is important to the investor. Insights into the market can be gained by studying historical data. These insights are used to determine appropriate investments and investment strategies.

Consider the following rates of return in Table 15.1:

TABLE 15.1	COMPARATIVE TOTAL RATES OF RETURN ON SPECIFIC SECURITY CLASSES		
Annual Total Return (% Change in Value Indices, December to December)			
Annual Returns	**T-Bills 91-Day (%)**	**Long-Term Bonds (%)**	**S&P/TSX Composite Stocks (%)**
1990	13.48	4.32	-14.80
1995	7.57	26.34	14.53
2000	5.49	12.97	7.41
2005	3.37	13.84	21.91
2006	4.16	4.08	10.69
2007	3.86	3.44	10.87
2008	0.83	2.10	-33.25

Source: Bloomberg

A study of Table 15.1 reveals that the highest rates of return were achieved by securities that had the greatest *variability* or risk as measured by **standard deviation**, a measure of risk that will be explained later.

While historical returns provide insight into the long-term performance of the market, it is obvious from the above that past performance is not necessarily indicative of future performance. Since it is extremely difficult to predict the future, an investor should employ the concept of diversification to reduce risk (discussed later in this chapter).

The above historical information serves to illustrate that risk and return are related. Figure 15.1 demonstrates this relationship graphically.

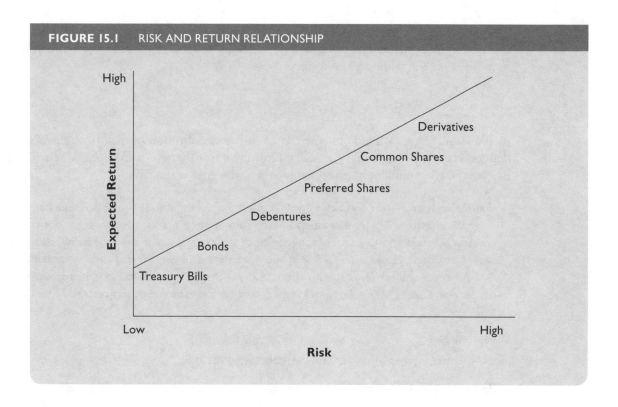

FIGURE 15.1   RISK AND RETURN RELATIONSHIP

NOMINAL AND REAL RATES OF RETURN

So far we have looked only at a simple rate of return (i.e., the nominal rate of return). For example, if a one-year GIC reports a 6% return, this 6% represents the nominal return on the investment. However, investors are more concerned with the real rate of return – the return adjusted for the effects of inflation.

The approximate real rate of return is calculated as:

Real Return = Nominal Rate – Annual Rate of Inflation

REAL RATE OF RETURN EXAMPLE

A client earned a 10% nominal return on an investment last year. Over the same period, inflation was measured at 2%. What was the client's approximate real rate of return on this investment?

The client earned a real rate of return of 8% on the investment, calculated as:

Real Return = 10% – 2% = 8%

THE RISK-FREE RATE OF RETURN

A study of historical returns reveals that Treasury bills usually keep pace with inflation and therefore provide a positive return. Since T-bills are considered essentially risk-free, all other securities must at least pay the T-bill rate plus a risk premium in order to entice clients into investing.

T-bills often represent the **risk-free** rate of return as there is essentially zero risk associated with this type of investment. The yield paid on a T-bill is roughly determined by estimating the short-term inflation and adding a real return.

Risk

As has already been pointed out, there is no universal definition of risk. In a statistical sense, it is defined as the likelihood that the actual return will be different from expected return. The greater the variability or number of possible outcomes, the greater the risk.

> *Example:* If an investor purchases a $500 Canada Savings Bond (CSB) and cashes the bond one year later, the investor will receive exactly $500 (plus any accrued interest). However, suppose the same investor purchased $500 worth of common stock at $25 per share in the expectation that the price would rise from $25 per share to $40 in one year's time. The investor may receive much more than $40 per share or much less than the original $25 per share. Common stocks would be defined as riskier than Canada Savings Bonds since the future outcomes are much less certain.

TYPES OF RISKS

There are many types of risk in the markets, these include:

Inflation rate risk: As explained previously, inflation reduces future purchasing power and the return on investments.

Business risk: This risk is associated with the variability of a company's earnings due to such things as the possibility of a labour strike, introduction of new products, and the performance of competing firms, among others. The uncertainty regarding a company's future performance is its basic business risk.

Political risk: This is the risk associated with unfavourable changes in government policies. For example, a government may decide to raise taxes on foreign investing, making it less attractive to invest in the country. Political risk also refers to the general instability associated with investing in a particular country. Investing in a war-torn country, for example, brings with it the added risk of losing one's investment.

Liquidity risk: A liquid asset is one that can be bought or sold at a fair price and converted to cash on short notice. A security that is difficult to sell suffers from liquidity risk, which is the risk that an investor will not be able to buy or sell a security at a fair price quickly enough due to limited buying or selling opportunities.

Interest rate risk: When an investor purchases a fixed-income security, for example, he or she expects to earn a certain return or yield on the investment. As we learned in the chapters on fixed-income securities, there is an inverse relationship between interest rates and bond prices. If interest rates rise, the investment will fall in value; on the other hand, it will rise in value if rates fall. Interest rate risk is the risk that investors are exposed to because of changing interest rates.

Foreign exchange risk: Foreign exchange risk is the risk of incurring losses resulting from an unfavourable change in exchange rates. Investors who invest abroad or businesses that buy and sell products in foreign markets are subject to this risk.

Default risk: When a company issues more debt to finance its operations, servicing the debt through interest payments creates a further burden on the company. The more debt the company acquires, the greater the risk that it may have difficulty servicing its debt load through its current operations. Default risk is the risk associated with a company being unable to make timely interest payments or repay the principal amount of a loan when due.

SYSTEMATIC AND NON-SYSTEMATIC RISK

Certain risks can be reduced by **diversification**. The risks known as **systematic risks** cannot be eliminated, as these risks affect all assets within certain classes. Systematic risk is always present and cannot be eliminated through diversification. This type of risk stems from such things as inflation, the business cycle and high interest rates.

Systematic (or market risk) is the risk associated with investing in each capital market: When stock market averages fall, most individual stocks in the market fall. When interest rates rise, nearly all individual bonds and preferred shares fall in value. Systematic risk cannot be diversified away; in fact, the more a portfolio becomes diversified within a certain asset class, the more it ends up mirroring that market.

Non-systematic risk, or **specific risk**, is the risk that the price of a specific security or a specific group of securities will change in price to a different degree or in a different direction from the market as a whole. Royal Bank of Canada may rise in price, for example, when the S&P/TSX Composite Index falls, or Royal Bank, Bank of Nova Scotia and Bank of Montreal (all financial companies) as a group may fall more than the Index.

Specific risk can be reduced by diversifying among a number of securities. This type of risk theoretically could be eliminated completely by buying a portfolio of shares that consisted of all S&P/TSX Composite Index stocks, using index funds or buying ETFs based on the Index. The fund manager could also be asked to create a fund that mirrors, but does not buy all of the securities included in, an index.

MEASURING RISK

Investors may expect a given return on an investment, but the actual results may be higher or lower. To get a better feel for the possible outcomes and their probability of occurrence, several measures of risk have been developed. The three common measures of risk are variance, standard deviation and beta.

Variance measures the extent to which the possible realized returns differ from the expected return or the mean. The more likely it is that the return will not be the same as the expected return, the more risky the security. When an investor purchases a T-bill, the return is predictable. The return cannot change as long as the investor holds the T-bill until maturity.

With other securities (e.g., equities), the outcomes are more varied. The price could increase, stay the same or decrease. The greater the number of possible outcomes, the greater the risk that the outcome will not be favourable. The greater the distance estimated between the expected return and the possible returns, the greater the variance. The risk of a portfolio is determined by the risk of the various securities within that portfolio.

Standard deviation is the measure of risk commonly applied to portfolios and to individual securities within that portfolio. Standard deviation is the square root of the variance. The past performance or historical returns of securities is used to determine a range of possible future outcomes. The more volatile the price of a security has been in the past, the larger the range of possible future outcomes.

The standard deviation, expressed as a percentage, gives the investor an indication of the risk associated with an individual security or a portfolio. The greater the standard deviation, the greater the risk.

Beta is another statistical measure that links the risk of individual equity securities or a portfolio of equities to the market as a whole. As we saw earlier, the risk that remains after diversifying is market risk. Beta is important because it measures the degree to which individual equity securities or a portfolio of equities tend to move up and down with the market. Once again, the higher the beta, the greater the risk.

Complete the following Online Learning Activity

Risk and Return - Individual Securities

There are different types of securities and funds to match the needs of investors who are prepared to accept different degrees of risk. GICs and government bonds are for investors seeking safety; equities and corporate bonds for those prepared to risk capital losses in the hope of achieving capital gains. The higher the risk, the greater the return that the investor will look for.

 Complete this activity to test your knowledge of **Risk and Return - Individual Securities**.

HOW ARE PORTFOLIO RISK AND RETURN RELATED?

Once you have a better understanding of the client's financial objectives and tolerance for risk (a more detailed discussion of these concepts follows later in this chapter), you will need to determine the broad categories from which investments will be selected. Chapter 16 provides a detailed discussion of asset allocation including the grouping of investment assets into three main asset classes: cash or near-cash equivalents; fixed-income securities; and equity securities.

A portfolio represents the securities held by an investor and may include securities from these three asset classes.

Calculating the Rate of Return on a Portfolio

The expected rate of return on a portfolio is calculated in a slightly different manner from the rate of return of a single security. Since the portfolio contains a number of securities, the return generated by each security has to be calculated.

PORTFOLIO RETURNS

The return on a portfolio is calculated as the weighted average return on the securities held in the portfolio. The formula is as follows:

Expected Return: $R_1(W_1) + R_2(W_2) + ... + R_n(W_n)$

Where:

R = The return on a particular security

W = The proportion (weight or %) of the security held in the portfolio based on the dollar investment

The following example illustrates:

RATE OF A RETURN ON A PORTFOLIO

A client invests $100 in two securities: $60 in ABC Co. and $40 in DEF Co.

The expected return from ABC Co. is 15% and the expected return from DEF Co. is 12%. To calculate the expected return of the portfolio, an advisor or investor would look at the rate expected to be generated by each proportional investment.

Since the total amount invested was $100, ABC Co. represents 60% ($60 ÷ $100) of the portfolio and DEF Co. represents 40% ($40 ÷ $100) of the portfolio. If ABC Co. earns a return of 15% and DEF Co. earns 12%, the expected return on the portfolio is:

$$\begin{aligned} \text{Expected return} &= (0.15 \times 0.60) + (0.12 \times 0.40) \\ &= 0.09 + 0.048 \\ &= 0.138 \text{ (or 13.8\%)} \end{aligned}$$

Measuring Risk in a Portfolio

While diversification is important, portfolio managers must also guard against too much diversification. When a portfolio contains too many securities, superior performance may be difficult to achieve and the accounting, research and valuation functions may be needlessly complex. It is estimated that virtually all non-systematic risk in an equity portfolio is eliminated by the time 32 securities are included in the portfolio.

Portfolio managers have developed a number of strategies for limiting losses on individual securities or on a portfolio. Most of these strategies involve the use of derivatives. For example, they may use put options on individual equities or on investments such as gold, silver, currencies, and so on. Additionally, the portfolio manager can hedge an entire portfolio by using derivatives on stock indexes, bonds or interest rates.

Combining Securities in a Portfolio

This section brings together the concepts of risk and return. Portfolio management recognizes the fact that while future returns are usually beyond the control of an individual or fund manager, risk to a certain extent can be managed.

Portfolio management stresses the selection of securities for inclusion in the portfolio based on the securities' contribution to the portfolio as a whole. This suggests some synergy or some interaction among the securities that results in the total portfolio being somewhat more than the sum of the parts.

If investors place all of their savings in a single security their entire portfolio is at risk. If the investment consists of a single equity security, the investment is subject to business risk and market risk. Alternatively, if all of the investor's funds are invested in a single debt security, the investment is subject to default risk and interest rate risk.

Some of these risks can be eliminated or reduced through diversification. However, diversification must be done carefully and the methodology for combining securities must be understood. Combining any two securities may not diversify the portfolio if the risk characteristics of the two securities are extremely similar.

CORRELATION

Correlation looks at how securities relate to each other when they are added to a portfolio and how the resulting combination affects the portfolio's total risk and return. To illustrate the concept, consider the following:

- An investor takes all of her savings and invests 100% of those savings in a gold mining stock. If the price of gold rises, the company does well and the client makes money. If the price of gold declines, the gold mining company does not do well and the investor loses money. In order to reduce this risk, the investor diversifies into another stock, which happens to be another gold mining company. Has the investor's portfolio been diversified?

- The investor's advisor points out that the portfolio has not been adequately diversified.

It is clear that the securities in the portfolio are linked – their value is tied to the fortunes of gold. The portfolio thus has a high correlation with the fortunes of gold. In fact:

- If the stock prices of the two gold mining companies move in the same direction each time (when one rises, the other also rises), they would have a perfect positive correlation, which is denoted as a correlation of +1.

- The investor does not reduce his or her risk by adding securities that are perfectly correlated with each other.

- Therefore, holding securities with perfect positive correlation does not reduce the overall risk of the portfolio.

What if the stock prices of two companies moved in opposite directions? Consider the following example:

• An investor creates a portfolio of two securities – an airline company stock and a bus company stock. In good economic times people fly, but in bad economic times they save money by taking the bus. In good times, the investor's airline company shares increase in value. In bad times, the airline stock declines but the loss is offset by an increase in the price of bus company shares.

• Since the stock prices move in the opposite direction each time (when one rises, the other falls), the investor earns a positive return with little risk (there is always the possibility of market risk). These securities have a perfect negative correlation, denoted as -1.

With perfect negative correlation, there is no variability in the total returns for the two assets – thus, no risk for the portfolio. Therefore, the maximum gain from diversification is achieved when securities held within the portfolio exhibit perfect negative correlation. In reality, however, it is very difficult to find securities with such a high level of negative correlation.

Research shows that adding poorly correlated securities to a portfolio does in fact reduce risk. However, each additional security reduces risk at a lower rate. In fact, an accepted view is that once there are 32 equities in the portfolio additional risk reduction is minimal. Since the securities in the portfolio are still positively correlated to some degree, the equity portfolio is left with one risk that cannot be eliminated – systematic or market risk.

Figure 15.2 shows how risk is reduced by adding securities to an equity portfolio.

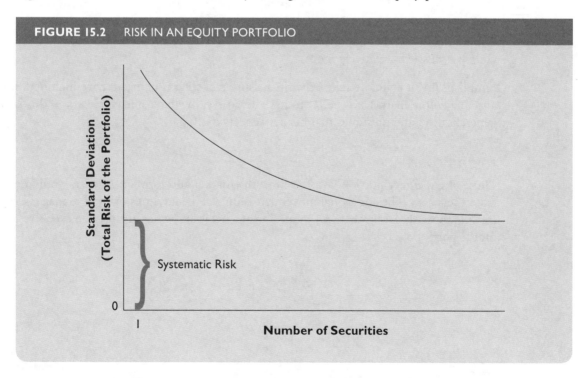

FIGURE 15.2 RISK IN AN EQUITY PORTFOLIO

The total risk of the portfolio falls quite significantly as the first few stocks are added. As the number of stocks increases, however, the additional reduction in risk declines. Finally, a point is reached where a further reduction in risk through diversification cannot be achieved. Therefore, the main source of uncertainty for an investor with a diversified portfolio is the impact of systematic risk on portfolio return.

PORTFOLIO BETA

As explained, the beta or *beta coefficient* relates the volatility of a single equity or equity portfolio to the volatility of the stock market as a whole. Specifically, beta measures that part of the fluctuation in price driven by changes in the stock market. **Volatility** in this context is a way of describing the changes in price over a long time frame. The wider the range in market prices, the greater the volatility and the greater the risk.

Any equity or equity portfolio that moves up or down to the same degree as the stock market has a beta of 1.0. Any security or portfolio that moves up or down more than the market has a beta greater than 1.0, and a security that moves less than the market has a beta of less than 1.0.

- If the S&P/TSX Composite Index rose 10%, an equity fund with a beta of 1.0 could be expected to advance by 10%.

- If the Index fell by 5%, the equity fund would fall by 5%.

- If an equity portfolio had a beta of 1.30, it would be expected to rise 13% (1.3 × 10%) when the Index rose 10%.

- An equity portfolio with a beta of 0.80 would be expected to only rise 8% when the Index rose 10%.

In real life, most portfolios have a beta between 0.75 and 1.40, indicating a positive correlation between equities and the stock market. Industries with volatile earnings, typically cyclical industries, tend to have higher betas than the market.

Defensive industries tend to have betas that are less than the market, that is, less than 1. This implies that when the market is falling in price, defensive stocks would normally fall relatively less and cyclical stocks relatively more.

Simplistically, it could be stated that in a rising market it is better to have high beta stocks and in a falling market it is better to have defensive, low beta stocks. However, this is an over-generalization and presumes that history repeats itself.

PORTFOLIO ALPHA

Quite often, equity portfolios outperform the market and move more than would be expected from their beta. The additional movement is due to the advisor's or fund manager's skill in picking those securities that will outperform. This is known as **alpha** - the excess return earned on the portfolio.

Complete the following Online Learning Activity

Risk and Return - Portfolio

Previously, you looked at the different types of risk that can affect a particular security and how to calculate the return on a single security. In this activity, you will look at how a mix of securities in a portfolio can affect both portfolio risk and return.

 Complete this activity to test your knowledge of **Risk and Return - Portfolio**.

WHAT IS THE PORTFOLIO MANAGEMENT PROCESS?

While securities are sometimes selected on their own merits, portfolio management stresses the selection of securities for inclusion in the portfolio based on that security's contribution to the portfolio as a whole. As the previous section on risk and return has shown, there is some synergy, or some interaction, among the securities, which results in the total portfolio effect being something more than the sum of its parts.

While the return of the portfolio will be the weighted average of the returns of each security, the risk of a portfolio is almost always less than the risks of the individual securities that make up the portfolio. This results in an improved risk-reward trade-off from using the portfolio approach.

Security selection decisions, then, are made in a context of the effect on the overall portfolio, rather than as discrete decisions that ignore the effect of one security on another in the portfolio.

For this reason, a portfolio approach is much more desirable than a series of uncoordinated decisions. The portfolio management process is a continuous set of six basic steps, with the word *process* indicating that when the sixth step is completed, work begins anew on the first step. The six parts to the portfolio management process are:

1. Determine investment objectives and constraints

2. Design an investment policy statement

3. Formulate an asset allocation strategy and select investment styles

4. Implement the Asset Allocation

5. Monitor the economy, the markets, the portfolio and the client

6. Evaluate portfolio performance

In this chapter, we focus on investment objectives and constraints and the investment policy statement. The remaining steps are described in Chapter 16.

Complete the following Online Learning Activity

Portfolio Management Process: Trisha's Journey

In this activity, you will be presented with Trisha's Case. Read through the whole portfolio management process and answer questions based on Trisha's Journey.

 Complete the **Portfolio Management Process** activity.

WHAT ARE INVESTMENT OBJECTIVES AND CONSTRAINTS?

The first step in the portfolio process is discovering the client's investment objectives and constraints to help determine the appropriate asset allocation for a client.

Clients usually do not communicate their goals to their advisors in terms of return, risk, etc. Instead, primary investment goals might be stated as a desire to retire at a certain age, the acquisition of a business, vacation property or sailboat, or the pursuit of some other tangible goal. With care and explanation to the client, the IA can translate such events into objectives with the client's full agreement and understanding.

Questions related to each of the objectives and constraints that follow can reveal a great deal about the client's objectives and constraints. However, there is also a place for a final overall question, such as, "Is there anything else that we haven't yet talked about, which might be important?" It is surprising what can come from such a question. The client might reveal pertinent facts such as a family member who is an insider (legal constraint), the presence of a serious illness (income and time horizon implications), or a pending marital breakup, which somehow did not get uncovered in previous conversation.

All the information learned from the client through interviews, questionnaires and follow-up discussions should be distilled into a return objective and a risk objective. These objectives must address the following questions:

• What rate of return does the client need to attain his or her goals?

• What risk is he or she willing and able to take to achieve them?

Return and Risk Objectives

The return objective is a measure of how much the client's portfolio is expected to earn each year on average. The return objective depends primarily on the return required to meet the client's goals, but it must also be consistent with the client's risk tolerance. An investor must determine whether a strategy of return maximization, in which assets are invested to make the greatest return possible while staying within the risk tolerance level, is preferable to a strategy in which a required minimum return is generated with certainty. The emphasis in the latter strategy is on risk reduction. In addition, the policy should be designed to take into account the client's tax position and needs with respect to the proportion of interest income, capital gains and dividend income to be generated.

The risk objective is a specific statement of how much risk the client is willing to sustain to meet the return objective. The risk objective is based on the client's risk tolerance, which in turn is dependent upon the client's willingness and ability to bear risk. Assessment of risk tolerance is a vital element in the ultimate design of the portfolio, as it will govern the selection of securities to be included.

Because the risk of a portfolio is less than the average risk of its holdings, the client's risk tolerance should be matched to the risk of the overall portfolio, and not to the risk of each security.

Although most retail clients will need some degree of inflation protection, the extent will vary. A retired person with a long time horizon and the goal of using the portfolio to generate income will be very concerned about the purchasing power of the cash flow from the portfolio.

The role of the portfolio process is to ensure that it generates returns while taking into account the investor's own particular level of risk tolerance. Therefore, managing risk is a major focus of portfolio management. While an increase in returns should result from an increase in risk, high-risk portfolios do not always turn out to be high-return portfolios.

Table 15.2 shows some of the alternatives available in constructing a portfolio. While grouping equities by level of risk is more subjective, the four definitions in Table 15.2 provide a basis for risk differentiation. The differences between the four equity risk categories are largely a function of differences in capitalization, earnings performance, predictability of earnings, liquidity and potential price volatility. Since these variables apply to all common shares in all industry groups, each industry may have companies whose securities could be ranked in any of the four groups. Also, because companies are not static, the risk in an individual security can change over time and may warrant a higher or lower ranking.

TABLE 15.2	SAMPLE RISK CATEGORIES WITHIN EACH ASSET CLASS
Cash or Cash Equivalents:	
1. Government issues (less than a year)	Lowest risk, highest quality
2. Corporate issues (less than a year)	Highest risk, lowest quality
Fixed-Income Securities:	
1. Short term (from one to five years)	Low risk, low price volatility
2. Medium term (from five to ten years)	Medium risk, medium price volatility
3. Long term (over ten years)	High risk, maximum price volatility
Equities	
1. Conservative	Low risk; high capitalization; predictable earnings; high yield; high dividend payouts; lower P-E ratios; low price volatility.
2. Growth	Medium risk; average capitalization; potential for above average growth in earnings; aggressive management; lower dividend payout; higher P-E ratios; potentially higher price volatility.
3. Venture	High risk; low capitalization; limited earnings record; no dividends; P-E of little significance; short operating history; highly volatile.
4. Speculative	Maximum risk; shorter term; maximum price volatility; no earnings; no dividends; P-E ratio not significant.

Investment Objectives

In general, investors have three primary investment objectives:

1. Safety of Principal

2. Income

3. Growth of Capital

And two secondary objectives:

4. Liquidity (or marketability)

5. Tax Minimization.

When necessary, the advisor can explain each objective to the client, and together, they can come to a joint conclusion as to the appropriate balance among the objectives. It may be difficult for clients to communicate their wishes in non-tangible ways, but allocation to each primary objective, on a percentage basis, is recommended. It adds clarity to both parties and will translate well into the **New Account Application Form** (**NAAF**) categories (refer to the copy of the NAAF shown in Chapter 26).

SAFETY OF PRINCIPAL OR PRESERVATION OF CAPITAL

One major objective is to have some assurance that the initial capital invested will largely remain intact. If this is the main concern among the three primary objectives, the client is effectively saying that, regardless of whether a small, large or nil return is generated on the capital, the advisor should try to avoid erosion of the amount initially invested.

If the highest degree of safety is required, it may be obtained by accepting a lower rate of income return and giving up much of the opportunity for capital growth. In Canada, a high degree of safety of principal and of certainty of income is offered by most federal, provincial and municipal bonds, if held to maturity. Shorter term bonds also offer a high degree of safety because they are close to their maturity dates. Government of Canada Treasury bills offer the highest degree of safety – they are virtually risk-free.

Examples of individual investors who might be seeking safety as a primary investment objective include:

- A young couple who are investing their savings for the eventual purchase of a house.

- A businessman who is temporarily investing the funds he will be using to buy out his partner in six months' time.

INCOME OBJECTIVE

This objective refers to the generation of a regular series of cash flows from a portfolio, whether in the form of dividends, interest or some other form. The taxation of dividends and interest income will be a major determinant of the split between income received from debt or equity securities. This split is decided at the time the asset mix is set.

An investor seeking to maximize the rate of income return usually gives up some safety if he or she purchases corporate bonds or preferred shares with lower investment ratings. In general, safety goes down as yield goes up.

Examples of investors who might emphasize income as a primary investment objective include:

*   A salaried individual who relies on the additional income from investments to meet the cost of raising and educating a family.

*   A retired couple whose pension income is insufficient to provide for all living expenses.

GROWTH OBJECTIVE

Growth of capital, or capital gains, refers to the profit generated when securities are sold for more than they cost to buy. When capital gains are the primary investment objective, the emphasis is on security selection and market timing. Capital gains are taxed more favourably than interest income (taxation is discussed in greater detail in chapter 25).

Examples of investors primarily seeking growth include:

*   A well-paid young executive with excess income who wishes to build his or her own pool of capital for early retirement.

*   A vice-president of a corporation who is seeking above average returns through common share investments.

Table 15.3, in very broad terms and disregarding inflation and its effects, shows the four major kinds of securities and evaluates them in terms of the three primary investment objectives.

TABLE 15.3	SECURITIES AND THEIR INVESTMENT OBJECTIVES		
Type of Security	**Safety**	**Income**	**Growth**
1. Short-Term Bonds	Best	Very steady	Very limited
2. Long-Term Bonds	Next best	Very steady	Variable
3. Preferred Stocks	Good	Steady	Variable
4. Common Stocks	Often the least	Variable	Often the most

LIQUIDITY (OR MARKETABILITY) OBJECTIVE

A secondary goal that may be sought by an investor is liquidity, also referred to as marketability, which is not necessarily related to safety, income return or capital gain. It simply means that at nearly all times there are buyers at some price level for the securities (usually at a small discount from fair value).

For some investors who may need money on short notice (i.e., liquidity), this feature is very important. For others, it may not be vital. Most Canadian securities (excluding some real estate–related securities) can be sold in reasonable quantities at some price, usually within one business day with settlement to follow within three business days.

TAX OBJECTIVE

When assessing the returns from any investment, the investor must consider the effect of taxation. The tax treatment of any investment varies depending on whether the returns are categorized as interest, dividends or capital gains. Thus, tax treatment of the returns influences the choice among investments.

Investment Constraints

Constraints provide some discipline in the fulfilment of a client's objectives. Constraints, which may loosely be defined as those items that may hinder or prevent the portfolio manager from satisfying the client's objectives, are often not given the importance they deserve in the policy formation process. Perhaps this is because objectives are a more comforting concept to dwell on than the discipline of constraints.

TIME HORIZON

A major factor in the design of a good portfolio is how well it reflects the **time horizon** of its goals. Fundamentally, the time horizon is the period of time from the present until the next major change in the client's circumstances. In other words, just because a client is 25 years of age and normal retirement is at age 60, this does not necessarily mean the time horizon is 35 years. Clients go through various events in their life, each of which can represent a time horizon and a need for a complete rebalancing of their portfolio.

> *Example:* Finishing university, planning for a career change, the birth of a child, the purchase of a home, and many other events besides retirement represent the end of one time horizon and the beginning of a new one.

While some major events in a client's life cannot be predicted, such as a serious health problem or loss of employment, a client's time horizon should still be the period of time from the present to the next major *expected* change in circumstances.

LIQUIDITY REQUIREMENTS

In portfolio management, liquidity means the amount of cash and near-cash in the portfolio. The cash component could be higher during certain parts of the market cycle, such as when securities are judged to be overpriced or too risky for that client, or when the yield curve is inverted and the returns on cash are high.

TAX REQUIREMENTS

An investor's marginal tax rate will dictate, in part, the proportion of income that should be received as dividends from Canadian corporations, which are eligible for a tax credit, versus interest income. Different marginal tax rates will help to dictate the proportion invested in preferred shares versus other fixed-income securities such as bonds. High tax rates, which significantly erode the final return on more traditional investments like GICs, are often a reason for a client to seek out the higher returns available from securities.

LEGAL AND REGULATORY REQUIREMENTS

Certainly, any investment activity that contravenes an Act, By-law, Regulation, Rule or the *Criminal Code* must be considered a constraint. For example, a client may be an insider or own a control position of a publicly-traded company and this client must comply with all applicable regulatory guidelines.

All firms have compliance personnel and many have legal counsel on staff. It is recommended that the investment advisor consult these resources when there is any question about legal issues.

UNIQUE CIRCUMSTANCES

Unique circumstances are specific to each client and must be considered in the creation of an effective investment policy. Examples of unique circumstances include the desire for ethically and socially responsible investing. For example, perhaps because of personal convictions, a client may instruct that no alcohol or tobacco stocks be purchased.

WHAT IS AN INVESTMENT POLICY STATEMENT?

The **investment policy statement (IPS)** contains the operating rules, guidelines, investment objectives and constraints, list of acceptable and prohibited investments, and method used for performance appraisal agreed to by the advisor and the client. It can be a lengthy, written and signed document, or it can be derived from the New Account Application Form in accordance with the Know Your Client rule. Regardless of its formality, the investment policy is the result of many complex inputs.

You can find a copy of a sample policy statement for a retail client in Module 16 of the course.

SUMMARY

After reading this chapter, you should be able to:

1. Describe the relationship between risk and return, calculate rates of return of a single security, identify the different types and measures of risk, and evaluate the role of risk in asset selection.

    *   Generally, to achieve higher returns, investors must be willing to accept a higher degree of risk.

    *   Returns from an investment can be measured in absolute dollars but are usually expressed as a percentage, or as a rate of return or yield. Historically, the highest rates of return have been achieved by securities that had the greatest variability or risk as measured by standard deviation.

    *   There is no universal definition of risk. In statistics, it is defined as the likelihood that the actual return will be different from the expected return. A variety of risks are present when investing. Systematic risk represents non-diversifiable risk, as it is always present and affects all assets within a certain class. Non-systematic risk is the risk that the price of a specific security or group of securities will change to a different degree or in a different direction from the market as a whole. Non-systematic risk can be reduced through diversification. Three common measures of risk are variance, standard deviation and beta:

        –   Variance measures the extent to which the possible realized returns differ from the expected return or the mean. The greater the variance, the greater the risk.

        –   Standard deviation is the square root of the variance. Expressed as a percentage, it gives an indication of the risk associated with an individual security or a portfolio. The greater the standard deviation, the greater the risk.

        –   Beta measures the degree to which equity securities or equity portfolios tend to move up and down with the market. The higher the beta, the greater the risk.

2. Explain the relationship between risk and return of a portfolio of securities, calculate and interpret the expected return of a portfolio, and identify strategies for maximizing return while reducing risk.

    *   Asset allocation involves determining the optimal division of an investor's portfolio among the different asset classes of cash, fixed income and equities to maximize portfolio return and reduce overall risk.

- There are a variety of measures available to assess the risk and return of a portfolio:

  - The return on a portfolio is calculated as the weighted average return on the securities held in the portfolio. While future returns are not controllable, risk can be managed to a certain extent by effective portfolio management.

  - Correlation looks at how securities relate to each other when they are added to a portfolio and how the resulting combination affects the portfolio's total risk and return.

  - An equity portfolio with a beta of 1.0 is considered as risky as the market; a beta less than 1.0 is less risky than the market; and a beta greater than 1.0 is more risky than the market.

  - Alpha measures the degree to which an equity portfolio performs better than would be expected from beta.

3. List the steps in the portfolio management process.

   - The six parts to the portfolio management process are: determining investment objectives and constraints; designing an investment policy statement; formulating an asset allocation strategy and selecting investment styles; implementing the asset allocation; monitoring the economy, the markets, the portfolio and the client; and evaluating portfolio performance.

4. Evaluate investment objectives and constraints and explain how to use them in creating an investment policy for a client.

   - An advisor must determine what rate of return a client needs to attain his or her goals, and what risk he or she is willing and able to take to achieve them.

   - In general, investors have three primary investment objectives: safety of principal, income and growth of capital. Two secondary objectives are liquidity and tax minimization.

   - Investment constraints are essentially considerations that may hinder or prevent the investment manager from satisfying the client's objectives, including time horizon, liquidity requirements, tax requirements, legal considerations and unique circumstances.

5. Describe the content of an investment policy statement and explain the purpose of an IPS.

- The investment policy statement contains the operating rules, guidelines, investment objectives and asset mix agreed on by the manager and the client. The policy statement forms the basis for the agreement between the manager and the client.

- Most investment policy statements cover the objectives and constraints of a portfolio, provide a list of acceptable securities and a list of prohibited securities, and outline the method to be used for performance appraisal.

Online Frequently Asked Questions

CSI has answered many frequently asked questions about this Chapter. Read through online Module 15 FAQs.

Online Post-Module Assessment

Once you have completed the chapter, take the Module 15 Post-Test.

Chapter *16*

The Portfolio
Management Process

16

The Portfolio Management Process

LEARNING OBJECTIVES

By the end of this chapter, you should be able to:

1. Describe the asset mix categories and evaluate strategies for setting the asset mix.
2. Compare and contrast the portfolio management styles of equity and fixed-income managers.
3. Discuss the benefits of asset allocation, distinguish strategic asset allocation from the types of ongoing asset allocation techniques, and differentiate active and passive management.
4. Describe the steps in monitoring and evaluating portfolio performance in relation to the market, the economy and the client.
5. Describe how portfolio performance is evaluated, calculate and interpret the total return and risk-adjusted rate of return of a portfolio.

PORTFOLIO ANALYSIS

Portfolio management is a process because financial markets and individual circumstances are ever changing, thus portfolio managers must be flexible to adapt to change. As we have seen before, there is no "one size fits all" solution to investing, and finding the right fit is critical to achieving financial objectives.

For an advisor, portfolio management involves analyzing a great deal of personal and financial information about a client to determine an asset mix that will best suit them. The asset mix can be allocated between cash, fixed-income securities and equities in any number of ways. A portfolio is never made up of one security; rather, it is a mix of a variety of securities that add up to something that is, or should be, more than the sum of its individual parts.

It is often quoted that the asset allocation decision has a significant impact on the overall return of a portfolio. Consequently, understanding what is involved with arriving at the asset mix decision is crucial for portfolio performance. When working with a client, an advisor must be able to explain the decisions and asset choices they made. Also, advisors must be prepared to react to changing markets, investor objectives and economic factors.

This chapter discusses some of the key theories, practices and measurement standards employed by the investment industry in the process of managing investment portfolios. Understanding this information is important because it can significantly contribute to how well an investor or advisor is able to comprehend and apply the language and skills of portfolio management.

🔑 KEY TERMS

Active investment strategy

Benchmark

Bottom-up analysis

Dynamic asset allocation

Indexing

Integrated asset allocation

Passive investment strategy

Sector rotation

Sharpe ratio

Strategic asset allocation

Tactical asset allocation

Top-down analysis

HOW IS AN ASSET MIX DEVELOPED?

After designing the investment policy (which you read about in Chapter 15), it is necessary to determine which investments will be selected.

To decide the exact make-up of the portfolio, i.e., to put together the appropriate asset mix, it is critical to understand the relationship between the equity cycle and the economic cycle and to use this understanding to plan the weighting to give to each asset class. In addition, it is essential to consider the individual characteristics and risk tolerance of the client.

The Asset Mix

The main asset classes are cash, fixed-income securities and equity securities. More sophisticated portfolios may also include alternative investments such as private equity capital funds, currency funds or hedge funds.

CASH

Cash includes currency, money market securities, Canada Savings Bonds, redeemable GICs, bonds with a maturity of one year or less, and all other cash equivalents. Cash is required to pay for expenses and to capitalize on opportunities, but is primarily used for liquidity purposes in case of emergencies.

In general terms, cash usually makes up at least 5% of a diversified portfolio's asset mix. Investors who are very risk averse may hold as much as 10% in cash. While cash levels may temporarily rise greatly above these amounts during certain market periods or portfolio rebalancings, normal long term strategic asset allocations for cash are often within the 5%–10% range.

FIXED-INCOME

Fixed-income products consist of bonds due in more than one year, strip bonds, mortgage-backed securities, fixed-income exchange-traded funds, and other debt instruments, as well as preferred shares. Convertible securities are not considered to be fixed-income products in the asset allocation process. The purpose of including fixed-income products is primarily to produce income as well as provide some safety of principal, although they are also sometimes purchased to generate capital gains.

From a portfolio management standpoint, preferred shares are simply another type of fixed-income security. They have a stated level of income, trade on a yield basis, are subject to the same protective provisions, and have a reasonably definable term. Although, legally, preferreds are an equity security, they are listed in portfolios as part of the fixed income component because of the price action and cash flow characteristics listed above.

Diversification can be achieved in this part of the asset mix in several ways:

- Both government and corporate bonds can be used, a range of credit qualities from AAA to lower grades can be chosen.

- Foreign bonds may be added to domestic holdings.

- A variety of terms to maturity, or *durations*, are often used (this is called *laddering*, with the various consecutive maturities mimicking rungs on a ladder).

- Deep discount or stripped bonds can be chosen alongside high-coupon bonds.

The amount of a portfolio allocated to fixed-income securities is governed by several factors:

- the need for income over capital gains
- the basic minimum income required
- the desire for preservation of capital
- other factors such as tax and time horizon

EQUITIES

Equities include not only common shares but also derivatives such as rights, warrants, stock and stock index options, equity exchange-traded funds, etc., and both convertible bonds and convertible preferreds. Although a dividend stream may flow from the equity section of a portfolio, its main purpose is to generate capital gains either through trading or long-term growth in value.

OTHER ASSET CLASSES

While portfolios of most retail clients consist of cash, fixed-income and equities, it is possible to diversify even further by adding other investments that do not lend themselves to being included in one of the major asset classes. Many portfolio managers believe that **hedge funds** should be considered a separate asset class.

It is also possible to invest directly in real estate, precious metals and collectibles, such as art or coins. Many of these investments, such as gold, are considered to be a good hedge against inflation.

Complete the following Online Learning Activity

Portfolio Mix

In this activity, you will learn how your portfolio mix may look like based on different objectives and risk tolerance profile.

 Complete the **Portfolio Mix** activity.

Setting the Asset Mix

The phases of the equity cycle (which traces movements in the stock market) are expansion, peak, contraction, trough and recovery. Understanding the equity cycle provides a useful approach for a general understanding of stock market movements.

Figure 16.1 shows the S&P/TSX Composite Index over the last few decades and illustrates (with shading) the different phases. It is important to note that within a stock market expansion phase, which may last several years, there are also serious setbacks or corrections to stock prices which may last as long as a year.

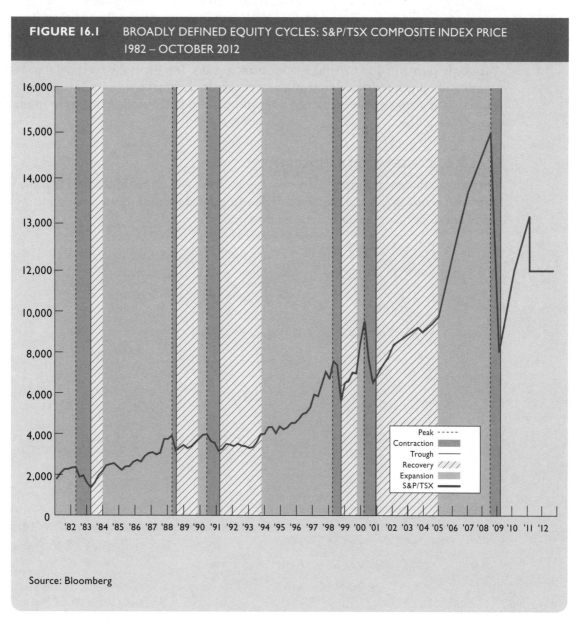

FIGURE 16.1 BROADLY DEFINED EQUITY CYCLES: S&P/TSX COMPOSITE INDEX PRICE 1982 – OCTOBER 2012

Source: Bloomberg

ASSET CLASS TIMING

The general framework that follows outlines the most basic strategies for investors who choose to time stock, bond and T-bill investments. The benefits from successfully timing asset class selections are impressive. However, this presupposes that the investor has successful asset mix analytic tools available that indicate when to make shifts between stocks, bonds and T-bills. In reality, most investors would have trouble determining whether a rise in interest rates is designed to slow economic growth or will actually lead to a recession and, therefore, a contraction phase in stock prices.

The rationale behind asset class timing is that investors who recognize when to switch from stocks to T-bills, to bonds and back to stocks can improve returns. In addition, if at the time in question bonds are the best asset class, then it should make sense to lengthen the term of bond holdings to maximize returns. Similarly, if stocks are the best asset class, then certain strategies can be implemented to maximize stock market gains. It is generally accepted that asset mix factors account for 90% or more of the variation in the total returns of investment portfolios. Investment analysts have developed sophisticated computer models that assist in the timing of asset class shifts.

THE LINK BETWEEN EQUITY AND ECONOMIC CYCLES

In order to understand stock market strategies, it is essential to understand that there is a link between equity cycles and economic cycles. In general, the equity and economic cycles are very similar except that the equity cycle tends to lead.

ECONOMIC GROWTH IN NOMINAL GDP

Figure 16.2 shows that the sustained economic growth in nominal GDP beginning in 1982 and 1996 fits closely the generally sustained rise in stock prices over that time. It is important to note that the beginning of the equity cycle actually preceded the beginning of the economic cycle by several months during 1982–1983 and 1996–1997. The equity cycle also preceded the beginning of the economic cycle in 2009, further underscoring the Toronto Stock Exchange's role as a leading indicator.

FIGURE 16.2 S&P/TSX COMPOSITE, CANADIAN GDP (AVERAGE ANNUAL % CHANGE) 1974 – OCTOBER 2012

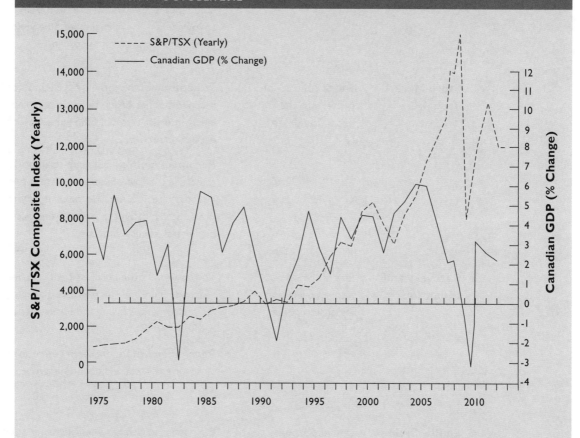

Source Bloomberg; Adapted from Statistics Canada

For investors who understand the relationship between economic and equity cycles, it is possible to follow the general investment strategies outlined in Table 16.1.

TABLE 16.1	GENERAL INVESTMENT STRATEGIES	
Equity Cycle	**Business Cycle**	**Strategy**
1. **Contraction Phase**	End of expansion through peak, into the contraction phase	• Recession conditions are apparent. Interest rates are high. • *Recommendation*: Lengthen term of bond holdings, e.g., sell short-term bonds and buy mid- to long-term. Try to maintain same yield (income). Avoid or reduce stock exposure
2. **Stock Market Trough**	End of contraction phase, into the expansion phase	• The bottom of the business cycle has not been reached but has begun to advance because of falling interest rates and the expectations of an economic recovery. • *Recommendation*: Sell long-term bonds since they rallied ahead of stocks in response to falling interest rates. Common stocks usually rally dramatically; often the largest gains occur in the higher-risk cyclical industries.
3. **Recovery and expansion**	End of trough, into recovery and expansion phase	• The bottom of the business cycle has been reached. Economy starts growing again, unemployment is falling and businesses are making profits. • *Recommendation*: Increase common stock exposure as sustained economic growth generally allows stocks to do well.
4. **Equity Cycle Peak**	Late expansion into peak phase	• Economic growth has been sustained; however, this has also led to higher interest rates and the Bank of Canada may be tightening its monetary policy. Short-term interest rates tend to be higher than long-term rates, i.e., the yield curve is inverted. • *Recommendation*: Reduce common stocks exposure and invest in short-term interest-bearing paper. The equity cycle peak is generally followed by the contraction phase.

The problem with these general strategies is that they do not account for the many important variations that occur during an equity cycle. These variations may dramatically affect stock and bond market performance for 12 months or longer.

> **Example:** During the expansion phase of 1982 to 1989, the stock market experienced sharp declines due to high interest rates for six months in 1984 and during the stock market crash of 1987. While the general strategies appear attractive, variations within a cycle can affect asset class performance.

Changes in the S&P/TSX Composite price level result, generally, from changes in interest rates or economic growth. The relationships between interest rate trends and economic trends (and therefore corporate profit trends) are of the greatest significance to equity price levels. These two factors, in combination, generally account for 80%–90% of the change in stock market prices.

As a result, these factors are often used together in asset mix models. As interest rates are used by central banks as a policy tool for managing economic growth, changes in rates tend to lead changes in economic growth.

WHAT ARE THE PORTFOLIO MANAGER STYLES?

Portfolio managers, and investors to some extent, tend to follow one of two investment strategies—active and passive.

The goal of an **active investment strategy** is to outperform a benchmark portfolio on a risk-adjusted basis. Investors can judge the success of their active strategies by comparing their portfolio's or asset class's performance to that of an appropriate benchmark or index.

> **Example:** the performance of an equity strategy that focuses on small-capitalization stocks should be gauged against a small-cap equity index.

Active equity investment strategies can be separated into two groups based on the approach used to select stocks for purchase or sale: bottom-up or top-down.

Bottom-up analysis begins with a focus on individual stocks. Investors or portfolio managers look at the characteristics of individual stocks and build portfolios of the best stocks in terms of forecasted risk-return characteristics.

Top-down analysis begins with a study of broad macroeconomic factors before it narrows the analysis to individual stocks. The classic approach to top-down analysis involves analyzing macroeconomic and capital market factors, then looking at industry-specific factors to evaluate a company's operating environment, and finally using company-specific factors to assess the value of a firm's common stock.

The two approaches are not mutually exclusive. A compelling recommendation about a particular stock or managed product should always include both external (macroeconomic and industry) and internal factors likely to affect the price of the security.

Managers using a passive investment strategy tend to replicate the performance of a specific market index without trying to beat it. Passive investment strategies can also be divided into two approaches: indexing and buy-and-hold.

Passive management is consistent with the view that securities markets are efficient – that is, securities prices at all times reflect all relevant information on expected return and risk. The passive portfolio manager does not believe that it is possible to identify stocks as underpriced or overpriced, at least to an extent that would achieve enough extra return to cover the added transactions costs. These managers use a buy-and-hold system.

Indexing is a portfolio management style that involves buying and holding a portfolio of securities that matches the composition of a benchmark index. This method does not require much trading or managerial expertise. The exception to this would be when the underlying stocks in the index change. Then the manager must trade, in order to keep the index fund matching the index.

Equity Manager Styles

GROWTH MANAGERS

Growth managers focus on stocks with above average potential for price increase.

In the bottom-up approach, growth managers focus on current and future earnings of individual companies, specifically earnings per share (EPS). Growth managers are looking for "earnings momentum" and they will pay more for companies if they feel the company's growth potential warrants the higher price. Stocks in this type of portfolio usually have a lower dividend yield, or provide no dividend at all, and managers may turn over the securities in the portfolio more often.

Risk Features

- If EPS falters, it can cause large percentage price declines.

- Reported EPS, above or below analysts' expectations, produces high portfolio volatility.

- These types of securities are highly vulnerable to market cycles.

Valuation

- High Price-Earnings Ratios

- High Price/Book Value

- High Price/Cash Flow

Long-term total return is gathered mostly through capital appreciation. Growth managers are usually not concerned with quarterly portfolio fluctuations. Clients must be more risk tolerant (i.e., they do not panic in down markets) and have long-term investment horizons.

The growth manager's challenge is to avoid paying too much. Growth investing is a matter of expectations and growth stocks seldom seem cheap today. But, if the company continues to grow as expected, then today's stock price will represent a good investment a year or two from now.

The growth style works best in rising markets. However, stocks with above-average prices are more vulnerable in bear markets. The style is appropriate for investors who are aggressive or who favour momentum investing, and who enjoy making spectacular gains in rising markets.

The growth style holds greater potential for capital appreciation because of faster earnings growth. Growth stocks tend to reinvest more of their earnings. However, this style has greater volatility, hence risk, since more of the total return of the portfolio is derived from capital appreciation rather than more stable dividend income. Also, growth stocks may fall more rapidly than other stocks in a declining market.

Since portfolio turnover tends to be higher, investors in taxable accounts may be liable for increased amounts of capital gains tax every year.

VALUE MANAGERS

For value investing managers, the focus is on specific stock selection. They are bottom-up stock pickers as well, with a research-intensive approach. Security turnover is typically low, as the manager will wait for a stock's intrinsic value to be realized. Since a stock is often cheap for a reason (it is out of favour), realizing its intrinsic value can take some time, if ever. Value managers seeks stocks that are often overlooked, disliked or out of favour with individual investors, institutional investors and equity analysts.

Risk Features

- Lower annualized standard deviation

- Lower historical beta

- Stock price is already low, so the downside is low

Valuation

- Low Price-Earnings ratios

- Low Price/Book Value

- Low Price/Cash Flow

- High dividend yield

Over the long term, value investing has produced total returns virtually identical to those of growth investing but with higher current dividend yield and less portfolio volatility. This style tends to perform best in down markets with some participation in up markets.

Because of the lower volatility associated with this style of management, value managers can be used as core managers for low-to-medium market risk tolerant clients with long-term investment horizons. This style of investing requires patience. The patience comes from waiting for the value of the underpriced bargains to be realized by the market.

By screening stocks for cheap fundamentals, and investigating a company's management, products or services, and competitive position, managers can buy stocks at discounts that should eventually rise in price. Because turnover in portfolios with a value bias tends to be low, investors incur fewer capital gains. Value investing largely ignores short-term market fluctuations.

A value manager's picks may not be immediately recognized as undervalued by the market. Value investing is more successful in inefficient markets, when stock prices may be out of line with corporate fundamentals, or in a stagnant or declining market, when there is greater emphasis on preserving capital or minimizing short-term losses.

One drawback to the value style of investing is that in efficient stock markets, the price of individual securities tends to reflect all that is known about them. Thus, an individual stock may be trading at a low price for a good reason that does not show up in its financial statements.

Because of the focus on "good value," value managers may be drawn to companies that are in need of a turnaround to overcome financial or competitive difficulties.

SECTOR ROTATION

Sector rotation applies a top-down approach, focusing on analyzing the prospects for the overall economy. Based on that assessment, the managers invest in the industry sectors expected to outperform. These managers typically buy large-cap stocks to maximize their liquidity. They are not as concerned with individual stock characteristics. Their primary focus is to:

• Identify the current phase of the economic cycle,

• The direction the economy is headed in, and

• The various sectors affected.

In other words, managers applying this strategy believe that industry selection is more important than stock selection, and therefore often try to identify emerging trends.

Risk features include high volatility caused by industry concentration and rotation between industries and greater risk if the manager's economic scenario is wrong and the favoured industries do not perform as expected.

Over short periods, managers and investors who use sector rotation may significantly underperform the market benchmark. The turnover for a sector rotation–style portfolio also tends to be high. This pushes up trading costs and the expenses charged to the fund. The higher turnover may create problems for taxable accounts, since there may be capital gains tax payable because of frequent trades. Also, the style's emphasis on industry sectors means that the merits of individual companies get less scrutiny and good individual stocks may be overlooked.

The emphasis on large, liquid companies that lead their particular sector also means that the actual stocks picked may not necessarily represent the performance of the entire sector. Stock-specific circumstances may cause an individual holding to behave very differently from its industry peers.

Sector rotation is concerned with trying to outperform the market averages such as the S&P/TSX Composite Index. For example:

• During the last stages of recession, bank stocks may rally first, to be followed by consumer growth stocks, consumer cyclical stocks, and thereafter those stocks that tend to benefit even later in an economic cycle, such as those for capital goods and commodity-based industries.

• Successfully shifting between these groups can produce greater returns than just buying and holding a diversified portfolio of stocks. However, industry rotation can be very complicated.

The most basic industry rotation strategy involves shifting back and forth between *cyclical* and *defensive* industries. During periods in which stock prices are falling, cyclical stocks tend to fall relatively faster. Defensive stocks, such as banks or utilities, tend to preserve capital by falling relatively more slowly. However, during periods in which stock prices are rising, cyclical industries, such as paper and forestry or integrated mines, tend to rise relatively faster because their profit growth is more robust during an economic expansion.

Industry rotation strategies become more complex once additional industry types are considered and variations in economic cycles are taken into account. For example:

- Some industry groups are *interest rate sensitive* and follow a pattern that conforms almost entirely to the interest rate cycle.

- However, growth industries may do consistently well in most economic environments because of sustained growth in corporate profits.

- A minority of industries are counter-cyclical or lag the market averages. For example, gold stocks are occasionally inversely related to the S&P/TSX Composite Index. Specifically, gold stock prices occasionally rise during recessions while stock market average price levels are falling.

Variations in the economic cycle can also have a dramatic bearing on the timing of sector rotation. Generally, two-thirds of a new economic recovery is being driven by an increase in consumer spending. This tends to lead to the need for businesses to add to plant and capacity, which results in an increased demand for capital goods and provides a boost for the stocks of capital goods makers.

Fixed-Income Manager Styles

Fixed-income managers invest in fixed-income products. Their choices may vary, depending on the term to maturity, credit quality, or their expectations of what will happen with interest rates and how this will affect the prices of the fixed-income products.

TERM TO MATURITY

Short-term managers will hold T-bills and short-term bonds with maturities less than five years. There is less volatility when interest rates rise since the portfolio has investments maturing that can be reinvested at the higher rates.

Medium-term managers' term to maturity will range from five to ten years. Mortgage funds are a good example. These funds generally invest in high-quality residential mortgages (usually NHA insured) with terms of five years.

Long-term managers will hold bonds with maturities of greater than ten years or longer.

CREDIT QUALITY

Bond quality of investment-grade bonds ranges from high (AAA) to low (BBB). High-quality issuers are typically federal and provincial governments and some very well-capitalized corporations. Generally, the lower the quality of the bond, the higher the yield it must have, so managers must balance the return potential with the risk of default. Many bond portfolios have predetermined credit quality limits under which they will not invest.

High-yield bonds are bonds that are not investment grade. They are often called junk bonds. Bonds in this category should have a higher yield, but they face greater credit risk. To mitigate this risk, managers often invest in high-yield bonds maturing in less than three years.

Because of the higher credit risk, corporate issues have higher yields than comparable Government of Canada issues. Thus, by selecting higher-quality corporate issues, a manager can improve a portfolio's yield without taking on much additional risk.

Another factor to consider with corporate issuers is liquidity. Lower-rated bonds have less liquidity than government issues. In a declining market, it may be difficult to find a buyer for this kind of debt.

INTEREST RATE ANTICIPATORS

Some managers feel they can add value by anticipating the direction of interest rates and structuring their portfolios accordingly.

- They will extend the average term on their bond investments when they anticipate a decrease in the general level of interest rates.

- If they anticipate an increase in interest rates, they will shorten the term.

Interest rate anticipation, sometimes also referred to as a form of duration switching, works best when the yield curve is normal – that is, there is a wide gap between short-term and long-term rates. If the yield curve is flat, it is not advantageous to extend the term to maturity of the portfolio. As explained in Chapter 7, the higher the duration of the portfolio, the greater the gain from falling interest rates and the greater the potential for capital gains.

WHAT IS ASSET ALLOCATION?

Asset allocation involves determining the optimal division of an investor's portfolio among the different asset classes. For example, depending on the client's tolerance for risk and the investment objectives, the portfolio may be divided as follows: 10% in cash, 30% in fixed-income securities, and 60% in equities.

It should be noted that clients' needs and objectives will change over their lifetimes. Asset allocation will have to be adjusted to take into account these shifting needs.

Portfolio managers and investors will also alter asset allocation to take advantage of changes in the economic environment. For example, when the economy enters a period of rapid growth, the portfolio manager must decide how best to take advantage of the market. He or she will likely decide that a heavier "weighting" in equities would generate better returns than holding more of the portfolio in fixed-income securities or cash.

Alternatively, if the portfolio manager believes the market is entering a recession, a heavier weighting in cash or fixed-income securities may be pursued to generate higher returns. This process of altering a portfolio's asset allocation to take advantage of changes in the economy is one meaning of the term market timing.

THE IMPORTANCE OF ASSET ALLOCATION

Investment returns are derived from:

- The choice of an asset mix
- Market timing decisions
- Securities selection
- Chance

Asset allocation is the single most important step in structuring a portfolio. It is estimated that it accounts for approximately 90% of the variation in returns on an investment portfolio.

All of the previous portfolio management process steps do nothing to benefit the client unless the portfolio is actually created by purchasing suitable securities. This selection stems from the equity and fixed-income analysis discussed in earlier chapters. Because the portfolio approach is being emphasized, an important consideration is how the securities interact with each other. Even more important is how the asset classes perform against each other, with each generating returns while offsetting some of the others' risks.

Table 16.2 demonstrates the importance of the asset mix in determining overall portfolio return.

In Part A, Annual Return by Asset Class, Portfolio Manager X outperforms Portfolio Manager Y by 22% in cash, 100% in fixed-income securities and 50% in equities.

However, Part B highlights the actual allocation of assets in each portfolio. Clearly, Portfolio Manager X invested more heavily in fixed-income securities whereas Portfolio Manager Y emphasized equities in his portfolio.

Part C shows the total return realized by each portfolio manager in a $1,000 portfolio. (Total return is calculated by multiplying the amount invested in each asset group by the rate of return for that group and adding the results.) Even though Portfolio Manager X significantly outperformed Manager Y in each asset class, the asset mix decision enabled Manager Y to achieve a higher total return in the portfolio.

TABLE 16.2 ASSET MIX & TOTAL RETURN			
Asset Group	**Index or Average**	**Portfolio Manager X**	**Portfolio Manager Y**
A. Annual Return by Asset Class			
Cash	10%	11%	9%
Fixed-Income Securities	6%	8%	4%
Equities	25%	30%	20%

Asset Group	Index or Average	Portfolio Manager X	Portfolio Manager Y
B. Actual Asset Mix			
Cash		5%	5%
Fixed-Income Securities		70%	25%
Equities		25%	70%
C. Total Return on a $1,000 Portfolio			
Cash		$5.50	$4.50
Fixed-Income Securities		56.00	10.00
Equities		75.00	140.00
Total Return		**$136.50**	**$154.50**
Total % Return		**13.65%**	**15.45%**

TABLE 16.2   ASSET MIX & TOTAL RETURN – *Cont'd*

The conclusion is clear. When seeking to maximize the total return of a balanced portfolio, it is more important to emphasize the correct asset group than to outperform an index or market average within an asset group. This is particularly true when capital markets are volatile.

Balancing the Asset Classes

The next step in the asset allocation process is to determine the appropriate balance among the selected asset classes. Using only cash, fixed-income and equity asset classes to make up a suitable portfolio, the following are examples of some approximate asset mixes. Note that they are provided for illustration only. The full set of client circumstances must be known to set an asset mix rather than simply choosing the closest example below.

- A young, healthy, single individual professional with good investment knowledge, high risk tolerance, moderate tax rate and a long time horizon:

Cash	5%
Fixed-Income	25%
Equities	70%
Allocation	100%

- A senior citizen in a low tax bracket with no income other than government pensions, a medium time horizon and low risk tolerance:

Cash	8%
Fixed-Income	67%
Equities	25%
Allocation	100%

- A middle-aged line factory worker, married with three teenaged children, who is a homeowner with great concerns about future employment and funding college education, and with limited investment knowledge:

Cash	10%
Fixed-Income	40%
Equities	50%
Allocation	100%

Strategic Asset Allocation

Investment management firms, both large and small, often have proprietary, highly sophisticated models to forecast security prices. Here we show how asset allocation is determined through historical results, as shown in Table 16.3. Considering only equities and fixed-income, and with 10% increments in the asset mix, the following are the expected returns for the various asset mixes.

TABLE 16.3	EXPECTED RETURNS FOR THE VARIOUS ASSET MIXES			
Asset Mix		**Historical Returns**		
Equities (%)	**Fixed-income (%)**	**Equities (%)**	**Fixed-income (%)**	**Expected Return on Portfolio (%)**
0	100	10.0	4.4	4.40
10	90	10.0	4.4	4.96
20	80	10.0	4.4	5.52
30	70	10.0	4.4	6.08
40	60	10.0	4.4	6.64
50	50	10.0	4.4	7.20
60	40	10.0	4.4	7.76
70	30	10.0	4.4	8.32
80	20	10.0	4.4	8.88
90	10	10.0	4.4	9.44
100	0	10.0	4.4	10.00

The table illustrates an analysis which considers equities/fixed-income combinations of 0% equities/100% fixed-income, 10%/90%, 20%/80%, and so on to 100% equities/0% fixed-income. The expected return of each asset mix combination is calculated by the manager. After viewing the possibilities outlined above, and considering the relative riskiness of stocks versus bonds, the manager will choose the optimal combination in consultation with the client. This asset mix is usually expressed in terms of percentage holdings, such as a 60/40 equities/fixed-income mix. If the manager chooses a 60/40 equities/fixed-income mix, the portfolio will have an expected return of 7.76%.

This base policy mix is called the **strategic asset allocation**. This is the long-term mix that will be adhered to by monitoring and, when necessary, rebalancing. As was just shown, to determine the strategic allocation, a limited number of asset mixes is analyzed to determine the expected return of each combination. In consultation with the client, the manager then reviews the range of outcomes and chooses one, to determine the long-term policy, or strategic, asset mix.

This base policy mix does not necessarily imply a buy-and-hold strategy, because shifting values of the asset classes will cause the allocation to "drift" from the strategic mix.

Example: Suppose a $100,000 portfolio is invested $60,000 in equities and $40,000 in fixed-income, for a 60/40 asset mix. If the stock market rose 10% while the bond market sagged 10%, the investor's portfolio mix would be higher than 60% equities, and lower than 40% fixed-income, after the change in market values. This is shown in Table 16.4 below.

TABLE 16.4   SECURITIES PRICE CHANGES AND ASSET MIX

Type of Security	Before Change	Change	After Change
Equities	$60,000	+$6,000	$66,000
Fixed-income	$40,000	-$4,000	$36,000
Asset Mix	60 / 40		64.7 / 35.3

Ongoing Asset Allocation

Once the asset mix is implemented, the asset classes will begin to change in value with fluctuations in the market. Dividends and interest income will flow into the cash component. As a result, the asset mix will begin to change.

Example: A portfolio starting out with an asset mix of 10% cash, 40% fixed-income and 50% equities could see its cash increase to 15% through cash flows from interest, dividends and maturing bonds, and the equity component could rise to 55% through capital gains.

Although the fixed-income class might be higher in value than before, proportionately it would now be underweighted, at only 30% of the total portfolio value versus the original 40%. This calls for a rebalancing back to the original policy mix of 10%/40%/50%. Investment managers rebalance in a disciplined manner, acting before the mix gets too out of balance, while remaining conscious of transaction costs. The manager will typically specify that an asset class must move more than a certain percentage (i.e., 5%) before it will be rebalanced.

DYNAMIC ASSET ALLOCATION

Dynamic asset allocation is a portfolio management technique that involves adjusting the asset mix to systematically re-balance the portfolio back to its long-term target or strategic asset mix. Re-balancing may be necessary for a variety of reasons:

- There is a build-up of idle cash reserves, possibly from dividends or interest income cash flows, that have not been re-invested.

- There are movements in the capital markets. These movements can cause abnormal returns, such as the 1987 market crash or the 1998 Asian financial crisis.

The portfolio manager follows a policy that places a limit on the degree to which each asset category can drift above or below the long-term target mix. Re-balancing becomes necessary once an asset category moves above or below this range. For example, the policy may call for a re-balancing if equities rise by more than 5% above their target weighting.

A dynamic re-balancing approach can be demonstrated using the example in Table 16.5. The strong performance in the stock market has altered the target asset mix to 64.7% equities and 35.3% fixed-income. One method of re-balancing the portfolio back to its target mix involves the direct buying and selling of the securities in the portfolio. The table demonstrates that to restore the target mix, a dynamic approach would involve:

- Selling $4,800 worth of equities

- Buying $4,800 worth of fixed-income

TABLE 16.5	DYNAMIC REBALANCING				
Asset Class	Asset Mix After Rise in Stock Market	New Asset Mix	Dynamic Re-balancing	Re-balanced Portfolio	New Asset Mix
Equities	$66,000	64.7%	-$4,800	$61,200	60%
Fixed-income	$36,000	35.3%	+$4,800	$40,800	40%
Asset Mix	$102,000	100.0%		$102,000	100%

Under the dynamic approach, re-balancing dampens returns in a strong market period since the portfolio manager is reducing the strongest-performing component. It enhances returns in a weak market period through the purchase of under-performing asset classes at reduced price levels.

The dynamic strategy is suitable for a more risk-averse investor, such as a retired individual with low risk tolerance. The tax situation of the investor should be reviewed carefully, as such active management will result in more realized capital gains and losses.

TACTICAL ASSET ALLOCATION

Strategic asset allocation need not be an absolutely rigid approach. While the investment policy statement may indicate a long-run mix of 60% equities and 40% fixed-income, the statement may also allow for some short-term, tactical, deviations from the strategic mix to capitalize on investment opportunities in one asset class before reverting back to the long-term strategic asset allocation. This is known as **tactical asset allocation**.

Example: If the bond market is depressed and poised for an upswing, the manager may overweight the portfolio in fixed-income products well over the strategic asset allocation for fixed-income for as long as a few months and then, having profited from this move, move back to the long-term strategic asset allocation. This enables the manager to exercise any market timing skills he or she may have, while investing for the expected return indicated by the strategic mix. In such a case, a strategic allocation could be considered a long-term strategy, with tactical deviations a short-term strategy.

Though not a passive strategy, this approach is only moderately active, and is appropriate for the long-term investor who is interested in market timing.

INTEGRATED ASSET ALLOCATION

All of the above types include consideration of capital market expectations, but only some take into account changes in capital markets or client risk tolerance. **Integrated asset allocation** refers to an all-encompassing strategy that includes all of these factors. The other asset allocation techniques are partial versions of the integrated approach.

Complete the following Online Learning Activity

Asset Allocation

One of the key steps in the asset allocation process is to determine the appropriate balance among the selected asset classes: Cash, Fixed Income and Equities. In these activities, you will review the different types of asset allocation strategy.

 Complete the **Asset Allocation** activity.

 Complete the **Trisha - Asset Allocation Strategy** activity.

WHAT IS PORTFOLIO MONITORING?

Having set the investment policy and designed and implemented an asset mix, the next step in the portfolio process is to monitor all fronts. The three key areas of focus are the market, the client and the economy.

Constructing a portfolio is only a beginning. Managing one is an ongoing process. It is, therefore, essential to develop a system to monitor the appropriateness of the securities that comprise the portfolio and the strategies that govern it. The process is twofold as it involves monitoring:

• The changes in the investor's goals, financial position and preferences; and

• Expectations for capital markets and individual securities.

Monitoring the Markets and the Client

Keeping informed of client objectives is critical. Investors may change their tolerance for risk, their need for liquidity, their need for savings, and their tax brackets. Therefore, client profiles must be updated on a regular basis. The New Account Application Form sets out the original profile of a client's income and asset levels, investment knowledge and goals.

These basic facts should be reviewed and kept current. If any significant change occurs, an amended New Account Application Form should be completed.

Capital markets are also constantly changing to reflect changes in government and central bank policies, economic growth or recession, and sectoral shifts in prosperity within the economy. The portfolio manager must be constantly alert to the direction of monetary policy, forecasts for GDP and the inflation rate, shifts in consumer demand and capital spending, and the potential impact of all these factors on the strategic asset mix or on individual holdings.

The challenge for the portfolio manager is to anticipate change and systematically adjust the portfolio to reflect both return expectations and the objectives of the client. The process of adjusting a portfolio follows the same methodology that is used when constructing it.

Monitoring the Economy

The asset mix decision involves an analysis of all capital markets and is complex. Virtually all information that may affect each asset class has to be incorporated into the decision-making process. The scope of this material includes expected activities in the private and public sectors, both nationally and internationally. It includes government policies, corporate earnings, economic analysis, existing market conditions and the forecaster's interpretation of the data.

Because of the complexity of the data and the subjectivity in interpretation, it is very difficult to make an accurate prediction about the magnitude of change in a particular asset class. For this reason, forecasts are sometimes expressed in ranges, with a minimum and maximum level. The use of a range not only reflects the unpredictability of capital markets, but it can also indicate the degree of risk anticipated.

The expected total returns for each asset group are calculated by adding the expected annual income to the expected capital gain or loss for each group.

> **Example:** If stock prices are expected to increase 10% and dividend yields are forecast to be 4%, then the expected total pre-tax return for equities would be 14%. (An example of a return forecast is provided in Module 16 of the CSC interactive online learning aid.)

Complete the following Online Learning Activity

Portfolio Monitoring

After the creation of a portfolio, the next step is the ongoing management of the portfolio. There are many factors that contribute to the change of a portfolio: the economy, the market and the client. In these activities, you will learn how the economy, the market and the client's situation can impact a portfolio.

 Work through the **Portfolio Monitoring** activity.

 Complete the **Portfolio Monitoring Scenario** activity.

HOW IS PORTFOLIO PERFORMANCE EVALUATED?

The success of a portfolio manager is determined by comparing the total rate of return of the portfolio being evaluated with the average total return of comparable portfolios. In this way, the portfolio manager and the client can compare their returns to industry norms and estimate their approximate ranking in relation to other portfolio managers.

For most individual investors, the ranking can be estimated most easily by comparing their performance with the averages shown in one of the surveys of funds appearing regularly in financial publications. Not only is it convenient, but many different funds are measured in the surveys and the portfolio manager can compare both the total return and the component returns of the portfolio. For example, the equity component of a diversified portfolio can be compared with the equity funds shown.

Managers are often measured against a predetermined **benchmark** that was specified in the investment policy statement. One common benchmark is the T-bill rate plus some sort of performance benchmark, perhaps the T-bill rate plus 4%. On portfolios that have low turnover to avoid capital gains taxes, performance against the market benchmark may not be appropriate. What investors are interested in is the protection and growth of their purchasing power.

Measuring Portfolio Returns

A simple method of computing total return is to divide the portfolio's total earnings (income plus capital gains or losses), or the increase (or decrease) in the market value of the portfolio, by the amount invested in the portfolio.

Example: Assume that in the course of a particular year a portfolio had a market value of $106,000 on January 1, and the market value of the portfolio on December 31 was $110,000. On this basis, the return for the portfolio for the year would be 3.77%, as calculated using the total return formula (pre-tax).

$$\text{Total Return} = \frac{\text{Increase in Market Value}}{\text{Beginning Value}} \times 100$$

$$= \frac{\$110,000 - \$106,000}{\$106,000} \times 100$$

$$= \frac{\$4,000}{\$106,000} \times 100$$

$$= 3.77\%$$

The above formula and calculation assumes no contributions to the portfolio by the client or withdrawals from the portfolio by the client.

When there are cash flows, a portion of the change in the value of the portfolio is the result of the cash flows themselves. For instance, if a portfolio is worth $100,000 at the start of the year and $150,000 at the end of the year, and the client added $15,000 in cash to the portfolio during the year, then $15,000 of the $50,000 increase in the value of the portfolio comes from the contribution, not return on investment. The return on a portfolio is affected by both the *amount* and *timing* of portfolio cash flows. There are several ways to deal with cash flows, and different portfolio reporting systems use different methods. These methods are explained fully in CSI's *Investment Management Techniques (IMT)* and *Wealth Management Essentials (WME)* courses.

Calculating the Risk-Adjusted Rate of Return

It is not enough merely to compare the returns of two portfolios to measure performance, without factoring in the risk assumed to earn those returns. The **Sharpe Ratio**, used by mutual fund companies and portfolio managers, compares the return of the portfolio to the riskless rate of return, taking the portfolio's risk into account. It measures the portfolio's risk-adjusted rate of return using standard deviation as the measure of risk.

$$S_p = \frac{R_p - R_f}{\sigma_p}$$

Where:

S_p = Sharpe Ratio

R_p = Return of the portfolio

R_f = Risk-free rate (typically the average of the three-month Treasury bill rate over the period being measured)

σ_p = Standard deviation of the portfolio

A good manager should be able to earn a risk-adjusted rate of return that is greater than the risk-free rate. If the risk-adjusted rate of return is lower than the risk-free rate, the portfolio is assuming more risk than is necessary.

If a manager is being measured against a benchmark, the portfolio's Sharpe ratio can be compared to the Sharpe ratio of the applicable benchmark. The larger the Sharpe ratio, the better the portfolio performed. A group of portfolios can therefore be ranked by their risk-adjusted performance. A money manager with a Sharpe ratio greater than the Sharpe ratio of the benchmark outperformed the benchmark. A portfolio's Sharpe ratio that is smaller than the benchmark's signals underperformance. A negative Sharpe ratio means the portfolio had a return less than the risk-free return.

Other Factors in Performance Measurement

Dissimilarities in portfolios also make accurate performance comparisons difficult. For example, portfolios may have different risk characteristics and/or special investor constraints or objectives. When such factors affect returns, the conclusions drawn from the performance comparisons should be adjusted to reflect the impact of the variables.

Because of the large number of variables in the management and measurement of portfolios, assessing investment performance is difficult. Regardless, when performance comparisons are made, investors should be concerned primarily with longer-term results since they best measure a manager's ability in all phases of the business cycle. Also of importance are consistency of results and the trend of performance as indicated by the results over the last few measurement periods.

SUMMARY

After reading this chapter, you should be able to:

1.   Describe the asset mix categories and evaluate strategies for setting the asset mix.

   • The basic asset classes are cash, fixed-income securities, and equities:

      – Cash includes currency, money market securities, Canada Savings Bonds, redeemable GICs, and bonds with a maturity of one year or less.

      – Fixed-income securities include bonds due in more than one year, mortgage-backed securities, fixed-income mutual funds, fixed-income exchange-traded funds, and other debt instruments, as well as preferred shares.

      – Equities include common shares, rights and warrants, equity exchange-traded funds, equity mutual funds, convertible bonds, and convertible preferreds.

   • Asset class timing is the practice of switching among industries and asset classes with a goal of maximizing returns and minimizing losses.

   • The link between equity and economic cycles allows investors to attempt to maximize returns on equity investments by acquiring or divesting holdings based on the stage of the equity and/or economic cycle.

2.   Compare and contrast the portfolio management styles of equity and fixed-income managers.

   • Active managers attempt to outperform the market by actively seeking stocks that will do better than the market and passive managers tend to replicate the performance of a specific market index without trying to beat it.

   • Equity growth managers use the bottom-up style of growth investing by focusing on current and future earnings of individual companies, with a key consideration being earnings per share (EPS).

   • Equity value managers focus on specific stock selection, buying stocks that research indicates are undervalued.

   • Equity sector rotators apply a top-down investing approach, focusing on analyzing the prospects for the overall economy. Based on that assessment, managers invest in the industry sectors expected to outperform.

   • Fixed-income managers make choices based on the term to maturity, credit quality, and their expectations of changes in interest rates and how this will affect the prices of fixed-income products.

3. Discuss the benefits of asset allocation, distinguish strategic asset allocation from the types of ongoing asset allocation techniques, and differentiate active and passive management.

   • Strategic asset allocation is the long-term asset mix that will be adhered to by monitoring and, when necessary, rebalancing a portfolio. It is the initial mix developed and is based on an evaluation of a client's personal and financial circumstances.

   • Dynamic asset allocation involves adjusting the asset mix to systematically rebalance the portfolio back to its long-term strategic asset mix.

   • Tactical asset allocation involves short-term, tactical deviations from the strategic mix to capitalize on investment opportunities in one asset class before reverting back to the long-term strategic allocation.

   • Integrated asset allocation is an all-encompassing strategy that takes into account changes in capital markets and client risk tolerance.

4. Describe the steps in monitoring and evaluating portfolio performance in relation to the market, the economy and the client.

   • Monitoring the markets and the client refers to evaluating portfolio decisions in light of changes in the investor's goals, financial position and preferences, relative to changing expectations for capital markets and individual securities.

   • Monitoring the economy refers to evaluating the changes in the economy as a whole and revisiting portfolio decisions based on changes in the economy.

5. Describe how portfolio performance is evaluated, calculate and interpret the total return and risk-adjusted rate of return of a portfolio.

   • The success of a portfolio manager is determined by comparing the total rate of return of the portfolio being evaluated with the average total return of comparable portfolios.

   • Managers are often measured against a predetermined benchmark specified in the investment policy statement.

   • One very simple method of computing total return is to divide the portfolio's total earnings (income plus capital gains or losses), or the increase in the market value of the portfolio, by the amount invested in the portfolio.

   • The Sharpe Ratio measures the portfolio's risk-adjusted rate of return using standard deviation as the measure of risk. Higher Sharpe Ratios are preferred.

Online Frequently Asked Questions

CSI has answered many frequently asked questions about this Chapter. Read through online Module 16 FAQs.

Online Post-Module Assessment

Once you have completed the chapter, take the Module 16 Post-Test.

SECTION *VII*

Analysis of
Managed Products

Chapter *17*

Fundamentals of Managed and Structured Products

17

Fundamentals of Managed and Structured Products

CHAPTER OUTLINE

What Factors are Driving the Growth of Managed and Structured Products?
- Recent Industry Developments - Meeting the Evolving Needs of Investors
- Regulatory Considerations

What Are Managed and Structured Products?
- Types of Managed and Structured Products

How do Managed and Structured Products Compare?
- Advantages of Managed Products
- Advantages of Structured Products
- Disadvantages of Managed Products
- Disadvantages of Structured Products
- Risks Involved With Managed and Structured Products

How is the Market Evolving for Managed and Structured Products?
- Outcome Based Investment Solutions
- Changing Compensation Models

Summary

LEARNING OBJECTIVES

By the end of this chapter, you should be able to:

1. List and describe the factors that are driving the growth of managed and structured products.

2. Differentiate between managed and structured products, including the advantages, disadvantages, and investment risks of structured products and managed products.

3. Describe how the growth of managed products has changed the role and compensation model of the Investment Advisor.

THE MARKET FOR MANAGED AND STRUCTURED PRODUCTS

Managed products have been around since the modern mutual fund was first created in the 1920s. Structured products are more recent financial instruments that were first introduced in the form of mortgage-backed securities during the 1970s.

Over the past 25 years, both managed and structured products have seen tremendous growth in the number of issues on the market and in the amount of assets under management. A greater and growing proportion of today's assets and daily trading activity is being funnelled into these types of products.

For example:

- The number of Toronto Stock Exchange (TSX) listed exchange-traded funds (ETFs) has grown from 1 in 1999 to 273 in September 2012 with a value of over $64 billion.

- The total market value of the 220 various other structured products listed on Toronto Stock Exchange is $30.5 billion.

- As of mid-2012, the value of market-linked GICs in Canada has grown to $34.1 billion, swelling in number after the market turmoil of 2008-09.

- Global assets under management in hedge funds, a form of managed product, has grown from US$450 billion in 1999 to an estimated US$2.2 trillion in 2012 (Source: Bloomberg).

In this chapter, we make a general comparison between the managed product market and the structured product market. First, we define managed products and structured products. Then, we examine the advantages and disadvantages each brings to the market. We also briefly list the various types of managed and structured products available. Next, we examine why managed and structured products have grown in popularity. Finally, we discuss how the increased use of managed and structured products has changed the role and compensation model for the Investment Advisor.

 **KEY TERMS**

Managed product

Separately managed account

Pooled account

Structured product

WHAT FACTORS ARE DRIVING THE GROWTH OF MANAGED AND STRUCTURED PRODUCTS?

The growth in the market for managed and structured products is due in part to a number of key factors, including:

The Search for Yield	• Short-term yields have fallen to multi-decade lows. • Retirees and institutional investors continue to seek alternatives to fill the return shortfall. • Many hedge funds, asset backed securities, and private equity funds have provided higher returns than standard stocks, bonds and conventional investment solutions.
Growth in Passive Investing	• The challenge faced by a majority of active investment managers to beat the market index year after year has driven many investors into index mutual funds and exchange-traded funds. • Demand for passive investing products that provide important return and risk management characteristics has also fuelled growth in index-linked GICs and index-linked PPNs (principal protected notes).
Demographics	• As baby boomers go through their life cycle of working, saving and eventual retirement, they continue to supply the world with a historic amount of investment capital. • All this capital is a source of huge pent-up demand for securities of all kinds.
The End of the Bull Market for Bonds	• The steady decline in interest rates since the 1980s fuelled one of the greatest periods of economic growth in world history until the credit and financial crisis of 2008/09. Since that time, interest rates appear to have hit rock bottom, providing little interest return to investors and posing ever increasing risk of capital loses as rates rise and return to more historical norms.
Product Innovations	• Retail investors can now access strategies and markets that were once only available to sophisticated institutional investors. • An individual with $1,000 or 100 shares, for example, can now get market exposure to foreign stocks or bonds, hedge fund strategies or commodities in a computer key stroke. This was unheard of 20 years ago.
Falling Commission Rates and Faster Computers	• The rise of discount brokerage firms, falling commission rates and ever faster computing speeds has meant faster and easier access, allowing the average investor to trade global markets like a portfolio manager. • This has fuelled growth in the need for more investing vehicles, and has improved the efficiency for managers in operating these vehicles. • This has in turn led to higher returns.

Recent Industry Developments - Meeting the Evolving Needs of Investors

Investors' needs continue to evolve, creating ongoing challenges and opportunities for advisors and the investment industry to meet those needs in an effective and timely manner. With the aging of the Baby Boomer generation, a large number of investors have, are or will be moving from the accumulation to the de-accumulation phase of their lives over a relatively short time frame. Their investment goals have driven, and will continue to drive, significant change in the investment industry.

Efforts by central bankers to stimulate growth through low interest rates in light of the financial crisis of 2008 and subsequent economic global slowdown, has meant that many traditional investments have seen their yields and returns decline to historically low levels. As a result, the search for greater yields and returns than those offered by traditional solutions such as mutual funds, bonds and Guaranteed Investment Certificates (GICs) has helped to fuel the creation of ever increasing new forms of investment solutions, including managed and structured products.

Regulatory Considerations

Mutual funds, one of the general public's most universal investment options, are regulated in Canada by National Instrument 81-102 (NI 81-102). Among other things, NI 81-102 forbids mutual funds from using leverage, and allows the use of derivatives only in certain non-speculative situations. Structured products, and some forms of managed products, can avoid the restrictions of NI 81-102 in an effort to provide the higher yields and returns sought by investors.

WHAT ARE MANAGED AND STRUCTURED PRODUCTS?

A **managed product** is:

- A pool of capital gathered to buy securities according to a specific investment mandate;

- The pool seeds a fund;

- The fund is managed by an investment professional that is paid a management fee to carry out the mandate.

The mandate of a fund can specify either *active* or *passive* management:

- *Active Management*: Active fund managers make investment decisions based on their outlook for the markets and securities in which they invest. Both of these outlooks should be clearly identified in the fund's investment mandate. In almost all cases, active fund managers intend to outperform the return on a specific benchmark index.

- *Passive Management*: Managers of passively managed funds do not make security selections. The manager seeks to assume only the systematic risk associated with investing in a particular asset class. The most common type of passively managed fund is one that attempts to replicate the returns of a market index.

Compared to the investment mandate of a structured product, the mandate of a managed product generally imposes more demands and restrictions on its fund manager, including:

* Specifying the types of securities that can or cannot be traded;

* Setting limits on the level of individual security concentration within the portfolio;

* Specifying the different sectors in which the fund can invest;

* Imposing rules and/or parameters on the use of leverage.

Examples of managed products include:

* Mutual funds

* Hedge funds

* Segregated funds

* Exchange traded funds (ETFs)

* Private equity funds

* Closed end funds

* Labour-sponsored venture capital corporations (LSVCC).

Managed products are offered in the following two account structures:

* Pooled accounts

* Separately managed accounts

In a **pooled account** structure:

* Investors' funds are gathered into a specific legal structure, usually a trust or corporation;

* An investor's claim to the pool's returns is proportional to the number of shares or units the investor owns;

* The pools are often open-ended, which means units are issued when there are net cash inflows to the fund, or units are redeemed when there are net cash outflows.

In a **separately managed account** structure:

* Individual accounts are created for each investor.

A **structured product** is a passive investment vehicle that is financially engineered to provide a specific risk and return characteristic. The value of a structured product tracks the returns of a reference security known as the *underlying asset*.

Underlying assets can consist of a single security, a basket of securities, foreign currencies, commodities or an index. Some examples of *underlying assets* include:

* Mortgage loans;

* Credit card receivables;

- Car loans;

- Equity indexes;

- Home equity loans.

Once constructed, a structured product is designed to have less risk than its underlying asset, but provide higher risk adjusted returns than conventional investments. Investors buy a share of the total pool of underlying assets.

The issuer of a structured product (e.g., a bank or a consumer finance firm) takes advantage of its economies of scale and market reach to package underlying assets that individuals could not cost effectively assemble on their own.

For example, an individual would not have access to a pool of mortgage loans with which to create a mortgage backed security (MBS). Individuals also lack the knowledge or expertise to evaluate each loan, or the ability to assemble them. But the bank that issued those mortgages would have the expertise, time and capital to assemble the loans into an MBS.

Types of Managed and Structured Products

Managed and structured products are available in a number of different types and formats, each with specific characteristics. Table 17.1 lists the various types of managed and structured products, with a short description of their investment objectives and underlying assets.

TABLE 17.1	TYPES OF MANAGED AND STRUCTURED PRODUCTS	
Name	**Description**	**Assets Held**
Mutual Funds	Pooled investment funds; highly regulated and unleveraged	Equity, fixed income, limited use of derivatives
Hedge Funds	Pooled investment funds; lightly regulated and leveraged	Equity, fixed income, derivatives, commodities
Exchange Traded Funds	Pooled investment funds; closely tracks underlying asset	Market Indexes, derivatives
Closed End Funds	Pooled investment fund with finite number of units	Equity, fixed income, derivatives, commodities
Listed Private Equity Funds	Pooled investment fund buying full ownership in private firms	Full or part ownership in private companies
Labour Sponsored Venture Capital Corporations	Equity shares that provide federal and provincial tax breaks	Ownership of private, small- to mid-size companies

TABLE 17.1	TYPES OF MANAGED AND STRUCTURED PRODUCTS – *Cont'd*	
Name	**Description**	**Assets Held**
Segregated Funds	Investment fund that combines a mutual fund with a life insurance policy	Equity and fixed income mutual funds
Principal protected notes	Debt-like security with equity linked returns	Derivatives, fixed income
Index-or mutual fund-linked GICs	Bank issued debt security with returns linked to an equity index	Hybrid instrument, often containing a derivative to track an underlying asset's return, like an index or a mutual fund
Split Shares	Equity securities with separate claims on the dividend and capital cash flow from a holding of underlying stocks	Dividend paying stocks
Canadian Originated Preferred Shares (COPrS)	Long term subordinated debt with features of preferred shares and corporate bonds	Unsecured (preferred shares)
Mortgage backed securities	Medium to long term bond with equal claim on the principal and interest cash flows from a pool of mortgages	Residential or commercial mortgages
Asset backed securities	Short to medium term bond with equal claim on the principal and interest cash flows from a pool of receivables	Consumer loans (home equity, student, auto, credit card)

HOW DO MANAGED AND STRUCTURED PRODUCTS COMPARE?

Table 17.2 provides you with a quick comparison of the main features of managed and structured products:

TABLE 17.2	COMPARISON OF MANAGED PRODUCTS AND STRUCTURED PRODUCTS	
	Managed Products	**Structured Products**
Structure	Mostly open ended	Closed ended
Maturity Date	Mostly none	Finite life
Holdings	Liquid and illiquid	Illiquid
Secondary market	Excellent to poor	Very poor
Management	Active or passive	Passive
Performance Goal	Absolute returns and/or risk reduction	Return and Risk reduction

Advantages of Managed Products

Let's begin the comparison by reviewing some of the advantages of owning managed products:

EXPERIENCE OF PROFESSIONAL MANAGEMENT

* Investors benefit from the specialized knowledge of investment professionals who create or manage these products.

* Investors also benefit from the access that these professionals have to analysts and experts in various fields.

ECONOMIES OF SCALE FROM POOLED INVESTMENT FUNDS

* The asset size of managed product funds allows negotiating of lower fees and transaction costs.

* Size also gives access to markets inaccessible to individuals, such as over-the-counter derivatives, new issues of foreign corporate bonds or commercial real estate deals.

DIVERSIFICATION

* Typically, managed products provide average investors the diversification they could not achieve with small account sizes.

* The variety of managed product options available also affords investors easy and quick exposure to any index or sector.

LIQUIDITY AND FLEXIBILITY

- Managed products such as mutual funds can be bought and sold at their net asset value at any time.

- ETFs can be easily bought and sold at their current market price in a size as small as a 100-share lot.

TAX BENEFITS

- Some structured products, like labour-sponsored venture capital corporations (LSVCCs), can provide investors with tax benefits. For example, LSVCCs can provide provincial and federal tax credits that can amount to 15-30% of the purchase price.

LOW COST INVESTMENT OPTIONS

- Products such as ETFs often have some of the lowest management expense ratios in the fund universe.

Advantages of Structured Products

As with managed products, owning structured products can provide investors with certain advantages, including:

- Experience of professional management;

- Economies of scale generated from pooling investment funds;

- Diversification.

Structured products, however, have other advantages that are unique to these products:

HIGHER YIELD

- Structured products offer higher yields at a given term-to-maturity compared to conventional fixed income instruments.

- Securitization enables structured products to combine high risk, illiquid securities into one lower risk, high yield security.

THE HIGH PROBABILITY OF RETURN OF PRINCIPAL

- Though there are some risks that could prevent the return of principal from being an absolute certainty, a structured product is generally much more likely to return 100% of the investors' principal than a managed product.

Disadvantages of Managed Products

Despite the advantages discussed above, there are disadvantages to owning managed and structured products.

Disadvantages of owning managed products:

LACK OF TRANSPARENCY

- Due to the largely unregulated and competitive nature of its business, entities like hedge funds rarely disclose their portfolio holdings on a timely basis.

- Details on a hedge fund's specific investment strategy are also often kept secret due to concerns that competitors could take advantage of the information.

- In certain cases, the lack of transparency makes it difficult to properly evaluate a hedge fund manager's performance, which increases the investor's chance that they could experience poor relative performance with their investment.

LIQUIDITY CONSTRAINTS

- Some managed product structures, such as hedge funds or private equity funds, offer liquidity only on a delayed basis.

- Certain funds may prevent an investor from accessing their funds until a specified time or only when certain conditions are met.

- In some cases, greater liquidity can come at a cost to the investor – for example, hedge funds may charge 1% – 2% of the investor's assets as a redemption fee.

HIGH FEES

- Active fixed income and foreign equity mutual funds can charge 2%–5% in management fees.

- This can represent a significant proportion of returns, especially in years where a fund may show a small return or a loss.

- Private equity and hedge funds typically charge a 20% performance fee on all profits above a certain stated threshold of return. For example, any returns above 10% in a given period are subject to a 20% additional fee above the on-going management fee.

VOLATILITY OF RETURNS

- Some managed products, such as closed end funds, hedge funds and private equity funds, may make use of leverage or invest in illiquid assets.

- While this can increase the chance of enhanced returns, it can also increase the chance of suffering enhanced losses.

Disadvantages of Structured Products

Similar to the above, here are some of the disadvantages of investing in structured products:

COMPLEXITY

- Some structured products, and particularly those that make significant use of derivatives, are complex financial instruments-this can make understanding their inherent risks too difficult to assess for investors.

HIGH COST

- To compensate for the return guarantee they provide, structured products, like principal protected notes (PPNs), often have a large built in cost structure.

- The investor can often be subject to selling commissions, management fees, performance fees, structuring fees, trailer fees and swap arrangement fees, just to name a few.

- For the investor to make a reasonable return through the investment a cost hurdle must be overcome.

ILLIQUIDITY OF THE SECONDARY MARKET

- Although some structured products, like principal protected notes (PPNs), are publicly (but thinly) traded, most structured products either lack an active secondary market or have a very thin one.

- Some PPN issuers provide a secondary market, but only on a best efforts basis.

- This can mean that in very active or volatile markets, the issuer will either step aside completely from making a market for the structured product or make a market with a very wide bid/ask spread.

Risks Involved With Managed and Structured Products

As with all types of investments, investors are exposed to various types of risk through managed and structured products. Here is a look at some of those risks:

Credit Risk	Credit risk can exist on several levels. For example, there is the chance of default on the consumer loans that make up the underlying holdings of asset-backed securities or on the mortgages within a pool backing MBS securities. There is also the chance of non-performance by corporate fixed income issuers, whose bonds are held in mutual fund portfolios. Credit risk also exists with the issuer of PPN principal guarantees, who may not be able to fulfill the guarantee.
Inflation Risk	Most structured products are essentially hybrid fixed income securities. Investors risk a loss of real purchasing power with structured products just as they might with conventional fixed income products.

Currency Risk	Managed or structured products that invest in non-Canadian dollar denominated assets and that do not hedge against currency risk can experience losses on the conversion back to Canadian dollars from the foreign currency if the Canadian dollar has strengthened against the foreign currency.
Prepayment Risk	If allowed based on the structure of the investment, some of the mortgages underlying MBS securities might be paid off earlier than expected. This will shorten the expected life of the MBS and could potentially leave the investor with a lower return over the life of the structured product.
Manager Risk	The returns of mutual funds, hedge funds and private equity funds are often contingent on the investment and organization skills of their managers. Investors risk losses or lower returns with poor management.

Complete the following Online Learning Activity

Managed and Structured Products

Managed and structured products have grown in popularity over the past decade as investor demand for alternative investment vehicles change. In this activity, you will review the similarities and differences between managed and structured products.

 Complete the **Managed and Structured Products – Comparing their Features** activity.

HOW IS THE MARKET EVOLVING FOR MANAGED AND STRUCTURED PRODUCTS?

Both managed and structured products have seen tremendous growth in the number of issues on the market and in the amount of assets under management over the past twenty five years. The financial services industry itself constantly evolves to meet ever-changing investor needs.

Outcome Based Investment Solutions

Over the last several years, investors experienced several periods of extreme volatility in capital markets. This has contributed to a lack of confidence in the ability of standard investment products to meet the needs of investors who are nearing or in the retirement stage of their lives. Protecting their assets and generating income from them has become more important than growing them.

Another consideration is that many of these investors are faced with different risks than investors in the accumulation stage of their lives, including:

- Health care risk

- Longevity risk

- Inflation risk

- Pension shortfall risk

Combined with the increasing wealth concentration of the Baby Boomers, this has led to a need for solutions that exhibit the following characteristics:

- *Greater certainty of return* to help clients secure a future lifestyle and offset longevity risk.

- *Security of assets* to help clients ensure at least a minimum lifestyle and provide peace of mind.

- *Flexibility* to help clients adapt to changes in their life situations.

The above noted risks and needs have led investors to desire more specific *outcome based* investment solutions than those that provide relative investment performance. The result has been a growing focus in the industry on achieving real-world outcomes, such as:

- Principal protection

- Target retirement dates

- Tax minimization

- Income generation

The types of solutions that are now being generated by the investment industry to meet the evolving needs of clients, and which are now outpacing the sale of standard mutual funds, include:

- Principal Protected Notes

- Annuities (including variable and longevity insurance)

- Target-date Funds

- Guaranteed Minimum Withdrawal Benefits (GMWBs)

- Inflation Indexed Investments

For advisors, it is important to note that these new products and solutions increase their role as a gatekeeper for their clients as the emphasis of the advisor role moves further away from securities selection and direct management of client assets. Many of these solutions have the same risks as noted for structured and managed products.

TARGET-DATE FUNDS

An investor would purchase a *target-date fund* (also known as *Life Cycle Fund*) to ensure that her savings are actively managed on her behalf towards a certain life goal or target date in the future (e.g., retirement). The fund manager will invest the fund's assets towards that goal, aiming to grow the fund in the earlier years and then to gradually reduce the risk of the fund as the target date approaches and the investor requires her savings to support her life goal. Another example of this type of solution is *target education funds*, where a specific date near or at the expected commencement of a child's post-secondary education is chosen by the investor. The fund manager then invests the fund's investments with that target date as their focus, focusing on growth in the early years and gradually reducing the risk of the fund as the target date approaches.

Example: A client purchases the ABC Life Cycle Fund 2025. The client selects the 2025 Fund because 2025 is the year that he plans to retire. In the earlier years, the ABC Life Cycle Fund 2025 will be managed more aggressively to generate higher returns and ideally grow the client's assets. However, as 2025 approaches, the fund will become gradually less growth focused and progressively more capital preservation focused, until in the last few years prior to the 2025 target date, when it will hold mostly cash and short term bonds.

Changing Compensation Models

The growth in managed and structured product offerings has changed compensation models for advisors and brokerage businesses. In recent years, a greater proportion of advisors and brokerage businesses have switched to fee-based programs and away from commission-based programs.

This trend towards fee-based business has been driven out of necessity. As individual investors became more empowered to make their own trading decisions (lower commissions, faster computers, widespread information), advisors and full-service brokerage firms had to find ways to add value to their client relationships, beyond the traditional way of picking securities for their portfolios.

One way advisors and brokerage firms have tried to add more value has been by acting as fund-of-fund managers. Their job has evolved to gathering assets and selecting the right combination of investment managers and products, in order to get a good balance of investment styles and sector exposures. The emphasis of knowledge has shifted from security analysis to manager analysis, and to finding the best ways to combine managers.

Example: A client is in need of small cap exposure. The advisor selects two to four suitable small cap growth and small cap value managers/products from the entire small cap universe to build the portfolio. Issues of security selection and portfolio management at the security level are left with the manager/product issuer. The advisor can now focus more on client specific issues and provide a more customized experience. As technological and product innovation advance, this trend is likely to continue well into the future.

SUMMARY

By the end of this chapter, you should be able to:

1. List and describe the factors that are driving the growth of managed and structured products.

    *   The growth in the market for managed and structured products is due in part to a number of key factors, including: the search for yield; growth in passive investing; demographics; the end of the bull market in bonds; product innovations; cheaper commissions and faster computers.

2. Differentiate between managed and structured products, including the advantages, disadvantages, and investment risks of structured products and managed products:

    *   A managed product is a pool of capital gathered to buy securities according to a specific investment mandate. The pool seeds a fund managed by an investment professional that is paid a management fee to carry out the mandate.

    *   Compared to the investment mandate of a structured product, the mandate of a managed product imposes far more demands and restrictions.

    *   A structured product is a passive investment vehicle financially engineered to provide a specific risk and return characteristic. The value of a structured product tracks the returns of reference security known as an underlying asset. The underlying assets can consist of a single security, a basket of securities, foreign currencies, commodities or an index.

    *   There is no active management of the underlying assets. The constituent underlying assets remain static.

    *   The structured product is a typically closed-ended structure.

3. Describe how the growth of managed products has changed the role and compensation model of the Investment Advisor.

    *   A greater proportion of advisors and brokerage businesses have switched to fee-based programs and away from commission-based programs.

    *   One way advisors and brokerage firms have tried to add more value has been by acting as fund-of-fund managers.

    *   Advisors and full-service brokerage firms had to find ways to add value to their client relationships, beyond the traditional way of picking securities for their portfolios.

Online Frequently Asked Questions

> CSI has answered many frequently asked questions about this Chapter. Read through online Module 17 FAQs.

Online Post-Module Assessment

> Once you have completed the chapter, take the Module 17 Post-Test.

Chapter *18*

Mutual Funds: Structure and Regulation

18

Mutual Funds: Structure and Regulation

What is the "Know Your Client" Rule?
- Suitability and Know Your Product
- The Role of KYC Information in Opening an Account

What are the Requirements when Opening and Updating an Account?
- Relationship Disclosure
- New Accounts
- Updating Client Information
- Distribution of Mutual Funds by Financial Institutions

Summary

 LEARNING OBJECTIVES

By the end of this chapter, you should be able to:

1. Define a mutual fund and describe the advantages and disadvantages of investing in mutual funds.

2. Compare and contrast mutual fund trusts and mutual fund corporations, explain and calculate how mutual fund units or shares are priced, calculate a fund's net asset value per share (NAVPS), and analyze the impacts of charges associated with mutual funds.

3. Define labour sponsored venture capital corporations (LSVCCs), discuss the advantages and disadvantages of LSVCCs, and contrast them with mutual funds.

4. Describe the mutual fund regulatory environment and the disclosure documents necessary to satisfy provincial requirements, identify mutual fund registration requirements, and discuss restrictions that sellers of mutual funds must observe.

5. Describe the "Know Your Client" rule within the context of suitability, the circumstances in which suitability of a client account must be re-assessed and knowing your product.

6. Describe "relationship disclosure information," list the elements that must be included in the client disclosure document, and the circumstances in which "Know Your Client" information requires an update.

INVESTING IN MUTUAL FUNDS

The Canadian mutual fund industry has experienced tremendous growth over the past decade, both in choice of products available to investors and in the dollar value of assets under management. Accordingly, the industry offers advisors and investors numerous opportunities and challenges. Are mutual funds ideal for all investors? As we have discussed previously in this course, there is no one perfect security that suits all investors; however, mutual funds have become important investment products for many investors.

Although they may seem simple and nearly universally available, mutual funds are in fact a complex investment vehicle. Available in a variety of different forms and through a variety of different distribution channels, they may be one of the most visible vehicles for many investors, from the smallest retail client to the largest institutional investor. The funds themselves are subject to a range of unique provisions and regulations; thus, it is important to ensure a full understanding of this particular investment vehicle.

Do you fully understand what funds can, and cannot, do for a portfolio? Can you provide an educated explanation about the different charges and fees that apply and what the implications are? Can you identify what needs to be done to stay within the regulations? In this first chapter on mutual funds, we explore the structure and regulation of the mutual fund industry.

KEY TERMS

Back-end load

Early redemption fee

F-class fund

Front-end load

Labour-sponsored venture capital corporations (LSVCC)

Management expense ratio (MER)

Money market

Mutual fund

National Instrument 81-101

National Instrument 81-102

Net asset value per share (NAVPS)

No-load fund

Offering price

Open-end trust

Pre-authorized contribution plan (PAC)

Redemption price

Simplified prospectus

Switching fee

System for Electronic Document Analysis and Retrieval (SEDAR)

Trailer fee

Unsolicited Orders

WHAT IS A MUTUAL FUND?

A **mutual fund** is an investment vehicle operated by an investment company that pools contributions from investors and invests these proceeds into a variety of securities, including stocks, bonds and money market instruments.

Individuals who contribute money become share or unitholders in the fund and share in the income, gains, losses and expenses the fund incurs in proportion to the number of units or shares that they own. Professional money managers manage the assets of the fund by investing the proceeds according to the fund's policies and objectives and based on a particular investing style.

Mutual fund shares/units are redeemable on demand at the fund's current price or **net asset value per share** (**NAVPS**), which depends on the market value of the fund's portfolio of securities at that time.

> The mutual funds industry in Canada has experienced tremendous growth since 1980. In 1980, mutual fund net assets totalled $3.6 billion in Canada. By September 2012, according to the Investment Funds Institute of Canada, mutual fund net assets under management grew to more than $827 billion. (source: "IFIC Industry Overview, September 2012" *http://www.ific.ca*).

A fund's prime investment goals are stated in the fund's prospectus and generally cover the degree of safety or risk that is acceptable, whether income or capital gain is the prime objective, and the main types of securities in the fund's investment portfolio.

Individuals who sell mutual funds, whether they are investment advisors or mutual fund sales representatives, must have a good understanding of the type and amount of risk associated with each type of fund. As is true with other financial services, the mutual fund representative must carefully assess each client profile to ensure that the type of mutual fund that is recommended properly reflects the client's risk tolerance and investment goals. The mutual fund representative also recognizes that a client's goals and objectives are never static and that the review process is ongoing, not transactional. Finally, he or she recognizes that proper diversification means that a client's portfolio will contain an asset mix allocated among: cash or near-cash investments, equity investments and fixed-income investments.

> **Note to students:** We use *mutual fund representative* to refer to those individuals who have met the regulatory requirements to advise on and sell mutual funds. Please be advised that the use of *dealing representative* is also used within the industry. For consistency, this course will use *mutual fund representative*.

Advantages of Mutual Funds

Mutual funds offer many advantages for those who buy them. Besides offering varying degrees of safety, income and growth, their chief advantages are:

LOW-COST PROFESSIONAL MANAGEMENT

The fund manager, an investment specialist, manages the fund's investment portfolio on a continuing basis. Both small and wealthy investors purchase mutual funds because they do not have the time, knowledge or expertise to monitor their portfolio of securities. This is an inexpensive way for the small investor to access professional management of their investments.

This is perhaps one of the main advantages that mutual funds offer. The fund manager's job is to analyze the financial markets for the purpose of selecting those securities that best match a fund's investment objectives. The fund manager also plays the important role of continuously monitoring fund performance as a way of fine-tuning the fund's asset mix as market conditions change.

DIVERSIFICATION

A typical large fund might have a portfolio consisting of 60 to 100 or more different securities in 15 to 20 industries. For the individual investor, acquiring such a portfolio of stocks is likely not feasible. Because individual accounts are pooled, sponsors of managed products enjoy economies of scale that can be shared with mutual fund share or unit holders. As well as having access to a wider range of securities, managed funds can trade more economically than the individual investor. Thus, fund ownership provides a low-cost way for small investors to acquire a diversified portfolio.

VARIETY OF TYPES OF FUNDS AND TRANSFERABILITY

The availability of a wide range of mutual funds enables investors to meet a wide range of objectives (i.e., from fixed-income funds through to aggressive equity funds). Many fund families also permit investors to transfer between two or more different funds being managed by the same sponsor, usually at little or no added fee. Transfers are also usually permitted between different purchase plans under the same fund.

VARIETY OF PURCHASE AND REDEMPTION PLANS

There are many purchase plans, ranging from one-time, lump-sum purchases to regular purchases in small amounts under periodic accumulation plans (called **pre-authorized contribution plans** or **PACs**). One of the main advantages of mutual funds is the low cost to invest. With as little as $100, an investor can begin to purchase units in a fund through a PAC. Again, with as little as $100 a month, they can continue to contribute. At redemption, there are also several plans from which to choose.

LIQUIDITY

Mutual fund shareholders have a continuing right to redeem shares for cash at net asset value. National Instrument 81-102 requires that payments be made within three business days in keeping with the securities industry settlement requirements.

EASE OF ESTATE PLANNING

Shares or units in a mutual fund continue to be professionally managed during the probate period until estate assets are distributed. In contrast, other types of securities may not be readily traded during the probate period even though market conditions may be changing drastically.

> The term 'estate' refers to all the assets owned by an individual at the time of death. Estate planning refers to planning for the administration and disposing of property of one's estate upon death. Probate is the process of validating an individual's will prior to distribution of estate assets.

LOAN COLLATERAL AND MARGIN ELIGIBILITY

Fund shares or units are usually accepted as security for a bank loan. They are also acceptable for margin purposes, thus giving aggressive fund buyers both the benefits *and risks* of leverage in their financial planning.

VARIOUS SPECIAL OPTIONS

Mutual funds consist of not only an underlying portfolio of securities, but also a package of customer services. Most mutual funds offer the opportunity to compound an investment through the reinvestment of dividends.

Sponsors of mutual funds file a variety of reports annually to meet their regulatory disclosure requirements. These reports include the annual information form (AIF), audited annual and interim financial statements and an annual report, among others. The reports must be provided to unitholders or any person on request. They are easily retrieved through **SEDAR** (the **System for Electronic Document Analysis and Retrieval**) at www.sedar.com. Increasingly, these reports contain useful educational features such as manager commentaries.

Other benefits associated with managed products include record-keeping features that save clients and their advisors time in complying with income tax reporting and other accounting requirements.

Disadvantages of Mutual Funds

COSTS

For most people, a weakness in investing in a mutual fund is the perceived steepness of their sales and management costs. Historically, most mutual funds charged a front-end load or sales commission and a management fee that was typically higher than the cost to purchase individual stocks or bonds from a broker. Competition in the market has subsequently reduced both load and management fees, and investors are now offered a wider choice of investment options.

UNSUITABLE AS A SHORT-TERM INVESTMENT OR EMERGENCY RESERVE

Most funds emphasize long-term investment and thus are unsuitable for investors seeking short-term performance. Since sales charges are often deducted from a plan holder's contributions, purchasing funds on a short-term basis is unattractive. The investor would have to recoup at least the sales charges on each trading transaction. This disadvantage does not apply to money market funds, which are designed with liquidity in mind.

With the exception of money market funds, fund holdings are generally not recommended as an emergency cash reserve, particularly during declining or cyclically low markets when a loss of capital could result from emergency redemption or sale.

PROFESSIONAL INVESTMENT MANAGEMENT IS NOT INFALLIBLE

Like equities, mutual fund shares or units can suffer in falling markets where unit values are subject to market swings (systematic risk). Volatility in the market is extremely difficult to predict or time, and is not controllable by the fund manager.

TAX COMPLICATIONS

Buying and selling by the fund manager creates a series of taxable events that may not suit an individual unitholder's time horizon. For example, although the manager might consider it in the best interests of the fund to take a profit on a security holding, an individual unit holder might have been better off if the manager had held on to the position and deferred the capital gains liability.

WHAT IS THE STRUCTURE OF MUTUAL FUNDS?

An investment fund is a company or trust engaged in managing investments for other people. By selling shares or units to many investors, the fund raises capital and the money raised is then invested according to the fund's investment policies and objectives. The fund makes money from the dividends and interest it receives on the securities it holds and from the capital gains it may make in trading its investment portfolio.

A mutual fund may be structured as either a trust or a corporation.

Mutual Fund Trust Structure

The most common structure for mutual funds is the unincorporated **open-end trust** (also referred to as 'open-ended'). The trust structure enables the fund itself to avoid taxation. Any interest, dividends or capital gains income, net of fees and expenses, flows-through directly to the unitholders. The income that flows through is taxed in the hands of the unitholder based on the type of income that the fund generated.

The **trust deed** establishing the open-ended mutual fund covers such things as the fund's principal investment objectives, investment policy, any restrictions on the fund's investments, who the fund's manager, distributor and custodian will be, among other things.

Other things to consider:

* With an open-ended structure, unitholders have the right to redeem their units at a price that is the same as, or close to, the fund's current net asset value per unit.

* Unitholders of a trust may or may not be given voting rights under the terms of the trust agreement. Voting rights, if any, should be clearly understood before purchase, by consulting the prospectus.

The governing policy for mutual funds requires that, in most cases, funds must convene a meeting of security holders to consider and approve specific issues. These issues include such matters as a change in the fund's fundamental investment objectives, a change in auditor or fund manager, or a decrease in the frequency of calculating net asset value.

Mutual Fund Corporation Structure

Mutual funds may also be set up as federal or provincial corporations provided they meet certain conditions set out in the *Income Tax Act*:

* The corporation's holdings must consist mainly of a diversified portfolio of securities.

* The income that it earns must be derived primarily from the interest and dividends paid out by these securities and any capital gains realized from the sale of these securities for a profit.

* Investors in mutual fund corporations receive shares in the fund instead of the units that are sold to investors in mutual fund trusts.

Investment funds established as corporations lack the flow-through status of investment fund trusts. However, the corporation can achieve a virtually tax-free status by declaring dividends during the course of the year that are equivalent to the corporation's net income after fees and expenses. These dividends are then taxed in the hands of the shareholder.

Organization of a Mutual Fund

We now move to highlight the typical structure and organization of a mutual fund.

Directors and Trustees	The directors of a mutual fund corporation, or the trustees of a mutual fund trust, hold the ultimate responsibility for the activities of the fund, ensuring that the investments are in keeping with the fund's investment objectives. To assist in this task, the directors or trustees of the fund may contract out the business of running the fund to an independent fund manager, a distributor and a custodial organization.
Fund Manager	The fund manager provides day-to-day supervision of the fund's investment portfolio. In trading the fund's securities, the manager must observe a number of guidelines specified in the fund's own charter and prospectus, as well as constraints imposed by provincial securities commissions.
	The manager must also maintain a portion of fund assets in cash and short-term highly liquid investments so as to be able to redeem fund shares on demand, pay dividends, and make new portfolio purchases as opportunities arise. A manager's ability to judge the amount of cash needed, and still have fund assets as fully and productively invested as possible, has a direct bearing on the success of the fund.

Fund Manager *– Cont'd*	Other responsibilities include:

- Calculation of the fund's net asset value
- Preparation of the fund's prospectus and reports
- Supervision of shareholder or unitholder recordkeeping
- Providing the custodian with documentation for the release of cash or securities.

The fund manager receives a management fee for these services. This fee is accrued daily and paid monthly. It is calculated as a percentage of the net asset value of the fund being managed.

Distributors

Mutual funds are sold in many ways: by investment advisors employed by securities firms, by a sales force employed by some organizations that control both management and distribution groups, by independent direct sales organizations and by "in house" distributors. The latter includes employees of trust companies, banks or credit unions who have duties other than selling.

In selling mutual funds, the distributor's representatives must explain the objectives and terms of various funds in language that is understandable to new, often unsophisticated investors. They also mail out confirmations of sales, handle client inquiries about features of the fund, and accept and transmit orders for fund share redemptions.

In the process, they offer clients financial planning assistance that involves "know your client" and suitability standards that are as important in mutual fund sales as they are in the general securities business. As compensation for these services, the distributor usually receives a sales fee.

Custodian

When a mutual fund is organized, an independent financial organization, usually a trust company, is appointed as the fund's **custodian**. The custodian collects money received from the fund's buyers and from portfolio income and arranges for cash distributions through dividend payments, portfolio purchases and share redemptions.

Sometimes the custodian also serves as the fund's **registrar** and **transfer agent**, maintaining records of who owns the fund's shares. This duty is complicated by the fact that the number of outstanding shares is continually changing through sales and redemptions. Fractional share purchases and dividend reinvestment plans further complicate this task.

Complete the following Online Learning Activity

Mutual Funds Fundamentals

In this activity, you will learn about the different ways mutual funds can be structured and the advantages and disadvantages of investing in mutual funds.

 Complete the **Mutual Fund Fundamentals** activity.

Pricing Mutual Fund Units or Shares

Mutual fund shares or units are purchased directly from the fund (often through a distributor) and are sold back to the fund when the investor redeems his or her units. Given that they cannot be purchased from or sold to anyone other than the fund, mutual funds are said to be in a continuous state of primary distribution. Similar to other new issues, a purchaser must be sent a prospectus.

The price an investor pays for a share or unit is known as its **offering price**. In the financial press the offering price is expressed as the **net asset value per share** or **NAVPS**. This price will be based on the NAVPS at the close of business the day the order was placed.

The NAVPS is the theoretical amount a fund's shareholders would receive for each share if the fund were to sell all its portfolio of investments at market value, collect all receivables, pay all liabilities, and distribute what is left to its shareholders. It is also used to calculate the **redemption price**, which is the amount (subject to redemption fees, if any) a shareholder receives when he or she redeems the shares.

If a mutual fund does not charge a sales commission to purchase a share or unit, an investor would pay the fund's current NAVPS. NAVPS is calculated as:

$$NAVPS = \frac{Total\ Assets - Total\ Liabilities}{Total\ Number\ of\ Shares\ or\ Units\ Outstanding}$$

Example: ABC fund has $13,000,000 in assets, $1,000,000 in liabilities and 1 million units outstanding. The offering price (the price paid by an investor for 1 unit) is calculated as:

$$NAVPS = \frac{\$13,000,000 - \$1,000,000}{1,000,000} = \$12\ per\ unit$$

This is also the redemption price if the fund does not levy any sales charges or fees.

Since most funds calculate an offering or redemption price at the *close* of the market each day, a specified deadline during the day is set.

• Orders received after the deadline are processed on the following business day.

• Mutual fund representatives are expected to transmit any order for purchase or redemption to the principal office of the mutual fund on the *same day* that the order is received.

- While payment for purchases is usually made in advance, payment for redeemed securities must be made within three business days, according to National Instrument 81-102, from the determination of the NAVPS.

The frequency with which mutual funds calculate NAVPS varies. Rules outlined in **National Instrument 81-102** state that *new* funds must calculate NAVPS at least once a week. At the same time, funds that computed NAVPS on a monthly basis when the Instrument came into effect continue to have the option to do so.

In reality, most large funds calculate NAVPS each business day after the markets have closed. If a fund computes its NAVPS less frequently than daily, sales and redemptions will be made at the next valuation date. If computed monthly, a fund may require that requests for redemption be submitted up to ten days before the date of the NAVPS computation. One exception to these rules is real estate funds. They must compute the NAVPS at least once a year, although most funds make the calculation on a quarterly basis.

Charges Associated with Mutual Funds

Mutual funds can be categorized on the basis of the type of sales commission or load that is levied.

- If loads are charged when the investor initially makes the purchase, they are called **front-end loads**.

- If they are charged at redemption, they are called **back-end loads**.

Most load funds have optional sales charges that let the investor choose between front-end or back-end charges. The actual level of the sales charge levied by load funds depends on the type of fund, its sponsor and method of distribution, the amount of money being invested, and the method of purchase (i.e., lump sum purchases versus contractual purchases spread out over a period of time).

A client may be able to negotiate with the representative over the front-end load, especially if a large amount of money is involved, as it is set by the distributor. The back-end load is set by the dealer and not negotiable.

> Trying to calculate the impact of the various types of fees on mutual funds can be very complicated. The Ontario Securities Commission and Industry Canada's Office of Consumer Affairs have developed a new online calculator that allows investors to determine the impact mutual fund fees have on investment returns over time. The Mutual Fund Fee Impact Calculator is located at *www.getsmarteraboutmoney.ca/tools-and-calculators/mutual-funds/default.aspx*.

NO-LOAD FUNDS

Many mutual funds, primarily those offered by direct distribution companies, banks and trust companies, are sold to the public on a no-load basis, with little or no direct selling charges. However, some discount brokers may levy modest "administration fees" to process the purchase and/or redemption of no-load funds. These funds, like other funds, do charge management or other administrative fees.

FRONT-END LOADS

A front-end load is payable to the distributor at the time of purchase. It is usually expressed as a percentage of the purchase price or NAVPS. The percentage typically decreases as the amount of the purchase increases.

Investors should be aware that the front-end load effectively increases the purchase price of the units, thereby reducing the actual amount invested.

> **Example:** A $1,000 investment in a mutual fund with a 4% front-end load means that $40 (4% × $1,000) goes to the distributor by way of compensation while the remaining $960 is actually invested.

Regulations require that front-end loads must be disclosed in the prospectus both as a percentage of the purchase amount and as a percentage of the net amount invested. In the example above, the prospectus would state that the front-end load charge would be 4% of the amount purchased ([$40 ÷ $1,000] ×100) and 4.17% ([$40 ÷ $960] × 100) of the amount invested.

CALCULATING A FRONT-END LOAD

To determine a fund's offering or purchase price when it has a front-end load charge, you must first determine the NAVPS and then make an adjustment for the load charge. Using a NAVPS of $12 and a front-end load of 4%, the offering or purchase price is calculated as:

$$\text{Offering or Purchase Price} = \frac{\text{NAVPS}}{100\% - \text{Sales Charge}}$$

So:

$$\text{Offering or Purchase Price} = \frac{\$12}{100\% - 4\%} = \frac{\$12}{1.00 - 0.04} = \frac{\$12}{0.96} = \$12.50$$

Note that the sales charge of 4% of the offering price is the equivalent of 4.17% of the net asset value (or net amount invested):

4% of $12.50 = $0.50

$$\frac{\$0.50}{\$12} = 4.17\%$$

BACK-END LOADS OR DEFERRED SALES CHARGES

A back-end load or deferred sales charge is payable to the distributor at the time of redemption or sale of the fund. The fee may be based on the original contribution to the fund or on the net asset value at the time of redemption.

In most cases, deferred sales charges on a back-end load fund decrease the longer the investor holds the fund. For example, an investor might incur the following schedule of deferred sales charges with this type of fund:

TABLE 18.1	BACK-END LOAD SCHEDULE
Year Funds Are Redeemed	**Deferred Sales Charge**
Within the first year	6%
In the second year	5%
In the third year	4%
In the fourth year	3%
In the fifth year	2%
In the sixth year	1%
After the sixth year	0%

CALCULATING A BACK-END LOAD

An investor purchases units in a mutual fund at a NAVPS of $10. If the investor decides to sell the units in the fourth year when the NAVPS is $15, the fund will charge a 3% back-end load or commission.

If the back-end load is based on the *original purchase amount*, the investor would receive $14.70 a unit, calculated as follows:

$$
\begin{aligned}
\text{Selling/Redemption Price} &= \text{NAVPS} - \text{Sales commission} \\
&= \text{NAVPS} - (\text{NAVPS} \times \text{sales percentage}) \\
&= \$15 - (\$10 \times 3\%) \\
&= \$15 - \$0.30 \\
&= \$14.70
\end{aligned}
$$

If the back-end load is instead based on the *NAVPS at the time of redemption*, the investor would receive $14.55, calculated as follows:

$$
\begin{aligned}
\text{Selling/Redemption Price} &= \$15 - (\$15 \times 3\%) \\
&= \$15 - \$0.45 \\
&= \$14.55
\end{aligned}
$$

TRAILER FEES

Another kind of fee is the **trailer fee**, sometimes called a service fee. This is a fee that a mutual fund manager may pay to the distributor that sold the fund. This fee is paid to the mutual fund representative annually as long as the client holds the funds. Trailer fees are usually paid out of the fund manager's management fee.

The justification for paying a fee is that the representative provides ongoing services to investors such as investment advice, tax guidance and financial statements. Some argue that the ongoing services are a valuable benefit to investors and that salespeople must be compensated for their work. Critics believe that such charges have the potential to produce a conflict of interest for the salespeople who could encourage investors to stay in the fund even when market conditions might indicate that they should redeem their shares.

Critics of trailer fees also argue that investors who hold funds for the long term end up paying higher overall fees than they would if they had paid a one-time front- or back-end load.

OTHER FEES

A small number of funds charge a set-up fee, on top of a front-end load or back-end load.

A variation of the redemption fee is the early redemption fee. Some funds, even no-load funds, note in the prospectus that funds redeemed within 90 days of the initial purchase may be subject to an early redemption fee, such as a flat fee of $100 or 2% of the original purchase cost. These fees are charged to discourage short-term trading and to recover administrative and transaction costs.

SWITCHING FEES

Switching fees may apply when an investor exchanges units of one fund for another in the same family or fund company. Some mutual fund companies allow unlimited free switches between funds, while others permit a certain number of free switches in a calendar year before fees are applied. In many cases, the financial advisor may charge a negotiable fee to a maximum of 2% of the amount being transferred, but an advisor may choose to waive this fee altogether. A common requirement for switching is that the funds involved are purchased under the same sales fee options.

In other words, clients generally aren't allowed to switch between a front-end fund and a back-end fund, or vice versa.

As well, switching fees generally do not apply if a fund merges with another or is being terminated for any other reason. In such cases, the investor would be allowed to transfer to the existing fund or withdraw the cash value of the contract without incurring withdrawal fees.

MANAGEMENT FEES

The level of management fees varies widely depending on the type of fund. In general, fees will vary depending on the level of service required to manage the fund.

- The management fees associated with money market funds are low, in the range of 0.50% to 1%.

- The management of equity funds (with the exception of index funds) requires ongoing research and therefore the management fees are higher, ranging from 2% to 3% (or higher).

- Index funds try to mirror the market with occasional rebalancing. Since this strategy is largely a passive buy-and-hold strategy, management fees are usually lower.

In all cases, the management fees charged would be outlined in the prospectus.

Management fees are generally expressed as a straight percentage of the net assets under management. For example, "an annual fee of not more than 2% of the average daily net asset value computed and payable monthly on the last day of each month." This method of compensation has been criticized because it rewards fund managers not on the performance of the fund, but on the level of assets managed. Of course, a fund that consistently underperforms will find that its assets will fall as investors redeem their holdings.

The management fee compensates the fund manager, but it does not cover all the expenses of a fund. For instance, other operating expenses like:

* Interest charges

* All taxes, audit and legal fees

* Safekeeping and custodial fees

* Provision of information to share or unitholders

are charged directly to the fund.

The **management expense ratio** (**MER**) represents the total of *all* management fees and other expenses charged to a fund, expressed as a percentage of the fund's average net asset value for the year. Trading or brokerage costs are excluded from the MER calculation because they are included in the cost of purchasing or selling portfolio assets.

MER is calculated as follows:

$$\text{MER} = \frac{\text{Aggregate Fees and Expenses Payable During the Year}}{\text{Average Net Asset Value for the Year}} \times 100$$

For example, if a fund with $500 million in assets has total annual expenses of $10 million, its MER for the year is 2% ($10 ÷ $500).

All expenses are deducted directly from the fund, not charged to the investor. As such, these fund expenses decrease the ultimate returns to the investors. For example, if a fund reports a compound annual return of 8% and a MER of 2%, it has a gross return of roughly 10%. This means that the MER, expressed as a percentage of returns, is 20% of the return ([2% ÷ 10%] × 100).

Published rates of return are calculated after deducting the management expense ratio, while the NAVPS of investment funds are calculated after the management fee has been deducted. Funds are required by law to disclose in the fund prospectus both the management fee and the management expense ratio for the last five fiscal years.

F–CLASS FUNDS

Many financial advisors are moving to providing fee-based, rather than commission-based, accounts. The client is charged a percentage of the assets under management, rather than a commission or fee for each transaction. Buying mutual funds within these programs was expensive, as the client was charged an MER that included compensation to the IA, as well as being charged the asset-based fee. To accommodate fee-based financial advisors, a number of mutual fund companies now offer F-class mutual funds. An F-class fund is identical to the regular fund, but charges a lower MER, thus reducing or eliminating the double charge.

Complete the following Online Learning Activity

Mutual Funds Fees

Individuals who sell mutual funds must have a thorough understanding and appreciation for all costs and fees of purchasing, owning and redeeming mutual fund units.

 Complete the **Mutual Fund Fees** activity.

WHAT ARE LABOUR-SPONSORED VENTURE CAPITAL CORPORATIONS?

Labour-sponsored venture capital corporations (LSVCCs) or **Labour-Sponsored Investment Funds (LSIFs)** are managed investment funds sponsored by labour organizations to provide capital for small to medium-sized and emerging companies. LSVCCs vary greatly in terms of size, risks and management style. Most are provincially based, although some are national.

Advantages of Labour-Sponsored Funds

The main attractions of LSVCCs are the generous federal and provincial tax credits that individuals receive for investing in them. Tax credits include a 15% federal credit on an annual investment up to and including $5,000, as well as an additional 15% provincial tax credit in some provinces. Therefore, depending on the type of fund and the residency requirements, LSVCCs generate a tax credit ranging from 15% to 30%.

(Investors should note that the Ontario government eliminated the 15% tax credit available on labour funds in 2010. In Alberta, only the 15% federal credit is available.)

> **Example:** Pierre invests $5,000 in an LSVCC in Québec, his province of residence. The fund is eligible for both federal and provincial tax credits. Pierre will receive a $750 federal tax credit (15% × $5,000) and a $750 provincial tax credit (15% × $5,000), for a combined tax credit of $1,500.

Although there is no maximum amount an investor may invest in an LSVCC, both the provincial and the federal tax credits are subject to annual maximum amounts. As mentioned, the federal tax credit is available on a maximum of $5,000 invested in any one year. A province may have a lifetime limit applicable to provincial tax credits.

The unused portion of the federal tax credits are not refundable and cannot be carried forward or back for application in subsequent or prior taxation years. An investor purchasing an LSVCC in the first 60 days of the calendar year can apply the tax credits either to the previous year's taxes or the current year's taxes.

Most LSVCC shares are eligible for RRSPs and RRIFs. In fact, buying an LSVCC investment within an RRSP, as most investors do, offers further tax savings. Shares can be purchased directly by an RRSP trust or may be purchased and then transferred to an RRSP or RRIF.

When LSVCC shares are purchased with money contributed to an RRSP, the contributor to the RRSP will receive the RRSP tax deduction as well as the LSVCC tax credits. The deduction of a sum equal to the purchase price in the case of a direct purchase, or a sum equal to the fair market value of the shares at the time of transfer, will be permitted, within the limits prescribed for contributions to an RRSP.

> **Example:** Pierre decides to invest $5,000 in an LSVCC for his RRSP. Assuming a 50% marginal tax rate, Pierre will realize additional tax savings of $2,500 ($5,000 × 50%) in addition to the $1,500 in LSVCC tax credits received on the purchase of the fund. Therefore, the effective after tax cost of his investment will be reduced to $1,000 ($5,000 − [$2,500 + $1,500]).

Disadvantages of Labour-Sponsored Funds

Because of the nature of the companies in which they invest, LSVCCs are considered a high-risk or speculative investment suitable only for investors who have a high risk tolerance. It is estimated that 80% of all new companies dissolve within five years of start-up.

The redemption of LSVCC shares is more complicated than the redemption of conventional mutual fund shares, since rules governing LSVCC redemptions differ from province to province and between provinces and the federal government. The *Income Tax Act* requires that the shares be held for eight years to avoid the recapture of federal tax credits. If redeemed before this minimum holding time, the investor must repay the tax credits received on the LSVCC when the fund was originally purchased.

> **Example:** If Pierre decides to redeem his LSVCC shares after holding the investment for only five years, he will have to repay the $750 federal tax credit and all of the $750 provincial credit he received.

Provincial requirements range from the right to redeem the shares immediately after purchase, to restrictions until a mandatory holding period has elapsed, to a ban on all redemptions.

Since venture capital investing is more labour-intensive than investing in liquid stocks, the costs of administering these funds, as reflected in management expense ratios, tend to be much higher than for conventional equity funds. In addition, these funds must maintain a large cash reserve to finance redemptions. This cash position can drag down fund performance in rising markets.

HOW ARE MUTUAL FUNDS REGULATED?

The Canadian securities industry is a regulated industry. Each province and territory has its own securities act and its own regulator who is responsible for regulating the underwriting and distribution of securities designed to protect investors and the industry. Securities regulations related to mutual funds are based upon three broad principles: personal trust, disclosure and regulation.

The success of these principles in promoting positive market activities relies largely on ethical conduct by industry registrants. The code of ethics establishes norms for duty and care that incorporate not only compliance with the "letter of the law," but also respect for the "spirit of the law." These norms are based upon ethical principles of trust, integrity, justice, fairness and honesty.

The code distills industry rules and regulations into five primary values:

- Mutual fund representatives must use proper care and exercise professional judgement.

- Mutual fund representatives should conduct themselves with trustworthiness and integrity, and act in an honest and fair manner in all dealings with the public, clients, employers and employees.

- Mutual fund representatives should conduct, and should encourage others to conduct, business in a professional manner that will reflect positively on the individual registrant, the firm and the profession, and should strive to maintain and improve their professional knowledge and that of others in the profession.

- Mutual fund representatives must act in accordance with the securities act of the province or provinces in which registration is held, and must observe the requirements of all Self-Regulatory Organizations (SROs) of which the firm is a member.

- Mutual fund representatives must hold client information in the strictest confidence.

Mutual Fund Regulatory Organizations

Investment firms that are members of one or more of the Canadian self-regulatory organizations (SROs), and the registered employees of such dealer members, are subject to the rules and regulation of these SROs (see Chapter 3). Furthermore, all securities industry participants are subject to the securities law in their particular provinces and in any other province where the relevant securities administrators may claim jurisdiction.

> Please note that reference to *province* or *provincial* encompasses Canada's 10 provinces and three territories.

The Mutual Fund Dealers Association (MFDA) is the mutual fund industry's SRO for the distribution side of the mutual fund industry. It does not regulate the funds themselves. That responsibility remains with the provincial securities commissions, but the MFDA does regulate how the funds are sold. The MFDA is not responsible for regulating the activities of mutual fund dealers who are already members of another SRO. For example, IIROC members selling mutual fund products will continue to be regulated by IIROC.

In Québec, the mutual fund industry is under the responsibility of the Autorité des marchés financiers and the Chambre de la sécurité financière. The Autorité is responsible for overseeing the operation of fund companies within the province, while the Chambre is responsible for setting and monitoring continuing education requirements and for enforcing a code of ethics. A co-operative agreement currently in place between the MFDA and the Québec regulatory organizations will help to avoid regulatory duplication and to ensure that investor protection is maintained.

National Instruments 81-101 and 81-102

Canadian funds fall under the jurisdiction of the securities act of each province. Securities administrators control the activities of these funds, and their managers and distributors, by means of a number of National and Provincial Policy Statements dealing specifically with mutual funds, and by provincial securities legislation applicable to all issuers and participants in securities markets. **National Instrument 81-101 (NI 81-101)** deals with mutual fund prospectus disclosure. **National Instrument 81-102 (NI 81-102)** and a companion policy contain requirements and guidelines for the distribution and advertising of mutual funds.

General Mutual Fund Requirements

Most mutual funds are qualified for sale in all provinces and are therefore registered for sale in each jurisdiction. With certain exceptions, the funds must annually file a full or simplified prospectus (described below) which must be acceptable to the provincial securities administrator. Most funds, particularly the smaller ones, file a prospectus or a simplified prospectus only in provinces where sales prospects appear favourable. Selling a fund's securities to residents of provinces in which the fund has not been qualified is prohibited. It is important, therefore, that mutual fund representatives deal only in those funds registered in their own jurisdiction.

Since mutual funds are considered to be in a continuous state of primary distribution, investors must receive a prospectus upon purchase. Mutual funds predominantly use the simplified prospectus system to qualify the distribution of mutual fund securities to the public. The actual requirements of this system are set out in NI 81-101.

The disclosure documents included as part of the simplified prospectus system consist of:

- A simplified prospectus
- The annual information form
- The annual audited statements or interim unaudited financial statements
- Other information required by the province or territory where the fund is distributed, such as material change reports and information circulars.

NI 81-101 requires only the delivery of the simplified prospectus to an investor in connection with the purchase of a mutual fund, unless the investor also requests delivery of the annual information form and/or the financial statements.

The Simplified Prospectus

A mutual fund prospectus is normally shorter and simpler than a typical prospectus for a new issue of common shares. Under the simplified prospectus system, the issuer must abide by the same laws and deadlines that apply under the full prospectus system. As well, the buyer is entitled to the same rights and privileges.

The **simplified prospectus** must be filed with the securities commission annually, but need not be updated annually unless there is a change in the affairs of the mutual fund. The simplified prospectus is written in plain language and set up in a specific format so that it is easier for the investor to find the information.

The mailing or delivery of the simplified prospectus must be made to the purchaser not later than midnight on the *second business* day after the purchase. This practice is followed because of the purchaser's rights of withdrawal and rescission and because the prospectus itself is an excellent sales tool, informing the buyer of the nature of the fund and its securities.

For further purchases of the same fund, it is not necessary to provide the simplified prospectus again unless it has been amended or renewed. If it has been amended or renewed, the investor has the right to withdraw from the investment within two business days after the document has been provided.

The simplified prospectus consists of two sections:

- **Part A** provides introductory information about the mutual fund, general information about mutual funds and information applicable to the mutual funds managed by the mutual fund organization.

- **Part B** contains specific information about the mutual fund.

The simplified prospectus may be used to qualify more than one mutual fund, as long as Part A of each prospectus is substantially similar and the funds belong to the same mutual fund family, administered by the same entities and operated in the same manner.

The simplified prospectus must contain the following information:

- Introductory statement describing the purpose of the prospectus and identifying the other information documents which the fund must make available to investors

- Name and formation of the issuer, including a description of the issuer's business

- Risk factors and description of the securities being offered

- Method used to set the price of the securities being sold or redeemed, and disclosure of any sales charges

- Method of distribution

- Statement of who has the responsibility for management, distribution and portfolio management

- Fees paid to dealers

- Statement of management fees and other expenses, including the annual management expense ratio for the past five years

- The fund's investment objectives and practices

- Information on the amount of dividends or other distributions paid by the issuer

- In general terms, the income tax consequences to individuals holding an investment in the fund

- Notice of any legal proceedings material to the issuer

- Identity of the auditors, transfer agent and registrar

- Statement of the purchaser's statutory rights

- Summary of the fees, charges and expenses payable by the security holder

The prospectus must be amended when material changes occur, and investors must receive a copy of the amendment.

Certain types of mutual funds may not use the simplified prospectus system under National Instrument 81-101. These are mutual funds that invest in real property and those that constitute a commodity pool program.

As part of the simplified prospectus system, a fund must provide its investors with financial statements on request. Annual audited financial statements must be made available to the securities commission(s) where the fund is registered on or before the deadline set by the commission(s). These statements must be made available to new investors.

Unaudited financial statements as at the end of six months after the fund year-end must also be submitted to the securities commissions, usually within sixty days after the reporting date. These statements must also be given to new investors.

THE ANNUAL INFORMATION FORM

Delivery of the **annual information form** (**AIF**) is available to investors on request. Much of the disclosure required in the AIF is similar to that provided in the simplified prospectus. The AIF contains, in addition to the above, information concerning:

- Significant holdings in other issuers

- The tax status of the issuer

- Directors, officers and trustees of the fund and their indebtedness and remuneration

- Associated persons, the principal holders of securities, the interest of management and others in material transactions

- The particulars of any material contracts entered into by the issuer

WHAT OTHER FORMS AND REQUIREMENTS ARE NECESSARY?

Other regulatory requirements include the following:

Registration Requirements for the Mutual Fund Industry

Mutual fund managers, distributors and mutual fund representatives must all be registered with the securities administrators in all provinces in which they operate. The commissions also insist that they be informed within five business days of any important change in personal circumstances, such as a change of address or bankruptcy.

Education qualifications: Mutual fund representatives must have successfully passed a mutual funds course such as the *Canadian Securities Course* (CSC), the *Investment Funds in Canada* (IFC) course, or another qualified education program.

Registration requirements: An application for registration is filed electronically with the **National Registration Database** (Form NRD 33-109F4), with the appropriate fee. Provincial securities acts set the requirements for initial and continuing registration. In Québec, the representative must register with the Autorité des services financiers.

These requirements include, but are not limited to, the following:

- Generally, mutual fund representatives must be employed by the distribution company.

- Mutual fund representatives are not permitted to carry on other forms of employment without the prior approval of the appropriate Administrator(s) and the industry association(s) of which their firms are members. Many provinces have issued policy statements permitting persons to be dually registered as mutual fund representatives and life agents.

- Applicants must complete a detailed application about their past businesses, employment and conduct and submit to a police review.

The application asks questions about the representative and any companies with which the representative has been associated in certain capacities, such as:

- Any action against the representative regarding any government licence to deal in securities or with the public in any other capacity requiring registration

- Any disciplinary action regarding an approval by any securities commission or other similar professional body

- Any past criminal convictions or current charges or indictments

- Any bankruptcies or proposals to creditors

- Any civil judgment or garnishment

Notices of changes: The mutual fund representative has the obligation to notify the provincial administrator within five business days (ten days in Québec) of any changes in the information required in their provincial application. These include:

- A change in address

- Disciplinary action of a professional body

- Personal bankruptcy (Ontario and Québec)

- Criminal charges or civil judgements

Transfer of registration: As soon as a mutual fund representative ceases to work for a registered dealer, registration is automatically suspended. The employer must notify the provincial Administrator of the termination of the employment and, in most provinces, the reason why. Before a representative's registration can be reinstated, notice in writing must be received by the Administrator from another registered dealer of the employment of the representative by that other dealer. The reinstatement of the registration must be approved by the Administrator.

If the Administrator does not receive a request for reinstatement and transfer to a new company within the permitted period of time, the registration lapses. The representative will have to apply again for registration. This period could be as short as 30 days or as long as 6 months (in Québec).

Mutual Fund Restrictions

The fund manager provides day-to-day supervision of the fund's investment portfolio. In trading the fund's securities, the manager must observe a number of guidelines specified in the fund's own charter and prospectus, as well as constraints imposed by provincial securities commissions.

PROHIBITED MUTUAL FUND MANAGEMENT PRACTICES

Some funds may have all the restrictions listed below, some may not. Restrictions that might be specified include:

* Purchases of no more than 10% of the total securities of a single issuer or more than 10% of a company's voting stock

* Funds cannot buy shares in their own company (for example, a fund owned by a bank cannot buy shares in that bank)

* Purchases of no more than 10% of the net assets in the securities of a single issuer or 20% of net assets in companies engaged in the same industry (specialty funds excepted)

* No purchases of the shares of other mutual funds, except in certain cases where no duplication of management fees occurs

* No borrowing for leverage purposes

* No margin buying or short selling

* Normally a prohibition on commodity or commodity futures purchases

* Limitations on the percentage holdings of illiquid securities such as those sold through private placement and unlisted stocks

USE OF DERIVATIVES BY MUTUAL FUNDS

Subject to strict regulatory controls, mutual fund managers are allowed to incorporate specific "permitted" derivatives as part of their portfolios. Recall that derivatives are contracts whose value is based on the performance of an underlying asset such as a commodity, a stock, a bond, foreign currency or an index. Options (puts or calls), futures, forwards, rights, warrants and combination products are among the permitted derivatives used by mutual fund managers.

The most prominent applications of derivatives among mutual fund managers are to hedge against risk and to facilitate market entry and exit. It is often cheaper and quicker to enter the market using derivatives rather than purchasing the underlying securities directly.

> **Example:** A fund manager may have experienced a rapid growth in the value of her portfolio, but is concerned that the market may fall. To protect herself against a fall in value, she purchases put options on the iUnits S&P/TSX 60 Index Fund (i60s). If the market declines, the fall in value of the portfolio is offset by an increase in the value of the put options. Other managers may sell call options on shares they already own in order to enhance the fund's income. When fund managers deal internationally, they may use futures contracts as protection against changes in currency values.

One focus of National Instrument 81-102 is to allow the use of derivatives to benefit investors by minimizing overall portfolio risk while, at the same time, ensuring that portfolio managers do not use derivatives to speculate with investors' money. This regulation covers such topics as:

- The total amount (10% maximum as a percentage of the net assets of a fund) that can be invested in derivatives

- How derivative positions must be hedged by the assets of the fund (based on daily portfolio valuations)

- Expiry dates on different option products

- Permitted terms

- The qualifications required by portfolio advisors to trade these instruments

There are exceptions to these rules. Hedge funds are exempted from these rules. As well, commodity pools are permitted to use derivatives in a leveraged manner for speculation.

The use of permitted derivatives must be described in a mutual fund's simplified prospectus. Briefly, the discussion must explain how the derivative(s) will be used to achieve the mutual fund's investment and risk objectives, and the limits of and risks involved with their planned use.

PROHIBITED SELLING PRACTICES

There are a number of sales practices that are clearly unacceptable to regulators. Engaging in these and other types of overselling and unethical behaviour could lead to a loss of registration.

Quoting a future price	When an investor places an order to buy or sell a mutual fund, the price per unit or share that he or she will be paying or receiving is not known. This is because the purchase or sale price is based on the net asset value on the next regular valuation date.
	Depending on the time of day in which the order is entered, the NAVPS may be priced at the end of the current business day or at the close of business on the next business day. Mutual fund companies specify the time by which a trade must be entered to receive the closing price for the current business day.
	Consequently, it is unlawful for a representative to backdate an order in an attempt to buy shares or units at a previous day's price.
Offer to repurchase	Representatives may not make offers to repurchase securities in an attempt to insulate investors from downturns in price. Of course, investors have the normal right of redemption should they wish to sell their mutual fund investments.

Selling without a licence	As mentioned, mutual fund representatives must be licenced in each province where they intend to sell mutual funds, and this requires registration with each provincial regulatory authority under which they intend to work. They must keep authorities informed of material changes in their personal circumstances that could affect their registration status.
	Furthermore, it is illegal for a mutual fund representative to sell products for which the representative is not registered. For example, a mutual fund representative cannot sell stocks, bonds or insurance unless licensed to do so in that province.
Advertising the registration	Mutual fund representatives may not advertise or promote the fact that they are registered with a securities authority, as this may imply that regulatory authorities sanction the representatives' conduct or the quality of the funds.
Promising a future price	Representatives may not make promises that a fund will achieve a set price in the future.
Sales made from one province into another province or country	While telecommunications have given access to the entire country, the filling of orders from non-provincial residents, even unsolicited, is not permitted unless the mutual fund representative is registered in the client's province. Selling mutual funds to clients in another province or to non-Canadian residents may result in the cancellation of the mutual fund representative's registration.
Sale of unqualified securities	Mutual funds must also be approved in the province in which mutual fund representatives are registered. It is forbidden to sell mutual funds that have not been approved by the provincial regulator. Fortunately, most mutual funds available on the market are approved in every Canadian jurisdiction.

GUIDELINES AND RESTRICTIONS

There are also guidelines and restrictions with respect to what distributor firms and fund managers are permitted to do. These guidelines obviously have an impact on the representative.

Prohibited sales practices include:

* The provision by fund managers of money or goods to a distributor firm or its representatives in support of client appreciation.

* While the rate of commission set for a new fund may differ from rates of commission set for already established funds, the rate of commission on a fund cannot be changed unless the prospectus for that fund is renewed.

* A fund manager may not provide co-operative funds for practices which are considered general marketing expenses, such as general client mailings.

* Fund managers may not financially subsidize skill enhancement courses such as effective communications, improving presentation skills, etc.

- There are strict guidelines with respect to the provision of non-monetary benefits. They are forbidden unless they are of such minimal value or frequency that the behaviour of a representative would not be influenced (such as pens, T-shirts, hats and golf balls).

This is not an all-inclusive list. It is the responsibility of the representatives to be aware of what is, and is not, allowed. The Investment Funds Institute of Canada (IFIC) puts out Sales Practices Bulletins, which interpret and give examples of acceptable and unacceptable sales practices.

SALES COMMUNICATIONS

NI 81-102 and NI 81-105 outline specific guidelines with respect to sales communications. The following is a brief summary of these policies, but a mutual fund representative should be familiar with both these instruments. These rules are common whether the communication comes from the representative, the representative's firm, the fund's promoter, manager or distributor, or anyone who provides a service to the client with respect to the mutual fund. When in doubt, the representative should always consult with their branch manager or compliance officer. Their approval is needed before any sales communications is sent out.

These guidelines apply to any type of sales communication, including advertising or any oral or written statements that the representative makes to a client.

Sales communications can include:

- A description of the fund's characteristics

- Comparisons between funds under common management, funds with similar investment objectives or a comparison of the fund to an index

- Performance information – there are very specific rules with respect to how this information must be calculated and presented

- Advertising that the fund is a no-load fund

Any information or comparisons must include all facts, that if disclosed, would likely impact on the decision made or conclusions drawn by the client.

Of paramount importance is that the communication cannot be misleading. The communication cannot make an untrue statement, omit any information that if omitted would make the communication misleading, nor present information in a way that distorts the information. All information must agree with the information found in the prospectus.

COMMUNICATING RATES OF RETURN TO CLIENTS

As with any communication delivered to the client, the expectation is that the client will be provided with "full, true and plain disclosure". This obligation extends to any communication provided to the client where an annualized rate of return is provided regarding a specific account or group of accounts. A client communication that includes an annualized rate of return must be accompanied with sufficient explanation regarding the method of calculating the rate of return and must be in accordance with standard industry practices. The definition of standard industry practices includes a time weighted or dollar-weighted return, such as the Dietz and/or Modified Dietz method, daily valuation and/or any method approved under the Global Investment Performance Standards as endorsed by the CFA Institute.

For those client accounts that have been opened for less than 12 months, the rate of return shown must be the total rate of return since the account was opened at the mutual fund dealer. It is also expected that any client communication that contains or makes reference to a rate of return has been reviewed and approved by appropriate supervisory staff at the mutual fund dealer.

CLIENT ACCOUNT PERFORMANCE REPORTING

In addition to communicating rates of return, clients must also be provided with information regarding the performance of their investments. As described under MFDA rule 5.3.5, the mutual fund representative must ensure that on an annual basis, clients are provided with a performance report that covers at a minimum, a 12-month period. Performance reporting provided to clients must include either:

- the market value of the assets held in the client account as at the start period and as at the end of the period covered by the performance report. If the market value of an investment is not readily attainable, sufficient explanation as to the basis for not including the investment in the performance report should be disclosed to the client as part of the performance report.

- total assets deposited and/or withdrawn during the period covered by the performance report. For example, money that has been deposited and withdrawn over the 12-month period or any funds or investments transferred from another mutual fund dealer should be reflected in the performance report.

- the gain or loss in the account as at the end of the period covered by the report. This should include any fees and charges to the account and any accruals for investments that earn interest income.

The mutual fund dealer may also elect to satisfy performance reporting by providing an annualized rate of return. As mentioned above, a client communication that contains an annualized rate of return must be calculated in accordance with standard industry practices with sufficient explanation to the client regarding the return method presented in the report.

Mutual Fund Dealers may elect to send performance reporting on a more frequent basis than that of every 12 months, but the minimum threshold for account performance reporting is no less that an annual basis, covering at a minimum, a 12-month period.

WHAT IS THE "KNOW YOUR CLIENT" RULE?

Prior to accepting a client account, securities regulations require that dealers and their mutual fund representatives obtain information about their client to ensure that the purchase of mutual funds is suitable. To meet this requirement, it is the responsibility of every mutual fund representative to use due diligence to:

- learn the essential facts relative to a client (i.e. age, net worth and earnings, investment knowledge, investment objectives, etc.) before opening an account and maintain this knowledge on an ongoing basis;

- learn the essential facts relevant to every order accepted and ensure that the order is within the bounds of good business practice;

- learn the circumstances behind each transaction, and

- ensure that the recommendations made for an account are appropriate for the client based on factors including the client's financial situation, investment knowledge, investment objectives and risk tolerance.

Clients purchasing mutual funds must provide "know your client" information, whether or not the mutual fund representative has made a recommendation to purchase mutual funds. This information must be obtained for all persons who have trading authority for the account as well as other persons with a financial interest in the account.

To assist in ensuring that all orders are suitable for the client, order forms may contain a "know your client" section (in some cases, the "Know Your Client Form" is a separate document that is to be completed by the purchaser). Separate KYC information should be obtained for each account a client has, as the investment objectives, risk tolerance and investment horizon of each account may differ. For example, the KYC information for an RRSP account of a 30-year-old will likely differ from a non-registered account the individual is using to save to buy a home in two or three years.

If the client refuses to provide this information, the client should be made aware that:

- collection of this information is required by law and by all other mutual fund dealers

- obtaining this information is for the client's benefit because it assists the representative in providing advice in choosing an appropriate mutual fund to meet the client's particular investment needs and objectives

If the client still refuses to provide know-your-client data, then the transaction cannot be processed.

Suitability and Know Your Product

As set out under the Know Your Client Rule, mutual fund representatives shall use due diligence to, among other things, ensure that the suitability of investments within each client account is assessed. This responsibility extends to:

- whenever the client transfers their account to the dealer, and/or

- whenever the dealer or mutual fund representative becomes aware of a material change in the "know your client" information, and/or

- any time where there has been a change in the mutual fund representative responsible for the client account.

MFDA Rules and Policies require that mutual fund dealers and their representatives maintain an adequate record of each order and of any other instruction, given or received for the purchase or sale of mutual funds, whether executed or unexecuted and that this review is completed in a reasonable time manner.

In addition to the initial suitability assessment, mutual fund representatives also have an on-going responsibility to assess that the investments in the client account continue to be suitable. This includes maintaining documented evidence of all suitability reviews and any follow-up action taken as a result of their review. It is also expected under MFDA Policy No.2 *"Minimum Standards for Account Supervision"*, that a representative's supervisor, Branch Manager and/or Branch Compliance Officer also perform a suitability review of the investments in a client's account and maintain evidence of that review and any follow-up action taken as a result of their review.

The suitability requirement applies to recommendations that a representative may make to a client and **unsolicited orders** (i.e., orders for mutual funds that have not been recommended by the representative but instead come from the clients). In the case of unsolicited orders to be accepted, the purchase must be reasonable given the client's investment objectives, risk tolerance, investment horizon and investment knowledge.

Where an unsolicited order is determined to be unsuitable for the client, the record of the order must include evidence that:

- the transaction was unsolicited
- a suitability review was performed
- the client was advised that the proposed transaction was unsuitable

Before proceeding with an unsuitable, unsolicited trade, representatives should consult with their Branch Manager and/or Branch Compliance Officer. Mutual fund dealers must have written procedures for dealing with unsuitable, unsolicited orders, and there is no obligation to accept an unsuitable purchase order from a client.

The Know Your Client rule provides a service to the client, the mutual fund representative and the dealer as well. By having complete details of a client's financial positions, investment objectives and risk tolerance, the representative is in a better position to determine the appropriateness of investments for their clients. Equally as important and to ensure that the representative is meeting their "know your client" obligation, the representative must also fully understand the products that are being recommended to clients (see MFDA Notice MR-0048 for "know your product" details).

The Role of KYC Information in Opening an Account

Know your client information is critical for opening accounts and taking orders. Information about individuals with a financial interest in an account, information about changes in the client's circumstances, and requirements relating to anti-money laundering and anti-terrorist financing laws must be obtained.

FINANCIAL INTEREST IN AN ACCOUNT

The investment experience and knowledge of all individuals who have trading authority over the account should be obtained, as well as KYC information for anyone with a financial interest in the account, such as joint account holders and beneficiaries of trusts and trust accounts for children. With a trust, the trustee has trading authority over the account, and therefore his or her investment experience and knowledge should be obtained, as well as the KYC of the beneficial owner of the account. For spousal RRSPs, the contributing spouse does not have a financial interest in the account, so KYC information is required for the non-contributing spouse only.

CHANGES IN CIRCUMSTANCES

Appropriate judgment should be used in determining whether sufficient KYC information has been obtained. MFDA Rules require that KYC information be updated whenever a representative or other dealer employee becomes aware of a material change in the client's circumstances. At least once a year the dealer must request, in writing, that each client notify the dealer of any material change in his or her circumstances.

ANTI-MONEY LAUNDERING AND ANTI-TERRORIST FINANCING LAWS

In addition, before opening any account, anti-money laundering and anti-terrorist financing requirements must be considered and met. Every mutual fund dealer is required to have processes and procedures in place for this purpose and provide appropriate training to all their employees, including representatives.

These processes generally focus on the verification of the identity of every person authorized to provide instructions regarding the account or who has a beneficial interest in the account. There also are procedures for freezing accounts of individuals and organizations that appear on a specific list published by FINTRAC, for reporting suspicious transactions and attempted transactions, and for client identification requirements that apply in special circumstances.

Cash transactions or a series of transactions on any given day of $10,000 or more for account holders should be reported to the dealer's Anti Money Laundering Compliance Officer (who often will be the Branch Compliance Officer).

WHAT ARE THE REQUIREMENTS WHEN OPENING AND UPDATING AN ACCOUNT?

The Mutual Fund industry is fortunate to conduct its business in a self-regulatory environment, but the primary responsibility for self-regulation rests with each mutual fund representative. The first step in ensuring compliance to the rules and policies that govern the mutual fund business is the accurate completion of documentation when opening new accounts. Maintaining accurate and current account documentation will allow the representative and the supervisory staff at the mutual fund dealer the necessary tools to perform a suitability assessment of the investments in the client account.

Relationship Disclosure

Securities regulation requires that for each new client account opened, the mutual fund dealer must provide the client with written "relationship disclosure information." This disclosure includes all the information that a reasonable client would consider important about their relationship with the mutual fund dealer and the representative. Relationship disclosure information may be provided in a standalone document or it may be included in the account opening documentation.

Regardless of the manner in which the relationship disclosure information is provided to the client, it must include the following information:

- a description of the nature or type of client account. This may include a statement that the client is ultimately responsible for investment decisions made in the account but that the client may rely on the investment advice provided by the representative.

- a description of the products and services offered by the mutual fund dealer and the representative. For example, whether only proprietary mutual funds are available (in-house mutual funds) or whether third-party mutual funds may be held in the client account.

- a description of the procedures at the dealer regarding the handling of cash and cheques.

- a description of the dealer's obligation to ensure that each order accepted or any recommendation made to the client is suitable and advise that even if investment direction is provided by the client that the representative remains responsible to ensure that the investment is suitable for the client.

  In addition to the above, the disclosure document must also outline the circumstances in which a suitability review will be made, this includes, a client's transfer of assets to the dealer, whenever there has been a material change in the "know your client" information previously provided and when there has been a change in the representative responsible for the client account.

- a description and explanation of the various terms with respect to "know your client" information collected by the dealer with a description of how this information will be used in assessing investments in the client account.

- a description of the content and frequency of client reporting for the account ; and

- a description of the nature of the compensation that may be paid to the dealer. For example, this may include a general statement on how the dealer is compensated with reference to more specific fee information which may be found in the client account documentation or a similar type of agreement.

Relationship disclosure provided in a standardized document should be approved by the dealers head office and/or branch office. Mutual fund dealers are also required to maintain evidence that relationship disclosure has been provided to the client. If relationship disclosure information is incorporated into account documentation and it is client-signed, maintaining a copy of the signed account documentation is sufficient evidence. In the event that the dealer chooses to provide relationship disclosure as a standalone document, the dealer may evidence client delivery by requesting a client signed acknowledgement or by maintaining copies of disclosure documents sent to the client in their respective file at the dealer. It is recommended that, for relationship disclosure documents that are not client-signed, the representative maintain detailed notes of client meetings and discussions evidencing that the relationship disclosure information has been provided.

As with any client account documentation, it is expected that when there is a significant change in the relationship disclosure information previously provided to the client that the dealer will take reasonable steps to notify the client of the change in a timely manner.

New Accounts

The first step in satisfying the Know Your Client Rule is to establish the client's account in accordance with securities regulation as well as the policies and procedures established at the mutual fund dealer. Each new client account accepted by the representative should be reviewed and approved by the person responsible at the dealer for approving new accounts within a reasonable time-frame. Account numbers should not be assigned until the client's full legal name and address is confirmed.

In addition, it is also expected that a New Account Application Form is completed for each new client account. Typically, the New Account Application Form will include the necessary Know Your Client ("KYC") information. If the KYC information is not included in the New Account Application Form, KYC information must be captured on a separate form. Regardless of how the KYC information is documented it must include, among other things, the client's personal information, financial information, risk tolerance, investment objectives, and disclosure of whether the client is an insider or significant shareholder of a public corporation. The information collected regarding risk tolerance and investment objectives should be sufficiently precise to enable the dealer and the representative to meet their suitability assessment obligations.

Updating Client Information

As discussed under the Know Your Client rule, every representative shall use due diligence to, among other things, learn the essential facts relative to a client before opening an account and maintain such knowledge on an ongoing basis. With respect to the latter obligation, material changes in an existing account require the completion of an updated KYC and for the account to be re-approved by the Branch Manager and/or the Branch Compliance Officer. All changes made to the KYC must be fully discussed with the client. Material changes include, but are by no means limited to, the following:

- risk tolerance
- investment time horizon
- investment objectives
- material change in assets or income

A client signature or other method to confirm client identity should be in place at the mutual fund dealer in order to evidence any change in client name, address or banking information.

The mutual fund representative is also expected to maintain evidence of client instructions regarding any material changes in client information and all such changes must be approved by the individual responsible at the dealer for approving new client accounts. MFDA rules required that at least annually, the mutual fund dealer in writing, request each client to notify them if the KYC information previously provided to the dealer has materially changed. The date of the request and the date upon which the client informs the representative that their KYC information has changed must be recorded and maintained.

Distribution of Mutual Funds by Financial Institutions

There are some rules that apply specifically to the distribution of mutual funds by financial institutions (such as banks, trust companies, insurance companies and loan companies).

The rules dealing with financial institutions' (FI) distribution of mutual funds require the following:

1. **Control of Registrant**: An FI can sell mutual fund securities in its branches only through a corporation ("dealer") which it controls directly or indirectly, or with which it is affiliated. The dealer must be registered in each province or territory where the mutual fund securities are sold.

2. **Registration of Employees**: Only registered mutual fund representatives can sell mutual funds.

3. **Dual Employment**: Employees of an FI who engage in financial services activities can also become registered as mutual fund representative of the dealer and therefore sell mutual fund securities, provided that dual employment is permitted by the legislation to which the FI is subject.

4. **Conflicts of Interest**: Conflicts of interest can arise as a result of dual employment. For example, FI employees who are compensated on the basis of their sales of mutual fund securities but not other products are motivated to sell mutual funds to a client, even if other products would be more suitable for the client. A conflict can arise even when dually employed representatives are paid on a salary-only basis where the representatives also have the ability to approve client loans (e.g., to fund mutual fund purchases).

   To address these concerns, dealers must have in place supervisory rules to prevent conflicts of interest arising as a result of dual employment of representatives. These supervisory rules must address potential conflicts and must be approved by the relevant provincial securities administrator unless such rules provide that:

   • Dually employed representatives are paid salary only; and either

   • A dually employed representative cannot make loans to finance purchases of mutual fund securities sold by that representative, or

   • Any loan made by a dually employed representative in order to finance the purchase of mutual fund securities sold by that representative must be approved by a senior lending officer of the FI.

5. **In-House Funds**: The requirements in these principles are based on the assumption that the only mutual fund securities traded by the dealer through branches of the FI will be those issued by a mutual fund sponsored by the FI (or a company controlled by or affiliated with the FI). If an FI wanted to sell mutual fund securities sponsored by a third party, this should be discussed with the relevant securities regulator to determine what amendments, if any, are needed to the rules regulating the sale of such securities.

6. **Proficiency**: Officers, directors and representatives of the dealer must satisfy normal proficiency requirements, which will be set out by the applicable securities commission.

7.   **Premises and Disclosure**: The dealer must carry on its business in such a way that it is made clear to clients that the business of the dealer and the FI are separate and distinct. Separate premises within a branch are not required, although adequate disclosure of the distinction must be made to customers of the FI.

The disclosure must advise clients that the dealer is a separate corporate entity from the FI and that the investment is not insured by the CDIC or any other government deposit insurer, is not guaranteed in whole or part by the FI, and is subject to fluctuations in market value. This disclosure must be printed in bold face type and must appear on the following documents:

- **Fund prospectuses**: The disclosure must be contained in the body of prospectuses; on renewals, the disclosure must appear on the face page;

- **Subscription or order forms**: If these forms are used (e.g., order forms may not be required for processing telephone transactions) then disclosure must appear on them;

- **Confirmation slips**;

- **Promotional material**: The disclosure must appear on all promotional material appearing or handed out in any branch of the FI.

The FI may lend money to a client in order to facilitate the purchase of mutual fund securities sold by the dealer. The dealer must disclose to the client that the full amount of the loan must be repaid even if the value of the mutual fund securities (purchased with the loan) decline in value.

> **Note:** The Nova Scotia provincial securities administrator may require further details of such a loan.

SUMMARY

After reading this chapter, you should be able to:

1. Define a mutual fund and describe the advantages and disadvantages of investing in mutual funds.

    *   A mutual fund is an investment vehicle operated by an investment company that pools contributions from investors and invests these proceeds in a variety of securities, including stocks, bonds and money market instruments. A professional money manager manages the fund and follows a particular investing style.

    *   Contributions from investors are pooled and invested in various asset classes according to the fund's policies and objectives.

    *   Individuals that contribute money become unitholders in the fund and share in the income, gains, losses and expenses the fund incurs in proportion to the number of units that they own.

    *   Mutual fund units are redeemable on demand at the fund's current net asset value per share (NAVPS), which depends on the market value of the fund's portfolio of securities at that time.

    *   Advantages of mutual funds include low-cost professional management, diversification, transferability, variety of purchase and redemption plans, liquidity, ease of estate planning, and eligibility for margin and as loan collateral.

    *   Disadvantages of mutual funds include costs, unsuitability as a short-term investment and/or emergency cash reserve, fallibility of professional management and tax complications.

2. Compare and contrast mutual fund trusts and mutual fund corporations, explain and calculate how mutual fund units are priced, calculate a fund's NAVPS, and analyze the impacts of charges associated with mutual funds.

    *   An open-end trust does not incur tax liability. Any income flows through to the unitholder to be taxed in the hands of the holder based on the type of income the fund generates.

    *   Mutual funds may also be set up as federal or provincial corporations and can be eligible for a special tax rate. This structure requires the holdings to be mainly a diversified portfolio of securities, and income must be derived primarily from capital gains, interest, and dividends generated by those securities.

    *   The corporation distributes income through dividends that are taxed in the hands of the unitholder, which allows the corporation to avoid paying taxes on income.

    *   Mutual fund units are purchased directly from the fund company, usually through a distributor, and are sold back to the fund when redeemed.

- The offering price is the net asset value per share and is the price an investor pays for a unit. This price is based on the NAVPS at the close of business on the day an order is placed.

- The NAVPS is calculated as:

$$\frac{\text{Total Assets} - \text{Total Liabilities}}{\text{Total Number of Units}}$$

- NAVPS is the amount a fund's unitholders would receive for each share if the fund were to sell its entire portfolio of investments at market value, collect all receivables, pay all liabilities, and distribute what is left to its unitholders.

- The redemption price is the price a shareholder receives when he or she redeems units, and is also based on the NAVPS.

- Purchases and redemptions can be subject to a range of fees that differ from fund to fund.
  - A front-end load is a percentage of the purchase price paid to a distributor or fund company at the time of purchase.

  - No-load funds are sold with low to no direct percentage selling charges; however, an administration fee may be charged for purchase and/or redemption.

  - Back-end load funds levy a fee at redemption, also referred to as a redemption charge or deferred sales charge. The fee may be based on the original contribution to the fund or on the net asset value at the time of redemption, and it may decline the longer an investor holds a fund.

3. Define labour sponsored venture capital corporations (LSVCCs), discuss the advantages and disadvantages of LSVCCs, and contrast them with mutual funds.

    - LSVCCs are investment funds sponsored by labour organizations to provide capital for small to medium-sized and emerging companies.

    - LSVCCs can be divided into two broad categories: funds that invest in a diverse range of industries and those that concentrate on specific sectors.

    - Advantages of LSVCCs can include:
      - Generous federal and provincial tax credits

      - RRSP and RRIF eligibility

- Disadvantages of LSVCCs can include:
  - A high level of risk
  - Complicated redemption rules
  - Possible recapture of tax credits on early redemption
  - Comparatively high management expense ratios
  - A reduction in performance in cases where managers need to maintain high levels of cash to fund potential redemptions

4. Describe the mutual fund regulatory environment and the disclosure documents necessary to satisfy provincial requirements, identify mutual fund registration requirements, and discuss restrictions that sellers of mutual funds must observe.

- The Mutual Fund Dealers Association (MFDA) is the industry's self-regulatory organization (SRO) for the distribution of mutual funds. In Québec, the mutual fund industry is the responsibility of the Autorité des marchés financiers and the Chambre de la sécurité financière.

- The regulation of Canadian mutual funds falls under the jurisdiction of the securities act of each province.

- National Instrument 81-101 regulates mutual fund prospectus disclosure. NI 81-102 and a companion policy contain requirements and guidelines for the distribution and advertising of mutual funds.

- Because mutual funds are in a continuous state of primary distribution, investors purchasing a mutual fund for the first time must be provided with the simplified prospectus, which is a shortened form of a full prospectus that contains certain specific components. Investors also need to receive any other information required by the province.

- Mutual fund managers, distributors and sales personnel must be registered with the securities commissions in all provinces in which they operate (and with the Autorité des marchés financiers if they operate in Québec).

- Mutual fund sales registration must be renewed annually. Registration is subject to employment status with a registered dealer and has the requirement of notification to the relevant administrator, within time limits, of any changes in specific information.

- The fund manager provides day-to-day supervision of the fund's investment portfolio and must observe a number of guidelines for securities trading as specified in the fund's charter and prospectus, and the constraints imposed by the securities commissions.

- Prohibited sales practices include, among others, quoting a future price, making an offer to repurchase, selling without a licence, advertising registration, promising a future price, selling from one province into another, and selling unqualified securities.

5.   Describe the "Know Your Client" rules within the context of suitability, the circumstances in which suitability of a client account must be re-assessed and knowing your product.

-   Securities regulations require that dealers and their dealing representatives know the objectives, investment knowledge, time horizon and risk tolerance of their clients by requiring the provision of "know your client" information in all cases.

-   This information must be obtained for all persons who have trading authority for the account as well as other persons with a financial interest in the account.

-   Suitability of investments held in the client account must be re-assessed whenever the client transfers their account to the dealer, or whenever the dealer or mutual fund dealing representative becomes aware of a material change in the KYC information previously provided and/or anytime where there has been a change in the mutual fund dealing representative responsible for the client account.

-   The suitability requirement applies to recommendations that a dealing representative may make to a client and unsolicited orders (i.e., orders for mutual funds that have not been recommended by the dealing representative but instead come from the clients).

-   Especially important is information about individuals with a financial interest in an account, information about changes in the client's circumstances, and requirements relating to anti-money laundering and anti-terrorist financing laws.

6.   Describe "relationship disclosure information," list the elements that must be included in the client disclosure document, and the circumstances in which "Know Your Client" information requires an update.

-   Relationship disclosure information is all the information that a reasonable client would consider important about their relationship with the mutual fund dealer and the dealing representative.

-   Specific information must be included in the relationship disclosure document, including a description of the nature or type of the account, a description of the products and services offered by the dealer and dealing representative, a description of the procedures at the dealer regarding the handling of cash and cheques, and a description of the dealer's obligations to ensure that each order accepted or any recommendation made is suitable

-   Know Your Client information requires an update where there has been a material change in the client information previously provided. Material changes include, but are by no means limited to, changes to the client's risk tolerance, investment time horizon, investment objectives of the client or a material change in the client assets or income.

-   There are specific rules that apply to the distribution of mutual funds by financial institutions (such as banks, trust companies, insurance companies and loan companies).

Online Frequently Asked Questions

CSI has answered many frequently asked questions about this Chapter. Read through online Module 18 FAQs.

Online Post-Module Assessment

Once you have completed the chapter, take the Module 18 Post-Test.

Chapter *19*

Mutual Funds: Types and Features

19

Mutual Funds: Types and Features

CHAPTER OUTLINE

LEARNING OBJECTIVES

By the end of this chapter, you should be able to:

1. Describe the types of mutual funds and discuss the risk-return trade-off of investing in each type.
2. Evaluate mutual fund management styles.
3. Calculate the redemption/selling price of a mutual fund, explain the tax consequences of redemptions, and describe the four types of withdrawal plans and the appropriate use of each plan for an investor.
4. Describe how mutual fund performance is measured and how the comparative performance of mutual funds is determined.

CHOOSING MUTUAL FUNDS

There are myriad choices for mutual fund investors and many factors to consider when selecting one or more funds for investment. Mutual funds can be categorized based on the types of investments held in the portfolio, the level of risk and reward, and how the fund is managed. It is important to understand the various categories and the implications of choosing a particular mutual fund, including the available methods of withdrawal and the tax implications.

Of course, both before and after an investor chooses a mutual fund, assessing that fund's performance is important. There a number of ways to measure fund performance and a number of different benchmarks. In Canada there are regulations about performance measures to help investors make comparisons between similar mutual fund investments.

There are literally thousands of funds to choose from. Understanding the risk and return characteristics of the different types of funds is important and necessary to make an intelligent, well-informed and effective decision on the type of mutual fund to invest in.

KEY TERMS

Adjusted cost base

Asset allocation fund

Balanced fund

Bond fund

Closet indexing

Daily valuation method

Dividend fund

Equity fund

Fixed-dollar withdrawal plan

Fixed-period withdrawal plan

Glide path

Index fund

Indexing

Modified Dietz method

Peer group

Ratio withdrawal plan

Systematic withdrawal plan

T3 Form

T5 Form

Target-date fund

Time-weighted rate of return (TWRR)

WHAT ARE THE DIFFERENT TYPES OF MUTUAL FUNDS?

Mutual funds offer different risks and rewards to investors and, as explained earlier, mutual fund representatives have a fiduciary obligation to match the appropriate fund with the needs of their clients.

Mutual funds are distinguished by their basic investment policy or by the kind of assets they hold. The Canadian Investment Funds Standards Committee (CIFSC) classifies Canadian domiciled mutual funds into six categories based on the types of assets under management. These categories include:

- Money Market Funds

- Fixed Income Funds

- Balanced Funds

- Equity Funds

- Specialty funds

- Target-date funds

Money Market Funds

As their name implies, these funds invest in the securities that trade in the money market. All of the assets of a money market fund are invested in cash, cash equivalent securities and short-term debt securities of an approved credit rating. Investments might include treasury bills, bankers' acceptances, high quality corporate paper and short-term bonds. Funds in this category include:

- Canadian money market

- U.S. money market

Money market funds add liquidity to a portfolio and provide a moderate level of income and safety of principal. They are considered the least risky type of mutual fund.

> To comply with National Instrument 81-102, funds designated as money market must maintain a minimum weighting of 95% of their total net assets in cash or cash equivalent securities.

A feature of these funds is a constant share or unit value, often $10. To keep NAVPS constant, the net income of the fund is calculated daily and credited to unitholders. The earned interest is paid out as cash or reinvested in additional shares on a monthly (or sometimes a quarterly) basis.

While risk is low, money market funds, as is true of all mutual funds, are not guaranteed. While fund managers try to maintain a stable NAVPS, rapid increases in interest rates could reduce the value of the shares or units. Money market funds are therefore subject to interest rate risk.

Distributions received from a money market fund are taxable as interest income when held outside of a registered plan. Investors would add the interest to their income and pay taxes at their marginal rate.

Fixed-Income Funds

Fixed-income funds are designed to provide a steady stream of income and safety of principal rather than capital appreciation. Funds in this category include:

- Canadian short-term fixed-income

- Canadian fixed-income

- Canadian long-term fixed-income

- Canadian inflation-protected fixed-income

- Global fixed-income

- High-yield fixed-income

Funds in this category must invest at least 95% of their non-cash assets in fixed-income securities.

Except for the high-yield fixed-income category, which invests in fixed-income securities with a non-investment-grade credit rating, fixed income funds invest primarily in high-quality government and corporate debt securities. Their degree of volatility is related to the degree of interest rate fluctuation, but fund managers will attempt to change the term to maturity, or duration, of the portfolio and the mix of low- and high-coupon bonds to compensate for changes in interest rates.

Interest rate volatility is the main risk associated with this type of fund. If the fund also invests in corporate bonds, the fund would also be exposed to default risk.

The primary source of returns from non-registered bond funds is in the form of interest income. The mutual fund investor may also receive a capital gain if the fund sells some of its bonds at a profit.

Balanced Funds

Balanced funds invest in both stocks and bonds to provide a mix of income and capital growth. These funds offer diversification, but unless the manager adds value by shifting investment proportions in anticipation of market conditions, investors might as well develop their own balanced portfolio by putting their money into more than one fund. Funds in this category include:

- Canadian equity balanced

- Canadian neutral balanced

- Canadian fixed-income balanced

- Global equity balanced

- Global neutral balanced

- Global fixed-income balanced

- Tactical balanced

The main investment objective of balanced funds is to provide a "balanced" mixture of safety, income and capital appreciation. These objectives are sought through a portfolio of fixed-income securities for stability and income, plus a broadly diversified group of common stock holdings for diversification, dividend income and growth potential.

The balance between defensive and aggressive security holdings is rarely 50-50. Rather, managers of balanced funds adjust the percentage of each part of the total portfolio in accordance with current market conditions and future expectations. In most cases, the prospectus specifies the fund's minimum and maximum weighting for each asset class. For example, a balanced fund may specify a weighting of 60% equity and 40% fixed income.

> According to the CIFSC, balanced funds can hold a range of 5% to 90% in equities and 10% to 95% in fixed-income securities.

Asset allocation funds have objectives similar to balanced funds, but they differ from balanced funds in that they typically do not have to hold a specified minimum percentage of the fund in any class of investment. The portfolio manager has great freedom to shift the portfolio weighting among equity, money market and fixed-income securities as the economy moves through the different stages of the business cycle.

An investor in balanced and asset allocation funds would be subject to market and interest rate risk, depending on the split between fixed-income and equity securities. Likewise, the tax implications are the same. The investor may receive a combination of interest, dividends and capital gains.

Equity Funds

The CIFSC divides equity funds into as many as 22 different categories. Funds in this category include:

- Canadian, U.S. and global equity

- Canadian dividend

- Canadian and U.S. small- and mid-cap equity

- International, European and Emerging markets equity

- Asia Pacific and Japanese equity

- Health care, precious metal, natural resources, and real estate equity

> Funds in this category must invest a minimum of 90% of their non cash assets in equity securities.

The main investment objective of equity funds is long-term capital growth. The fund manager invests primarily in the common shares of publicly traded companies. Short-term notes or other fixed-income securities may be purchased from time to time in limited amounts for liquidity and, occasionally, income. The bulk of assets, however, are in common shares in the pursuit of capital gains. Because common share prices are typically more volatile than other types of securities, prices of equity funds tend to fluctuate more widely than those funds previously mentioned, and are therefore considered riskier.

Investments in markets outside of Canada are subject to foreign exchange rate risk. As with common stocks, equity funds range greatly in degree of risk and growth potential. These funds are all subject to market risk.

Some equity funds are broadly diversified holdings of blue chip income-yielding common shares and may, therefore, be classified at the conservative end of the equity fund scale. Other equity funds adopt a slightly more aggressive investment stance, for example, investing in young growing companies with an objective of above-average growth of capital.

Other equity funds are of a more speculative nature – aggressively seeking capital gains at the sacrifice of safety and income by investing in certain sectors of the market (precious metals, health care, biotechnology) or certain geographical locations (China, Latin America, Japan).

The tax implications are the same as for any fund that holds equity securities. The distributions will be in the form of capital gains and dividends and are taxed accordingly.

SMALL-CAP AND MID-CAP EQUITY FUNDS

Canadian equity funds that limit investments to companies with capitalization below those of the hundred largest Canadian companies are considered to be small- to mid-cap Canadian equity funds. Because smaller companies are considered to have higher potential for growth than large, well-established ones, these funds offer opportunities that theoretically differ from general Canadian equity funds. Small-cap companies generally have a market capitalization of $250 million to $1 billion and mid-caps are in the range of $1 billion to $9 billion. These companies do not usually pay dividends, as they are young and reinvest profits into expansion.

Along with the potential for greater gains, there is more volatility than is typically experienced with an equity fund that invests in mature blue chip equities. Distributions in this type of fund will be primarily in the form of capital gains.

DIVIDEND FUNDS

Canadian dividend funds provide tax-advantaged income with some possibility of capital appreciation. Dividend funds invest in preferred shares as well as high-quality common shares that have a history of consistently paying dividends. The income from these funds is in the form of dividends, which have the tax advantage of receiving the dividend tax credit. There may be capital gains as well.

The price changes that lead to capital gains or losses on dividend funds are driven by both changes in interest rates (interest rate risk) and general market trends (market risk). Price changes in the preferred share component of the fund are driven by interest rate changes, while general upward or downward movements in the stock market most heavily affect the common share component. Recall that preferred shares rank ahead of the common shares but below bondholders, in the event of bankruptcy or insolvency. Consequently, dividend funds are considered riskier than bond funds, but less risky than equity funds.

Specialty Funds

Not all funds fit easily into one of the above categories. Some funds are more narrowly focused and concentrate their assets into one main area – a specific industry or region, for example. Funds in this category may include:

- Retail venture capital

- Alternative strategies

- Miscellaneous – which are further subdivided to include:
    - Income and real property
    - Leveraged
    - Commodity
    - Geographic
    - Sector

Specialty funds seek capital gains and are willing to forgo broad market diversification in the hope of achieving above-average returns. Because of their narrower investment focus, these funds often carry substantial risk due to the concentration of their assets in just one area.

While still offering some diversification, these funds are more vulnerable to swings in the industry in which they are specializing or, if they have a portfolio of foreign securities, in currency values. Many, but not all, tend to be more speculative than most types of equity funds.

Index Funds

An index fund sets out to match the performance of a broad market index, such as the S&P/TSX Composite Index for an equity index fund or the DEX Universe Bond Index for a bond index fund. While index funds are not specifically listed in the above categories, they are categorized under the type of asset class they tend to replicate.

> *Example:* If ABC Fund tends to replicate the DEX Universe Bond Index, the fund would be categorized as Fixed-Income Fund – Canadian Fixed-Income.

The fund manager invests in the securities that make up the index they imitate, in the same proportion that these securities are weighted in the index.

> *Example:* If the chosen index is the S&P/TSX Composite Index and the Bank of Montreal represents 0.75% of the Index, the index fund must include 0.75% of Bank of Montreal stock.

Overall, the management fees associated with index funds are usually lower than those of other equity or bond funds. As a result, investing in an index fund represents a low-cost way for an investor to pursue a passive investment strategy.

The investment objective of an equity index fund is to provide long-term growth of capital. Equity index funds are subject to market risk because the portfolio is tied to the performance of the market. With a bond index fund, the main risk is interest rate risk.

The distributions will depend on the type of index being matched. A fund matching a bond index will obviously have primarily interest income, with some capital gains. An index fund matching an equity index may have dividend and capital gains distributions.

Target-date Funds

In 2005, a new type of fund was introduced: **target-date funds** (also referred to as target-based funds or life-cycle funds). These funds have two characteristics that distinguish them from other mutual funds: a maturity date and a glide path.

Investors who buy this product generally select maturity dates that match a certain life goal or target date in the future (e.g., date of retirement).

The **glide path** refers to changes in the fund's asset allocation mix over time which allows the fund to pursue a growth strategy by holding more risky assets in the early years of the fund's life and then gradually reduce the risk of the fund as the target date approaches. The adjustment is made automatically by the fund manager without any action from fund holder. Target-date funds are structured on the assumption that risk tolerance declines as investors grow older.

These funds have their own category under the CIFSC classification. Upon maturity, target-date funds are moved out of the target-date group and included in the appropriate fixed income or balanced fund category.

> **Example:** An investor who plans to retire in 2025 could buy a 2025 target-date fund. The asset allocation may gradually move from 80% equity and 20% fixed income in the early years to an asset allocation of 20% equity and 80% fixed-income by the target date.

The increase in popularity of target-date funds is driven by demographics—baby boomers in Canada will retire in significant numbers over the next 15 to 20 years.

Comparing Fund Types

As the discussion above highlights, the mutual fund industry has created a variety of funds designed to meet the diverse needs of the Canadian investing public. Because each fund type or group will hold different types of securities and will pursue different investment objectives, the risk and return between the various funds will also differ.

Figure 19.1 illustrates the risk-return trade-off between the different categories of mutual funds.

FIGURE 19.1   RISK AND RETURN BETWEEN DIFFERENT TYPES OF MUTUAL FUNDS

Specialty Funds

Equity Funds

Balanced Funds

Fixed Income Funds

Money Market Funds

Return

Low   High

Risk

It is important to note that there is a large range of risk-return profiles within a fund category. For example, for two equity funds, a Canadian dividend fund may have a risk/return profile that is significantly different than an emerging markets equity fund. Also, we have not included target-date funds here as the risk profile of this type of fund changes over the life of the fund.

Complete the following Online Learning Activity

Risk/Return on Mutual Funds

In order to recommend appropriate mutual funds to your clients, you need to be aware of the risk-return potential associated with the different types of funds. This activity will help you to evaluate your knowledge of the different risks associated with the mutual fund types.

⚙ Complete the **Risk/Return on Mutual Funds** activity.

WHAT ARE THE DIFFERENT FUND MANAGEMENT STYLES?

The absolute and relative return of a portfolio can be attributed first to the choice of asset class, and second to the style in which it is managed. Understanding investment styles is important in measuring fund performance. Managers employing a particular strategy may outperform or underperform others using a different strategy over the same periods.

Management style can be divided into two broad categories: passive and active.

- A **passive investment strategy** involves some form of indexing to a market or customized benchmark. In contrast, most equity styles are active. Active managers try to outperform the market benchmarks.

- There are many different **active investment** styles. At any one time, several of these styles may be in favour and others may be out of favour. Overall, funds that follow a passive strategy generally report lower management expense ratios (MERs) while funds that pursue an active strategy typically report higher MERs.

Active management may involve individual company selection, or over-weighting in favoured segments of industry sectors, or country selection for regional funds. In choosing to take an active approach, advisors may diversify their clients' portfolios by growth, value or other management style. This same strategy holds true with mutual funds. To diversify a client's portfolio, an advisor may recommend both a value mutual fund and a growth mutual fund. In this way, volatility is reduced, and there continues to be an opportunity for higher returns than those made by the market as a whole.

The various equity and fixed-income manager styles were described in Chapter 16, and these styles also apply to mutual funds. We discuss two other mutual fund manager styles below.

Indexing and Closet Indexing

Indexing represents a passive style of investing that attempts to buy securities that constitute or closely replicate the performance of a market benchmark such as the S&P/TSX Composite Index or the S&P 500 Composite Index. The indexing style is a low-cost, long-term, buy-and-hold strategy. There is no need to conduct individual securities analysis. Many index funds, particularly those that provide foreign exposure, rely on a combination of stock index futures and Canadian treasury bills.

Closet indexing does not replicate the market exactly, but sticks fairly closely to the market weightings by industry sector, by country or region, or by average market capitalization. Some active managers are closet indexers. This can be determined by how closely their returns, their volatility and their average market capitalization correspond to the index as a whole.

The concept of index funds is generally simpler for investors to understand than other management styles. These funds simply buy the same stocks as the index. Because they do not need analysts for stock selection, management fees are lower than for actively managed funds. A final advantage is that indexing makes for low portfolio turnover, which is an advantage for taxable accounts.

The indexing style, being essentially a strategy to mirror the market, represents a loss of opportunity to outperform it. Also, after the payment of fees and expenses, index mutual funds or indexed segregated funds return somewhat less than the market benchmark in the long term. Another disadvantage of this style is that distributions in the form of derivative-based income are taxable as income, rather than as capital gains.

HOW ARE MUTUAL FUND UNITS OR SHARES REDEEMED?

After acquiring shares in a mutual fund, the investor may wish to dispose of his or her shares or units and use the proceeds. The mechanics of disposing of fund units are fairly straightforward.

- The client contacts his/her advisor (or discount brokerage) and makes a request to sell or redeem fund units.

- The broker then places the trade request with the fund, or the fund's distributor.

- At the end of the valuation day, the fund calculates the net asset value and the proceeds are sent to the investor.

Most funds also offer the investor a variety of methods of receiving funds if the investor does not want to redeem a specific number of shares or units. These withdrawal methods are called systematic withdrawals and will be discussed shortly.

Tax Consequences

Mutual funds redeem their shares on request at a price that is equal to the fund's NAVPS. If there are no back-end load charges, the investor would receive the NAVPS. If there were back-end load charges or deferred sales charges, the investor would receive NAVPS less the sales commission. Mutual funds can generate taxable income in a couple of ways:

- Through the distribution of interest income, dividends and capital gains realized by the fund

- Through any capital gains realized when the fund is eventually sold

ANNUAL DISTRIBUTIONS

When mutual funds are held outside a registered plan (such as an RRSP or RRIF – discussed in detail in Chapter 25), the unitholder of an unincorporated fund is sent a **T3 form** and a shareholder is sent a **T5 form** by the respective funds. This form reports the types of income distributed that year – foreign income and Canadian interest, dividends and capital gains, including dividends that have been reinvested. Each is taxed at the fund holder's personal rate in the year received.

> **Example:** An investor purchases an equity mutual fund for $11 per share and in each of the next five years receives $1 in annual distributions, composed of $0.50 in dividends and $0.50 in distributed capital gains. Each year the investor would receive a T5 from the fund indicating that the investor would have to report to the Canada Revenue Agency an additional $1 in income. The T5 may indicate offsetting dividend tax credits (from dividends earned from taxable Canadian corporations).

It is sometimes difficult for mutual fund clients to understand why they have to declare capital gains, when they have not sold any of their funds. There is, however, a simple explanation. The fund manager buys and sells stocks throughout the year for the mutual fund. If the fund manager sells a stock for more than it was bought, a capital gain results. It is this capital gain that is passed on to the mutual fund holder. Unfortunately, capital losses that arise when selling a stock for less than it was bought cannot be passed on to the mutual fund holder. The losses are held in the fund and may, however, be used to offset capital gains in subsequent years.

DISTRIBUTIONS TRIGGERING UNEXPECTED TAXES

During the year a mutual fund will generate capital gains and losses when it sells securities held in the fund. Capital gains are distributed to the fund investors just as interest and dividends are distributed. If the distribution of capital gains is carried out only at year end, it can pose a problem for investors who purchase a fund close to the year end.

Consider an investor who purchased an equity mutual fund through a non-registered account on December 1 at a NAVPS of $30. This fund had a very good year and earned capital gains of $6 per share. These capital gains are distributed to the investors at the end of December either as reinvested shares or as cash.

As is the case with all distributions, this caused the NAVPS to fall by the amount of the distribution, to $24 (see Exhibit 19.1 below). At first glance, one might think that the investor is just as well off, as the new NAVPS plus the $6 distribution equals the original NAVPS of $30.

Unfortunately, the $6 distribution is taxable in the hands of the new investor, even though the $6 was earned over the course of the full year. For this reason, some financial advisors caution investors against buying a mutual fund just prior to the year-end without first checking with the fund sponsor to determine if a capital gains distribution is pending. Exhibit 19.1 provides an example.

EXHIBIT 19.1   DISTRIBUTIONS AND TAXES

An investor with a marginal tax rate of 40% purchases a mutual fund with a NAVPS of $30. The portfolio is valued at $30. The fund distributes $6 as a capital gains dividend or distribution. The value of the investor's portfolio after the distribution and the tax consequences would be:

Value of portfolio before distribution:	$30.00
Value of portfolio after distribution:	
NAVPS	$24.00
Cash or Reinvested Dividends	$ 6.00
	$30.00

Tax Consequences:

Assuming that the $6 was a net capital gain: 50% × $6.00 × 40%

= $1.20 Taxes Payable

Note: Even though the fund may call this distribution a "dividend" it is simply a distribution of capital gains. No dividend tax credit would apply.

Transactions that occur WITHIN the fund (such as the fund buying and selling individual securities such as stocks and bonds) could result in income distributions such as a capital gain to fund investors in the year the distribution occurs.

If you are a mutual fund investor and you sell your shares this transaction is yours and does not occur WITHIN the fund. You simply sell your shares and receive the cash. This transaction could result in a capital gain (but resulted from your own action – not the actions of the fund itself).

CAPITAL GAINS

When a fund holder redeems the shares or units of the fund itself, the transaction is considered a disposition for tax purposes, possibly giving rise to either a capital gain or a capital loss. Only 50% of net capital gains (total capital gains less total capital losses) is added to the investor's income and taxed at their marginal rate.

Suppose a mutual fund shareholder bought shares in a fund at a NAVPS of $11 and later sells the fund shares at a NAVPS of $16, generating a capital gain of $5 per share on the sale. The investor would have to report an additional $2.50 per share in income for the year (50% × $5 capital gain). This capital gain is not shown on the fund's T5, as this was not a fund transaction.

ADJUSTING THE COST BASE

A potential problem may arise when an investor chooses to reinvest fund income automatically in additional non-registered fund units. The complication arises when the fund is sold and capital gains must be calculated on the difference between the original purchase price and the sale price. The total sale price of the fund will include the original units purchased plus those units purchased over time through periodic reinvestment of fund income.

This mix of original and subsequent units can make it difficult to calculate the **adjusted cost base** of the investment in the fund. If careful records have not been kept, the investor could be taxed twice on the same income. Many investment funds provide this information on quarterly or annual statements. If these statements are not kept, it may be very time consuming to attempt to reconstruct the adjusted cost base of the investment.

Consider the case where an investor buys $10,000 of fund units. Over time, annual income is distributed and tax is paid on it, but the investor chooses to reinvest the income in additional fund units. After a number of years, the total value of the portfolio rises to $18,000 and the investor decides to sell the fund.

A careless investor might assume that a capital gain of $8,000 has been incurred. This would be incorrect, as the $8,000 increase is actually made up of two factors: the reinvestment of income (upon which the investor has already paid taxes) and a capital gain.

The portion of the increase due to reinvestment must be added to the original investment of $10,000 to come up with the correct adjusted cost base for calculating the capital gain. If, for example, the investor had received a total of $3,500 in reinvested dividends over the course of the holding period, the adjusted cost base would be $13,500 (the original $10,000 plus the $3,500 in dividends that have already been taxed). The capital gain is then $4,500, not $8,000.

Complete the following Online Learning Activity

Tax Consequences

When income from a mutual fund is automatically reinvested, it increases the adjusted cost base of the investment and thus affects tax status. Also important is factoring in the reinvested distributions when calculating return on a mutual fund investment.

This activity will help you to better understand both the method of calculating the adjusted cost base of a mutual fund and the tax consequences when units are redeemed. Review the method and then try the examples for yourself.

 Complete the **Tax Consequences** activity.

Reinvesting Distributions

Many funds will, unless otherwise advised, automatically reinvest distributions into new shares of the fund at the prevailing net asset value without a sales charge on the shares purchased. Most funds also have provisions for shareholders to switch from cash dividends to dividend reinvestment, and vice versa.

The reaction of the NAVPS to a distribution of funds is similar to that of a stock the day it begins to trade ex-dividend. The NAVPS will fall by an amount proportionate to the dividend. Since most investors receive their dividends in the form of more units rather than cash, the net result of the distribution is that the investor owns more units, but the units are each worth less.

For example, the NAVPS of a fund is $9.00 the day before a dividend distribution. The fund decides to pay a dividend of $0.90 per unit. After the distribution is made, the NAVPS of the fund will fall by $0.90 to $8.10. As Table 19.1 shows, if this fund had 1,000,000 units outstanding, the NAVPS before the distribution would be $9,000,000 ÷ 1,000,000 = $9.00. The NAVPS after the distribution would be $8,100,000 ÷ 1,000,000 = $8.10.

TABLE 19.1	IMPACT OF A DISTRIBUTION ON TOTAL NET ASSETS		
	Before Distribution	**After Distribution**	**When Distributions Are Reinvested**
Assets			
Portfolio	$8,075,000	$8,075,000	$8,075,000
Cash	950,000	50,000*	950,000
Liabilities			
Expenses	(25,000)	(25,000)	(25,000)
Total Net Assets	**$9,000,000**	**$8,100,000**	**$9,000,000**

* Distributions payable: $950,000 cash – ($0.90 dividend × 1,000,000 units outstanding).

Because the investors receive their distribution in new units, the fund now has 1,111,111.11 units worth $8.10 each ($900,000 ÷ $8.10 = 111,111.11 plus the original 1,000,000 units). Total fund assets are still $9,000,000. The $900,000 never actually leaves the company, but is reinvested in the fund.

What impact does this have on the individual investor? As stated above, the investor ends up with more units worth less each. The net effect is that the investor's portfolio is worth the same amount. Table 19.2 illustrates this. Assume that the investor owned 1,000 units of the fund. The investor would receive a distribution worth $900.00 (1,000 units × $0.90). The distribution is invested into new units. These new units now have a NAVPS of $8.10. The investor would receive $900 ÷ $8.10 = 111.11 units. The investor now has a total of 1,111.11 units (1,000 + 111.11).

TABLE 19.2	IMPACT OF DISTRIBUTION ON VALUE OF INVESTMENT	
	Before Distribution	After Distribution
1,000 units × $9.00	$9,000	
1,111.11 × $8.10		$9,000

Withdrawal Plans

A mutual fund's shareholders have a continual right to withdraw their investment in the fund simply by making the request to the fund itself and receiving in return the dollar amount of their net asset value. This characteristic is known as the **right of redemption** and it is the hallmark of mutual funds.

Withdrawal plans have evolved to meet the needs of investors who require regular income and tax efficiency – such as retiring and retired investors – and who do not want to withdraw their entire investment in a lump sum. To meet these needs, many funds offer one or more systematic withdrawal plans. In simple terms, instead of withdrawing all of one's holdings from a fund, the investor instructs the fund to pay out part of the capital invested plus distributions over a period of time. Withdrawals may be arranged monthly, quarterly or at other predetermined intervals.

If the fund invests its assets successfully and its portfolio increases in value, the increased worth of the fund's shares helps offset the reduction of principal resulting from the planned withdrawal over the specified period. However, if the investment decreases in value, there is a possibility that the investor's entire investment will be extinguished earlier than expected. This is a real risk that must be explained to investors contemplating withdrawal plans.

RATIO WITHDRAWAL PLAN

Here the investor receives an annual income from the fund by redeeming a specified percentage of fund holdings each year. The percentage chosen for redemption usually falls between 4% and 10% a year depending on the amount of income the investor requires. Obviously, the higher the percentage, the more rapid the rate of depletion of the investor's original investment. And, since the payout is a set percentage of the value of the fund, the amounts will vary each time.

Table 19.3 shows an example of a ratio withdrawal plan. We have assumed in this example, and each of the examples that follow, that the portfolio will grow by a steady 8% per year. In this example, we have also assumed that the investor wishes to withdraw 10% at the beginning of each year.

TABLE 19.3	RATIO WITHDRAWAL PLAN								

The value of each withdrawal will vary from year to year.

	Value at Beginning of Year				Value of Withdrawal				Value at End of Year
Year 1	$100,000	×	10%	=	$10,000	($90,000	×	1.08	=	97,200)
Year 2	$97,200	×	10%	=	$9,720	($87,480	×	1.08	=	94,478)
Year 3	$94,478	×	10%	=	$9,448	($85,030	×	1.08	=	91,833)
Year 4	$91,833	×	10%	=	$9,183	($82,650	×	1.08	=	89,262)
Year 5	$89,262	×	10%	=	$8,926	($80,336	×	1.08	=	86,763)

FIXED-DOLLAR WITHDRAWAL PLAN

This plan is similar to a ratio withdrawal plan except that the fund holder chooses a specified dollar amount to be withdrawn on a monthly or quarterly basis. Funds offering this type of plan often require that withdrawals be in "round amounts" (e.g., $50 or $100, etc.). If the investor's fixed withdrawals are greater than the growth of the fund, the investor will encroach upon the principal.

Table 19.4 shows an example of a fixed-dollar withdrawal plan.

TABLE 19.4	FIXED-DOLLAR WITHDRAWAL PLAN							

In this case, a constant or fixed amount of $10,000 is withdrawn at the beginning of each year.

	Value at Beginning of Year		Value of Withdrawal					Value at End of Year
Year 1	$100,000	–	$10,000	($90,000	×	1.08	=	$97,200)
Year 2	$97,200	–	$10,000	($87,200	×	1.08	=	$94,176)
Year 3	$94,176	–	$10,000	($84,176	×	1.08	=	$90,910)
Year 4	$90,910	–	$10,000	($80,910	×	1.08	=	$87,383)
Year 5	$87,383	–	$10,000	($77,383	×	1.08	=	$83,574)

When amounts withdrawn are greater than the increases in the portfolio, the principal can be encroached upon and eventually may reach zero.

FIXED-PERIOD WITHDRAWAL PLAN

Here a specified amount is withdrawn over a pre-determined period of time with the intent that all capital will be exhausted when the plan ends. For example, if an investor wished to collapse a plan over five years, he would withdraw: 20% of the remaining capital in year one, 25% in year two, 33% in year three, 50% in year four and 100% in the final year.

Table 19.5 shows an example of a fixed-period withdrawal plan.

TABLE 19.5	**FIXED-PERIOD WITHDRAWAL PLAN**							
In this case, a specific fraction is withdrawn at the beginning of each year.								
	Value at Beginning of Year		% of Capital Withdrawn		Value of Withdrawal				Value at End of Year
Year 1	$100,000	×	20%	=	$20,000	($80,000	×	1.08	=	86,400)
Year 2	$86,400	×	25%	=	$21,600	($64,800	×	1.08	=	69,984)
Year 3	$69,984	×	33%	=	$23,328	($46,656	×	1.08	=	50,388)
Year 4	$50,388	×	50%	=	$25,194	($25,194	×	1.08	=	27,209)
Year 5	$27,209	×	100%	=	$27,209				$0

The above assumes that the plan will be collapsed over five years.

LIFE EXPECTANCY–ADJUSTED WITHDRAWAL PLAN

This type of plan is a variation of a fixed-period withdrawal plan. Payments to the fund holder are designed to deplete the entire investment by the end of the plan, while providing as high an income as possible during the fund holder's expected lifetime. However, to accomplish this, the amount withdrawn on each date is based on periods of time, which are continually readjusted to the changing life expectancy of the plan holder, taken from mortality tables. Thus, the amounts withdrawn vary in relation to the amount of capital remaining in the plan and the plan holder's revised life expectancy.

Table 19.6 shows an example of a life expectancy–adjusted withdrawal plan.

TABLE 19.6	LIFE EXPECTANCY–ADJUSTED WITHDRAWAL PLAN

Using actuarial tables it is assumed that the client is expected to live to age 85 and is currently age 75. Using the formula:

$$\frac{\text{Value of the Portfolio}}{\text{Life Expectancy} - \text{Current Age}}$$

	Value at Beginning of Year			Value of Withdrawal					Value at End of Year
Year 1	$100,000	$\dfrac{\$100,000}{85-75}$	=	$10,000	($90,000	×	1.08	=	$97,200)
Year 2	$97,200	$\dfrac{\$97,200}{85-76}$	=	$10,800	($86,400	×	1.08	=	$93,312)
Year 3	$93,312	$\dfrac{\$93,312}{85-77}$	=	$11,664	($81,648	×	1.08	=	$88,180)
Etc.									

Suspension of Redemptions

As with all rules, there are exceptions. Securities commissions require all Canadian mutual funds to make payment on redemptions within a specified time; however, redemption suspensions can be permitted. Almost all funds reserve the right to suspend or defer a shareholder's privilege to redeem shares under certain highly unusual or emergency conditions. For example, a suspension might be invoked if normal trading is suspended on securities that represent more than 50% of securities owned by the fund. Obviously, if the fund cannot determine the net asset value per share, it cannot determine the redemption price of a unit or share.

HOW IS MUTUAL FUND PERFORMANCE COMPARED?

Once a mutual fund has been selected, the investor must be able to measure and evaluate the fund's performance, particularly over a certain time period. By doing so, the investor can evaluate how well the mutual fund manager has done over the evaluation period relative to the cost of management.

Performance measures include tools and techniques used to judge the historical performance of mutual funds, either in isolation or in comparison to other mutual funds. Although past performance is never a guarantee of future performance, performance measures can reveal certain historical trends or attributes that offer some insight into future performance.

Performance data is available from the mutual fund companies themselves, the websites of popular independent research firms such as Morningstar and Globe Fund, and special monthly mutual fund sections in the *National Post* and *The Globe and Mail*. In addition to their free services, Morningstar, Globe Fund and others offer more in-depth research and analysis for a fee.

Reading Mutual Fund Quotes

There are many financial sources that report the current net asset values of mutual funds on either a daily or weekly basis. The financial press sometimes includes simple and compound rates of return, the variability (or degree of volatility) of each fund, the expense ratio, and the maximum sales or redemption charge of each fund.

A typical quotation for a mutual fund that traded in the last 52-week period would be presented as follows:

EXHIBIT 19.2 READING MUTUAL FUND QUOTATIONS

				– Friday data –				– Rate of Return –				– Weekly Data –			
High	Low	Fund	Vty	Cls	$chg	%chg	1mo	1yr	3yr	5yr	High	Low	Cls	$chg	%chg
16.73	14.50	ABC Growth	4	16.62	-.06	-.36	4.0	6.3	10.0	7.9	16.73	16.62	16.62	.01	.06

This quotation is complex but very useful and may vary in format among financial newspaper quotation sections. This quotation shows that:

- The NAVPS of ABC Growth has traded as high as $16.73 per share and as low as $14.50 during the last 52 weeks.

- Vty is a measure of fund volatility (i.e., the variability in returns over the previous three-year period compared with other funds in this asset class). The scale is from 1 to 10. Funds with a Vty of 1 have the lowest variability in returns and funds with a Vty of 10 have the highest variability in returns.

- During the day under review, ABC closed at a NAVPS of $16.62. The fund closed down $0.06 from the previous trading day, representing a -0.36% fall over the previous day.

- ABC had a 1-month rate of return of 4%, a 1-year return of 6.3%, a 3-year return of 10% and a 5-year return of 7.9%. The rate of return assumes that all dividends have been reinvested in the fund.

- Over the previous week, ABC traded at a high of $16.73 and at a low of $16.62, finally closing at a NAVPS of $16.62 for a dollar increase of $0.01 and a percentage increase of 0.06% from the previous week.

The performance of money market funds is presented somewhat differently. Because of the relatively fixed NAVPS that these funds maintain, newspapers do not bother to report the NAVPS, but rather report each fund's current and effective yield. The current yield reports the rate of return on the fund over the most recent seven-day period expressed as an annualized percentage. The effective yield is the rate of return that would result if the current yield were compounded over a year, thereby allowing comparison with other types of compounding investments.

Investors who follow the performance of their funds in the daily paper should realize that dividends and interest earned by a fund's investments are distributed periodically. Many investors use these distributions to automatically purchase additional units in the fund. When distributions are made, the NAVPS is decreased by the amount of the distribution. This can be disconcerting to investors, but they should recognize that under automatic reinvestment plans, the distributions are used to purchase additional shares, with the net effect that they are just as well off as they were before the distribution decreased the NAVPS.

Measuring Mutual Fund Performance

Performance measurement involves the calculation of the return realized by a portfolio manager over a specified time interval called the evaluation period.

The most frequently used measure of mutual fund performance is to compare NAVPS at the beginning and end of a period. Usually this method is based on several assumptions, including the reinvestment of all dividends. The increase or decrease at the end of the period is then expressed as a percentage of the initial value. Consider the following example:

Beginning NAVPS	$19.50
Ending NAVPS	$21.50
Gain:	[($21.50 − $19.50)/ $19.50] × 100 = 10.26%

This calculation assumes that the investor made no additions to or withdrawals from the portfolio during the measurement period. If funds were added or withdrawn, then the portfolio return as calculated using this equation may be inaccurate.

When measuring the return on a mutual fund, it is important to minimize the effect of contributions and withdrawals by the investor, because they are beyond the control of the portfolio manager. This is best accomplished by using a time-weighted rate of return, which measures the actual rate of return earned by the portfolio manager.

TIME-WEIGHTED RATE OF RETURN

A **time-weighted rate of return** (**TWRR**) is calculated by averaging the return for each sub-period in which a cash flow occurs to create a return for the reporting period. Therefore, unlike a total return, it does account for cash flows such as deposits, withdrawals and reinvestments.

Methods of calculating a time-weighted return include the daily valuation method and the Modified Dietz method.

Daily valuation method: With the daily valuation method, the incremental change in value from day to day is expressed as an index from which the return can be calculated. This is beneficial for mutual funds, which generally calculate NAVPS daily, so their return calculation at the end of the month is greatly simplified. The main drawback is the need to value the portfolio every day, which can become difficult when trying to price the market value of real estate, mortgage-backed securities, illiquid issues, etc.

Modified Dietz method: The Modified Dietz method reduces the extensive calculations of the daily valuation method by providing a good approximation. It assumes a constant rate of return through the period, eliminating the need to value the portfolio on the date of each cash flow. The Modified Dietz method weights each cash flow by the amount of time it is held in the portfolio.

STANDARD PERFORMANCE DATA

To ensure that that mutual fund returns are comparable across different funds and fund companies, Canadian regulators have instituted standard performance data that specify which return measures, at a minimum, mutual fund companies must include, and how they are to be calculated. If these measures are presented in sales communications, they must be printed as prominently as any other performance data the mutual fund company provides.

For mutual funds other than money market funds, standard performance data includes compounded annual returns for one-, three-, five- and ten-year periods, as well as the total period since inception of the fund. For money market funds, the standard performance data include the current yield and the effective yield.

Mutual fund advisors should look at periods of three to five years or more as well as individual years. Periods of less than one year are not very meaningful. Nor is a one-year return conclusive, although it is reasonable to ask questions if the fund is falling well short of the average in its category. Always keep in mind, however, that past performance is not indicative of future performance.

COMPARATIVE PERFORMANCE

Return data is useful in telling us how much a particular fund earned over a given period. However, its usefulness is limited because it does not indicate whether the fund was performing well or poorly, especially relative to other funds in its group.

To determine the quality of fund performance, it is necessary to compare the return against some standard. For mutual funds, there are two general standards of comparison: the return on a fund's benchmark index and the average return on the fund's peer group of funds.

BENCHMARK COMPARISON

All mutual funds have a benchmark index against which their return can be measured, for example, the S&P/TSX Composite Index for broad-based Canadian equity funds or the DEX Universe Bond Index for bond funds. The benchmark indexes are used in the following ways:

- If a fund reports a return that is higher than the return on the index, we can say that the fund has outperformed its benchmark.

- If a fund reports a return that was lower than the return on the index, we can say that the fund has underperformed its benchmark.

Morningstar Canada has developed a series of mutual fund benchmarks that summarize average rates of return for Canadian bond, Canadian equity, U.S. equity, global bond and international equity funds. These indexes are available on their website at www.morningstar.ca. They provide a benchmark that investors may use to measure the relative performance of various funds.

A **peer group** is made up of mutual funds with a similar investment mandate. To measure the performance of a fund, its return is compared to the average return of the peer group. So if a fund posted a one-year return of 12% while the average return of its peer group over the same period was 9%, we can say that the fund outperformed its peer group over the evaluation period.

Issues that Complicate Mutual Fund Performance

When comparing mutual fund performance, one must avoid comparing the performance of two funds that are dissimilar (e.g., a fixed-income fund versus a growth equity fund) or comparing funds that have differing investment objectives or degrees of risk acceptance.

One complicating factor occurs when the name or class of fund does not accurately reflect the actual asset base of the fund. Investors should be aware, for example, that funds classified as Canadian equity funds may at times have significant portions of their assets invested in equities other than Canadian stocks. This is not to suggest that the fund manager is doing something wrong. Each manager must consider market trends and adjust the timing of the fund's investments. It does, however, suggest that the published results are often comparing apples with oranges.

This discrepancy between a fund's formal classification and its actual asset composition can impair attempts to create a portfolio. For example, an investor who wished to allocate 10% of a portfolio to gold stocks might be surprised to find that, at some points, gold mutual funds are holding 50% of their assets in cash. This results in an actual asset allocation of 5% in gold rather than the desired 10%.

RISK

Another factor that complicates comparisons between funds is that there is often no attempt to consider the relative risk of funds of the same type. One equity fund may be conservatively managed, while another might be willing to invest in much riskier stocks in an attempt to achieve higher returns.

Any assessment of fund performance should consider the volatility of a fund's returns. There are a number of different measures of volatility, but each attempts to quantify the extent to which returns will fluctuate. From an investor's standpoint, a fund that exhibits significant volatility in returns will be riskier than those with less volatility. Measures used to quantify volatility include:

*   the standard deviation of the fund's returns
*   beta
*   the number of calendar years it has lost money
*   the fund's best and worst 12-month periods
*   the fund's worst annual, quarterly or monthly losses

Standard deviation measures how volatile a fund has been over a past period to give an indication of how it might behave in the future. If a fund has consistently earned a 5% return per year over the past 20 years, although there is no guarantee, it would be reasonable to expect that the fund will earn 5% in the future. If, however, a fund's annual return fluctuated from a negative 20% to a positive 20% over a period of 20 years, it is much less likely that the fund will earn a return of 5% in the coming year. Standard deviation is a common measure of the consistency of a fund's return. The higher the standard deviation, the more volatile or unpredictable the return may be.

Other methods, which look at different time periods, can be used to calculate best-case and worst case scenarios. Ratings systems based on multiple periods avoid placing too much emphasis on how well or poorly the fund did during a particular short-term period.

An advisor who deals with mutual funds should be aware of how the fund tends to perform relative to the stock market cycle. Some will outperform others in rising markets, but do worse than average in bear markets. The beta, available on most fund performance software, measures the extent to which a fund is more or less volatile than the underlying market in which it invests. The greater the variation in the fund's returns, the riskier it tends to be. Particular attention should be paid to periods during which the fund lost money.

PITFALLS TO AVOID IN JUDGING MUTUAL FUND PERFORMANCE

There are a number of pitfalls to avoid in judging a mutual fund's performance.

- Past performance is not indicative of future performance and there is no guarantee that any fund will be able to maintain or improve upon past performance, especially in a general market downturn. Mutual fund advisors scrutinize the past and attempt to predict future performances, although they are not correlated. Software products that permit advisors to review performance and sort funds according to various criteria include: Globe HySales and PALTrak.

- Some observers argue that the performance of a fund is a direct reflection of the skill of the portfolio manager. These observers suggest that historical performance must be discounted when there is a change in portfolio manager.

- While average returns for a peer group of funds are useful measures, averages may be artificially high because of "survivorship bias." This means there is a tendency for poorly performing funds to be discontinued or merged. Because of survivorship bias, the average returns of surviving funds do not fully reflect the past performance of the entire spectrum of funds.

- Mutual fund performance evaluations should take into account both the type of fund and its investment objectives. Bond funds cannot be compared with equity funds, and even equity funds with different investment objectives cannot be compared.

- Beta relates the change in the price of a security to the change of the market as a whole. Mutual funds with high betas are considered riskier than comparable funds with lower betas.

- Standard deviation is a statistical test that measures the dispersion of historic prices of a specific stock, or class of investments, around the historic average of that particular stock or class. A larger standard deviation is indicative of greater volatility.

- There is no single appropriate time horizon for rating risks and returns, and the practices of industry analysts vary considerably. For long-term funds, a three-year period is generally regarded as a bare minimum. More weight can be attached to longer periods of five to ten years, or at least two market cycles.

- Advisors should be wary of selective reporting of performance periods, or periods for which there are no comparable numbers for the performance of a market benchmark or a peer group of competing funds.

Complete the following Online Learning Activities

Measuring Mutual Fund Performance

Evaluating mutual fund performance is part of an advisor's job. Practise evaluating the funds presented in this exercise.

 Complete the **Measuring Mutual Fund Performance** activity.

Mutual Funds Study Guide

To help you learn all the material in this chapter, you may want to create an outline with key points. Try the one we've created for this module, adding your own notes to make a complete module outline.

Complete the **Mutual Funds Study Guide** to help you study for the module.

SUMMARY

After reading this chapter, you should be able to:

1. Describe the types of mutual funds and discuss the risk-return trade-off of investing in each type.

- Canadian mutual funds fall into six categories: money-market, fixed-income, balanced, equity, specialty funds, and target-date funds.

    - Money market funds invest in cash and near-cash securities or money market instruments. They generally have a constant share or unit value. The net income of the fund is calculated daily and credited to unitholders, then paid out as cash or reinvested in additional shares on a regular basis.

    - Fixed-income funds are designed to provide a steady stream of income rather than capital appreciation. Interest rate volatility is the main risk associated with this type of fund. Interest income is the primary source of return.

    - Balanced funds invest in both stocks and bonds to provide a mix of income and capital growth. A new type of balanced fund has emerged in recent years: target-date funds. These funds have a maturity date and the risk of the fund decreases as the maturity date approaches.

    - Equity funds are invested primarily in the common shares of publicly traded companies with an investment objective of long-term capital growth. Funds vary greatly in degree of risk and growth potential, and are all subject to market risk.

    - Specialty funds seek capital gains and are willing to forgo broad market diversification in the hope of achieving above-average returns. Because of their narrower investment focus, these funds often carry substantial risk due to the concentration of their assets in just one area.

- An index fund is a passive investment strategy designed to match the performance of a specific market index through direct investment in the securities that make up the specified index.

- Risk and return can be seen as a scale with the lowest risk/lowest return funds category being money market funds and the highest risk/highest return funds category generally being specialty funds. Within that range there are (lower to higher risk) fixed-income funds, balanced funds, and equity funds.

2. Evaluate mutual fund management styles.

    •   The two broad categories of management style are passive and active. Passive management generally involves some form of indexing to a market or customized benchmark. Active managers try to outperform market benchmarks using active asset allocation and selection.

    •   Other styles include closet indexing, where the portfolio fairly closely follows the market weightings of the benchmark. Refer to Chapter 16 for the discussion on the other equity and fixed-income manager styles.

3. Calculate the redemption or selling price of a mutual fund, explain the tax consequences of redemptions, and describe the four types of withdrawal plans and the appropriate use of each plan for an investor.

    •   Mutual funds are redeemed at a price equal to a fund's net asset value per share (NAVPS). Mutual funds redeemed while held in registered funds do not have any immediate tax consequences.

    •   Investors holding mutual funds in non-registered accounts are subject to tax on capital gains realized when the fund is sold and on annual distributions of income and capital gains earned within the fund.

    •   Many funds offer one or more systematic withdrawal plans: based on investor instructions, a partial payout of capital invested plus distributions reinvested are made at a specific time and/or interval.

        –   In a ratio withdrawal plan, the investor receives annual income from the fund by redeeming a specified percentage of fund holdings on each withdrawal date.

        –   In a fixed-dollar withdrawal plan, the investor receives a specified dollar amount on each withdrawal date.

        –   In a fixed-period withdrawal plan, a specified amount is withdrawn over a pre-determined period of time with the intent that all capital be exhausted when the plan ends.

        –   In a life expectancy–adjusted withdrawal plan, the goal is to deplete the entire investment by withdrawing amounts adjusted to reflect the portfolio's current value and the changing life expectancy of the plan holder.

4. Describe how mutual fund performance is measured and how the comparative performance of mutual funds are determined.

    *   Performance is measured by calculating the return realized by a portfolio manager over a specified time interval called the evaluation period.

    *   One approach is to calculate the percentage change in the NAVPS from the beginning to the end of a period, using specific assumptions including reinvestment of all dividends and no cash withdrawals or deposits.

    *   A time-weighted rate of return better measures the actual rate of return earned by a portfolio manager because it minimizes the effect of contributions and withdrawal by investors.

    *   The daily valuation method measures the incremental change in fund value from day to day and this is expressed as an index from which the return can be calculated.

    *   The Modified Dietz method is a more accurate way to measure the return on a portfolio because it identifies and accounts for the timing of all interim cash flow while a simple geometric return does not.

    *   Canadian regulations require standardized performance data, including which return measures are to be calculated, how often they must be calculated, and the way they must be calculated.

    *   Quality of fund performance is determined by comparison against a relevant standard, which is either a fund's benchmark index or the average return on the fund's peer group of funds.

Online Frequently Asked Questions

CSI has answered many frequently asked questions about this Chapter. Read through online Module 19 FAQs.

Online Post-Module Assessment

Once you have completed the chapter, take the Module 19 Post-Test.

Chapter *20*

Segregated Funds and Other Insurance Products

20

Segregated Funds and Other Insurance Products

CHAPTER OUTLINE

LEARNING OBJECTIVES

By the end of this chapter, you should be able to:

1. Identify and describe the various features of segregated funds.
2. Describe the tax considerations of investing in segregated funds.
3. Discuss the regulation of segregated funds, including the role played by OSFI, Assuris and other regulatory agencies.
4. Describe the features of guaranteed minimum withdrawal plans and other insurance products.

ROLE OF INSURANCE PRODUCTS

Segregated funds are unique in that they are insurance-based investment products with special features and benefits. Although they share many similarities with mutual funds, the insurance features make them quite different.

In the previous chapter we learned about the features and risks of investing in mutual funds. Investors must realize that the value of their investment can certainly increase when markets do well, but if markets do poorly or if the fund is poorly managed, there is also the opportunity for loss. Segregated funds give you the upside potential of market gains, but also in certain circumstances protect you from the loss of your investment.

Because one needs to be a licensed life insurance agent to sell segregated funds in Canada, this chapter provides you with an overview of the product, including the features and benefits and some of the background needed to assess the tax and regulatory aspects of investing in segregated funds. Understanding the risk and return characteristics of the different types of funds is important and necessary to make an intelligent, well-informed and effective decision on the type of product to invest in.

KEY TERMS

Allocation

Annuitant

Assuris

Beneficiary

Canadian Life and Health Insurance Association
  Incorporated (CLHIA)

Contract holder

Creditor protection

Death benefit

Guaranteed minimum withdrawal benefit plans

Individual variable insurance contracts (IVICs)

Insurable interest

Irrevocable beneficiary

Maturity guarantee

Notional units

Probate

Reset

Revocable beneficiary

Segregated fund

WHAT ARE THE DIFFERENT SEGREGATED FUND FEATURES?

Segregated fund contracts and other widely held investment funds offer professional investment management and advice, the ability to invest in small amounts, regular client statements, and other services. They combine investments and related services in an integrated package. In the case of segregated fund contracts, investments and certain elements of insurance contracts are combined.

Segregated funds, however, also have unique features that enable them to meet special client needs, such as maturity protection, death benefits and creditor protection. Unlike other types of investment funds, segregated funds are regulated by provincial insurance regulators because they are insurance contracts contracts – known as **individual variable insurance contracts** (**IVICs**), between a contract holder and an insurance company.

> *It is worthwhile noting that individuals must be licensed to sell life insurance in order to sell segregated funds.*

Because of the insurance benefits they offer, segregated funds are more expensive than uninsured funds, particularly in the form of higher MERs, an important point to consider when advising on or investing in a segregated fund.

Because of their legal structure, segregated funds do not issue actual units or shares to investors, since this would imply ownership. Instead, an investor is assigned **notional units** of the contract, a concept that measures a contract holder's participation and benefits in a fund. This concept also makes it possible to compare the investment performance of segregated funds with those of mutual funds.

Essentially, the contract covers the following three parties:

The Contract Holder	The person who bought the contract.
	A segregated fund contract can be held within registered plans such as RRSPs, RESPs and RRIFs.
	When the contract is held outside a registered plan such as an RRSP, the contract holder does not have to be the person whose life is insured by the contract. When the contract is held in a registered plan, the contract holder and the annuitant must be the same person.
The Annuitant	The person on whose life the insurance benefits are based.
	There are restrictions on whose life a contract holder can base a contract. The general rule in most provinces is that the contract holder, at the time that the contract is signed, must have an "insurable interest" in the life or health of the annuitant. Otherwise, the proposed annuitant must consent in writing to have his or her life insured.

The Beneficiary	The person who will receive the benefits payable under the contract upon death of the annuitant. (A contract may have more than one beneficiary.)
	The contract holder may designate one or more beneficiaries, or may designate his or her estate as the beneficiary. The beneficiary does not have to be a person. It could, for instance, be a charitable organization.
	A **revocable designation** offers greater flexibility, because the contract holder can alter or revoke the beneficiary's status. In the case of an **irrevocable designation**, the contract holder cannot change the rights of a beneficiary without the beneficiary's consent.

Maturity Guarantees

One of the fundamental contractual rights associated with segregated funds is the promise that the contract holder or the beneficiary will receive at least a partial guarantee of the money invested. In fact:

- Provincial legislation requires that the **maturity guarantee** be at least 75% of the amount invested over a contract term of at least a ten-year holding period or upon the death of the annuitant.

- To offer greater capital protection, many insurers have increased the minimum statutory guarantee to 100% of the amount invested. The 100% guaranteed funds feature higher management expense ratios than the 75% guaranteed funds, reflecting the higher risks of offering full maturity protection after ten years.

These guarantees – whether full or partial – appeal to people who want specific assurances about their potential capital loss.

With a maturity guarantee, a client may participate in rising markets without setting a limit on potential returns. At the same time, subject to the ten-year holding period, the client's invested capital is protected from loss.

AGE RESTRICTIONS

Insurance companies offering ten-year maturity guarantees that exceed the statutory requirement of 75% may impose restrictions on who qualifies for the enhanced guarantee.

Example: The restriction might be that the individual on whom the death benefits are based must be no older than 80 at the time that the policy is issued. Alternatively, the purchaser might receive a reduced level of protection under the policy once he or she reaches a certain age.

RESET DATES

Although segregated fund contracts have at least a ten-year term, they may be renewable when the term expires, depending on the annuitant's age. If renewed, the maturity guarantee on a ten-year contract would "reset" for another ten years. A **reset** allows contract holders to lock in the current market value of the fund and set a new ten-year maturity date.

Reset dates can be anywhere from daily to once a year. The daily reset feature benefits clients in rising or falling markets. In a rising market, when the net asset value of fund units is increasing, daily resets enable contract holders to continually lock in accumulated gains. In a falling market, when net asset values are falling, contract holders will also be protected, because the guarantee is based on the previous high.

Table 20.1 provides a simplified example of how the daily reset works when the market value of a fund's assets is either rising or falling:

TABLE 20.1   DAILY RESET VALUES

Date	Accumulated Value	Guaranteed Maturity Value	Impact of Reset	New Maturity Date
Jan. 4, 2013	$10,000	$10,000	None	Jan. 4, 2023
Jan. 5, 2013	$9,900	$10,000	Protects against $100 market loss	Jan. 5, 2023
Jan. 6, 2013	$10,125	$10,125	Locks in $125 market gain	Jan. 6, 2023

Death Benefits

The **death benefits** associated with segregated funds meet the needs of clients who want exposure to long-term asset classes while ensuring that their investments are protected in the event of death.

The principle behind the death benefits offered by a segregated fund is that the contract holder's beneficiary or estate is guaranteed to receive payouts amounting to at least the guaranteed amount, excluding sales commissions and certain other fees. The amount of the death benefit is equal to the difference, if any, between the guaranteed amount and the net asset value of the fund at death.

Table 20.2 illustrates the death benefits when the market value of the units held in the segregated fund is below, the same as, or higher than the original purchase price. To simplify the illustration, it is assumed that the fund has been held long enough that any deferred sales charges are no longer applicable.

TABLE 20.2   DEATH BENEFITS

Guaranteed Amount	Market Value at Death	Death Benefit	Total Amount Paid to Beneficiary
$10,000	$8,000	$2,000	$10,000
$10,000	$9,000	$1,000	$10,000
$10,000	$10,000	None	$10,000
$10,000	$11,000	None	$11,000

As the table shows, death benefits are paid only when the market value of the fund is below the guaranteed amount.

- When the market value of the segregated fund at death is $9,000, the beneficiary will receive the market value and a death benefit payment of $1,000 above the market value. Therefore, in addition to the payment of the $9,000 market value of the fund, the total payment to the beneficiary is $10,000.

- When the market value at death is above the guaranteed amount, there is no death benefit payable because the beneficiary receives the full market value of the investment which is higher than the guaranteed amount.

Creditor Protection

Segregated funds may offer protection from creditors in the event of bankruptcy. This protection is not available through other managed investment products such as mutual funds. Creditor protection is available because segregated funds are insurance policies. The fund's assets are owned by the insurance company rather than the contract holder. Insurance proceeds generally fall outside the provisions of bankruptcy legislation.

Creditor protection can be a valuable feature for clients whose personal or business circumstances make them vulnerable to court-ordered seizure of assets to recover debt. Business owners, entrepreneurs, professionals or other clients who have concerns about their personal liability are among those who might welcome the creditor protection offered by a segregated fund.

> *Example:* Suppose that a self-employed professional died and left a non-registered investment portfolio of $300,000 and business-related debts of $150,000. If the portfolio were made up of mutual funds, creditors would have a claim on half of the portfolio, leaving only $150,000 for the surviving family members. In most provinces, except Québec, the estate would also be subject to probate fees based on the size of the estate.
>
> If the entire portfolio had been held in segregated funds, $300,000 would be payable directly to the deceased person's beneficiaries. Creditors could claim nothing, and the beneficiaries would receive their money promptly and without having to deduct a portion for probate fees.

Creditor protection does not apply under all circumstances. In order for the assets held in the contract to be eligible for creditor protection, the purchase must not be made with the intention of avoiding potential creditor action, and a beneficiary must be named.

Bypassing Probate

Segregated funds can help clients avoid the costly **probate** fees levied on assets held in investment funds. Probate refers to the legal process of administering the estate of a deceased person. The ability to bypass probate is one of the key estate-planning advantages of segregated funds.

Segregated fund contracts are not regarded as part of the deceased's estate. The proceeds of segregated funds pass directly into the hands of the beneficiaries. There is no waiting for probate to be completed. Nor can payment be delayed by a dispute over the settlement of the estate. Moreover, by passing assets directly to beneficiaries through a segregated fund, contract holders can ensure that their beneficiaries save on fees paid to executors, lawyers and accountants.

Cost of the Guarantees

In addition to the costs incurred by mutual funds, such as sales fees, switching fees, trailer fees and management expense ratios, segregated funds have added costs related to death benefits and maturity guarantees.

Assessing the true value of the insurance in segregated funds is a difficult issue. Certainly the management expense ratios for segregated funds are higher than those of comparable mutual funds.

Bankruptcy and Family Law

Under federal bankruptcy law, segregated funds are not normally included in the property divided among creditors. For example, a bankruptcy trustee cannot change a beneficiary designation to make the proceeds of the contract payable to the contract holder's creditors.

Under the federal *Bankruptcy and Insolvency Act*, the proceeds of a segregated fund may be subject to seizure if it can be proven that the purchase was made within a certain period before the bankruptcy, normally within one year. But if the client was legally insolvent when the contract was purchased, the segregated fund purchases could be challenged as far as five years back.

Complete the following Online Learning Activity

Segregated Funds Review

 Complete the **Segregated Funds Review** activity to learn more about the features of segregated funds.

Comparison to Mutual Funds

Table 20.3 highlights some of the key similarities and differences between segregated funds and mutual funds.

TABLE 20.3	SIMILARITIES AND DIFFERENCES BETWEEN SEGREGATED FUNDS AND MUTUAL FUNDS	
Features	**Segregated Funds**	**Mutual Funds**
Legal status	Insurance contract	Security
Who owns assets of fund	Insurance company	Fund itself, which is a separate legal entity
Nature of fund units	Units have no legal status, and serve only to determine value of benefits payable	Units are legal property which carry voting rights and rights to receive distributions

TABLE 20.3	SIMILARITIES AND DIFFERENCES BETWEEN SEGREGATED FUNDS AND MUTUAL FUNDS – *Cont'd*	
Features	**Segregated Funds**	**Mutual Funds**
Who regulates their sale	Provincial insurance regulators	Provincial securities regulators
Who issues them	Mainly insurance companies; also a small number of fraternal organizations	Mutual fund company
Main disclosure document	Information folder	Prospectus
How often valued	Usually daily, and at least monthly	Usually daily, and at least weekly
Redemption rights	Right to redeem is based on contract terms	Redeemed upon request
Required financial statements	Audited annual financial statement	Audited annual financial statement and semi-annual statement for which no audit required
Sellers' qualifications	Licensed life insurance agents; BC, Saskatchewan and PEI also require successful completion of a recognized investment course, such as those offered by the CSI, IFIC or potentially by CAIFA	Licensed mutual fund representatives or registered brokers
Maturity guarantees	Minimum of 75% of deposits after 10 years. Companies may offer guarantees up to 100%	None
Government guarantees	None	None
Protection against issuer insolvency	Assuris, a not-for-profit organization, provides up to $60,000 per policyholder per institution in compensation against any shortfalls in policy benefits resulting from the insolvency of a member firm (restricted to death benefits and maturity guarantees)	The Mutual Fund Dealer Association (MFDA) Investor Protection Corporation (IPC), a not-for-profit corporation, provides protection up to $1,000,000 to eligible customers of MFDA members as a result of a member's insolvency
Death benefits	Yes, may be subject to age or other restrictions	None
Creditor protection	Yes, under certain circumstances	None
Probate bypass	Yes, proceeds of contract held by deceased contract holder may be passed directly to beneficiaries, avoiding probate process	None

Complete the following Online Learning Activity

Comparison between Segregated Funds and Mutual Funds

Review and print this **Comparison between Segregated Funds and Mutual Funds** summary sheet.

HOW ARE SEGREGATED FUNDS TAXED?

Segregated funds are insurance contracts, but are taxed as if they were trusts. The insurance company itself, which is the legal owner of the assets of the segregated fund, does not pay taxes on income earned by the fund.

The fund's net income – whether in the form of dividends, capital gains or interest – is deemed to be the contract holder's income. In non-registered accounts, this income is taxable in the current year. The amount of income deemed to have been earned by each contract holder is calculated using a procedure known as **allocation**. A percentage of the fund's total income is allocated to each unit, according to the terms of the segregated fund contract.

Most funds allocate income to a contract holder based on the number of units held, and the proportion of the calendar year during which those units are held. For instance, a segregated fund contract held for six months of the year would receive half the per-unit allocations accorded to a contract held for the full year.

Impact of Allocations on Net Asset Values

The different ways in which mutual funds and segregated funds flow through income to unit holders is reflected in what happens to the net asset values (NAV) of the funds.

With a mutual fund:

- Net asset values fall when a distribution is made, because income and capital gains may accumulate inside the fund and are then paid out.

- Periodically (usually annually or quarterly), the mutual fund makes distributions to existing unit holders, each time deducting the value of the distribution from the fund's assets.

- The NAVPU declines by the amount of the distribution. Most distributions are reinvested in the fund, and the new units are issued to the unit holders.

- Therefore, although the NAVPU declines, the unit holder owns more units.

With segregated funds:

- The fund does not suffer a decline in the NAV after an allocation of income.

- Instead, the segregated fund contract receives additional income, which is allocated to existing units.

- In most cases, these allocations are held in the policy, though they may also be redeemed by the contract holder and received as cash.

Although the calculation of the tax impact of the allocation method is beyond the scope of the course, we can say that:

- Segregated fund NAVPU is the same for all contract holders at any given point in time.

- The NAVPU at which an investor purchases a segregated fund varies depending on when during the year the fund is purchased.

- Income allocations do not reduce the NAVPU of a segregated fund.

- Segregated fund allocations per unit are paid throughout the year.

One of the advantages of segregated fund contracts over mutual funds is the fact that capital losses, as well as capital gains, can be passed on to the contract holder. This is not true of mutual funds, where capital losses cannot be flowed through to unit holders. They must be kept in the fund and used in future years to offset capital gains.

Tax Treatment of Guarantees

Payments from a segregated fund contract's maturity guarantees are taxable. If the proceeds of the contract (after commissions) are less than the adjusted cost base, income tax is payable on the guaranteed amount. However, the contract holder can use the difference between the market value of the segregated fund and the adjusted cost base as a capital loss.

The net effect is zero if the guarantee is considered to be a capital gain. If the guarantee paid is considered to be income, then the policyholder must pay tax on the full amount, but can use only 50% of any capital loss declared.

If the proceeds exceed the adjusted cost base, the contract holder is taxed on the difference.

The following examples illustrate the amount of tax payable under three different scenarios:

- Scenario I: The maturity value exceeds the original cost of the contract.

- Scenario II: The maturity value is less than the guaranteed amount.

- Scenario III: A reset provision has been used, making the maturity guarantee $30,000 higher than in the original contract. Resetting the maturity guarantee extends the policy over a new ten-year period. Even if the reset is used to lock in a capital gain, it does not constitute redemption and therefore does not trigger a taxable event.

Under each scenario, it is assumed that $100,000 was invested in a lump sum on a deferred sales charge basis, and that the policy was held long enough that there are no redemption fees applicable when the policy is surrendered. The calculations are based on a 100% maturity guarantee.

EXHIBIT 20.1

	Invested Amount	Maturity Guarantee	Market Value at Redemption	Maturity Guarantee Paid	Capital Gain	Taxable Capital Gain
Scenario I	$100,000	$100,000	$130,000	$0	$30,000	$15,000
Scenario II	$100,000	$100,000	$95,000	$5,000	$0	$0
Scenario III	$100,000	$130,000	$110,000	$20,000	$30,000	$15,000

Scenario I

Client redeems $100,000 deposit after ten years for proceeds of $130,000. The market value of the policy at maturity exceeds the adjusted cost base.

Tax consequences: 50% of the capital gain of $30,000 is taxable in the year of redemption.

Scenario II

Client redeems $100,000 deposit after ten years for proceeds of $95,000 in current market value. Since the net market value at maturity is less than the adjusted cost base, the client is paid $5,000 as the maturity guarantee.

Tax consequences: The maturity guarantee of $5,000 is taxable as a capital gain, but it is reduced to $0 by the $5,000 capital loss incurred because the client's $100,000 deposit is now worth only $95,000.

Scenario III

Client chooses to reset the maturity guarantee after five years, locking in the gain in market value to $130,000 and extending the policy. Ten years after the reset date, the policy matures at a market value of $110,000. The client receives a $20,000 maturity guarantee, for total proceeds of $130,000.

Tax consequences: No capital gains liability is triggered at the time of the reset. However, at the time of redemption (15 years after the original deposit), the capital gain of $30,000 ($10,000 from the increase in market value and $20,000 from the maturity guarantee) is taxable in the year in which it is paid out.

These are very simplified examples, as they assume there were no distributions paid by the issuing company over the period specified. In reality, distributions would likely be paid every year. Tax is paid on these distributions in the year that they were paid and cannot be taxed twice. Fortunately, the issuing company keeps track of these distributions and the adjusted cost base is reported on the recipient's T3 slip.

Tax Treatment of Death Benefits

When the insured person dies, the contract is terminated and the beneficiaries receive the market value of the segregated fund plus death benefits, if any. If the contract holder is not the same person as the annuitant, the contract remains in force when the contract holder dies, but the deceased owner is deemed to have disposed of the contract at fair market value. This deemed disposition will normally trigger a capital gain or a capital loss.

If the contract holder took advantage of the provision allowing his or her spouse to be named as the successor owner, the contract can be transferred to the spouse at its adjusted cost base, thereby deferring any capital gains liability. If the contract owner and annuitant is the same person, the gain or loss will be reflected on the owner's terminal tax return for the year of death.

> **Example:** A client purchases a segregated fund contract for $100,000. The contract provides for a 100% guarantee at death. Five years later, the client dies. At the time of the client's death, the market value of the segregated fund is $80,000. The death benefit payment would be $20,000. Assuming the fund was held in a non-registered plan, the client would report a $20,000 gain, but the client would also have an offsetting capital loss of $20,000. Because the fund declined from $100,000 to $80,000, there would be no tax impact as the two would cancel each other out.

HOW ARE SEGREGATED FUNDS REGULATED?

For the most part, segregated fund contracts are subject to the provincial legislation governing all life insurance contracts. Each province and territory has accepted the **Canadian Life and Health Insurance Association Inc.** (**CLHIA**) guidelines as the primary regulatory requirements. Federal insurance regulators do not regulate the sale of segregated funds.

Monitoring Solvency

The Office of the Superintendent of Financial Institutions (OSFI) is responsible for ensuring that federally regulated insurance companies are adequately capitalized under the requirements of the federal *Insurance Companies Act*.

OSFI's key requirements for segregated fund contracts include:

- The maturity guarantee payable at the end of the term of the policy cannot exceed 100% of the gross premiums paid by the contract holder. (This rule also applies to contracts carrying reset features, which allow the contract holder to lock in gains and set a new ten-year term to maturity.)

- The initial term of the segregated fund contract cannot be less than ten years.

- There can be no guarantee of any amounts payable on redemption of the contract before the annuitant's death or the contract maturity date.

The Role Played by Assuris

Assuris is the insurance industry's self-financing provider of protection against the loss of policy benefits in the event of the insolvency of a member company. Assuris is financed by assessments levied on its members, and is incorporated federally as a nonprofit organization.

The federal government, along with most provinces, requires life insurers to be members of Assuris and to pay its levies.

The Assuris guarantee covers only the death benefits and maturity guarantees in a segregated fund contract. The assets of the funds themselves are not eligible for Assuris protection, because they are segregated from the general assets of the insurance company.

Segregated fund holders therefore enjoy a built-in form of protection against an insurance company's insolvency. Assuris' role is to "top up" any payments made by a liquidator to fulfill the insurance obligations under a segregated fund contract.

The maximum compensation that can be awarded under an individual segregated fund policy is up to $60,000 or 85% of the promised guaranteed amounts, whichever is higher. These limits apply both to amounts held by individuals in registered plans, such as RRSPs, RRIFs and life income funds, and to contracts held outside registered plans.

Complete the following Online Learning Activity

Segregated Fund, Features and Tax Considerations

Segregated funds and mutual funds are different in many ways: structure, benefits, costs, tax treatment, distribution and regulation. Sometimes one fund is more appropriate than another fund for a given client. Under which circumstances is one fund more appropriate than the other? In these activities, you will test your understanding of segregated funds.

 Complete these **Scenarios** and **True and False** activities.

WHAT ARE OTHER INSURANCE PRODUCTS?

In the past, segregated funds were the domain of insurance companies. Recently, the entry of mutual fund companies and the growing popularity of segregated funds for investors have led to significant product expansion in segregated funds. The result has been variations of and enhancements to the basic structure of the traditional segregated fund contract.

Guaranteed Minimum Withdrawal Benefit Plans

When clients near their retirement, losses in their portfolio can be particularly serious. Earlier in the investment cycle, good years can balance off bad years, but in retirement the extra return from later good years can be lost, since part of the portfolio has to be withdrawn for income.

To counter the risk of retirement funds being impaired by a few bad years at the wrong time, insurance companies have developed **guaranteed minimum withdrawal benefit (GMWB) plans**.

A GMWB is similar to a variable annuity.

With a variable annuity the amount of monthly payment to the annuitant varies according to the value of the investments in a segregated fund into which premiums are placed. Many variable contracts provide a "floor" below which benefits may not fall. The floor for benefits is usually equal to 75% of premiums paid, regardless of what happens to the value of the variable annuity fund.

GMWB plans provide a guaranteed minimum annual payout – typically 5% to 7% of the amount invested – no matter how the investments perform. Every three years, throughout the term of the plan, if the underlying fund has increased in value, the guaranteed amount is reset upwards. If the investment value is reset higher, the guaranteed payout increases or the plan withdrawal schedule is extended. If the investment value drops, however, the payout amount is guaranteed and cannot be reduced.

GMWB plans are a combination of investments and insurance. They can be bought in lump sum by transferring registered or non-registered savings plans to the GMWB. The insurance company then provides a variety of investment funds to choose from. The underlying investments can be based on a variety of indexes, funds, etc.

These plans have another advantage besides guaranteeing principal repayment and the possibility of sharing in the increased value of a mutual fund – an annual 5% guaranteed bonus allocated to the account for each calendar year that the client does not make any withdrawals.

> ***Example:*** If a client buys the plan several years before withdrawals begin, the guarantee increases by a 5% bonus each year until withdrawals start, even if the fund decreases in value. During this period, if the market rises, the three-year reset is in effect. This reset compounds the value of the 5% increases in the guarantee.

If a client starts to take payments immediately after purchasing the plan, she will be susceptible to earlier losses in the portfolio. In other words, she may never be able to receive more than the principal repayment.

It is necessary to purchase the plan several years in advance of withdrawal, in order to build up the guarantee. The bonuses come in those years regardless of the behaviour of the underlying fund.

These plans are especially suitable for clients with 5 to 10 years to retirement, who cannot afford significant losses in their portfolio during that time. These clients also want to be able to share in the growth of selected financial markets.

GMWB plans provide the potential for growth but with a guaranteed income floor that provides a secure income stream as a base. The income stream can also be assured for the life of the investor. This provides further peace of mind, knowing that the investment can provide income for life.

GMWB plans come with fees levied to manage the underlying mutual fund(s) and fees levied to fund the GMWB guarantee. The investor may have to pay sales charges when depositing or withdrawing from the contract depending on the sales charge option of the fund(s) chosen.

During the course of 2012, several insurance companies significantly modified their GMWB plans, many also suspended the sales GMWB due to adverse market conditions.

Portfolio Funds

Portfolio funds, which invest in other funds instead of buying securities directly, allow investors to hold a diversified portfolio of segregated funds through a single investment. The responsibility for choosing or rebalancing the asset mix usually rests with the fund company.

Management expenses for portfolio funds are generally higher than for stand-alone segregated funds and guaranteed investment funds, because the investor pays for the asset allocation service, on top of the management costs for the underlying funds.

SUMMARY

1. Identify and describe the various features of segregated funds.

    *   A segregated fund is a life insurance product that shares many similarities with mutual funds. The insurance component offers such features as maturity protection, death benefits and creditor protection.

    *   The contract holder is the person who bought the segregated fund contract. The annuitant is the person on whose life the insurance benefits are based. The beneficiary is the person or persons who will receive the benefits payable under the contract on the death of the annuitant.

    *   In registered plans only, the contract holder and the annuitant must be the same person.

    *   Provincial regulations require that beneficiaries receive a guarantee of at least 75% to a maximum 100% of the return of the money invested over a contract term of at least a ten year holding period.

    *   Depending on the annuitant's age, the contract may be renewable when the term expires. If renewed, the maturity guarantee on a ten-year contract would reset for another ten years.

    *   If a contract holder dies, the holdings in the fund bypass probate and pass directly to the beneficiaries.

    *   Creditor protection is available because segregated funds are insurance policies. The fund's assets are owned by the insurance company rather than the contract holder, and insurance proceeds generally fall outside the provisions of bankruptcy legislation.

    *   To benefit creditor protection, the purchase must not be made with the intention of avoiding potential creditor action, and a beneficiary must be named.

    *   The management expense ratio (MER) on a segregated fund is typically higher than that on a comparable mutual fund because of the insurance components.

2. Describe the tax considerations of investing in segregated funds.

    *   Net income earned from a segregated fund is deemed to be the contract holder's income and is taxable in the current year.

    *   The appropriate percentage of the income is allocated to the contract holder, generally based on the number of units held and the proportion of the calendar year in which the units were held.

    *   The allocations are reported annually on a T3 slip, although they are made throughout the year.

- Payments from maturity guarantees are taxable. The amount taxed is the proceeds, less sales charges, minus the cost of the contract (which is the original amount deposited plus any allocations).

3. Discuss the regulation of segregated funds, including the role played by OSFI, Assuris and other regulatory agencies.

- Generally, segregated fund contracts are subject to the provincial legislation governing life insurance contracts, but there are some differences between jurisdictions.

- The contracts are subject to the guidelines on guarantee provisions of The Office of the Superintendent of Financial Institutions (OSFI).

- In the case of insolvency of a fund, Assuris guarantees cover the death benefits and maturity guarantees of the fund contract and will top up any payments made by a liquidator to fulfill these insurance obligations.

- All communications considered advertisements are governed by Canadian Life and Health Insurance Association (CLHIA) guidelines.

4 Describe the features of guaranteed minimum withdrawal plans and other insurance products.

- Guaranteed minimum withdrawal plans are similar to variable annuities in that the amount of the monthly payment varies according to the value of investments. The GMWB option gives the planholder the right to withdraw a certain fixed percentage of the initial deposit every year until the entire principal is returned, no matter how the fund performs.

- Portfolio funds invest in other funds instead of buying securities, thus allowing investors to hold a diversified portfolio of segregated funds through a single investment.

Online Frequently Asked Questions

CSI has answered many frequently asked questions about this Chapter. Read through online Module 20 FAQs.

Online Post-Module Assessment

Once you have completed the chapter, take the Module 20 Post-Test.

Chapter *21*

Hedge Funds

21

Hedge Funds

CHAPTER OUTLINE

How has the Market for Hedge Funds Evolved?
- Comparisons to Mutual Funds
- Investing in Hedge Funds
- Size of the Hedge Fund Market
- Tracking Hedge Fund Performance

What are the Benefits and Risks of Hedge Funds?
- Benefits
- Risks
- Due Diligence

What are the Different Hedge Fund Strategies?
- Relative Value Strategies
- Event-Driven Strategies
- Directional Funds

What are Funds of Hedge Funds?
- Advantages
- Disadvantages

Summary

LEARNING OBJECTIVES

By the end of this chapter, you should be able to:

1. Define hedge fund, compare and contrast hedge funds with mutual funds and institutional investors with retail investors in hedge funds, summarize the history and growth of the hedge fund market and discuss how hedge fund performance is tracked.

2. Evaluate the benefits, risks and due diligence requirements of investing in hedge funds.

3. Identify the three categories of hedge fund strategies and describe how the specific strategies within each category work.

4. Describe the advantages and disadvantages of investing in a fund of hedge funds (FoHF) structure versus individual hedge funds.

ROLE OF HEDGE FUNDS

For many investors, hedge funds are a relatively new investment product. Popular awareness of hedge funds in Canada is recent and has grown markedly since 2001. Even though several high-profile hedge funds have failed over the years, bringing negative attention to the industry, hedge fund assets continue to grow.

Investors should realize, however, that hedge funds are not for everyone. They are commonly described as lightly regulated pools of investment capital that have greater flexibility in their investment strategies. Some hedge funds are conservative, others are more aggressive. Despite the popular name, some funds do not hedge their positions at all. Therefore, it is best to think of a hedge fund as a type of fund structure rather than a particular investment strategy.

These investments are less regulated, less controlled and less standardized than the majority of investments, but they also offer opportunities that cannot be ignored.

Part of the attraction of investing in hedge funds lies in the flexibility that allows them to pursue investment opportunities not available to mutual funds or segregated funds because of regulatory restrictions. Individual investors could also find it difficult to replicate the strategies because they may be prohibitively expensive or simply logistically impossible.

Because hedge fund managers have tremendous flexibility in the types of strategies they can employ, the manager's skill is more important in hedge funds than in almost any other managed product. This makes the amount of due diligence performed before recommending or investing in a hedge fund of significant importance. Thus, understanding the particular strategy the manager is employing and the manager's track record is critical to the success of the investment decision.

The chapter begins with an overview and history of hedge funds in Canada and then reviews the various hedge fund strategies. The chapter ends with a discussion of how to track hedge fund performance and the different types of hedge fund structures that have evolved recently.

KEY TERMS

Accredited investor

Commodity pool

Convertible arbitrage

Directional hedge fund

Event-driven hedge fund

Expected return

Fund of hedge funds (FoHFs)

Hedge fund

High-water mark

Incentive fee

Limited partnership

Lockup

Offering memorandum

Principal-protected notes (PPNs)

Relative value hedge fund

HOW HAS THE MARKET FOR HEDGE FUNDS EVOLVED?

Hedge funds are lightly regulated pools of capital whose managers have great flexibility in their investment strategies. These strategies are often referred to as alternative investment strategies, although this term may also be used to describe investments in private equity, real estate and commodities/managed futures.

Hedge fund managers are not constrained by the rules that apply to mutual funds or commodity pools. The managers can take short positions, use derivatives for leverage and speculation, perform arbitrage transactions, and invest in almost any situation in any market where they see an opportunity to achieve positive returns.

Some hedge funds are conservative; others are more aggressive. Despite the name, some funds do not hedge their positions at all. Therefore, it is best to think of a hedge fund as a type of **fund structure** rather than a particular investment strategy.

Comparisons to Mutual Funds

Like mutual funds, hedge funds:

*   are pooled investments that may have front-end or back-end sales commissions
*   charge management fees
*   can be bought and sold through an investment dealer

Despite these similarities, there are many differences, summarized in Table 21.1.

TABLE 21.1 COMPARING MUTUAL FUNDS TO HEDGE FUNDS	
Mutual Funds	**Hedge Funds**
• Can take limited short positions when regulatory authority has been granted	• No restrictions on short positions
• Can use derivatives only in a limited way	• Can use derivatives in any way
• Are usually liquid	• May have liquidity restrictions
• Are sold by prospectus to the general public	• Are generally sold by offering memorandums to sophisticated or accredited investors only
• Are subject to considerable regulatory oversight	• As private offerings are subject to less regulation
• Charge management fees but usually have no performance fees	• Charge management fees and in most cases performance fees
• "Relative" return objective; performance is usually measured against a particular benchmark	• "Absolute" return objective; fund is expected to make a profit under all market conditions
• Most are valued daily	• Most are valued monthly

TABLE 21.1	COMPARING MUTUAL FUNDS TO HEDGE FUNDS – *Cont'd*
Mutual Funds	**Hedge Funds**
• Quarterly or annual disclosure to unitholders	• Annual disclosure to unitholders
• Cannot take concentrated positions in the securities of a single issuer	• Can take concentrated positions

Investing in Hedge Funds

The market for hedge funds can be split into (a) funds targeted toward high-net-worth and institutional investors, and (b) funds and other hedge fund-related products targeted toward the broader individual investor, or "retail" market.

Hedge funds targeted toward high-net-worth and institutional investors are usually structured as **limited partnerships** or trusts, and are issued by way of private placement. Instead of issuing a prospectus, these hedge funds usually issue an **offering memorandum**, which is a legal document stating the objectives, risks and terms of investment involved with a private placement.

To invest in these funds, investors must be considered either **sophisticated** or **accredited**. Sophisticated and accredited investors must meet certain minimum requirements for income, net worth, or investment knowledge. For example, to be considered an accredited investor in any province:

- A person must own, alone or with a spouse, net financial assets having an aggregate realizable value exceeding $1,000,000

  or

- Have had net income before taxes exceeding $200,000 (or $300,000, if combined with a spouse) in each of the two most recent years, and a reasonable expectation of exceeding the same net income level in the current year

For the broader individual investor, alternative investment strategies are increasingly being used in hedge funds and hedge-fund products structured as something other than a limited partnership. These structures include commodity pools, closed-end funds and principal-protected notes.

1. **Commodity pools**: Commodity pools are a special type of mutual fund that can use leverage and engage in short selling using derivatives. Unlike conventional mutual funds, commodity pools must be sold under a long-form prospectus. Also, special requirements are imposed on mutual fund salespersons who sell them. Commodity pools are one way that retail investors can gain access to some hedge fund strategies.

2. **Closed-end funds**: To avoid mutual fund investment restrictions, a hedge fund may be structured as a closed-end fund (which means that redemptions by the fund, if any, occur only once a year or even less frequently). Closed-end funds can be offered to retail investors by prospectus, but are not subject to the investment restrictions that apply to mutual funds. Closed-end funds are often listed on the TSX, which allows retail investors access to the fund through the secondary market.

3. **Principal-protected notes (PPNs)**: Principal-protected notes provide investors with exposure to the returns of one or more hedge funds and a return of principal on maturity that is guaranteed by a bank or other highly rated issuer of debt securities (the Canadian Wheat Board and Business Development Bank are two examples). These products are not defined as "securities" and therefore are not subject to the rules and restrictions of securities law. As a result, this a popular structure for providing retail investors access to hedge fund strategies.

Complete the following Online Learning Activity

Hedge Funds Structure and their attributes

 Review the **Hedge Fund Structures and their attributes** summary sheet.

EXHIBIT	HISTORY OF HEDGE FUNDS

Alfred Jones is recognized as the father of hedge funds. In 1949, he created a fund with a goal to offer protection from a declining equity market while achieving superior returns. He did this by taking two speculative tools, short selling and leverage, and merging them into a conservative investing strategy.

Jones's model was based on the premise that performance depends more on stock selection than market direction. He believed that in a rising market a successful manager should:

• Buy or go long securities that will rise more than the market; and

• Sell or go short securities that will rise less than the market.

Conversely, in a falling market a successful manager should:

• Sell or go short securities that will decline more than the market; and

• Buy or go long securities that will fall less than the market.

Based on this premise, Jones believed that his fund could produce a net profit in both up and down markets.

In addition to using short sales, Jones also used a small amount of leverage and, in a revolutionary move, set up the fund as a general partnership with performance-based fee compensation. Jones also invested most of his own money in the fund, since he did not expect investors to take risks with their money that he was not comfortable assuming himself.

Jones was very successful with his hedge fund and outperformed the best mutual funds consistently through most of the 1950s and 1960s. His success led to the entry of many new hedge funds into the marketplace. Initially, these new hedge funds followed Jones's long/short strategy, but innovations in derivatives and technology, together with new liquid markets abroad, allowed for the creation of new hedge fund styles, such as arbitrage funds, event-driven funds and macro funds.

Size of the Hedge Fund Market

Hedge funds have experienced tremendous growth in assets over the last several years. By some estimates, there are about 9,000 hedge funds trading worldwide with combined assets in excess of US$1.6 trillion, up from $400 billion in 2001. For comparison purposes, there were only about 600 hedge funds in 1990 (Source: Bloomberg).

Tracking Hedge Fund Performance

There are many different hedge fund indexes, each of which tracks different groups of hedge funds. None of the indexes is exhaustive, since hedge funds are not required to report any information or even to disclose their existence. Any given hedge fund index does not, therefore, give a complete picture of the hedge fund industry.

That being said, hedge fund indexes are a valuable source of information, because most investors are interested in the performance of larger, more well-known funds that are tracked by indexes.

One of the best-known hedge fund indexes is the Credit Suisse/Tremont Hedge Fund Index. The index draws upon the Tremont TASS database, which tracks 2,600 funds and managers. TASS tracks only those funds that have $10 million or more under management and that have current audited financial statements. This index includes most of the major hedge funds in the U.S. and provides a good picture of the mainstream hedge fund market. It is interesting to note that historically the Credit Suisse/Tremont Hedge Fund Index has had a low correlation with major U.S. stock market indexes, including the Dow Jones Industrial Average, the NASDAQ Composite Index and the S&P 500 Index.

The Credit Suisse/Tremont Hedge Fund Index is also broken down into nine strategy sub-indexes, including the Credit Suisse/Tremont Long/Short Equity Index, the Credit Suisse/Tremont Equity Market Neutral Index and others. All told, Credit Suisse/Tremont claims to track more than 5,500 hedge funds. More information can be found online at *www.hedgeindex.com*.

Complete the following Online Learning Activity

Introduction to Hedge Funds

 Complete the **Introduction to Hedge Funds** activity.

WHAT ARE THE BENEFITS AND RISKS OF HEDGE FUNDS?

Benefits

Hedge fund benefits include:

Correlation with traditional asset classes: Although correlations can change over time, hedge fund returns usually have a low correlation to the returns on traditional asset classes, such as equity and debt securities. If these low correlations are maintained over time, hedge funds can provide diversification benefits and help lower overall portfolio risk. The extent to which a hedge fund provides diversification benefits depends on the type of hedge fund and on market conditions.

Risk minimization: Many hedge funds attempt to minimize risk. For example, the Credit Suisse/Tremont Hedge Fund Index tends to have a low standard deviation relative to equities, as measured by the Dow Jones World Index and S&P 500.

Absolute returns: Many investors underestimate the impact of negative years on overall wealth creation. Hedge fund managers seek to achieve positive or absolute returns in any market condition (up, down or trendless), not just returns that beat a market index, which is the goal of most mutual funds.

Potentially lower volatility and higher returns: With their potential for higher returns and generally lower standard deviations, hedge funds as a group usually outperform other asset classes on a risk adjusted basis.

That being said, investors should not expect all hedge funds to have the same or even a similar return. Expected returns depend significantly on the type of hedge fund strategy.

Also, since hedge funds generally have a low correlation with stocks and bonds, including hedge funds in a portfolio with these traditional asset classes may improve returns while reducing overall risk. When hedge funds perform well, the benefit to the portfolio's overall risk-adjusted return can be substantial.

Risks

Hedge fund risks include:

Light regulatory oversight: As hedge funds are generally offered as private placements, they are not required by securities laws to provide the comprehensive initial and ongoing information associated with securities offered through a prospectus. This lack of transparency may create a situation in which hedge fund investors may not always know how their money is being invested.

> **Example:** It is possible that an unscrupulous hedge fund manager could be covering up losses by reporting inflated earnings. This type of fraud may not be identified until it is too late. Also, hedge fund managers may stray from the fund's stated investment strategy, engaging in a practice known as style drift. Once again, because of the lack of an ongoing reporting requirement, investors may not find out that this has happened until long after the fact.

To avoid these types of situations, the onus is on investors and their advisors to conduct thorough due diligence on hedge fund managers and their funds prior to investing in them. Due diligence checks should include a review of audited financial statements to support representations of historical performance and a detailed review of a fund's offering memorandum. There is more on due diligence later in this chapter.

Manager and market risk: The management of mutual funds has evolved to the point where the investor's performance expectation is usually defined by the benchmark against which the manager is measured. In other words, the manager's performance is measured against a particular index. Hedge funds do not seek to produce returns "relative" to a particular index, but strive to generate positive returns regardless of market direction.

A mutual fund manager's performance is more likely to reflect the general performance of the markets where they are trading, whereas a hedge fund manager's performance largely depends on the manager. In light of this, investors and their advisors should clearly understand the manager's targets, including the expected return, expected risk (as measured by the standard deviation), Sharpe ratio, overall percentage of positive months, etc. This way, investors and their advisors can measure the manager's performance against their stated targets instead of an index that is not related to the underlying strategies used by the hedge fund manager.

Investment strategies: Even if hedge fund managers try to mitigate risk, the methods they use may be difficult to understand. As a result, there is a risk that investors may not fully understand the techniques being used. It is the responsibility of investors and advisors to understand the strategies and investment products used by the hedge fund manager, as well as the fund's risk profile.

Liquidity constraints: Unlike mutual funds, hedge funds are typically not able to liquidate their portfolios on short notice. Holding less liquid investments often produces some of the excess returns generated by hedge funds. This liquidity premium is part of the trade-off against traditional investments.

In light of this, there are often various forms of liquidity constraints imposed on hedge fund investors.

LOCKUP PERIOD

A **lockup** refers to the time period that initial investments cannot be redeemed from a hedge fund. For example, some hedge funds may charge an early redemption fee if the initial investment is redeemed within the first three months to one year. Once the lockup period is over, the investor is free to redeem shares on any liquidity date specified in the offering memorandum.

Similar to traditional mutual funds, a hedge fund manager can refuse redemptions if there is an occurrence in the markets that prevents the orderly liquidation of the hedge fund's investments.

Incentive fees: In addition to management and administration fees, hedge fund managers often charge an incentive fee based on performance. Incentive fees are usually calculated after the deduction of management fees and expenses and not on the gross return earned by the manager. This detail can make a significant difference in the net return earned by investors.

The calculation of incentive fees can be subject to a high-water mark, a hurdle rate or both.

High-water mark	A **high-water mark** ensures that a fund manager is paid an incentive fee only on net new profits. In essence, a high-water mark sets the bar (based on the fund's previous high value) above which the manager earns incentive fees. It prevents the manager from "double dipping" on incentive fees following periods of poor performance. ***Example:*** A new hedge fund is launched with a net asset value per unit of $10. At the end of the first year, the fund's net asset value per unit rises to $12. For the first year, the manager is paid an incentive fee based on this 20% performance. By the end of the second year, the fund's net asset value per unit has fallen to $11. The fund manager is paid no incentive fee for the second year and will not be eligible to receive an incentive fee until the fund's net asset value per unit rises above $12.
Hurdle rate	A hurdle rate is the rate that a hedge fund must earn before its manager is paid an incentive fee. For example, if a fund has a hurdle rate of 5%, and the fund earns 20% for the year, incentive fees will be based only on the 15% return above the hurdle rate, subject to any high-water mark. Hurdle rates are usually based on short-term interest rates.

It is important to determine whether the high-water mark is perpetual over the fund's life, or whether the manager has the authority to reset the level annually. If a fund has both a hurdle rate and a perpetual high-water mark, then incentive fees are paid only on the portion of the fund's return above the return needed to reach the perpetual high-water mark plus the hurdle rate.

> ***Example:*** A hedge fund needs to earn a 10% return this year to reach its perpetual high-water mark. The fund also has a 5% hurdle rate. In this case, incentive fees will be paid only on the portion of the fund's return in excess of 15% (10% + 5%).

Before buying a hedge fund, investors should confirm that there is a high-water mark, and ensure they understand how it is calculated and whether the hedge fund manager has the power to reset it. Note that management fees and expenses are paid regardless of the fund's performance.

Tax implications: The taxation of hedge funds is as varied as the structures used to offer them. Some hedge funds, such as limited partnerships and domestic trusts, are subject to full taxation annually. Others offer full tax deferral by using offshore structures to defer tax until disposition. In addition, some parts of the return may be taxed as income, while others are considered capital gains for tax purposes.

The tax structure is an important factor when selecting hedge funds, and investors and their advisors should ensure they understand the tax implications of the specific hedge fund structure.

Short selling and leverage: Unlike most mutual funds, hedge funds can both short sell and use leverage. Since security prices can, in theory, rise without limitation and since it may be difficult to buy back certain securities, hedge funds that use unhedged short-selling techniques to make directional bets may be risky.

Hedge funds may borrow several times the fund's invested capital. Although leverage can accentuate profits, it can also magnify losses.

Business risk: One of the biggest, and most overlooked, risks to investors is the business risk associated with hedge fund investing. Unlike large, well-capitalized mutual fund organizations, hedge fund companies are often start-up businesses. Investors assess the capitalization of the company and whether the manager has any experience running a business. A hedge fund manager may be a competent investment manager, but lack the skill or ability to run a business.

Due Diligence

Since most hedge funds provide investors with limited information, advisors and investors should fully research hedge funds before investing in them. Hedge funds are complex financial vehicles, and it is the advisors' responsibility to evaluate different hedge funds and select those suitable for each individual client.

Advisors have access to information about the hedge fund industry that clients do not. For example, they can participate in conference calls with hedge fund managers, and attend seminars and conferences featuring presentations by hedge fund managers. Most hedge fund managers allow advisors to phone and ask them questions about their funds.

Advisors should contact hedge fund managers, not only before buying into a fund, but routinely as part of an ongoing due diligence process. Hedge funds can change over time, and it is the advisor's responsibility to keep on top of these changes.

Advisors could develop a scoring system to assess a hedge fund's "risk profile" (like a "risk profile" for the client). The following questions should be addressed when assessing a hedge fund's risk profile (this list is not exhaustive):

MANAGER'S INVESTMENT PROCESS AND STRATEGY

- What is the hedge fund's investment process, philosophy and style?

- Is leverage used, and if so, how much? How is it employed?

- Does the fund use hedging strategies? Are derivatives used to hedge or to speculate?

- What risk controls does the hedge fund have in place?

- Have profits been made evenly across investments/strategies, or by a few more concentrated "home run" positions?

- Have losses come from a high number of trades, high expenses, from a small number of bad trades or positions, and/or for other market reasons?

- Does the fund have foreign exchange risk?

- At the initiation of a position, does the manager have a maximum loss tolerance, and if so, does the manager use a stop-loss rule?

- What type of market environment is required for the manager's investment strategy to work? Is there something happening in the markets right now that makes this investment strategy more or less attractive?

- What is the worst type of market environment that could negatively affect the manager's trading strategy?

FUND DETAILS

- Are audited financial statements available for the fund?

- What is the fund's lockup period?

- What is the fund's liquidity risk?

- How does the high-water mark for this fund work?

- What are the hedge fund's subscription and redemption policies?

INVESTORS' LEGAL AND TAXATION ISSUES

- What are the legal/taxation issues for fund investors?

- Where is the fund domiciled and how is its income treated for tax purposes?

- Is the hedge fund registered with or subject to regulation by any securities authority?

- What is the fund's legal structure and does it create any risk of personal liability to investors?

BUSINESS ISSUES

- Does the current manager have a long-term track record for the fund's strategies?

- How much capital has the manager personally invested in the fund?

- Is the hedge fund company profitable at their current level of assets under administration?

- How stable and well financed is the hedge fund company?

Advisors can also use hypothetical questions to assess how a particular set of circumstances could affect a hedge fund. Advisors can ask:

- How changes in market factors, such as prices, volatilities, and correlations, would affect the fund.

- About the fund's "credit risk," and how declines in the creditworthiness of entities in which the fund invests would affect the fund.

- About the fund's "liquidity risk," and how a decline in market liquidity could affect the value of the fund's investments.

Complete the following Online Learning Activity

> **Hedge Funds and Portfolio Risk**
>
> Hedge funds employ different types of investment options, including short selling, leveraging and the use of derivatives. Some experts would say that a hedge fund decreases portfolio risk; whereas others would say a hedge fund increases portfolio risk. Which is correct?
>
> In strict terms, hedging is performed to minimize risk and limit the possibility of loss. The products and methods used for hedging are also used for speculating. Speculating is the acceptance of high risk levels to achieve maximum return in a short to medium time frame.
>
> Which attributes of hedge funds or which hedge fund strategies contribute to decreasing and increasing portfolio risk?
>
> Complete the **Hedge Funds and Portfolio Risk** activity.

WHAT ARE THE DIFFERENT HEDGE FUND STRATEGIES?

While there are many different hedge fund strategies, there is no standardized industry classification for hedge funds. However, hedge funds can generally be broken down into three major categories based on the strategies they use – relative value, event-driven and directional, listed in order of increasing expected return and risk.

Table 21.2 shows the three major categories and the specific hedge fund strategies that fall within each one of these categories.

TABLE 21.2	MAJOR HEDGE FUND CATEGORIES		
Hedge Fund Category	**Objective of the Strategy**	**Market Exposure to the Underlying Market Direction**	**Specific Strategies**
Relative Value Strategies	Attempt to profit by exploiting inefficiencies or arbitrage opportunities in the pricing of related stocks, bonds or derivatives.	Low or no exposure	• Equity market neutral • Convertible arbitrage • Fixed-income arbitrage
Event-Driven Strategies	Attempt to profit from unique events such as mergers, acquisitions, stock splits, and buybacks.	Medium exposure	• Merger or risk arbitrage • Distressed securities • High-yield bond

TABLE 21.2	MAJOR HEDGE FUND CATEGORIES – *Cont'd*		
Hedge Fund Category	**Objective of the Strategy**	**Market Exposure to the Underlying Market Direction**	**Specific Strategies**
Directional Strategies	Bet on anticipated movements in the market prices of equity securities, debt securities, foreign currencies and commodities. Hedge funds using these strategies have high exposure to trends in the underlying market.	High exposure	• Long/short equity • Global macro • Emerging markets • Managed futures • Dedicated short bias

Relative Value Strategies

EQUITY MARKET-NEUTRAL

An equity market-neutral strategy is designed to exploit equity market inefficiencies and opportunities by creating simultaneously long and short matched equity portfolios of approximately the same size. The goal of equity market-neutral investing is to generate returns that do not depend on the direction of the stock market. Well-designed equity market-neutral portfolios hedge out the risks related to industry, sector, market capitalization, currency and other exposures. Leverage is applied to enhance returns.

The reasoning behind this strategy is that long positions will rise more in price than short positions in rising markets and short positions will fall more in price than long positions in declining markets, resulting in a net positive outcome, no matter the market direction.

CONVERTIBLE ARBITRAGE

A convertible arbitrage strategy is designed to identify and exploit mispricing between convertible securities (convertible bonds or preferred shares) and the underlying stock.

Convertible securities have a theoretical value that is based on a number of factors, including the value of the underlying stock. When the trading price of a convertible bond moves away from its theoretical value, an arbitrage (or profitable) opportunity exists.

This strategy typically involves buying undervalued convertible securities and hedging some or all of the underlying equity risk by selling short an appropriate amount of the issuer's common shares. Properly executed, this strategy creates a net position with an attractive yield that can be almost completely unaffected by broader equity market movements. Interest income on the convertible bond added to the interest on the short sale proceeds contributes a relatively steady return.

FIXED-INCOME ARBITRAGE

A fixed-income arbitrage strategy attempts to profit from price irregularities between related interest rate securities and derivatives, including government and non-government bonds, mortgage-backed securities, options, swaps and forward rate agreements. High leverage is normally used to help generate returns well beyond transaction costs. Leverage for this type of fund can range from 10 times to up to 30 times the capital employed.

EXHIBIT 21.1

Probably the most famous (or infamous) example of fixed-income arbitrage was the hedge fund run by Long Term Capital Management (LTCM). The managers engaged in fixed-income arbitrage strategies that often involved buying and selling bonds of different sovereign nations. Part of LTCM's downfall was that they began to trade in markets in which they had limited knowledge or experience. As well, they began using excessive leverage to enhance returns.

LTCM's strategy is best explained by Paul Krugman, a professor of economics at MIT, in his 1998 article "Rashomon in Connecticut. What Really Happened to Long-Term Capital Management?" (*www.slate.com*).

Imagine two assets – say, Italian and German government bonds – whose prices usually move together. But Italian bonds pay higher interest. So someone who "shorts" German bonds – receives money now, in return for a promise to deliver those bonds at a later date – then invests the proceeds in Italian bonds, can earn money for nothing. Of course, it's not that simple. The people who provide money now in return for future bonds are aware that if the prices of Italian and German bonds happen not to move in sync, you might not be able to deliver on your promise. So they will demand evidence that you have enough capital to make up any likely losses, plus extra compensation for the remaining risk. But if the required compensation and the capital you need to put up aren't too large, there may still be an opportunity for an exceptionally favorable trade-off between risk and return.

In fact, it's still more complicated than that. Any opportunity that straightforward would probably have been snapped up already. What LTCM did, or at least claimed to do, was find less obvious opportunities along the same lines, by engaging in complicated transactions involving many assets. For example, suppose that, historically, increases in the spread between the price of Italian compared with German bonds were correlated with declines in the Milan stock market. Then the riskiness of the bet on the Italian-German interest differential could be reduced by taking out a side bet, shorting Italian stocks – and so on. In principle, at least, LTCM's computers, programmed by Nobel laureates, allowed the firm to search for complex trading strategies that took advantage of even subtle market mispricing, providing high returns with very little risk.

As an example of one of its trades, LTCM, based on its computer models, went long Russian bonds against U.K. and U.S. bonds. In August 1998, the ruble was devalued, while U.K. and U.S. interest rates fell, meaning that LTCM lost on both ends of the trade. Since a considerable amount of leverage was used for this strategy, LTCM lost billions of dollars. Given the systemic risk to the global financial system, in August 1998, the Federal Reserve Board summoned 14 banks to set up emergency loans to meet margin calls while LTCM unwound their positions.

The moral of the story is that no matter how sophisticated the computer model or how smart the manager(s), volatile and unpredictable markets, combined with heavy leverage, can be a dangerous combination. It should be noted, however, that LTCM was not a typical hedge fund, given its sheer size. Today, most fixed-income arbitrage funds use leverage in the range of 20 to 30 times their capital.

Event-Driven Strategies

MERGER OR RISK ARBITRAGE

A merger or risk arbitrage strategy invests simultaneously in long and short positions in the common stock of companies involved in a proposed merger or acquisition. The strategy generally involves taking a long position in the company being acquired and a short position in the acquiring company. The hedge fund manager attempts to take advantage of the differential between the target company's share price and the offering price. Typically, the share price of the target company rises and the share price of the acquiring company drops after a takeover or merger announcement.

The returns on merger arbitrage are largely uncorrelated to the overall stock market. In general, equity risk is managed because the hedge fund manager is dealing with the probable outcomes of specific transactions rather than predicting the overall market.

DISTRESSED SECURITIES

A distressed securities strategy invests in the equity or debt securities of companies that are in financial difficulty and face bankruptcy or reorganization. Distressed securities generally sell at deep discounts, reflecting their issuers' weak credit quality. Many institutional investors are not permitted to own securities that are rated less than investment grade. Therefore, downgrading the credit rating of an issuer or security below the permissible minimum can precipitate a wave of forced selling that depresses the security's value below fair market value. Hedge fund managers attempt to profit from the market's lack of understanding of the true value of deeply discounted securities or the inability of institutional and other investors to hold these securities.

HIGH-YIELD BONDS

A high-yield bond strategy invests in high-yield debt securities (also known as junk bonds) of a company the manager feels may get a credit upgrade or is a potential takeover target. In general, these funds use little or no leverage.

Directional Funds

LONG/SHORT EQUITY

The long/short equity strategy is the most popular type of hedge fund strategy, constituting more than 75% of the hedge fund activity in Canada. These funds are classified as directional funds, because the manager has either a net long or net short exposure to the stock market. The manager is not trying to eliminate market effects or market trends completely, as would be the case with an equity market-neutral strategy; rather, he or she takes both long and short positions simultaneously, depending on the outlook of specific securities.

With a long/short equity strategy, managers try to buy stocks they feel will rise more in a bull market than the overall market, and short stocks that will rise less. In a down market, good short selections are expected to decline more than the market and good long selections will fall less.

In a long/short equity strategy, the fund is exposed to market risk based on the extent of the net exposure – either long or short. Compared to a long-only fund, this type of fund is often better able to profit in a declining market, as it can short stocks and manage the fund's net exposure to the market.

A long/short equity fund's net exposure is calculated as follows:

$$\frac{\text{Long exposure} - \text{Short exposure}}{\text{Capital}}$$

EXAMPLE

Suppose a hedge fund manager feels that the shares of General Motors are underpriced relative to the shares of Ford Motor Company. The manager, with $1,000 in capital, buys shares in General Motors worth $1,000 and, at the same time, goes short shares in Ford worth $600.

This position can be viewed as having two components: a $600 "hedged" component and a $400 "unhedged" component.

In the "hedged" component, the manager has an equal dollar amount ($600) of long General Motors shares and short Ford shares, theoretically eliminating the market risk on this portion of the fund. The only risk that the hedged component is exposed to is stock selection risk, which is the risk that Ford's shares will outperform GM's shares.

The "unhedged" component consists of a directional bet on the likelihood that shares of General Motors will rise, since the fund is exposed to market risk on 40% of the portfolio.

With the additional bet made on General Motors, the fund's net market exposure is calculated as follows:

$$\text{Net exposure} = \frac{\$1,000 - \$600}{\$1,000}$$

$$= 40\%$$

If the stock market declines by 20%, the long/short equity fund's net exposure to this decline is only 40% of the market decline, or 8% (20% × 40%).

Of course, there is no free lunch: the price of protection from downside market movements is that the performance in rising markets will be lower than if the fund had not had a short Ford position. If the stock market rises by 20%, the fund's net exposure (or participation) to this increase will be only 40%. The portfolio of two stocks (GM and Ford) will rise by only 8%, or 40% of the 20% market increase.

CALCULATING LEVERAGE – *For information only*

Many long/short funds use some leverage. One method of calculating the fund's leverage is to add the fund's short market value to the long market value (this sum is called the fund's gross exposure) and then divide by the net capital invested. In this example, the fund's leverage is 1.6 times its capital.

$$\text{Leverage} = \frac{\$1,000 + \$600}{\$1,000}$$

$$= \frac{\$1,600}{\$1,000}$$

$$= 1.6 \text{ times}$$

As leverage can amplify both risk and return, hedge fund investors must understand the degree of leverage that the fund manager is using, as part of their due diligence before investing in a fund.

GLOBAL MACRO

The global macro strategy is one of the most highly publicized hedge fund strategies, although it constitutes only a small percentage of the strategies used by today's hedge funds.

Rather than make investments on events that affect only specific companies, funds using a global macro strategy make bets on major events affecting entire economies, such as shifts in government policy that alter interest rates, thereby affecting currency, stock and bond markets.

Global macro funds participate in all major markets including equities, bonds, currencies and commodities. They use leverage, often through derivatives, to accentuate the impact of market moves.

EXHIBIT 21.2

Examples of global macro hedge fund success stories include George Soros's Quantum Fund, which in 1992 bet – successfully as it turned out – US$10 billion, much of it leveraged, on the British pound being devalued, and David Gerstenhaber's Argonaut Fund, which in 1996 bet that interest rates in Italy and Spain would converge downward with the expected European Monetary Union. Both funds made spectacular returns.

Examples of global macro hedge fund disasters include the Niederhoffer Investments Fund, which was wiped out following some bad bets against the Thai baht and stock index futures in 1997.

EMERGING MARKETS

Emerging markets hedge funds invest in equity and debt securities of companies based in emerging markets. The primary difference between an emerging markets hedge fund and an emerging markets mutual fund is the hedge fund's ability to use derivatives, short selling and other complex investment strategies. However, since some emerging markets do not allow short selling and do not have viable derivative markets, these funds may not be able to hedge. As a result, performance can be very volatile.

DEDICATED SHORT BIAS

Up to 1997 this strategy was known as "dedicated short selling." However, the bull run of the late 1990s reduced the number of these funds and led the rest to change their strategy to a "short bias." To be classified as short bias, the fund's net position must always be short. In other words, the fund may have long positions, but on a net basis, the fund must constantly be short.

EXHIBIT 21.3

One of the better-known short-bias funds, which was closed out because of a continued increase in stock prices, was run by Julian Robertson of Tiger Management. Throughout most of the late 1990s, his fund was short several billion dollars' worth of technology stocks. He finally pulled the plug in early 2000 following the continued run-up in the NASDAQ Composite Index. Unfortunately, his timing could not have been worse. Shortly after closing out his fund, the NASDAQ Composite Index began a descent where it lost 60% of its value in the following nine months.

MANAGED FUTURES FUNDS

A managed futures fund invests in listed financial and commodity futures markets and currency markets around the world. Fund managers are usually called Commodity Trading Advisors (CTAs).

Most managed futures fund managers apply a systematic approach to trading, using technical and statistical analysis of price and volume information to determine investment decisions. Once the manager has developed the system, trading decisions are largely mechanical, and little or no discretion is involved. Other fund managers make discretionary decisions according to current economic and political fundamentals.

In Canada, managed futures funds are often established as commodity pools. Following a November 2002 Canadian Securities Administrators ruling (NI 81-104), these commodity pools can be sold as mutual funds to the general investor (not only accredited or sophisticated investors), and use derivatives in a leveraged manner for speculation. However, regulators require greater disclosure from and higher proficiency in the mutual fund companies and the agents who sell these products, compared to what is required of conventional mutual funds.

Complete the following Online Learning Activity

Hedge Fund Strategies

There are a number of hedge fund strategies, each with very different investment return, volatility and risk profile. This activity will help you become proficient at identifying different types of hedge funds based on the management strategy employed.

 Complete the **Hedge Fund Strategies** activity.

WHAT ARE FUNDS OF HEDGE FUNDS?

A fund of hedge funds (FoHF) is a portfolio of hedge funds, overseen by a manager who determines which hedge funds to invest in and how much to invest in each. There are two main types of FoHF:

- Single-strategy, multi-manager funds invest in several funds that employ a similar strategy, such as long/short equity funds or convertible arbitrage funds.

- Multi-strategy, multi-manager funds invest in several funds that employ different strategies.

Advantages

Funds of hedge funds have the following advantages:

- **Due diligence**. The task of selecting and monitoring hedge fund managers is time-consuming and requires specialized analytical skills and tools. Most individual and institutional investors do not have the time or the expertise to conduct thorough due diligence and ongoing risk monitoring for hedge funds. FoHFs constitute an effective way to outsource this function.

- **Reduced volatility**. By investing in a number of different hedge funds, a FoHF should provide more consistent returns with lower volatility or risk than any of its underlying funds.

- **Professional management**. An experienced portfolio manager and his or her team evaluates the strategies employed by the various fund managers and establishes the appropriate mix of strategies for the fund. Selecting funds that make up a low- or non-correlated portfolio requires detailed analysis and substantial due diligence. Ongoing monitoring is also required on each underlying fund to ensure performance objectives continue to be met.

- **Access to hedge funds**. Most hedge funds do not advertise and many are not sold through traditional distribution channels. Information on some hedge funds is closely held and hard to get hold of. Many successful hedge funds have reached their capacity limitations and either do not accept new money or only accept money from existing investors. Using their experience and contacts within the industry, reputable FoHF managers will know how to get hold of a hedge fund manager, or obtain information on a particular fund, and even reserve capacity with a fund. These are important qualities that a fund of funds manager brings to the table.

- **Ability to diversify with a smaller investment**. FoHFs increase access by smaller investors to hedge funds. While there are many Canadian hedge funds that accept as little as $25,000 from accredited investors, some funds have a minimum investment threshold of US$1 million, with some as high as US$5 million or more. An investor would need to commit significant funds to achieve the equivalent diversification offered by a fund of funds.

- **Manager and business risk control**. As hedge funds are less regulated than more mainstream investments, many investors believe that some hedge fund management firms may terminate their activities for business or other reasons at any time. This risk is based on the fact that hedge fund management firms tend to be relatively small business concerns, the success of which often rests upon one or a small number of managers and partners. Moreover, some hedge funds pursue riskier investment strategies, and may be more likely to experience problems, with some likelihood of having to terminate the fund. This "blowup risk" can be diversified away through a FoHF, as any individual fund likely represents only a relatively small fraction of the total assets invested. Additionally, the FoHF manager's duty is to continuously monitor and manage underlying funds in order to mitigate business risk.

For these reasons, funds of funds are increasingly the preferred hedge fund investment of choice for both institutional and retail investors.

Disadvantages

Funds of hedge funds do, however, have certain disadvantages and risks:

- **Additional costs**. Competent FoHF managers can be expensive to retain. Additional fees cover the management and operating expenses of the FoHF organization as well as its margins. Most FoHFs charge a base fee and an incentive fee, in addition to the fees (both base and incentive) charged for the underlying hedge funds. A typical FoHF charges a 1% management fee and a 10% incentive fee, plus fund expenses.

- **No guarantees of positive returns**. FoHFs do not constitute guaranteed investments and cannot be assured of meeting their investment objectives. In fact, during certain periods, FoHF asset values will probably decline. Investors and advisors need to understand that the FoHF is simply the sum of its component hedge fund investments. Despite the claims of some hedge fund marketers, investors should not, and cannot, expect positive returns in every reporting period.

- **Low or no strategy diversification**. Some FoHFs are strategy-specific and invest only in one type of hedge fund, such as long/short equity or convertible arbitrage. Such FoHFs fill a specific role in the portfolio, and may contribute less diversification than multi-strategy, multi-manager FoHF.

- **Insufficient or excessive diversification**. The number of hedge funds in a FoHF can vary dramatically, from 5 to more than 100 hedge funds. Some may not provide adequate diversification, depending on the objectives sought by the investor. Others may dilute returns and provide more diversification than the investor needs.

- **Additional sources of leverage**. Some FoHFs add a second layer of leverage to enhance the FoHF's return potential (above leverage used by the underlying hedge fund managers). This adds to the costs and risk of the FoHF and needs to be understood and agreed upon by the investor.

Complete the following Online Learning Activity

Myth or Reality

Hedge funds are aggressive. Hedge funds are risky. Are these statements myths or realities? Learn more about the reality of hedge funds.

 Complete the **Hedge Fund Myths and Realities** activity.

SUMMARY

After reading this chapter, you should be able to:

1. Define hedge fund, compare and contrast hedge funds with mutual funds and institutional investors with retail investors in hedge funds, summarize the history and growth of the hedge fund market and discuss how hedge fund performance is tracked.

    - Hedge funds are lightly regulated pools of capital whose managers have great flexibility in their investment strategies, including using derivatives for leverage and speculation, arbitrage, and investing in almost any situation in any market.

    - Mutual funds are far more regulated and restricted in terms of permitted investments, valuation and reporting practices.

    - Institutional and high-net-worth investors are generally targeted by funds structured as limited partnerships or trusts that are issued as private placements.

    - Alternative ways of providing access to hedge fund opportunities, including commodity pools, closed-end hedge funds and principal-protected notes, are targeted at retail investors.

    - Hedge fund performance is tracked against market indexes, although finding exactly correlated indexes is problematic because of variance among funds and the lack of regulatory requirements for funds to publicly report performance figures.

2. Evaluate the benefits, risks and due diligence requirements of investing in hedge funds.

    - The benefits of investing in hedge funds include low correlation to traditional asset classes, low standard deviation in relation to equities, a management theory in which managers seek to achieve positive or absolute returns in all market conditions, higher returns and generally lower standard deviations that equate to higher performance than other asset classes on a risk-adjusted basis.

    - The risks of investing in hedge funds include light regulatory oversight, manager and market risk, complex investment strategies that may not be fully visible to potential investors, liquidity constraints, incentive fees, tax implications, capital risk as a result of short selling and leverage, and business risk.

    - As most hedge funds provide investors with limited information, advisors recommending these funds as investments must perform thorough research to fulfill requirements of due diligence.

3. Identify the three categories of hedge fund strategies and describe how the specific strategies within each category work.

   • Relative value strategies (equity market-neutral, convertible arbitrage, fixed-income arbitrage): exploiting inefficiencies or arbitrage opportunities in the pricing of related stocks, bonds or derivatives.

   • Event-driven strategies (merger or risk arbitrage, distressed securities, high-yield bonds): profiting from unique events such as mergers, acquisitions, stock splits and buybacks.

   • Directional strategies (long/short equity, global macro, emerging markets, dedicated short bias, managed futures funds): investing based on anticipated movements in the market prices of equity securities, debt securities, foreign currencies and commodities.

4. Describe the advantages and disadvantages of investing in a fund of hedge funds (FoHFs) structure versus individual hedge funds.

   • A fund of hedge funds is a portfolio of hedge funds overseen by a manager.

   • Single-strategy, multi-manager funds invest in several funds that employ a similar strategy.

   • Multi-strategy, multi-manager funds invest in several funds that employ different strategies.

   • FoHFs have certain advantages: reduced need for due diligence, reduced volatility, professional management, ease of access, diversification with smaller amounts of capital, and lower manager and business risk.

   • FoHFs can also have certain disadvantages: additional costs, no guarantees of positive returns, low or no strategy diversification, insufficient or excessive diversification, and increased risk because of additional layers of leverage.

Online Frequently Asked Questions

CSI has answered many frequently asked questions about this Chapter. Read through online Module 21 FAQs.

Online Post-Module Assessment

Once you have completed the chapter, take the Module 21 Post-Test.

Chapter *22*

Exchange-Listed Managed Products

22

Exchange-Listed Managed Products

CHAPTER OUTLINE

What are Closed-End Funds?
- Advantages of Closed-End Funds
- Disadvantages of Closed-End Funds

What are Income Trusts?
- Real Estate Investment Trusts (REITs)
- Business Trusts

What are Exchange-Traded Funds?
- Trading ETFs
- Recent Trends in ETFs
- Regulatory Issues

What is Listed Private Equity?
- Structure of Listed Private Equity Companies
- Advantages and Disadvantages of Listed Private Equity

Summary

LEARNING OBJECTIVES

By the end of this chapter, you should be able to:

1. Define closed-end funds and discuss the advantages and disadvantages of investing in closed-end funds.
2. Define income trust, differentiate among the types of income trusts, and describe their features.
3. Describe the advantages, disadvantages, and features of exchange-traded funds (ETFs).
4. Explain how to invest in private equity through a listed equity (private equity firm).

EXCHANGE-LISTED PRODUCTS

Since the early 1990s, managed products have become popular investment vehicles for many investors, particularly those who consider direct investing in bonds or equities too complex or risky. Managed products are often appropriate for investors who have a limited amount of money to invest but want the benefits of diversification and professional investment management.

As we learned in the previous chapters, managed products include more than just mutual funds. The one constant in the investment industry is change. Continual innovation in financial markets, products, and the wealth management industry in general has resulted in an overwhelming number and variety of managed products, which makes the process of making investment decisions all the more challenging. With more choice, investors have more homework to do before investing. Advisors are responsible for understanding the characteristics and features of these investment options to assess their suitability for clients.

This chapter continues to demonstrate one of the consistent themes we have presented in this course – investors are not limited to simply stocks and bonds for their investment choices. This chapter provides an overview, a discussion of the advantages and disadvantages, and the suitability of the many different types of managed products.

KEY TERMS

Closed-end discretionary fund

Closed-end fund

Exchange-traded fund (ETF)

Income trust

Interval fund

Private equity

Real Estate Income Trust (REIT)

WHAT ARE CLOSED-END FUNDS?

Closed-end funds are pooled investment funds that initially raise capital by selling a limited or fixed number of shares to investors. The number of shares or units in closed-end funds remains fixed, except in rare cases of an additional share offering, share dividend or share buy-back.

The manager of the fund uses the fixed pool of capital to purchase and manage a basket of securities according to a specific investment mandate, for which the manager is paid a management fee. In general, the management fee charged by a closed-end fund is lower than the management fee of a mutual fund with a similar investment objective.

Once issued, closed-end fund units are listed for trading on a stock exchange. Investors who wish to buy or sell units of the fund must do so through a stock exchange. Investors also pay a commission on the transaction rather than a front-end load or back-end load.

The prices of closed-end funds are based on market supply and demand, as well as underlying asset value. Closed-end funds can trade at a discount, at par or at a premium relative to the combined net asset value of their underlying holdings. Historically, most closed-end funds trade at a discount to their NAVPS.

An increase or decrease in the discount can indicate market sentiment. The greater the relative discount, all other things being equal, the more attractively priced the fund. However, it is important to find out whether the discount at which a fund is trading is below historical norms. A widening discount could indicate underlying problems in the fund, such as disappointing results from an investment strategy, a change in managers, poor performance by the existing managers, increased management fees or expenses, or extraordinary costs such as a lawsuit.

The underlying assets in a closed-end fund are quite varied, examples include:

- Preferred shares of Canadian financial institutions

- Diversified holdings of a basket of foreign-based manufacturing companies

- A portfolio of income producing securities, including business trusts, real estate investment trusts, and utility income trusts

Funds that have the flexibility to buy back their outstanding shares periodically are known as **interval funds** or **closed-end discretionary funds**. They are more popular in the United States. In Canada, closed-end funds may also be structured with buyback or termination provisions. For example, a fund could be structured to terminate on June 30, 2012, at which time the proceeds will be distributed to unitholders. However, the fund manager could propose to continue the fund after this date, subject to unitholder approval.

Advantages of Closed-End Funds

Diversification can reduce the risks associated with the varying discounts of closed-end funds. A portfolio of closed-end funds that have a low degree of correlation with each other will smooth out the adverse effects of closed-end discounts.

Closed-end funds offer certain opportunities for investment returns not available to investors in open-end investment funds, such as short selling. Thus closed-end funds can provide a boost to an investor's total returns. Typically a closed-end fund is more fully invested than an open-end fund. Open-end funds must keep a certain percentage of their funds liquid, in case of redemptions. Closed-end funds do not have this constraint. For instance, in addition to capital appreciation of the underlying assets, the trading discount to net asset value may shrink or the fund may trade at a premium.

In working with a closed-end structure, money managers have the flexibility to concentrate on long-term investment strategies without having to reserve liquid assets to cover redemptions.

Because the number of units of a closed-end fund is generally fixed, capital gains, dividends and interest distributions are paid directly to investors rather than reinvested in additional units. Therefore, tracking the adjusted cost base of these funds may be easier than for open-end mutual funds. Moreover, because there is only a fixed number of units to be administered, investors in closed-end funds may benefit from lower management expense ratios (MERs) than open-end funds with similar objectives.

Disadvantages of Closed-End Funds

Like stocks and unlike open-end funds, closed-end funds do not necessarily trade at net asset value. In bear markets, closed-end unitholders or shareholders may suffer as the value of the underlying assets declines, and the gap between the discount and the net asset value widens. Furthermore, since closed-end funds are not widely used in Canada, they may trade for extended periods at prices that do not reflect their intrinsic or true value.

Partly because of the divergence of trading prices from net asset value, closed-end funds are less liquid than open-end funds. Buyers and sellers must be found in the open market. The fund itself does not usually issue or redeem units. Commissions are paid at the time of purchase and at the time of sale.

Unlike the deferred sales charge option available on many open-end funds, there is no schedule of declining redemption fees. In fact, if closed-end shares appreciate, the commission payable on sale could be higher than it was at the time of purchase, since it would be based on the share's ending value.

Since many closed-end funds do not provide for automatic reinvestment of distributions (a feature of most open-end funds), the unitholder is responsible for reinvesting cash that may build up in his or her account.

For closed-end funds that trade on foreign exchanges, any dividend income earned is considered foreign income and is not eligible for the federal dividend tax credit.

WHAT ARE INCOME TRUSTS?

An **income trust** is similar in some ways to a closed-end fund. Investors purchase ownership interests in the trust, which in turn holds interests in the operating assets of a company – e.g., seafood processing, office rentals, shopping centres, etc. These securities are exchange-traded and trade on the Toronto Stock Exchange.

Generally speaking, income trusts are divided into two primary categories:

- **Real Estate Investment Trusts (REITs)** purchase real estate properties and pass the rental incomes through to investors.

- **Business income trusts** purchase the assets of an underlying company, usually in the manufacturing, retail or service industry, in such diverse areas as peat moss extraction, restaurants, industrial appliances, canning and distribution.

> It is important to note that the type of businesses that operate within the same category may be very different. One REIT may operate shopping centres and another REIT may own senior housing. Although these two types of income trusts are REITs, the comparison between the two is not relevant. One must compare an income trust with other income trusts that operate in a niche that is relatively similar.

Income trusts react to changing interest rates, similar to fixed-income securities, but trade on an exchange, like equities.

Because they are backed by the specific revenue-generating properties or assets held in the trust, they face the same risks as common equities. The underlying business is affected by market conditions and economic cycles, as well as management performance. Depending on their structure, the priority and security of trusts typically rank below those of subordinated debentures.

Real Estate Investment Trusts (REITs)

Real Estate Investment Trusts (REITs) consolidate the capital of a large number of investors to invest in and manage a diversified real estate portfolio. REITs are usually specialized in one real estate sector, such as shopping centres, senior housings, office or industrial rentals, or residential rentals. Investors participate by buying "units" in the trust. REITs allow small investors to invest in commercial real estate previously available only to corporate or more affluent and sophisticated investors.

REITs generally pay out a high percentage of their income, typically 95%, to their unitholders.

REITs are publicly traded companies that may be structured as either open-end or closed-end funds. If they meet the stringent standards set out under the *Income Tax Act*, REITs may qualify as registered investments for RRSPs and RRIFs.

REITs face many of the risks typical of real estate investments:

- Quality of the properties

- State of the rental markets and tenant leases

- Costs of debt financing

- Natural disasters and access to liquidity.

REIT managers generally minimize risk by avoiding real estate development and instead invest primarily in established income-producing properties.

Liquidity is a major benefit of REIT ownership. REIT units are much more liquid than real estate. However, investors should determine the liquidity of any particular REIT before investing, since some, especially the more specialized REITs, have thin trading volumes, despite being exchange traded. As publicly traded instruments, REITs are also subject to full disclosure rules giving the investor access to more complete information for decision-making purposes.

When interest rates rise, REIT trading values may fall – higher borrowing costs make the purchase of new properties less profitable. On the other hand, REITs represent a good hedge against inflation; in an inflationary environment the value of the underlying real estate owned by REITs may appreciate.

Because rental income is fairly stable, REITs generally yield high levels of income but usually lack the potential for large capital gains or losses possible with equities. As with any investment, it may be necessary to accept lower yields to ensure a high-quality portfolio underlying the yield.

Buying REITs gives investors access to professional management. REITs, however, are just as susceptible to ineptitude on the part of management as any other company. The keys to minimizing risk lie in sound research before purchase and in diversification.

Business Trusts

Business trusts are as varied as the types of companies listed on a stock exchange. It is in this category that you see many examples of companies with strong, stable earnings, but little growth potential. Management uses the income trust structure to make an offering more attractive, since the company would be less attractive as a common share IPO.

Income trusts work best in markets where new competitors are unlikely to spring up – ideally a monopoly or a quasi-monopoly or a company operating in a protected niche.

The types of businesses held by business trusts are diverse and include:

- Forest products

- Storage facilities

- Natural gas processing

- Restaurants and food distributors

- Fish processing, sardine canning

- Aircraft parts, industrial washing machines, and biotechnology.

It is difficult to make generalizations about the risks of business trusts because of the diversity of the underlying businesses. Business income trusts are subject to the same interest rate risk as fixed income securities. They are, however, also subject to the same risks as equity securities. Although they tend to be more stable than the equity market because the underlying business assets provide regular, stable income, they are still subject to market and economic risk.

INCOME TRUST TAXATION

One of the key advantages of an income trust was the ability of the trust to avoid paying tax by passing the income generated by the trust directly to the trust unitholders. The revenue generated by the income trust was therefore taxed in the hands of investors.

However, the federal government changed the taxation of income trust distributions in late 2006. Beginning in 2007, a new tax became applicable to distributions from publicly traded income trusts established after October 31, 2006. Trusts already in existence on that date were not subject to the new tax until their 2011 taxation year. Since 2011, the tax treatment is now more like that of corporations – income trusts pay tax and the distributions from an income trust are taxed in the hands of the investor in the same manner as dividends received from taxable Canadian corporations.

After this change in tax treatment, many income trusts converted back into corporations, since there was no longer any tax advantage to remain as an income trust. However, it is important to note that Canadian REITs are still exempt from these tax changes, and continue to operate under the rules that were in place before 2007.

Complete the following Online Learning Activity

Key Characteristics of Income Trusts

To better appreciate the characteristics of income trusts, it is important to understand their structure and the type of business income trusts are in. In this activity, you will review the concept of income trusts.

 Read the **Overview of Income Trusts**.

WHAT ARE EXCHANGE-TRADED FUNDS?

Exchange-traded funds (ETFs) are investment vehicles that combine some of the features of mutual funds and individual stocks. They are structured as open-ended mutual fund trusts and are similar to index mutual funds because they represent a portfolio of securities that track specific market indexes – the S&P/TSX 60 Index or the S&P 500 Index for example.

The units of the trust are listed and traded on stock exchanges, much like individual stocks representing a key difference with mutual funds. The fund holds an underlying basket of securities (equities, bonds, commodities or derivatives).

In Canada, there has been significant growth in the number of ETFs and the companies that offer them. The leading sponsors of ETFs include the following:

* I-Shares (Blackrock)

* Powershares Canada

* BMO ETFs (BMO Financial Group)

* Horizons ETFs

* Vangard Canada

Trading ETFs

Like stocks, ETFs trade throughout the trading day and investors can employ the same kinds of trading strategies used with stocks, such as the use of derivatives and short selling. Income generated by the securities in the ETF (i.e., dividends, interest or capital gains) flows through to the investor, so that it maintains its original characteristics.

Most investors use ETFs in one of two ways. Some investors use ETFs as a core passive investment in an index or underlying asset, with the intention of holding the ETF for a long time. Others, particularly active investors, use ETFs to implement their short-term forecast for a particular index, sector, or underlying asset. These investors sometimes trade ETFs frequently, and they may intend to maintain a position for only a short amount of time.

ETFs are attractive investments because they offer instant diversification opportunities and significantly lower MERs when compared to traditional mutual funds. Although brokerage commissions are a factor when buying and selling ETF shares, the lower MERs may offset the brokerage costs over the long term.

ETFs are also structured to minimize capital gains distributions through lower portfolio turnover compared to actively managed mutual funds. This makes them a more tax efficient investment relative to mutual funds.

Table 22.1 illustrates the key differences between ETFs and conventional mutual funds.

TABLE 22.1	COMPARING ETFS AND INDEX MUTUAL FUNDS	
	ETFs	**Index Mutual Fund**
Pricing	Close to net asset value at any time during the day	Once per day using the closing price of the fund's net asset value
Management Fees	Very low MERs Commissions to buy and sell	Low MERs May have front or rear loads
Portfolio Turnover	Low – lower taxable capital gains distributions lead to greater tax efficiency	Low – lower taxable capital gains distributions lead to greater tax efficiency
Short Selling	Yes	No
Use of Leverage	Yes	No
Ease of Trading	Yes	No

Globally, the ETF market is huge business. From no issues in 1989, Europe and the U.S. now each have more than 700 listed ETFs while Canada boasts more than 160 (Fall 2012). This is phenomenal growth considering Canada had only 1 ETF in 1990.

EXAMPLE	ISHARES S&P/TSX 60 INDEX FUND

A popular ETF in Canada is the iShares S&P/TSX 60 Index Fund. This ETF holds a basket of stocks that represents the S&P/TSX 60 Index and trades under the symbol XIU on the Toronto Stock Exchange. The ETF consists of 60 of the largest (and most liquid) securities by market capitalization traded on the TSX.

The market price of the Fund fluctuates directly with changes in the market prices of the securities comprising the S&P/TSX 60 Index. The actual price at which the Fund trades may deviate slightly from the net asset value due to market fluctuations. Prices are quoted daily in the financial press in the same manner as other equities.

The Fund also provides dividend income for unitholders. Dividends are paid quarterly and consist primarily of dividends received from the companies held by the fund, interest on cash balances, and securities lending income, minus fund expenses.

Recent Trends in ETFs

One outcome of the phenomenal growth in the global ETF marketplace is the variety of ETF products available to the retail investor. No longer limited to country or industry sectors, there are now ETFs that track currencies, commodities, pursue active management, among many others. We discuss some of these new structures in the next sections.

COUNTRY-BASED ETFs

Investors hoping to access greater diversification, or to implement a tactical investment into a specific region, found it hard to access various specific countries. ETFs worked to fill this gap by offering region-based and country-based offerings on a low cost basis.

SEGMENTATION OF THE BROAD MARKETS INTO SECTORS

The growing number of ETFs that segment the market can now be used to target exposures. For example, investors who do not want to invest in the broader market, or who want to increase their holdings in a sector, can select ETFs that focus only on one sector of the market. In some cases, segmentation is further refined down to a specific industry.

VARIOUS STYLES OF COMMODITIES ETFs

There are many styles of commodity-based ETFs, including equity- or futures-based ETFs. Gold and silver investors can access ETFs that hold the underlying physical commodity. Although these ETFs also tend to follow an index, they all have challenges in tracking the spot price of a respective commodity. However, commodities ETFs do provide an efficient way to access a commodity investment strategy.

MUTUAL FUNDS OF ETFs

In addition to advancements in individual ETFs, a growing trend is to include ETFs within a mutual fund. This hybrid investment is done either on an individual basis, where a mutual fund will buy one ETF as its holding, or on a portfolio basis, where several ETFs are purchased at once within a portfolio. The mutual fund ETF portfolio can be either static or tactical with the investment mix. Some of these investment mixes can comprise either all passive investments or a mix of passive and active management. This approach combines the traditional benefits of mutual funds with the advancements in ETFs. It also makes the features of ETFs accessible to all licensed investment individuals, including mutual fund licensed individuals.

ACTIVE MANAGEMENT ETFs

Active ETFs are constructed according to the fund manager's investment philosophy, for example a value, growth, top down, or bottom-up strategy. The active portion of the fund is created and managed no differently than any other actively-managed open-ended mutual fund. What might be different is when trading activity in each takes place. An active mutual fund manager will trade whenever market conditions and opportunities permit. The manager of an active ETF may be permitted, for example, to make portfolio changes only at the end of a day or week. Active ETFs charge significantly less in MERs than open-ended mutual funds managing a similar portfolio, but generally more than other passive ETFs.

INVERSE AND LEVERAGED ETFs

An inverse ETF moves in the opposite direction of the index or benchmark it tracks. The ETF profits when the underlying index falls and posts a loss when the index rises.

A leveraged ETF is designed to achieve returns that are multiples of the performance of the underlying index they track. The use of leverage, or borrowed capital, makes them more sensitive to market movements. The fund uses borrowed capital, in addition to investor equity, to provide a higher level of exposure to the underlying index. Typically, a leveraged ETF will use $2 of leverage for every $1 of investor capital. The goal is to generate a return made with the borrowed capital that exceeds what it cost to acquire the capital itself. For example, a leveraged ETF might attempt to achieve a daily return that is two times the daily return of the S&P 500.

Inverse and leveraged ETFs use derivatives to gain exposure to the market. Because these ETFs focus on daily movements, their performance is impacted by the volatility of the markets. As such, these types of ETFs are more suitable for short-term trading than for a longer-term hold. Given the complexities of these products, specific training is recommended, before offering these ETFs to clients.

INVERSE LEVERAGED ETFs

This type of ETF follows closely to the structure of a leveraged ETF in that the ETF will seek to achieve a return that is a multiple of the inverse performance of the underlying index it is tracking.

> **Example:** An ETF is constructed to return 2 times the inverse daily return on the S&P/TSX 60 Index – meaning that the fund will gain double the loss of the Index on a daily basis (i.e., if the Index drops 10% on the day, the ETF will post a 20% gain for that trading day, or will lose 20% if the index rises 10%).

Investors should realize that leveraged and inverse leveraged ETFs are complex financial products that employ sophisticated trading strategies. These ETFs expose investors to much greater risk compared to the traditional, passively managed ETF.

THE DANGERS OF INVERSE LEVERAGED ETFs

The use of inverse leverage in periods of market volatility can add significant risk to the investment. To illustrate, consider the following simplistic two-day example showing the effect of market volatility on inverse leveraged ETFs.

Example 1

The index rises from 1,000 to 1,010 on the first day but falls back to close at 1,000 on the second day. For this example, let's assume the ETF opens at 100 on the first day and commissions are excluded.

	Index	Index Return	Return Calculation	Inverse ETF Return	Inverse ETF Value
End of Day 1	1,010	+1%	$\dfrac{(1,010 - 1,000)}{1,000}$	-1%	99
End of Day 2	1,000	-0.99%	$\dfrac{(1,000 - 1,010)}{1,010}$	+0.99%	99.98

At the end of Day 2, the index is back to its original value and the inverse ETF lost 0.02%.

Example 2

The index goes from 1,000 to 1,100 on the first day and back down to close at 1,000 on the next day. The ETF opens at 100 on the first day.

	Index	Index	Index Return	Inverse ETF Return	Inverse ETF Value
End of Day 1	1,100	$\dfrac{(1,100 - 1,000)}{1,000}$	+10%	-10%	90
End of Day 2	1,000	$\dfrac{(1,000 - 1,100)}{1,100}$	-9.09%	+9.09%	98.18

At the end of Day 2, the index is back to its original value and the inverse ETF lost 1.82%. Note the difference between the loss in scenario 1 (- 0.02%) compared to the loss in scenario 2 (-1.82%) given the volatility of the index.

As you can see, the greater is the market volatility the greater is the impact on inverse leveraged ETFs. While the index may be back to its original value after a big market swing, the inverse leveraged ETF has lost value during the process.

COMMODITY ETFs

A commodity ETF can be structured in one of two ways. The ETF can have a physical holding of the commodity or it can hold derivatives to replicate a physical holding of a commodity. For example, the fund may have physical holdings of precious metals, such as the SPDR Gold Shares ETF that holds, in its London vaults, physical gold bars. Or, the ETF could make use of forward contracts to replicate the NGX Canadian Natural Gas Index.

Regulatory Issues

IIROC dealer members act as gatekeepers for investors. Dealer members facilitate access for investors who want products in the marketplace. In the case of products that are new or complex variants of existing ones, dealer members have responsibilities to understand their features, risks and benefits and to make sure their customers understand likewise so they can make appropriate choices.

> For more information, see IIROC's notice 09-0172, "Sales Practice Obligations Relating to Leveraged and Inverse Exchange-Traded Funds" dated June 11, 2009 (*www.iiroc.ca*).

Dealer member obligations extend from product due diligence before the sale to monitoring and review during and after the sale. For example, before an inverse leveraged or active ETF is first introduced, dealer members should understand how the fund works, what risks and rewards are offered to an investor and what risks and rewards are provided to the dealer. Doing so will enhance the firm's ability to detect and avoid conflicts and inappropriate recommendations before they occur.

KNOW YOUR CLIENT OBLIGATIONS

As ETFs now span the entire risk spectrum it is more important than ever for advisors to adhere to KYC obligations. Each ETF is suitable only to a specific audience and every advisor recommending an ETF needs to know if clients' objectives and constraints match what the ETF offers.

For instance, leveraged ETFs are more suitable for tactical purposes and are not appropriate for long term buy and hold investors. ETFs tracking commodities or foreign stock indexes may not be appropriate for more risk averse investors. Finally, investors in high tax brackets should probably avoid ETFs with high turnover and large taxable distributions in non-registered accounts.

Complete the following Online Learning Activity

Exchange-Traded Funds

Exchange-traded funds have become a popular investment vehicle for investors. In this activity, you will learn more about exchange-traded funds and how they are alike and how they differ from mutual funds and stocks.

 Complete the **Exchange-Traded Funds** activity.

WHAT IS LISTED PRIVATE EQUITY?

A listed private equity company is an investment company that uses its capital to purchase or invest in a wide range of other companies. The shares of a listed private equity company are publicly-traded on a stock exchange. Investment holdings could include companies that are publicly-traded on a stock exchange or are privately held (a privately held company does not trade on a stock exchange).

For example, the investment holdings of a private equity company could include the shares of a small-capitalization energy stock that trades on the TSX, a start-up restaurant chain that requires additional funding, an established real estate developer that is privately held, among others.

Traditionally, investment in private equity occurred through companies that were not listed on a stock exchange. They were privately held and used their own invested capital to purchase and invest in other businesses. Over the past decade, an increasing number of private equity companies have started listing on stock exchanges. Reasons for this transformation include better access to capital, improved liquidity, and transparency. These listed companies trade like common shares and are subject to the same regulatory and reporting requirements as other publicly-traded companies. The allure for the investor is the opportunity to invest in a diversified company whose investment holdings would not typically be available for investment by the average retail investor.

Structure of Listed Private Equity Companies

Private equity is the financing of firms unwilling or unable to find capital using public means. The term "private equity" is a bit of a misnomer, though, because the private equity asset class really encompasses both debt and equity investments. Long-term returns on private equity exceed returns on most other asset classes. But in exchange for these returns, private equity also exposes investors to far higher risks.

There are several means by which private equity finances firms.

Leveraged Buyout	A leveraged buyout is the acquisition of a company, financed with equity and debt. Buyouts are one of the most common forms of private equity.
Growth Capital	Growth capital is used to finance the acquisitions by or the high growth rates of expanding firms.
Turnaround	Turnaround financing is investment in underperforming or out of favour industries that are in financial need or are undergoing restructuring.
Early Stage	Early-stage investments are made in firms that are in the earliest stages of developing products or services in high-growth industries such as healthcare or technology. These firms usually have a limited number of customers.
Late Stage	The financing of firms that are better established but still not profitable enough to be self-sufficient is considered late-stage investment. Revenue growth is still very high in these companies.

Distressed Debt	The purchase of debt securities of private or public companies that are trading below par because of financial trouble is called distressed debt.
Infrastructure	Infrastructure debt finances the construction or improvement of utility networks or transportation assets, such as bridges or tunnels.

Here is an example of a hypothetical structure of a listed private equity company.

Example: ABC Corp. is a private equity firm that trades on the TSX. The company is highly diversified and conducts business through various autonomous subsidiaries operating in multiple industries including holdings in the real estate, financial, and healthcare sectors. ABC is led by a team of 30 partners who manage corporate investments, private equity portfolios, and various other assets.

ABC uses their investment capital to purchase companies they feel offer the potential for long-term capital gains. The company focuses on a wide range of small to mid-size privately-held investment opportunities.

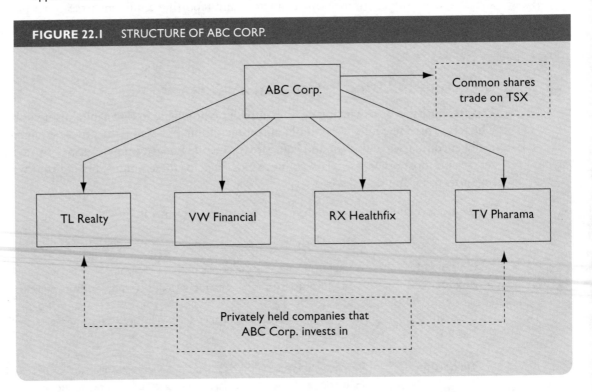

FIGURE 22.1   STRUCTURE OF ABC CORP.

For investors, purchasing shares in a listed private equity company is straightforward. You can buy and sell the shares in the same way as you would purchase the shares of any other publicly-traded company.

Private equity companies may also structure themselves as a private equity fund. These funds are pools of privately-managed capital formed for the purposes of making investments in other companies. The funds are typically managed by a promoter and this manager earns a fee for performing the investment management function. Investors will typically commit to invest a certain amount of capital when the fund is established, for example a minimum investment of $20,000. As the manager identifies suitable investments for the fund, these investors are required to advance the capital they have committed to invest.

Advantages and Disadvantages of Listed Private Equity

As with any type of investment, there are advantages and disadvantages of investing in a listed private equity company. A couple key advantages include:

- **Access to Legitimate Inside Information**: Because private equity managers are often buying majority ownership in a company, a much greater depth of information on possible investments is available to them. This information helps to more accurately assess the likely success of a company's business plan and helps investors follow proper post-investment strategy. The greater level of disclosure significantly reduces uncertainty and risk in private equity investment. Equivalent information in the public markets would be considered inside information.

- **Influence over Management and Flexibility of Implementation**: To improve the odds of realizing superior returns on their investments, private equity managers generally seek active participation in a company's strategic direction. Such participation could include development of a business plan, selection of senior executives and identification of eventual acquirers of the firm. Furthermore, as owners, private equity managers can implement their business plan without answering to other shareholders or regulators.

Disadvantages include:

- **Illiquid Investments**: Lack of liquidity is one of the key disadvantages faced by private equity investors. For example, when a venture capital firm purchases shares in a private company, the holding period is three to seven years, on average. Venture capital fund investors are locked in to their investment during this period. It is possible to sell partnership shares to a third party, but at a significantly discounted price.

- **Dependence on Key Personnel**: Private equity funds usually depend on the general partners and a relatively small staff for all key investment decisions. Also, private equity managers often take an active role in the management of companies in which they invest, including participation on the company's board of directors. For this reason, the inability of one or more key people to carry out their duties could have a significant adverse effect on a partnership and on the return on its investment.

Complete the following Online Learning Activity

Exchange-Listed Managed Products Summary

This activity lists the main characteristics of Exchange-listed managed products.

 Review the **Exchange-Listed Managed Products summary**.

SUMMARY

After reading this chapter, you should be able to:

1. Define closed-end funds and discuss the advantages and disadvantages of investing in closed-end funds.

    *   Closed-end funds are pooled investment funds that issue a limited or fixed number of shares and trade on an exchange.

    *   Fund prices are based on market demand and underlying asset value.

    *   Funds can trade at a discount, at par or at a premium relative to the combined net asset value of their underlying holdings.

    *   Advantages of closed-end funds include:
        *   Diversification

        *   Ability to short-sell

        *   Increased investment flexibility for managers

        *   Ease in tracking an adjusted cost base

        *   Potentially lower management expense ratios than for open-ended funds

    *   Disadvantages of closed-end funds include:
        *   Lack of liquidity

        *   Possibility of trading below net asset value

        *   Paying regular commissions

        *   Possibility of lack of availability of income reinvestment plans

        *   Highly taxed income from funds that trade on foreign exchanges

2. Define income trust, differentiate among the types of income trusts, and describe their features.

    *   Income trusts are asset-back securities that have been created to purchase and hold interests in the operating assets of a company.

    *   Real estate investment trusts (REITs), which can be open or closed-end funds, consolidate the capital of a large number of investors to invest in and manage a diversified real estate portfolio. Rental incomes (as much as 95% of that generated) are passed through to investors who buy units in the trust. The units are more liquid than buying real estate directly.

    *   Business income trusts purchase the assets of an underlying company, usually in the manufacturing, retail or service industry.

3.   Describe the advantages, disadvantages and features of exchange-traded funds (ETFs).

- Exchange-traded funds (ETFs) are investment vehicles that combine some of the features of mutual funds and individual stocks. They trade on recognized exchanges and hold the same stocks in the same proportion as those included in a specific index.

- The key advantages to holding ETFs are the diversification opportunities and the significantly lower MERs when compared to traditional mutual funds.

- Active ETFs are constructed according to the fund manager's investment philosophy, for example a value, growth, top down, or bottom up strategy. The active portion of the fund is created and managed no differently than any other actively-managed open-ended mutual fund.

- An inverse ETF moves in the opposite direction of the index or benchmark it tracks. The ETF profits when the underlying index falls and posts a loss when the index rises. The inverse ETF is designed to hedge exposure to or profit from downward moving markets.

- A leveraged ETF is designed to achieve returns that are multiples of the performance of the underlying index they track. The use of leverage, or borrowed capital, makes them more sensitive to market movements.

- Inverse leveraged ETFs seek to achieve a return that is a multiple of the inverse performance of the underlying index it is tracking.

- Inverse and leveraged ETFs expose investors to much greater risk compared to the traditional, passively managed ETFs.

4.   Explain how to invest in private equity through a listed equity (private equity firm).

- A listed private equity company is an investment company that uses its capital to purchase or invest in a wide range of other companies. The shares of a listed private equity company are publicly-traded on a stock exchange.

- These listed companies trade like common shares and are subject to the same regulatory and reporting requirements as other publicly-traded companies.

- Private equity is the financing of firms unwilling or unable to find capital using public means. The term "private equity" is a bit of a misnomer, though, because the private equity asset class really encompasses both debt and equity investments.

- Private equity companies may also structure themselves as a private equity fund. These funds are pools of privately-managed capital formed for the purposes of making investments in other companies.

Online Frequently Asked Questions

CSI has answered many frequently asked questions about this Chapter. Read through online Module 22 FAQs.

Online Post-Module Assessment

Once you have completed the chapter, take the Module 22 Post-Test.

Chapter *23*

Fee-Based Accounts

23

Fee-Based Accounts

LEARNING OBJECTIVES

By the end of this chapter, you should be able to:

1. Differentiate the features, advantages and disadvantages of the various types of fee-based accounts.
2. Describe the various types of managed accounts.

THE CHANGING COMPENSATION MODEL

There is an ongoing shift in the securities industry. The industry is moving away from the traditional advisor/client relationship model, which compensates the advisor with commissions, to a model that bundles various services into a fee based on the client's assets under management. The types of accounts created in this new model are referred to as **fee-based accounts**. Typically, these accounts apply to affluent or high-net-worth clients.

This chapter focuses on the various types of fee-based accounts available in the marketplace. What's important to recognize here is that as we approach the end of the course the products discussed in this chapter clearly show how the compensation model of the Investment Advisor continues to evolve. As this chapter demonstrates, the traditional stock picker role is changing dramatically.

KEY TERMS

Discretionary accounts

Fee-based accounts

Managed accounts

Multi-disciplinary accounts

Multi-manager accounts

Mutual fund wraps

Overlay manager

Private family office

Separately managed accounts

Single-manager accounts

Unified managed account

WHAT ARE THE DIFFERENT FEE-BASED ACCOUNTS?

The past decade has seen tremendous growth in the availability and types of **fee-based accounts**. These types of accounts have also significantly outpaced the growth of traditional commission-based accounts. Some of the key reasons for this shift in the advisor/client relationship model include:

1.   Advisors are focused on trading in the traditional commission-based model. This focus generally comes at the expense of the time they can devote to a client's financial planning and wealth management needs. In most cases, the planning needs for affluent or high net worth clients have moved beyond simple stock and bond picking to include advice on risk management, estate planning, debt management, insurance and retirement planning. Affluent clients who want these planning needs addressed want access to their advisor's skill set without being limited to simple trading strategies.

2.   Market surveys have shown that affluent clients approve of having a portion of the advisor's fee linked to the performance of their portfolio. Since program fees are tied to assets under management, the fee will vary with the performance of the investment. This approach puts both the client and the advisor on the same side as a fee-based business and erases the potential for conflict of interest, inherent in commission-based selling.

3.   Affluent clients appreciate the clear disclosure that comes with a fee-based account. The fees are paid directly by the client and are transparent, shown on the client's regular account statements. Therefore, advisors are limited in selling products that contain hidden compensation, such as trailer fees, back end loads and referral fees.

4.   The fee-based model provides the affluent client with more confidence in the advisor. Under a commission-based structure, the client might wonder if the advisor is suggesting investments because the product carries a higher commission. Under a fee-based account relationship, the client has complete confidence that the advisor is recommending securities that are in the best interests of the client.

There are two broad categories of fee accounts: managed and non-managed. Within the category of managed fee accounts, clients have several alternatives, depending on their desired level of customization and amount of investable assets.

Figure 23.1 shows the various types of fee-based accounts that we will discuss in this chapter.

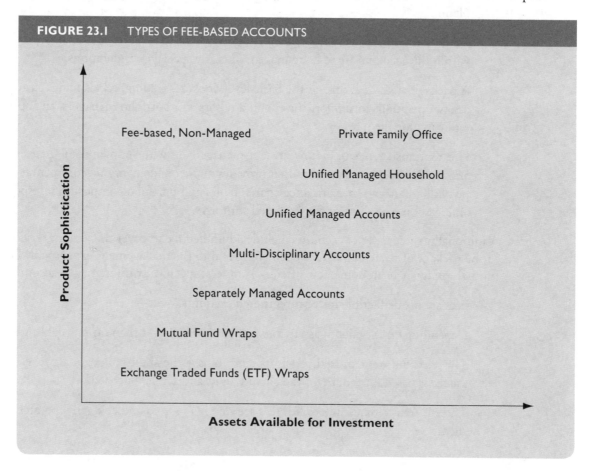

FIGURE 23.1   TYPES OF FEE-BASED ACCOUNTS

Managed Accounts

Managed accounts have become a significant part of the investment services available in the marketplace. They consist of almost 15% of a firm's overall revenues. In fact, they have grown about six times faster than commission-based assets during the middle part of the last decade (Source: Investor Economics, Retail Brokerage Report 2008).

Managed accounts get their name from the discretionary nature of the services provided. Clients elect to have a licensed portfolio manager decide and execute investment decisions on their behalf. This means that the manager has the discretion to make investment decisions that are suitable for the client.

Managed accounts typically have the following features in common:

- Professional investment management by a licensed portfolio manager with discretionary authority over the account.

- Assets within the account held exclusively for the client. The client has direct ownership of the investments within the account. The assets are not pooled, as they are with a mutual fund, and the investment management is provided to the client—not to the trust.

- Services beyond investment management that include wealth management and financial planning.

- An Investment Policy Statement allowing the client to specifically outline how the assets within the accounts are to be managed, plus any special considerations.

- A package of services that, at the basic level, includes trading, rebalancing, custody of the assets, operations to support the client, advisors and portfolio managers, and specialized reporting for clients.

- Greater transparency of the investment management with supplemental quarterly reports and a year-end summary that often provides market and economic commentary from the portfolio managers, performance charts, tables and portfolio composition, respective gains and losses per security, and a fee-based summary.

Additionally, these types of accounts include a bundled fee to cover the various services included in the package of related services. When compared to the management expense ratio (MER) on mutual funds, there are some key differences in fees, specifically for managed accounts, as follows:

- Fees are tax deductible for non-registered accounts.

- Depending on the client's assets, the fees tend to be lower than on mutual funds.

- The fee is not standardized. Advisors tend to have the ability to negotiate fees. In most cases, the fee is based on the size of the client's assets and services needed.

- There is transparency in fees. All fees are clearly reported and charged separately to the client.

Fee-Based Non-Managed Accounts

Non-managed fee accounts are full-service brokerage accounts that provide clients with financial planning services combined with a fixed or unlimited number of trades, all bundled into a fee charged on the client's assets under management.

Fees for these types of accounts range from 1.0% to 2.5% of the assets under management. In most cases, the annual fee is paid quarterly out of cash held in the account. The fee depends on the following criteria:

- Dollar size of account

- Estimated number of trades

- Type of investment (equity, bond, money market, mutual fund, GIC etc.)

Some large investment dealers offer two levels of fee-based accounts. The higher level typically offers more or unlimited free trading.

Advantages and Disadvantages of Fee-Based Accounts

Fee-based accounts enable advisors to provide financial planning and wealth management services to clients and to continue recommending securities and third-party mutual funds, without regard for the commissions they normally carry. Advisors need no longer shun passive investment vehicles, such as low-cost index funds and the fast-growing array of exchange-traded funds.

However, not everyone in the industry feels that the move to fee-based brokerage accounts is necessarily positive. Opponents of fee-based brokerage accounts cite the following possible disadvantages:

- **Potentially more expensive**: If clients buy and hold their investments, they may not fully benefit from this type of account, given that trades are part of the packaged service.

- **Limited number of trades**: Some fee-based accounts have a limit on the number of trades in the account. The maximum depends on the firm, and on the size and the type of account.

- **Neglect by the Investment Advisor**: There is a chance that the advisor could become lazy due to the continuing stream of income regardless of time and effort put into the account. Most advisors would avoid this type of behaviour, given that they would likely lose the client over time.

- **Extra fees charged**: In some circumstances, the client can be charged two fees. In addition to the fee charged on the account, the client can be charged extra fees from investments that have fees or commissions buried into their price, such as a structured product or mutual fund with a trailer fee. Given the full disclosure requirements to clients, the instance of these types of accounts is very low.

- **Trading and research time requirements**: Advisors are still required to spend significant amounts of time trading and researching securities.

Discretionary Accounts

As well as managed accounts, investors can also access **discretionary accounts**. Both types of accounts allow the client to empower someone else with discretion to make investment decisions on the client's behalf. However, there are some key differences between these two types of accounts:

- With managed accounts, the client's investment portfolios are managed on a continuing basis by the investment dealer. These programs tend to use model portfolios. The model is applied to similar clients tailored to the client's individual needs.

- Discretionary accounts are usually opened for a short period of time. They serve as a matter of convenience for clients who are unwilling or unable to attend to their own accounts, for example, through illness or absence from the country. Given their short-term nature, these programs tend not to use a model portfolio, but rather simply monitor an existing account of securities.

The New Account Application Form provides for the identification of discretionary authority over an account. This form should be used to indicate the category of the account (i.e., discretionary or managed).

The exchanges and IIROC have adopted rules for discretionary and managed accounts. Some of these rules include the following:

- Discretionary authority with respect to a managed account must be given by the client in writing and accepted in writing by a partner or director. The authorization must specify the client's investment objectives.

- Discretionary authority for discretionary accounts may not be solicited, whereas managed accounts may be solicited.

- Investment Advisors other than partners or directors may not accept authorization for a simple discretionary account.

According to IIROC rules, Investment Advisors may make investment recommendations for simple discretionary accounts. However, the decision to implement the recommendation rests with a partner or director, and the Investment Advisor receives written approval from the partner or director prior to carrying out the recommendation.

In managed accounts, discretionary authority may not be exercised by a member, or any person on a member's behalf, unless the person responsible for the management of the account is designated and approved as a portfolio manager.

WHAT ARE THE DIFFERENT TYPES OF MANAGED ACCOUNTS?

There are many different types of fee-based managed accounts. We will discuss three of these accounts, which have many similarities:

- Single-Manager
- Multi-Manager
- Private Family Office

Single-Manager Accounts

Single-manager accounts are directed by a single portfolio manager who focuses considerable time and attention on the selection of securities, the sectors to invest in and the optimal asset allocation. The portfolio manager often maintains a model portfolio and then executes bulk purchases and sales based on their investment decisions. The manager then allocates the sales and purchases to their respective clients' accounts.

Client accounts can be tailored with security exclusions. The client also benefits from the manager's use of tax loss selling. This is a temporary deviation from the model portfolio to realize a capital loss for the benefit of the specific client, to offset some of the gains. While each account program has specific advantages, the primary disadvantage with this type is the lack of an independent professional approach to evaluate the ongoing performance and risk of the respective portfolios.

ADVISOR OR INVESTMENT COUNSELLOR

With these types of accounts, the advisor providing the account servicing also provides the investment management. The advisor is required to be licensed as a portfolio manager in order to make the investment decisions on behalf of the client. The actual securities are held within the client's account in amounts that follow the advisor's portfolio model.

The portfolios offered tend to focus on the advisor's area of specialty, and leverages the advisor's skills in either fundamental or technical analysis. In each case, a client's risk tolerance is determined. The advisor/portfolio manager establishes the portfolio that is aligned with a suitable model. Often, the model portfolios are guided by the firm's security selections and portfolio construction.

The key advantages of this type of program include:

- Lower costs since no other parties are involved with the account.

- An intimate understanding of a client's needs is combined with a tailored investment management program.

PROPRIETARY MANAGED PROGRAM

Firms help advisors focus on servicing their clients and growing their business by providing them access to a centralized investment management service. Advisors partner with the firm's portfolio managers to select from a list of model portfolios of specific securities. The actual securities are held within the client's account in amounts that follow the firm's portfolio model. The portfolio manager directs the changes to the securities within the model. The advisor maintains the client relationship, outlining any required customization or life events that may cause changes to a client's portfolio model.

ETF WRAPS

Exchange-traded fund (ETF) wraps are often directed by a single portfolio manager who creates the model for a specific managed account. The managed account holds a basket of exchange-traded funds for security selection. While the underlying ETFs tend to be passive in the investment management, the value added comes from the asset allocation and sector selection. This value added service can be either passive or active, as follows:

- **Passive approach**: The portfolio manager determines the client's risk tolerance and then sets the optimal asset allocation and establishes the portfolio, with ongoing rebalancing back to the set asset mix.

- **Active approach**: The portfolio manager again determines the client's long term risk tolerance, but then applies a short-term tactical approach by actively overweighting or underweighting the sector and the client's asset allocation in order to take advantage of changing market conditions. The portfolio manager has greater discretion in rebalancing the portfolio to take advantage of the market.

The key advantages of the active approach are:

- Lower cost of the underlying investment management tends to provide a reduced cost base and likely lower client fees. Therefore, the program has a lower cost than most multi-manager programs.

- More efficient use of the advisor's time results in better focus on wealth management and servicing the client, while knowing the portfolio manager is researching and trading securities daily.

- Firms normally provide advisors with marketing support.

Multi-Manager Accounts

Multi-manager accounts offer clients and their advisors more choice in terms of product and services. These accounts focus on providing access to elite institutional portfolio managers. Often, clients are aligned with two or more portfolio models from these portfolio managers. Each portfolio model is a component of the client's greater diversified holdings.

For example, one portfolio model can focus on fixed-income, while another focuses on Canadian equities. To provide oversight to the program, the portfolio managers are considered sub-advisors to the firm's portfolio manager of record (also known as the overlay manager).

ROLE OF THE OVERLAY MANAGER

The **overlay manager** plays a number of key roles in the management of a client's portfolio, including:

- The overlay manager conducts ongoing due diligence reviews of each of the underlying portfolio managers (the sub-advisors). As a manager of managers, he or she sets the metrics for ongoing evaluations, evaluates new managers and removes poorly performing ones from the program. This provides affluent clients with a higher level of confidence in their investment program. The client gains peace of mind knowing that professional oversight is governing the quality of the underlying portfolio managers, ensuring discretionary money management is on track with the stated objectives.

- The overlay manager sets the overall optimal asset mix and the proportions for each sub-advisor to manage what will maximize performance and mitigate risk. The client may have a customized investment portfolio that increases in complexity, given the wealth of the client and the need to derive higher levels of optimization.

- The overlay manager also conducts ongoing monitoring of the client's investments and the composition of the overall investment portfolio.

- The overlay manager coordinates the efforts of the sub-advisors and sometimes conducts rebalancing.

- The overlay manager provides market insight to advisors. He or she coordinates the views of the sub-advisors and reflects on the broader picture of the markets, which is then conveyed to the advisors and their clients.

The overlay manager works with the advisors in servicing clients. This is not a referral but a partnership, in which the advisor retains the client's assets. This provides a superior offering for the affluent or high-net-worth client. The service incorporates the existing trusted relationship of the advisor, whom the client has become comfortable dealing with.

Each type of program has specific advantages. The primary advantage is the direct access clients have to elite industry professionals. More importantly, however, this access allows advisors to change their business model. They redirect time previously spent on research and security selection to servicing their clients, and to focus on the complex wealth management needs of the affluent client. The fees for multi-manager accounts cover the underlying investment management, the oversight functions of the overlay manager, custody, and the aspects of wealth management and financial planning.

MUTUAL FUND WRAPS

Mutual fund wraps are established with a selection of individual funds managed within a client's accounts. Mutual fund wraps differ from funds of funds. The client holds the actual funds within their account, as opposed to a fund that simply invests in other funds. In most cases, a separate account is established for the client and the selected funds are held inside that dedicated account.

The composition and weighting of individual funds within the account are directed by the overlay manager, while the investment management of the underlying funds is conducted by the sub-advisors. The overlay manager plays an active role by rebalancing the client's holdings back to their target asset mix, or by adding and removing funds based on the quality of the investment management the funds offer.

The key advantages of mutual fund wraps include:

- A coordinated investment account optimized on the asset allocation and selection of managers.

- Ongoing oversight management of the funds.

SEPARATELY MANAGED ACCOUNTS

A client who has more than $150,000 to $500,000 in an account has the option of moving beyond pre-packaged and standardized mutual funds. The client can opt for a portfolio management service where the model of investments is held directly by the individual investor. With **separately managed accounts**, the sub-advisors control a dedicated account for the portfolio model. Each client has a separate dedicated account to hold the selected investments.

As the sub-advisor makes the investment decisions, the actual securities are debited and credited to the client's dedicated account within the firm. The overlay manager establishes a collection of these dedicated accounts for the client, reflecting the optimal asset mix to help the client attain the overall investment objectives, while mitigating risk.

Since the client holds the underlying securities, the portfolio models can be set to exclude investments or sectors in which the client prefers not to invest. The portfolio can also factor in investments where the client already has exposure and does not want additional exposure. Therefore, whereas the sub-advisors direct the investment of hundreds of client accounts, the clients still have the ability to tailor their holdings, which are held separate from all other clients' investments. In addition to the security exclusions, an investor's distinctive tax situation is taken into consideration.

The key advantages of separately managed accounts include:

- Separately managed accounts provide access to elite portfolio managers under the oversight of an overlay manager.

- The client directly holds the securities in the account. In addition, the client avoids the risk of being forced to prematurely sell long-term positions to meet the cash needs of other investors, and avoid distributions that are related to funds (capital gain distributions).

- Supplemental reports collectively report on the performance of each separate account. The performance is specific to the investor and to other factors in the holdings, including when the holdings are purchased and sold, and deposits and withdrawals of specific securities within the accounts.

MULTI-DISCIPLINARY ACCOUNTS

Multi-disciplinary accounts are an evolution of separately managed accounts, all with the same benefits. The key difference is the format in which the portfolio models are held. With separately managed accounts, the optimal asset mix is held in separate accounts dedicated for each sub-advisor's model. With multi-disciplinary accounts, separate models are combined into one overall portfolio model in a single account. The overlay manager takes the investment decisions of the underlying sub-advisors and combines them into one overall balanced portfolio model for the single account.

Multi-disciplinary accounts hold a mix of securities selected in the models of the sub-advisors, which are then combined with selected mutual funds and ETFs. By combining the models of sub-advisors with mutual funds and ETFs, higher levels of optimal asset allocations can be created.

UNIFIED MANAGED ACCOUNT

A further evolution of separately managed accounts is the **unified managed account**. This type of account includes the same benefits as multi-disciplinary accounts. This model has additional enhancements, however, including performance reports from the respective sub-advisors, outlining distinct models contained within the single custody account. These models are held within the account in *sleeves* to effectively combine detailed reporting of separately managed accounts, while maintaining the enhancement of the single custody account, as in a multi-disciplinary account.

EXHIBIT 23.1   UNIFIED MANAGED HOUSEHOLD ACCOUNTS

The unified managed household account is a concept that is still being defined. However, many industry experts are working toward providing such a holistic level of service to high net worth clients.

The account focuses on two levels, using the following two different approaches:

- The first approach aims to provide investment management across firms. Accounts held at multiple firms are coordinated into one overall managed account view. This approach has many advantages. However, it will likely take some time to work through the compliance issues. There is also limited incentive for competing firms to cooperate. Most firms would be reluctant to relinquish control and risk the inevitable consolidation of accounts.

> **EXHIBIT 23.1** UNIFIED MANAGED HOUSEHOLD ACCOUNTS – *Cont'd*
>
> • The second approach has more potential to succeed. This consists of the coordination of holdings across a family or household. In this approach, one overall portfolio model is used to coordinate investment management within and across accounts for the family or the household. This application can provide better tax management and inclusion of all of the holdings, regardless of size or format of the account. In a Canadian setting, the ideal account would take a balanced portfolio model and allocate the fixed income within an RRSP, placing the equities in a Canadian cash account and the international equities in a U.S. cash account.

Private Family Office

A **private family office** is an extension of the advisor's client servicing approach. In this approach, instead of having only one advisor, a team of professionals handles all of an affluent client's financial affairs within one central location. The client's portfolio may include investments, trust and estates, philanthropy, corporate planning, tax planning and filing, legal work, basic account servicing, including bill paying, and others. The investment management is unique for each family. This account is managed by institutional portfolio managers, similar to the managing of pensions. Generally, access to a family office is for clients with more than $50 million in an account. Typically, this service is conducted for a fee on the assets under management.

The key advantages of the family office service include:

*   High net worth clients are completely free to concentrate on matters other than their financial affairs.

*   Given that all professionals are concentrated in one service, they are aligned with the recommendations on the client's investments, taxes, legal, estate and corporate needs.

Complete the following Online Learning Activity

Definitions

Many different types of fee-based accounts have emerged over the past several years. This activity will reinforce your understanding of the various fee-based accounts discussed in this chapter.

 Complete the **Definitions** activity.

SUMMARY

1. Differentiate the features, advantages and disadvantages of the various types of fee-based accounts.

   - Managed accounts offer professional portfolio management services whereby the manager has discretionary authority over the account. In this way, the manager plays an active role in making and carrying out investment decisions.

   - Managed accounts typically offer a bundled fee to cover the various services included in the package of related services.

   - Non-managed accounts are full-service brokerage accounts that provide clients with financial planning services combined with a fixed or unlimited number of trades, all bundled into a fee charged on the client's assets under management.

   - Discretionary accounts are usually opened for a short period of time. They serve as a matter of convenience for clients who are unwilling or unable to attend to their own accounts, for example, through illness or absence from the country.

   - Discretionary authority with respect to a managed account must be given by the client in writing and accepted in writing by a partner or director. The authorization must specify the client's investment objectives.

2. Describe the various types of managed accounts.

   - Single-manager accounts are directed by a single portfolio manager who focuses considerable time and attention on the selection of securities, the sectors to invest in and the optimal asset allocation. The portfolio manager often maintains a model portfolio and then executes bulk purchases and sales based on their investment decisions.

   - With an advisor/investment counsellor account, the advisor providing the account servicing also provides the investment management. The advisor is licensed as a portfolio manager and tends to focus on the advisor's area of specialty. The advisor/portfolio manager establishes the portfolio that is aligned with a suitable model.

   - Exchange-traded fund (ETF) wraps are often directed by a single portfolio manager who creates the model for a specific managed account. The managed account holds a basket of exchange-traded funds for security selection and can be either a passive or active approach.

   - Multi-manager accounts offer clients and their advisors more choice in terms of product and services. These accounts focus on providing access to elite institutional portfolio managers. Each portfolio model is a component of the client's greater diversified holdings. To provide oversight to the program, the portfolio managers are considered sub-advisors to the firm's portfolio manager of record (also known as the overlay manager).

- The overlay manager works with the advisors in servicing clients. This is not a referral but a partnership, in which the advisor retains the client's assets. The overlay manager conducts ongoing due diligence reviews of each of the underlying portfolio managers (the sub-advisors). As a manager of managers, he or she sets the metrics for ongoing evaluations, evaluates new managers and removes poorly performing ones from the program.

- Mutual fund wraps are established with a selection of individual funds managed within a client's accounts. Mutual fund wraps differ from funds of funds. The client holds the actual funds within their account, as opposed to a fund that simply invests in other funds.

- With separately managed accounts, the sub-advisors control a dedicated account for the portfolio model. Each client has a separate dedicated account to hold the selected investments. As the sub-advisor makes the investment decisions, the actual securities are debited and credited to the client's dedicated account within the firm. The overlay manager establishes a collection of these dedicated accounts for the client, reflecting the optimal asset mix to help the client attain the overall investment objectives, while mitigating risk.

- With multi-disciplinary accounts, separate models are combined into one overall portfolio model in a single account. The overlay manager takes the investment decisions of the underlying sub-advisors and combines them into one overall balanced portfolio model for the single account.

- Multi-disciplinary accounts hold a mix of securities selected in the models of the sub-advisors, which are then combined with selected mutual funds and ETFs. By combining the models of sub-advisors with mutual funds and ETFs, higher levels of optimal asset allocations can be created.

- A unified managed account includes performance reports from the respective sub-advisors, outlining distinct models contained within the single custody account. These models are held within the account in *sleeves* to effectively combine detailed reporting of separately managed accounts, while maintaining the enhancement of the single custody account, as in a multi-disciplinary account.

- A private family office is an extension of the advisor's client servicing approach. In this approach, instead of having only one advisor, a team of professionals handles all of an affluent client's financial affairs within one central location. The client's portfolio may include investments, trust and estates, philanthropy, corporate planning, tax planning and filing, legal work, basic account servicing, including bill paying, and others. The investment management is unique for each family.

Online Frequently Asked Questions

CSI has answered many frequently asked questions about this Chapter. Read through online Module 23 FAQs.

Online Post-Module Assessment

Once you have completed the chapter, take the Module 23 Post-Test.

Chapter *24*

Structured Products

24

Structured Products

LEARNING OBJECTIVES

By the end of this chapter, you should be able to:

1. Describe the features, risks and benefits of principal-protected notes (PPNs).
2. Explain the structure, risks associated with and the tax implications of Index-, Mutual Fund- and Hedge Fund-Linked guaranteed investment certificates (GICs).
3. Explain the structure, risks associated with and the tax implications of split shares.
4. Describe the features of asset-backed securities including asset-backed commercial paper and the securitization process.
5. Discuss the structure and benefits of mortgage-backed securities.

STRUCTURED PRODUCTS: AN OVERVIEW

Structured products provide investors with risk, return, tax and diversification characteristics not available from conventional investments. The pricing of these products can reference a single security, a basket of securities, an index, commodities or a combination of assets. They can be designed to provide enhanced yield, capital protection and/or tax efficiency.

Structured products were created as an alternative financing method for companies to raise capital on better terms than other more conventional methods, such as issuing regular bonds. To attract investors, they have to be designed to meet needs not fulfilled by other types of standard investments. Structured products are not currently subject to National Instrument 81-102, the regulation that governs many aspects of mutual funds. Therefore, they can improve returns by using leverage, derivatives or strategies not available to mutual funds.

The first structured products were designed to provide returns related or referenced to well-known securities, indexes or investments (i.e., S&P 500 Equity Index, price of gold bullion). These reference securities are called underlying assets. Over time, the underlying assets of structured products have become more varied to attract more capital. As investor interest in the advantages that structured products offer grew, so has the number of them available. Their ability to meet the unique needs of a more and more sophisticated investor market has undoubtedly been one of the factors that has contributed to the successful growth of the structured product market.

KEY TERMS

Asset-backed securities

Asset-backed commercial paper (ABCP)

Capital shares

Index-linked guaranteed investment certificates (GICs)

Mortgage-backed securities (MBSs)

Pass-through securities

Prepayment risk

Principal-protected notes (PPNs)

Roll-over risk

Special purpose vehicle (SPV)

Split shares

Tranches

WHAT ARE PRINCIPAL-PROTECTED NOTES?

In Canada, a **principal-protected note** (**PPN**) is a debt-like instrument with a maturity date. The issuer agrees to repay investors the amount originally invested (the principal) plus interest. The interest rate is tied to the performance of an underlying asset, such as a portfolio of mutual funds or common stocks, fixed-income investments, a market index, a hedge fund or a portfolio of hedge funds. PPNs guarantee only the return of the principal. Although many PPNs are most often issued by chartered banks, they are not protected by the Canada Deposit Insurance Corporation (CDIC).

PPNs are not issued under a prospectus and are not considered securities. In most provinces, special licensing is not required to sell them. Although some PPNs have been designed as income-producing investments, most do not make interim distributions of income. The term to maturity of a PPN varies according to the issue, typically ranging from five to 12 years from the date of issue.

The three main types of PPNs are:

1. **Index-linked notes** are certificates usually offered in three-year to five-year terms by major banks. Index-linked notes are non-transferable and cannot be redeemed prior to maturity. Any return is linked to the performance of a stock market index. However, the note may have a market participation clause or a maximum gain cap that limits the product's return potential.

2. **Mutual fund-linked notes** derive their return from an underlying mutual fund or set of mutual funds and often have a longer term of maturity (six to eight years).

3. **Hedge fund-linked notes** allow investors to participate in hedge fund returns without the large minimum account size normally required for direct investment and without the downside volatility.

PPN Guarantors, Manufacturers and Distributors

Generally, the following three entities are involved in bringing a PPN to market:

GUARANTOR

The guarantor or issuer of the PPN is the entity that guarantees the principal at maturity. In Canada, most PPNs are issued by Schedule I and Schedule II chartered banks.

MANUFACTURER

The manufacturer helps the issuer design the notes and market them to investors and distributors. The big six Schedule I banks all have large distribution networks, including bank branch networks and investment dealers. These banks usually serve as both the issuer and manufacturer of their own PPNs.

DISTRIBUTOR

Investment dealers and mutual fund dealers, which employ advisors to sell PPNs, act as distributors. The distributor receives a commission for each PPN sold. The commission is shared with the advisor according to a prearranged formula.

Given the overlap in Canada between the banking system and the investment industry, one bank may fulfill all three functions, especially in the case of a Schedule I bank. Alternatively, three separate entities may be involved in issuing a PPN. All three entities receive a share of the fees associated with the PPN.

Complete the following Online Learning Activity

Key Features

PPNs are structured in many different ways and with a variety of features. This activity will help you better understand the different features available on PPNs.

 Complete the **Features of PPNs** activity.

The Structure of PPNs

A PPN can potentially offer equity-like returns while at the same time lowering or even eliminating long-term capital risk that is typically present when equities are held outright.

However, this complexity can come at the expense of transparency. Even experienced, highly knowledgeable dealers, advisors and investors may not fully understand how these products work, where the source of return lies and how the principal is protected.

Although an analysis of the structure of PPNs is beyond the scope of the CSC, what follows is a general overview. (More advanced courses offered by CSI provide a more detailed discussion.)

Let's consider two of the more popular structures:

ZERO-COUPON BOND PLUS CALL OPTION STRUCTURE

The simpler of the two structures is the combination of a zero-coupon bond (which matures at par) plus one or more call options. The PPN issuer invests most of the proceeds in a zero-coupon bond that has the same maturity as the PPN. The zero-coupon bond guarantees the return of principal on maturity. The remainder of the proceeds is invested in a call option on the underlying asset. The call option portion of the PPN provides the potential return.

> **EXAMPLE**   HOW THE ZERO-COUPON BOND PLUS CALL OPTION STRUCTURE WORKS
>
> A bank issues a 5-year PPN based on the price of ABC stock. Terms of the PPN are that the principal is guaranteed and the investor participates 100% in the price of ABC stock above $35. The bank raises $50 million from investors. Of the $50 million, $42 million is invested in a 5-year zero-coupon bond with a face value of $50 million. Another $8 million is invested in a 5-year call option on ABC that gives the investor the right to buy the stock at $35. At maturity, investors receive their principal from the maturity of the zero-coupon bond. Any extra return derives from the value of the call option. The call option has value if the price of ABC at the note's maturity is greater than $35 a share.

CONSTANT PROPORTION PORTFOLIO INSURANCE (CPPI) STRUCTURE

In a CPPI structure, the portfolio manager shifts the portfolio's allocation between a riskier asset and a risk-free asset in response to changes in interest rates and the value of the risky asset:

- As the value of the risky asset increases or interest rates rise, the allocation to the risky asset increases and the allocation to the risk-free asset decreases.

- Likewise, as the value of the risky asset falls or interest rates fall, the allocation to the risky asset falls and the allocation to the risk-free asset rises.

The goal of a CPPI structure is to guarantee a minimum payout on a certain date in the future, while providing the opportunity to outperform the minimum payout. With a CPPI structure, instead of buying the zero-coupon bond, the issuer continually tracks how much it would cost to buy the zero-coupon bond to guarantee the principal. As long as the note's assets remain above this floor value, the issuer can invest the assets with the objective of matching the performance of, or in some cases outperforming, the underlying asset.

Complete the following Online Learning Activity

PPN Structures

PPNs can be structured using a CPPI or a Zero-coupon bond plus option structure. There are some key differences between the two that you need to be able to recognize. This activity will test your understanding of these two structures.

 Complete the **Performance Factors** activity.

Risks Associated with PPNs

PPNs often are perceived as risk-free investments because the principal is guaranteed at maturity. While potentially lower-risk than an equity investment, PPNs carry their own unique set of risks, as outlined in Table 24.1.

TABLE 24.1	RISKS ASSOCIATED WITH PPNs
Liquidity Risk	Almost all PPNs offer investors the opportunity to redeem their investment in the PPN before maturity. This gives PPNs a distinct advantage over many conventional GIC-based products, which must be held until maturity.
	A PPN is often constructed with illiquid securities, typically over-the-counter derivative contracts. The PPN sponsor can take the opposite side of these contracts in the secondary market. Frequently, because of the illiquidity of the underlying securities, the sponsor will charge a wide bid-ask spread for the inconvenience of providing a secondary market for the investor. It is important to note that, although the issuer may offer to facilitate a secondary market, they are under no obligation to do so.
Performance Risk	The performance of the PPN may not resemble the performance of the underlying asset, especially in the early years following the issue of the PPN. Many factors are involved in pricing a PPN, including interest rates, the actual performance of the underlying asset, and various explicit and implicit fees. Investors should realize, therefore, that they are not going to fully participate in the underlying asset's returns with the benefit of a principal-protection feature. Principal protection costs money, and the return from a PPN is unlikely to exactly match the returns of the underlying asset.
Call Risk	In certain cases, the issuer may redeem the PPN before maturity. For instance, this may occur when the PPN delivers the advertised return prior to maturity. Having the PPN called earlier than the maturity date can cause an investor to lose the opportunity to continue to enjoy an investment that was presumably meeting their investment needs. It may also expose them to reinvestment risk, as appropriate investment opportunities at the time of the calling of the PPN may be less advantageous relative to what they were at the time of the original investment date.
Credit Risk	The issuer may be unable to return the investor's principal at maturity. PPNs are guaranteed by the banks that issue them. While most are large global institutions that present no serious credit risk, that may not be the case with all guarantors. Advisors and investors are advised to always check the credit ratings of the PPN issuer to ensure the institution can back the guarantee, if necessary.
Currency Risk	PPNs may be structured to track the returns from a foreign currency-denominated underlying asset or assets. Unless specified otherwise in the PPN's offering documents, a PPN based on a foreign asset exposes investors to currency risk.

IMPORTANT FACTORS TO CONSIDER WITH PPNs

PPNs are not appropriate for investors who:

- Rely on a regular and predicable investment income to fund their lifestyle: Although some newer PPNs are designed to provide income, the income stream is not guaranteed. Many PPNs specifically exclude interim income distributions.

- Require liquidity: Liquidity is not guaranteed with these products. Also, although the issuer may offer to facilitate a secondary market, it is under no obligation to do so. Even if it does facilitate a secondary market on a regular basis, the bid price may not accurately reflect the economic performance or value of the note before maturity. Therefore, an investor who buys a PPN should really be prepared to hold it until its maturity date.

Considering recent market volatility, the idea of a principal-protected investment may seem appealing for investors. However, they must determine if they really need the protection PPNs offer. An investor with average or above-average tolerance for risk, and a sufficiently long time horizon, may find that a properly diversified portfolio outperforms a PPN over the long run and avoids their inherent risks, while keeping volatility at an acceptable level.

Tax Implications of PPNs

The tax treatment of these investments has generated some controversy. Principal-protected notes fall into a category known as market-linked deposit notes, which are fully eligible for investment inside registered plans. Normally, non-registered accounts attract tax on three sources of return: net realized capital gains, interest income, and dividend income. However, only the first two of these (net realized capital gains and interest income) apply to PPNs.

EXAMPLE NET REALIZABLE CAPITAL GAINS

A realized capital gain arises when an asset is sold (or otherwise disposed of) for a higher price than the owner originally paid for it (or, the adjusted cost base (ACB)). Similarly, a realized capital loss occurs when an asset is sold for a lower price than the owner originally paid for it.

When an investor realizes both capital gains and capital losses in a particular year, only the difference between the two, the net realized capital gain, is taxable. Investors can carry forward realized capital losses not used in previous years to offset capital gains in later years.

Net realized capital gains are preferable to other sources of return because they generally attract the lowest tax rate, depending upon the taxpayer's income. In Canada, only half of net realized capital gains are taxable at the investor's marginal tax rate.

TAX TREATMENT OF PPNs HELD TO MATURITY

It is generally accepted that any return from a PPN held to maturity will be taxed as interest income. For example, if a PPN originally issued with an NAV of $10 is redeemed at maturity at an NAV of $18, the $8 gain will be treated as interest in the year in which the note was redeemed.

This tax treatment is spelled out in the PPN's offering document, usually found under the heading "Certain Canadian Income Tax Considerations." An example of the wording you might find in such a document is:

> *The excess of the Maturity Redemption Amount over the Principal Amount of a Note, which is payable to a Holder, cannot be determined prior to the date on which the final NAV is determined, and the right to such excess arises only at the Maturity Date. The amount of such excess, if any, will be included in the Holder's income, as interest, in the taxation year in which the Maturity Date occurs.*

In short, a PPN held to maturity may not be tax-effective depending upon the investor's tax situation, as the return is taxed as regular income instead of the generally more tax-advantaged capital gains or dividends.

TAX TREATMENT OF PPNs REDEEMED BEFORE MATURITY

As discussed earlier, most of today's PPN products offer at least limited liquidity before maturity. Typically, PPNs can be liquidated on a weekly basis, at the discretion of the issuer or its agent. If the PPN is sold at a profit, that profit is taxed as a capital gain. If it is sold at a loss, the loss is considered to be a capital loss for tax purposes. Consequently, many investors sell or redeem their PPNs prior to maturity to maximize the tax advantages of capital gains taxation and avoid being taxed at the marginal tax rate applied to interest income.

WHAT ARE LINKED GUARANTEED INVESTMENT CERTIFICATES?

Guaranteed Investment Certificates (GICs) are a type of fixed-income security that offers fixed rates of interest for a specific term. The advantage of this product for the investor is the guarantee by the issuing institution of both principal and interest payments and the eligibility for CDIC insurance coverage for the investor. Customization in the GIC market now provides investors with more choice, for example linking the returns on a GIC to the return on an underlying stock index, mutual fund or hedge fund.

Structure of Linked GICs

Indexed-, mutual fund- and hedge fund-linked GICs combine the guarantee of the principal invested with some of the growth potential of an equity investment. With the recent market volatility and historically low interest rates, they have grown in popularity, particularly among conservative investors who are concerned with safety of capital but who are seeking yields greater than the low interest rates offered on standard interest bearing GICs or other term deposits in today's market.

These instruments offer risk-averse investors exposure to stock market returns combined with the guaranteed safety and security of a GIC. They are insured by the CDIC. They are typically offered with three- and five-year terms. They may be indexed to domestic or global indexes or to a combination of benchmarks, as well as mutual funds with various mandates and hedge funds with specific strategies. Also, they are usually non-redeemable until maturity.

While the principal is guaranteed, the total return on the instrument is not known until maturity, and this may be limited either by a maximum cap on returns or by a participation rate, depending on the issuer:

- A maximum cap on returns means the investment cannot yield more than the maximum return allowed by the issuer.

    Example: ABC Market Linked GIC is based on the performance of the S&P/TSX Composite Index. The total return on the investment is capped at a maximum of 30% — if the stock market is up 40% over the five-year term of the ABC Market Linked GIC, the maximum return the client can enjoy is 30%.

- A participation rate means the performance of the linked GIC will be equal to a predetermined percentage of the performance of the underlying asset.

    Example: ABC Market Linked GIC is based on the performance of the S&P/TSX Composite Index. The total return on the investment has a participation rate of 60% of the Index return — if the stock market is up 40% over the five-year term ABC Market Linked GIC maximum return for the investor is 24% (60% of 40%).

The caveat is that if the underlying index, mutual or hedge fund falls in value over the term the instrument is held, all that is returned to the investor is the original principal invested. Investors must, therefore, weigh the risks that the underlying asset could decline over the period that the instrument is held.

How Returns are Determined

The calculation of the overall return on a linked GIC may vary among issuers. For the sake of simplicity, we will use index-linked GICs as an example, and the following generally holds true:

The main variables used to determine the overall return include:

- The initial index level

- The ending index level

- Index growth over the term

- Any maximum cap on returns or a participation rate

As an example, let's consider the return on a five-year XYZ Market-Linked GIC that is based on the performance of the S&P/TSX Composite Index and has a 60% participation rate. A 60% participation rate means the return the investor earns will be equal to 60% of the underlying market index return. Table 24.2 illustrates the overall return on this instrument:

TABLE 24.2	OVERALL RETURN ON THE DEF MARKET LINKED GIC			
Initial Index Level	**Ending Index Level**	**Index Growth over the Period**	**Participation Rate**	**Overall Return**
8,600	12,000	39.53%	60%	23.72%

Index Growth   =   (Ending Index Level – Initial Index Level) / Initial Index Level x 100

Overall Return   =   Index Growth x Participation Rate

To calculate the total return earned over the term, simply multiply the amount of the principal invested by the Overall Return. Let's consider a $10,000 investment in the five-year ABC Market-Linked GIC.

Total interest earned   =   Principal x Overall Return

          = $10,000 x 23.72%

          = $2,372

Performance comparisons are difficult, but some features can and should be compared in determining whether to invest in index-linked GICs. Along with having different underlying benchmarks, the terms of these securities vary:

- Some tie returns to the level of the index on a particular date.

- Some base the return on the average return for a number of periods during the GIC's term.

- Others allow investors to lock in returns as of a given period.

- Still others allow early redemptions at specific dates, such as a one-year anniversary.

Although averaging provisions reduce the effect of a sharp market plunge just before maturity, they also reduce the investor's returns in a gradually rising market.

Risk Associated with Linked GICs

Linked GICs set out to boost returns by providing investors with exposure to the performance of various equity investments. Although the principal is protected, investors must accept the risks associated with an investment that tracks the performance of the stock market, a mutual or hedge fund.

For investors, the main risk scenario is what happens when there is no index or fund growth, or the index or fund falls over the term of the holding. Regardless of what happens to the underlying investment, at the end of the term, 100% of the principal will always be returned.

In most cases, investors cannot redeem these linked GICs prior to the maturity date. This type of investment is designed for investors who are prepared to hold the instrument to maturity and have a willingness to accept the risk that the investment may generate no return at all.

Tax Implications

The returns, if any, on linked GICs are classified as interest income. If the instrument is purchased outside of a registered retirement savings plan, the gains will be added to income and taxed at the investor's marginal tax rate. And because the return is deferred to the maturity of the GIC, the interest income realized is all taxed in the year of maturity. Consequently, depending upon the investor's tax situation, these linked GICs are not the most tax efficient investments and may be better suited for registered plans such as RRSPs and TFSAs.

WHAT ARE SPLIT SHARES?

A **split share** is a security that has been created by a corporation (usually an investment trust) to divide (or split) the investment attributes of an underlying portfolio of common shares into separate components that satisfy different investment objectives.

The split share corporation takes the proceeds from the sale of the split share units to investors and purchases the equivalent amount of common shares of one or more common stock issuers. The split share corporation then issues two types of shares as follows:

Preferred shares	The preferred shares receive the majority of the dividends from the common shares held by the split share corporation. Preferred shares appeal to equity investors willing to sacrifice capital gain in favour of dividend income.
Capital Shares	The capital shares receive the majority of any capital gains on the common shares. Capital shares appeal to equity investors willing to sacrifice dividend income in favour of capital gains.

In a typical split-share issue, the preferred share has a priority claim on all available dividends from the underlying portfolio of common shares. The preferred share is also entitled to a priority claim on the capital of the portfolio up to a certain value. The capital share receives all the capital appreciation on the portfolio above what the preferred share is entitled to. The capital share may also receive dividends after the preferred share dividend has been paid.

In many ways split shares are akin to two investors teaming up to buy a single stock. One investor (the preferred share investor) chooses the priority claim on the dividends in exchange for capital protection, while the other (the capital share investor) relinquishes the first claim on dividends in exchange for all the price appreciation above a certain value. The capital share investor is willing to give up dividends on the underlying common shares in exchange for a leveraged investment in those shares.

Split shares are issued for a specific term stated in the prospectus; at the end of the term the split-share company will redeem the shares. At that point, once the owners of the preferred shares have received back their principal investment and once other obligations have been paid, the capital shares receive the remaining value. Split-share terms range from three to more than 10 years.

> **EXAMPLE   HOW SPLIT SHARES ARE CREATED**
>
> Assume that the common shares of ABC Corp. trade at $50 and pay an annual dividend of $1.50 (representing a 3% dividend yield). To create a split share based on ABC Corp., an investment dealer purchases ABC's common shares and places them in an investment trust called ABC Split Corp. The trust then issues one ABC Split preferred share at a price of $25 for each ABC common share the trust holds. Holders of the preferred shares receive the entire $1.50 dividend from the ABC Corp. common share. This gives the preferred share a dividend yield of 6%, which is twice the yield on the common shares because only half as much money is required to receive the full common share dividend. In exchange for the higher yield, the preferred share is entitled to only the first $25 of the value of each ABC Corp. common share that ABC Split Corp. owns.
>
> ABC Split Corp. also issues one ABC Split capital share for each common share held in the trust. The capital share is priced at $25 and its owners are entitled to all the capital appreciation of ABC Corp. above $25 per share for the term of the split-share corporation.

Risks Associated with Split Shares

Both capital and preferred shares are influenced by the financial health of the underlying portfolio shares. Both types of shares also depend on good management of the split-share corporation – in particular, keeping costs down and monitoring the underlying portfolio vigilantly. Some managed funds use options and borrowing for investment to increase profit (i.e., leverage). Doing so increases risk for the investors, but can also improve their opportunities for profit.

CAPITAL SHARE RISKS

Capital shares are much riskier than preferred shares are. Capital shares are ranked after preferred shares in priority in the event that the split-share corporation is wound up, and they are not paid until after obligations to preferred holders and other liabilities are paid.

Inherent Leverage: Investors in capital shares can lose the entire value of their investment if the underlying portfolio of common shares declines sufficiently. Capital share investors need to be comfortable with both the investment outlook for the common shares that constitute the underlying split-share portfolio and with the capital share's leverage factor.

Volatility: Since capital shares provide a leveraged investment in a portfolio of underlying common shares, they are volatile. A study of price volatility (reported by Scotia Capital) reveals that capital shares tend to be significantly more volatile than the common shares held in the underlying portfolio and therefore carry more risk.

Dividend Cuts: Although capital shares may not receive dividends, they are susceptible to dividend cuts, especially when the corresponding preferred shares have a guaranteed dividend. A rate cut means that more portfolio shares have to be sold to pay the dividends, which results in less value for holders of capital shares.

PREFERRED SHARE RISKS

Early Closing: A split-share corporation often reserves the right to wind up earlier than the stated maturity date and redeem the shares if the asset value falls below a specific level. If the corporation is wound up, holders of preferred shares will face the prospect of finding replacement investments with comparable yields.

Early Redemption: Investors should note the risk of early redemption and, if paying a price higher than redemption value for a split preferred share, be sure to know its yield-to-call. This is necessary because investors will lose the premium when the shares are redeemed.

Credit Risk: Credit risk involves any potential change in the creditworthiness of the preferred share issuer as defined by a credit-rating agency. A reduction in the rating will tend to lower the price of preferred shares because the yield demanded by the market will increase.

Decline in Value of Underlying Portfolio: A significant decline in the value of the underlying portfolio can reduce the price of split preferred shares. However, split preferred shares are afforded a fairly generous degree of protection at issue, represented by the value of the capital share. As well, a decline in the value of the underlying common shares would have to be sustained over the life of the split preferred share. Investors can measure the amount of downside protection by comparing the split-share unit's net asset value with the redemption price of the split preferred share.

Reinvestment Risk: Investors in split preferred shares lock in a rate of return on purchase of a preferred share but are subject to reinvestment risk if the shares are redeemed prior to maturity. Investors would then be forced to seek other investments which may not provide the same yields and tax advantages of the existing structure.

Taxation Risks: An attractive feature of preferred shares is that the tax rate applied to dividend income they earn is lower than that applied to interest income. The relative appeal of this feature, however, depends on the investor's marginal tax bracket and province of residence.

Investors must be aware that preferred shares' tax rate could change if the government were to alter the shares' status as flow-through entities. The tax rules for dividends and capital gains could also change. As well, any change in taxation rates in general could alter the relative attractiveness of these shares.

Dividend Cuts: If the dividends on the underlying shares are cut or eliminated, the value of the split preferred shares is reduced, especially when the split-share dividend is tied to the portfolio dividend.

If a split preferred share has a fixed dividend, and portfolio dividends are too low to cover that dividend, portfolio shares must be sold to top up the dividend. Because this reduces the net asset value of the corporation, the downside risk of the preferred shares is increased.

Tax Implications

Split-share corporations are mutual fund corporations or trusts. This means that once they have covered all costs to running the corporation, they pay out all remaining profits to their unit holders. They pay no income tax when they pass on their net income to unit holders. The income they earn is taxed in the unit holder's hands. Thus, even if capital shares are designed to receive no income until the end of their term, they may still receive dividends from profits that are not owed to preferred holders. These profits may arise from portfolio sales required as a result of a merger or from rising dividends.

CANADIAN ORIGINATED PREFERRED SECURITIES (COPRS)

Canadian Originated Preferred Securities (COPrS) were introduced to the Canadian market in March 1999 (they are a trademark of Merrill Lynch). COPrS are long-term junior subordinated debt instruments issued by Canadian corporations. These hybrid securities offer features that resemble both long-term corporate bonds (debt) and preferred shares (equity). Similar to debt instruments, COPrS' quarterly distributions are treated as regular interest income for taxation purposes. Similar to preferred shares, COPrS trade cum dividend (an ex-date is declared) in that accrued interest is not added to the market price. COPrS rank ahead of common and preferred shares but are ranked below senior and other subordinated debt of the corporation. COPrS trade on listed stock exchanges and trade like preferred shares.

With most COPrS, the issuer has the right to defer payment for up to 20 consecutive quarterly periods. Deferred interest will accrue, but not compound. Most issues are redeemable by the issuer at a redemption price equal to 100% of the principal amount of the securities to be redeemed plus accrued and unpaid interest. Yields tend to be much higher on COPrS than on comparable fixed-income instruments to compensate investors for the advantages of the issuer.

Because payments from COPrS are treated as interest income for tax purposes, the payments do not receive the preferential dividend tax treatment. This makes them particularly suitable for inclusion in an income tax-sheltered registered account, such as an RRSP, RRIF or TFSA.

WHAT ARE ASSET-BACKED SECURITIES?

Asset securitization is a process that aggregates and transforms financial assets such as mortgages, loans and other receivables into marketable securities. Securitization dates back to the 1970s, when residential mortgages were pooled by government agencies and distributed primarily to institutional investors as fixed-income investments. By the early 1980s, the great success of this market led to the securitization of other income producing assets such as automobile loans and credit card receivables.

Numerous financial institutions use securitization to transfer the credit risk of the assets they originate from their balance sheets to investors, such as life insurance companies, pension funds and hedge funds. Given their financial expertise, these institutional investors are able and willing to assume the risk of the underlying assets and the unique characteristics of the securities in which they are "packaged". Often the incentive for the financial institution to package and sell their receivables in this way is that it reduces their need to establish capital reserves for these balance sheet assets. By relinquishing these assets, they free up capital to pursue business opportunities and make further loans.

The Securitization Process

In its most basic form, securitization is a two-step process, as follows:

1. The originator, a company with income producing assets, groups together assets it wants to remove from its balance sheet. It pools together these assets into a reference portfolio and sells them to a separate legal entity controlled by the issuer, called a **special purpose vehicle (SPV)**, which has been set up for the sole purpose of purchasing the assets to take them off the originator's balance sheet.

2. The issuer finances the purchase of these assets by the SPV by selling marketable securities, called **asset-backed securities (ABS)**, to investors such as large financial institutions, and to managers of large pools of capital such as pension plans and mutual funds.

Typically, the originator services the original income producing assets for a fee, and then passes the net amount of interest directly to the SPV. The SPV then redistributes this net amount to the various investors who own the ABS issued by the SPV. The investors receive payments, often either fixed or floating-rate.

With the cash received from the SPV, in exchange for the sale of the reference assets, the originator is now able to expand its loan or asset portfolio and repeat the securitization cycle or process once again. Conversely, the ABS investor now has a claim on the cash flows emanating from the assets owned by the SPV. These cash flows might be unique when compared to the other types of assets or securities also held by the ABS investor, which serves to diversify their investments.

The securitization process is depicted in Figure 24.1.

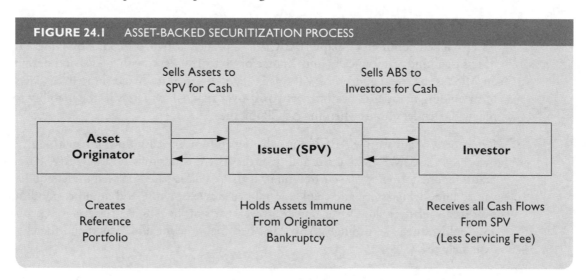

FIGURE 24.1 ASSET-BACKED SECURITIZATION PROCESS

In its most basic form, the SPV issues only one class of ABS. Accordingly, each ABS investor has a simple pro rata claim on the SPV's assets and cash flows. This claim is in direct proportion to the amount of the ABS issue each investor owns.

However, with increasing investor interest, the ABS market has become more sophisticated, and ABS design has become more complex. Most ABS securities now divide the reference portfolio into a number of classes, commonly referred to as **tranches**, each of which has different income characteristics (e.g., fixed or variable rate of return) and levels of credit risk associated with it.

These tranches are sold separately to investors who seek the appropriate risk-return opportunity from the SPV's assets.

Both the investment return (principal and interest payments) and losses are allocated among the various tranches according to their seniority in the SPV. For example:

- The most creditworthy tranche has the first claim on any income generated by the SPV.

- Until this tranche is fully paid, no other tranche is entitled to any interest payments.

- Investors in the least creditworthy tranche hope that there will be sufficient interest payments remaining to satisfy their claims when their time comes.

The standard securitization scheme assumes the following 3-tier tranche hierarchy:

- Senior
- Mezzanine
- Junior

The senior tranche, normally the largest of the three tranches, has the least amount of credit loss risk associated with it and attracts the most credit-sensitive type of investor.

The junior tranche, normally the smallest of the three tranches, has the greatest amount of credit risk and attracts a somewhat smaller group of investors who are more comfortable in assessing and taking more risk in the ABS. This tranche, however, anticipates being compensated for the higher risk with a higher rate of return than investors in the other ABS tranches.

Asset-Backed Commercial Paper

Asset-backed commercial paper (**ABCP**) is a particular type of ABS. ABCP has a maturity date of less than one year, typically in the range of 90 to 180 days, with a legal and design structure of an ABS (as discussed above). ABCP was initially designed to match short-lived assets with short term funding in order to minimize any **roll-over risk**, which refers to the inability to refinance or renew the lender's funds when the ABCP matures.

Repayment of a maturing ABCP normally depends on the cash flows emanating from the assets owned by the SPV, as well as the ability of the ABCP issuer to issue a new ABCP to replace the maturing one (or renew the current one). If the ABCP is based on well understood and easily valued underlying assets, and stable capital markets exist with good liquidity conditions, the roll-over risk is relatively low. Over time, however, parts of the ABCP market have become complex and sophisticated. Accordingly, ABCP has become more misunderstood and thereby potentially extremely risky.

EXHIBIT 24.1 CANADIAN ABCP CRISIS – *For information only*

Canada experienced its own financial crisis in 2007, when a number of issuers of non-bank managed ABCP announced that it was not possible to renew or roll-over outstanding ABCP due to unfavourable conditions in the Canadian capital markets.

Apparently, an increasing number of ABCP trusts held an ever increasing share of U.S. residential mortgage loans. As the housing and mortgage crisis grew and the news of the imploding U.S. prime market spread, investors in Canadian ABCP became concerned that Canadian ABCP issuer SPVs could face material credit losses as a direct result of their subprime mortgage exposure.

Many investors were not aware of the nature and type of investments underlying their ABCP investment. This lack of transparency is one of the hallmarks of ill-designed investment vehicles. This understanding should be of paramount concern for advisors and their clients when considering new investment vehicles such as structured products and hedge funds.

In response to deteriorating market conditions, many ABCP issuers and sponsors decided to extend the maturity date on ABCP that had extension date features. Unfortunately, most banks declined requests for liquidity on the basis that current capital market conditions did not constitute or satisfy the market disruption clauses in their liquidity guarantee agreements. This left most SPVs unable to repay holders of ABCP on their stated maturity date.

The decision by the non-bank ABCP liquidity guarantors formed the core of the Canadian ABCP crisis. The vast majority of these non-bank ABCP liquidity providers were domestic branches or affiliates of various foreign banks (Schedule II banks).

Most large Canadian Schedule I banks also issued ABCP securities, using the same bankruptcy-remote SPV structure employed by the non-bank, third-party ABCP issuers. Despite the legal remoteness of their ABCP SPVs, Schedule I banks decided to voluntarily honour all redemption and maturity-related aspects of their ABCP issues. They did this to help ensure the stability of the ABCP market, to avoid possible spillover panic into other areas of the money and short-term funding markets and to avoid reputation risk issues.

The Canadian ABCP market is divided into two parts:

• ABCP issued and guaranteed by chartered banks (Schedule I)

• ABCP issued by SPVs sponsored or guaranteed by non-banks (non-Schedule I)

At its peak in early 2007, the total Canadian ABCP market was estimated at over $120 billion. The ABCP liquidity crisis was quite extensive. The non-bank, or third-party, sponsored portion of the Canadian ABCP market was estimated at about $32 billion.

Although several factors contributed to the ABCP crisis, the three most important were as follows:

1. A mismatch between the maturity of the ABCP and the maturity dates of the associated underlying assets (in the SPV).

2. ABCP investment in assets, and derivatives on those assets, that had substantial credit risk.

3. Common product design legal terms not sufficiently clear regarding proper interpretation of non-bank, third-party liquidity guarantee clauses; in particular, a definition of *market disruption*.

Complete the following Online Learning Activity

Asset-Backed Commercial Paper (ABCP)

Canada experienced its own financial crisis in 2007, when a number of issuers of non-bank managed ABCP announced that it was not possible to renew or roll-over outstanding ABCP due to unfavourable conditions in the Canadian capital markets. This case study will provide further insight into this crisis.

 Complete the **Asset-Backed Commercial Paper (ABCP)** activity.

WHAT ARE MORTGAGE-BACKED SECURITIES?

Mortgage-backed securities (MBS) are another class of income-producing structured product.

Mortgage-backed securities (**MBSs**) are bonds that claim ownership to a portion of the cash flows from a group or pool of mortgages. They are also known as mortgage **pass-through securities**. A servicing intermediary collects the monthly payments from the issuers of the mortgages and, after deducting a fee, passes them through (i.e., remits them) to the holders of the security. The MBS provides liquidity in an otherwise illiquid market. Every month, holders receive a proportional share of the interest and principal payments associated with those mortgages.

As we learned previously, all bonds have interest rate risk. Longer term to maturity bonds have greater interest rate risk than shorter term to maturity bonds. Bond prices and interest rates are inversely related. When interest rates rise, the market price of bonds drop, and visa-versa. All bonds carry some degree of credit risk, the risk that the issuer might encounter financial difficulty and be unable to make timely payment of the bond's coupons and principal at the maturity date. However, not all bonds have **prepayment risk**, which is the risk that the issuer of the bond might prepay or redeem early some or all principal outstanding on the loan or mortgage.

Many MBS securities have prepayment risk, particularly those issued in the U.S. bond market and a portion of those issued in the Canadian market. This is due to the nature of the residential mortgages (home owners may elect to pay-down a portion of their mortgage principal) that form part of the pools of mortgages that underlie the MBS.

In both the Canadian and U.S. mortgage-backed securities market, the vast majority of the MBS are assumed to be of AAA credit quality. This is because they are issued with either an explicit or implicit government guarantee of timely payment of interest and principal in the event of delinquency or default of the borrower.

Exhibit 24.2 provides a brief look at the history of the MBS market.

EXHIBIT 24.2   BACKGROUNDER ON THE MBS MARKET – *For information only*

Mortgage-backed securities were first created in the United States in 1970 by the Government National Mortgage Association (GNMA), commonly known as Ginnie Mae. MBS securities issued by GNMA carry a *full faith and credit guarantee,* the implicit promise of timely payment of interest and principle by the federal U.S. government, no matter the underlying credit risks.

However, in addition to GNMA, the majority of all U.S. MBS are guaranteed by two U.S. government sponsored entitles (GSEs). The first of these is the Federal Home Loan Mortgage Corporation (FHLMC), commonly known as Freddie Mac. The other is the Federal National Mortgage Association (FNMA), commonly known as Fannie Mae. It is assumed that the U.S. government will support these MBS securities if either GSEs is unable to do so due to financial difficulties.

U.S. MBS were imitated in Canada by the issuance of mortgage-backed securities in 1987, insured by the Canada Mortgage and Housing Corporation (CMHC) under the National Housing Act (NHA). These are known as NHA MBSs.

Structure and Benefits of MBS

In an MBS, the security backing the mortgages is residential properties (single-family, multi-family and social housing), which are fully insured as to interest, principal and timely payment by CMHC. There is no limit to the size of holding that can be insured. These securities trade in the secondary market. Introduced in 1986, MBS issues have become a routine part of the mortgage industry.

NHA MBSs can be structured with an open or a closed pool. Because mortgages may have provisions for prepayment, which have significant effects on the cash flows and yields, MBSs are composed separately of pre-payable (open) and non-pre-payable (closed) mortgages.

In an open NHA MBS, the owners of the underlying properties can prepay the principal. Therefore, the return and pricing of open MBS is somewhat uncertain because of the unsteady or unpredictable cash flows. When interest rates are falling, it is profitable for property owners to prepay their open mortgages and refinance the property at a lower rate. The realized yields on the pre-payable MBS will be lower than expected from the interest rates on the component mortgages.

The closed mortgage pools are made up of social housing and multiple-family home mortgages. Since prepayment of principal is not allowed with closed NHA MBS, cash flows and pricing are more certain than with open mortgage pools.

The income stream of an MBS is a combination of interest and scheduled principal payments. It can also include prepayments and any prepayment penalties. Deductions are made for servicing and guarantee fees as well.

Terms of an MBS can be as short as 3-5 years or longer than 10 years. Any principal not yet prepaid at maturity is returned to the investor. Monthly payments actually occur at the 15th day of each month because of the time delay in collecting mortgage payments and calculating the new outstanding mortgage balances. This payment method has a cost at the end of term, when the remaining principal is finally returned to the holders after two weeks. A significant forgone return can be incurred on a large holding.

One of the primary benefits of a MBS is its monthly income stream, which makes it well suited to provide retirement income. Furthermore, the only part of the income stream that is taxable is the interest income part. The return of principal is not taxable. MBS are fully marketable and can be sold at market value at any time.

Investors buy an MBS because it effectively places their money in real estate (in the form of mortgages) without facing the risk of default (with the benefit of CMHC's guarantee), or the problems of collections and credit appraisal.

The most common are the five-year pools that are denominated in multiples of $5,000. MBSs earn returns that are comparable to GICs and are typically higher than Treasury bills or other Government of Canada bonds with similar terms.

Because the Government of Canada stands behind the CMHC guarantee, MBSs are roughly equal in security to Government of Canada T-bills and bonds. As such, one would expect the yields to be virtually the same as on government bonds. In fact, there is a clear yield premium on the MBS.

Table 24.3 shows the benefits and risks of NHA MBS.

TABLE 24.3	BENEFITS AND RISKS OF NHA MORTGAGE-BACKED SECURITIES
Benefits	**Risks**
• They are fully guaranteed by the Government of Canada as to principal, interest and timing of payments when held to maturity.	• The prepayment possibility on pre-payable MBSs introduces reinvestment risk. If rates decline, it may not be possible to find the same attractive yield.
• The CMHC guarantee does not limit the holding's size.	• For a pre-payable MBS issue, increased payments might be received when unscheduled payments are made by the borrowers. Extra payments may also include bonuses or penalties. Both these situations reduce future interest payments.
• Guaranteed monthly payments are provided.	
• Yields are higher than the equivalent maturity Government of Canada bonds.	• If a mortgage loan goes into default, all MBS investors may receive the full payment of the principal of a mortgage loan before the scheduled maturity date, which brings interest payments from that property to an end.
• They are very liquid.	
• A low minimum investment is required (usually $5,000).	
• They are eligible to be held within an RRSP, RRIF or a TFSA.	• Similarly, if the mortgage property is damaged, legal action may result in the liquidation of the loan from the NHA MBS pool.
	• Although MBSs are liquid, a capital loss might be incurred when they are sold, if market rates have increased and there is still a considerable time to maturity.

SUMMARY

By the end of this chapter, you should be able to:

1. Describe the features, risks and benefits of principal-protected notes (PPNs).

    *   A PPN is a debt-like instrument with a maturity date, whereby the issuer agrees to repay investors the amount originally invested (the principal) plus interest.

    *   Although many PPNs are issued by chartered banks, they are not protected by Canada Deposit Insurance Corporation (CDIC).

    *   The guarantor or issuer of the PPN is the entity that guarantees the principal at maturity. The manufacturer helps the issuer design the notes and market them to investors and distributors. The investment dealers and mutual fund dealers, which employ advisors to sell PPNs, act as distributors. The distributor receives a commission for each PPN sold.

    *   In the zero-coupon bond plus call option, the PPN issuer invests most of the proceeds in a zero-coupon bond that has the same maturity as the PPN. The zero-coupon bond guarantees the return of principal on maturity. The remainder of the proceeds is invested in a call option on the underlying asset.

    *   In a CPPI structure, the portfolio manager shifts the portfolio's allocation between a riskier asset and a risk-free asset in response to changes in interest rates and the value of the risky asset. As the value of the risky asset increases or interest rates rise, the allocation to the risky asset increases and the allocation to the risk-free asset decreases.

    *   PPNs are not appropriate for investors who rely on a regular and predicable investment income to fund their lifestyle.

    *   It is generally accepted that any return from a PPN held to maturity will be taxed as interest income.

2. Explain the structure, risks associated with and the tax implications of Index-, Mutual Fund- and Hedge Fund-Linked guaranteed investment certificates (GICs).

    *   Index-, Mutual Fund- and Hedge Fund-Linked guaranteed investment certificates (GICs) are hybrid investment products that combine the safety of a deposit instrument with some of the growth potential of an equity investment.

    *   While the principal is guaranteed, the total return on the instrument is not known until maturity, and this may be limited either by a maximum cap on returns or by a participation rate, depending on the issuer.

    *   Along with having different underlying investments or benchmarks, the terms of these securities vary. Some tie returns to the level of the index or fund on a particular date. Some base the return on the average return for a number of periods during the GIC's term.

- Although the principal is protected, investors must accept the risks associated with an investment that tracks the performance of the stock market, mutual or hedge fund.

- In most cases, investors cannot redeem these linked GICs prior to the maturity date.

- The return on linked GICs is classified as interest income. If the instrument is purchased outside of a registered retirement savings plan, the gains will be added to income and taxed at the investor's marginal tax rate.

3. Explain the structure, the risks associated with and the tax implications of split shares.

- A split share is a security that has been created to divide (or split) the investment attributes of an underlying portfolio of common shares into separate components that satisfy different investment objectives: preferred share and capital share components.

- The preferred shares receive the majority of the dividends from the common shares held by the split share corporation. This structure is of interest to equity investors seeking yield.

- The capital shares receive the majority of any capital gains on the common shares. Capital shares interest equity investors willing to sacrifice dividend income in favour of capital gains.

- The preferred share has a priority claim on all available dividends from the underlying portfolio of common shares.

- Split shares are issued for a specific term stated in the prospectus; at the end of the term the split-share company will redeem the shares.

4. Describe the features of asset-backed securities including Asset-Backed Commercial Paper and the securitization process.

- Asset securitization is a process that aggregates and transforms financial assets such as mortgages, loans and other receivables into marketable securities.

- Numerous financial institutions use securitization to transfer the credit risk of the assets they originate from their balance sheets to those investors, such as life insurance companies, pension funds and hedge funds.

- The originator of the security will group assets together to remove from its balance sheet. The assets are pooled into a reference portfolio and then sold to a separate legal entity called a special purpose vehicle. Marketable securities are then sold against the SPV.

- Most ABS securities now divide the reference portfolio into a number of classes, commonly referred to as tranches, each of which has different levels of risk and reward associated with it. These tranches are sold separately to investors who seek the appropriate risk-return opportunity from the SPV's assets.

- Asset-Backed Commercial Paper (ABCP) is a particular type of ABS — it has a maturity date of less than one year, typically in the range of 90 to 180 days, with a legal and design structure of an ABS (as discussed above).

- Repayment of a maturing ABCP normally depends on the cash flows emanating from the assets owned by the SPV, as well as the ability of the ABCP issuer to issue a new ABCP (or renew the current one).

5. Discuss the structure and benefits of mortgage-backed securities.

- Mortgage-backed securities (MBSs) are bonds that claim ownership to a portion of the cash flows from a group or pool of mortgages. They are also known as mortgage pass-through securities.

- Many MBS securities have prepayment risk, particularly those issued in the U.S. bond market and a portion of those issued in the Canadian market. This is due to the nature of the residential mortgages that form part of the pools of mortgages that underlie the MBS.

- The security backing the mortgages is residential properties (single-family, multi-family and social housing) fully insured as to interest, principal and timely payment by CMHC.

- NHA MBSs can be structured with an open or a closed pool. Because mortgages may have provisions for prepayment, which have significant effects on the cash flows and yields, MBSs are composed separately of pre-payable (open) and non-pre-payable (closed) mortgages.

Online Frequently Asked Questions

CSI has answered many frequently asked questions about this Chapter. Read through online Module 24 FAQs.

Online Post-Module Assessment

Once you have completed the chapter, take the Module 24 Post-Test.

Working With the Client

Chapter *25*

Canadian Taxation

25

Canadian Taxation

LEARNING OBJECTIVES

By the end of this chapter, you should be able to:

1. Describe the features of the Canadian income tax system, calculate income tax payable, and differentiate the tax treatment of interest, dividends and capital gains (and losses).
2. Calculate capital gains and capital losses and assess strategies for minimizing tax liability.
3. Describe and differentiate the different tax deferral plans and their uses.
4. Identify basic tax planning strategies and discuss their advantages.

TAXES AND INVESTMENTS

It is often said that there are only two certainties in life: death and taxes. Taxes are a reality of life for Canadians and they affect many personal and investment decisions. Complicating matters is the differential tax rates for income, dividends, and capital gains, not to mention continually changing legislation announced each year in the Federal Budget. The taxation of investment income also affects retirement planning through tax-favoured investments such as registered retirement savings plans (RRSPs).

Investors and advisors must have a working knowledge of the taxation of investment income. Does this mean you need to become a tax expert? No. Most advisors rely on the professional input of accountants and tax experts when a decision on a specific tax matter is needed.

So why is there a section on taxation in this course? Because understanding the basic principles and practices of taxation, and some of the key strategies and opportunities, is necessary. Ignoring this area when making investment decisions could mean more tax is paid than necessary, or that a tax planning strategy is missed. This chapter also highlights when to contact a tax expert for more specific advice. Making mistakes related to the taxation of investments can be costly and can even result in an unexpected visit to a court of law!

KEY TERMS

Annuity

Attribution rules

Canada Education Savings Grant (CESG)

Capital loss

Carrying charge

Contribution in kind

Deemed disposition

Deferred annuity

Defined Benefit Plans (DBP)

Defined Contribution Plan (DCP)

Fiscal year

Income splitting

Marginal tax rate

Money Purchase Plans (MPP)

Past Service Pension Adjustment (PSPA)

Pension Adjustment (PA)

Pooled Registered Pension Plan (PRPP)

Registered Education Savings Plan (RESP)

Registered Pension Plan (RPP)

Registered Retirement Income Fund (RRIF)

Registered Retirement Savings Plan (RRSP)

Self-directed RRSP

Spousal RRSP

Stock savings plan (SSP)

Superficial loss

Tax Free Saving Account (TFSA)

Tax loss selling

HOW DOES THE CANADIAN TAXATION SYSTEM WORK?

This section discusses the fundamentals of taxation in Canada only. Individuals seeking advice or information should seek assistance from the Canada Revenue Agency (CRA, *www.cra-arc.gc.ca*).

Proper tax planning should be a part of every investor's overall financial strategy. The minimization of tax, however, must not become the sole objective nor can it be allowed to overwhelm the other elements of proper financial management. The investor must keep in mind that it is the after-tax income or return that is important. Choosing an investment based solely on a low tax status does not make sense if the end result is a lower after-tax rate of return than the after-tax rate of return of another investment that is more heavily taxed.

While all investors wish to lighten their individual tax burden, the time and effort spent on tax planning must not outweigh the rewards reaped. Tax planning is an ongoing process with many matters being addressed throughout the year. The best tax advantages are usually gained by planning early and planning often, allowing reasonable time for the plan to work and to produce the desired results.

While the tax authorities do not condone tax evasion, *tax avoidance* by one or more of the following means is completely legitimate:

- Full utilization of allowable deductions;

- Conversion of non-deductible expenses into tax-deductible expenditures;

- Postponing the receipt of income;

- Splitting income with other family members, when handled properly; and

- Selecting investments that provide a better after-tax rate of return.

Although this discussion will highlight some of the taxation issues that affect taxpayers, none of the suggestions made here should be considered specific recommendations. As tax plays a significant part in the overall financial plan and can affect the choice of investments greatly, every attempt should be made to keep abreast of the ever-changing rules and interpretations.

The Income Tax System in Canada

The federal government imposes income taxes by federal statute (the *Income Tax Act*, often referred to as the *ITA*). All Canadian provinces have separate statutes which impose a provincial income tax on residents of the province and on non-residents who conduct business or have a permanent establishment in that province. The federal government collects provincial income taxes for all provinces except two:

- Quebec, which administers its own income tax on both individuals and corporations; and

- Alberta, which administer their own income tax on corporations.

Canada imposes an income tax on world income of its residents as well as certain types of Canadian source income on non-residents. Companies incorporated in Canada under federal or provincial law are usually considered resident of Canada. Also, foreign companies with management and control in Canada are considered resident in Canada and are subject to Canadian taxes.

TAXATION YEAR

All taxpayers must calculate their income and tax on a yearly basis. Individuals use the calendar year while corporations may choose any **fiscal year**, as long as this time period is consistent year over year. No corporate taxation year may be longer than 53 weeks.

CALCULATION OF INCOME TAX

Calculating income tax involves four steps:

- Calculating all sources of income from employment, business and investments

- Making allowable deductions to arrive at taxable income

- Calculating the gross or basic tax payable on taxable income

- Claiming various tax credits, if any, and calculating the net tax payable

Once total income has been determined, there are a number of allowable deductions and exemptions that may be made in calculating taxable income.

Types of Income

There are four general types of income. Each is treated differently under Canadian tax laws.

Employment income	Employment income is taxed on a *gross receipt basis*. This means that the taxpayer cannot deduct for tax purposes all the related costs incurred in earning income as a business does. However, employees are permitted to deduct a few employment-related expenses such as pension contributions, union dues, child care expenses and other minor items.
Capital property income	Includes assets purchased solely for investment purposes, such as stocks, bonds, and mutual funds. The income from these investments – dividends and interest for example – is considered income from capital property.
Business income:	Business income arises from the profit earned from producing and selling goods or rendering services. Self-employment income falls in this category. Business income is taxed on a *net-income basis*.
Capital gains and losses:	A capital gain or loss is the gain or loss resulting from the sale of capital property. A capital gain occurs when the property is sold at a price higher than its original cost (or lower than its cost in the case of a capital loss). Costs of the sale or disposition are also included in arriving at a capital gain or capital loss.

Calculating Income Tax Payable

Basic tax rates are applied to taxable income. Rates of federal tax applicable to individuals in 2012 (excluding tax credits) are as follows:

TABLE 25.1 FEDERAL INCOME TAX RATES FOR 2012 – *For information purposes only*	
Taxable Income:	**Tax**
• on the first $42,707	15%
• on the portion of taxable income over $42,707 and up to $85,414	22%
• on the portion of taxable income over $85,414 and up to $132,406	26%
• on the portion of taxable income over $132,406	29%

Source: Adapted from Canada Revenue Agency website: *www.cra.gc.ca*.
Readers are advised that the CRA website (*www.cra.gc.ca*) should be consulted for current tax related information.

Currently, all provinces levy their own tax on taxable income. Provincial amounts are calculated in essentially the same way as federal tax.

Adding the provincial rate to the federal rate gives the taxpayer's combined marginal tax rate. The **marginal tax rate** is the tax rate that would have to be paid on any additional dollars of taxable income earned.

Given an investor's marginal tax rate, the tax consequences of certain investment decisions can be estimated. In this way an advisor can respond to a client's need to minimize taxes and select securities for the portfolio that offer the investor a higher after-tax rate of return.

Taxation of Investment Income

INTEREST INCOME

For investments not held in registered plans taxpayers are required to report interest income (from such investments as CSBs, GICs and bonds) on an annual accrual basis, regardless of whether or not the cash is actually received.

> While the income of products like zero-coupon bonds are received only at maturity or at sale, taxes will be charged annually on these investments if they are not held inside a registered plan. IAs must be cautious about taxes due on amounts not yet received.

DIVIDENDS FROM TAXABLE CANADIAN CORPORATIONS

Individual taxpayers receive preferential tax treatment on dividends received from Canadian corporations. The preferential treatment reflects the fact that corporations pay dividends from after-tax income—i.e., from their profits. The amount included in a taxpayer's income is 'grossed-up' to equal approximately what the corporation would have earned before tax. The taxpayer then receives a tax credit that offsets the amount of tax the corporation paid.

> *For information purposes only:* There are two types of dividend tax credits available to Canadian corporations—one for privately-held and one for publicly-traded corporations. We discuss the dividend tax credit available to most Canadian publicly traded companies below.

Eligible Canadian dividends are grossed-up by 38% to arrive at the *taxable amount of the dividend* and then the taxpayer receives a federal dividend tax credit of 15.02% on this amount. Dividend tax credits are also available at varying provincial levels.

> *Example:* An individual receives a $300 eligible dividend from a Canadian corporation. The individual would report $414 ($300 × 38% plus $300 or 138% of $300) in net income for tax purposes. The additional $114 is referred to as the gross up and the $414 is the taxable amount of the dividend.
>
> The taxpayer calculates net income using the $414 amount, and can then claim a federal dividend tax credit in the amount of 15.02% of the taxable amount of the dividend, which is $62.18 in this example (15.02% × $414).

The dividend gross-up and federal tax credit are shown on the T5 form sent annually to shareholders. Who issues and sends the T5 depends on how the shares are held. Registered shareholders receive the T5 from the dividend-paying corporation itself; investment dealers holding shares in street name issue the T5 to the beneficial owners. Quite often the investment dealer will combine all dividends paid to the investor during the year and issue just one T5 for all of them.

Stock dividends and dividends that are reinvested in shares are treated in the same manner as cash dividends.

DIVIDENDS FROM FOREIGN CORPORATIONS

Foreign dividends are generally taxed as regular income, in much the same way as interest income. Individuals who receive dividends from non-Canadian sources usually receive a net amount from these sources, as non-resident withholding taxes are applied by the foreign dividend source. Such investors may be able to use foreign tax credits to offset the Canadian income tax otherwise payable. The allowable credit is essentially the lesser of the foreign tax paid or the Canadian tax payable on the foreign income, subject to certain adjustments. Details on what foreign tax is allowed as a deduction are available from the CRA.

MINIMIZING TAXABLE INVESTMENT INCOME

Dividends from taxable Canadian corporations (but not foreign corporations) are subject to less tax than interest income. Accordingly, a shift from interest bearing investments into dividend-paying Canadian stocks may reduce taxes and improve after-tax yield.

Depending on the tax rate, the tax on Canadian dividends can be higher or lower than the tax payable on capital gains. This is illustrated in Tables 25.2 and 25.3. At a marginal federal tax rate of 29%, federal taxes owed on capital gains are lower than tax owed on the same amount of Canadian dividends. But at a marginal tax rate of 22%, the taxes owed on dividends are less than taxes owing on the same amount of capital gains. In both cases, there is a substantial difference between the tax owed on interest and the tax owed on capital gains and dividends.

TABLE 25.2 COMPARISON OF TAX CONSEQUENCES OF INVESTMENT INCOME IN A 29% MARGINAL TAX BRACKET

	Interest Income	Canadian Dividend Income	Capital Gains Income
Income Received	$1,000.00	$1,000.00	$1,000.00
Taxable Income	$1,000.00	$1,380.00 (Grossed up by 38%)	$500.00 (50% of $1,000)
Federal Tax (29%)	$290.00	$400.20	$145.00
Less Dividend Tax Credit (15.02%)	–	$207.28	–
Federal Tax Owed	**$290.00**	**$192.92**	**$145.00**

TABLE 25.3 COMPARISON OF TAX CONSEQUENCES OF INVESTMENT INCOME IN A 22% MARGINAL TAX BRACKET

	Interest Income	Canadian Dividend Income	Capital Gains Income
Income Received	$1,000.00	$1,000.00	$1,000.00
Taxable Income	$1,000.00	$1,380.00 (Grossed up by 38%)	$500.00 (50% of $1,000)
Federal Tax (22%)	$220.00	$303.60	$110.00
Less Dividend Tax Credit (15.02%)	–	$207.28	–
Federal Tax Owed	**$220.00**	**$96.32**	**$110.00**

Tax-Deductible Items Related to Investment Income

CARRYING CHARGES

Tax rules permit individuals to deduct certain carrying charges for tax purposes. Acceptable carrying charge deductions include:

- Interest paid on funds borrowed to earn investment income such as interest and dividends.

- Fees for certain investment advice.

- Fees paid for management, administration or safe custody of investments.

- Safety deposit box charges.

- Accounting fees paid for the recording of investment income.

The following charges cannot be deducted from investment income:

- Interest paid on funds borrowed to buy investments that can generate capital gains only.

- Brokerage fees or commissions paid to buy or sell securities. Instead, these fees or commissions affect the cost base of the investment.

- Interest paid on funds borrowed to contribute to a registered retirement savings plan, a registered education savings plan, a registered disability savings plan, or a tax-free savings account (TFSA);

- Administration, counselling and trustee fees for regular or self-directed registered retirement savings plan or registered retirement income fund.

- Fees paid for advice such as financial planning.

BORROWED FUNDS

A taxpayer may deduct the interest paid on funds borrowed to purchase securities if:

- The taxpayer has a legal obligation to pay the interest

- The purpose of borrowing the funds is to earn income

- The income produced from the securities purchased with the borrowed funds is not tax exempt

If the interest earned on a fixed-income debt security is greater than the rate paid to borrow the funds used to purchase the security, the interest amount paid for the borrowed funds is generally deductible. However, in the case of convertible debentures, normally all carrying charges are deductible since the debentures may be converted into common shares which could theoretically pay unlimited dividends.

Complete the following Online Learning Activities

The Canadian Tax System

Tax planning is an important element of any client's financial plan. Although the financial planner is in charge of co-ordinating the overall plan, the advice of an accountant or tax specialist is essential when choosing a strategy for tax reduction and tax deferral.

 Complete the **Tax Basics** activity to review the key features of the Canadian tax system.

Calculating Tax Payable

Can you calculate how much tax is owed on income from various sources? In this short quiz you will have an opportunity to practice calculating tax payable for a fictional investor.

 Complete the **Calculating Tax Payable** quiz.

HOW ARE INVESTMENT GAINS AND LOSSES CALCULATED?

Investors and their advisors should have a general understanding of the concepts of capital gains and losses when developing an investment strategy.

A capital gain occurs when capital property, such as the shares of a company, is sold for more than its cost (i.e., the selling price is higher than the cost price).

Note: The CRA uses the technical term 'disposition' to refer to the sale of a security, capital property, etc. We use the two terms ('disposition' and 'sale') interchangeably in this chapter.

For tax purposes, however, the calculation may not be so simple because:

*   Additional costs are often involved in the purchase and sale of property other than the cost price, e.g., commissions paid on the purchase and sale of listed securities.

*   The past value of certain properties on which capital gains are calculated is difficult to determine, e.g., real estate held for many years.

Although capital gains result in an additional tax burden to the taxpayer, only part of a capital gain is taxed.

Generally, the CRA treats the sale of shares as being capital in nature. However, an exception may occur if the taxpayer's actions, indicated by intention, show that the taxpayer is in the business of trading securities to realize a speculative profit from the shares. In this case, the CRA may argue that gains realized are fully taxable as ordinary income (and losses fully deductible). Factors which the CRA would review in assessing whether trading is speculative (their definition) in nature include:

*   Short periods of ownership

*   A history of extensive buying and selling of shares or quick turnover of securities

*   Special knowledge of, or experience in, securities markets

*   Substantial investment of time spent studying the market and investigating potential purchases

- Financing share purchases primarily on margin or some other form of debt

- The nature of the shares (i.e., speculative, non-dividend type)

Although none of these individual factors alone may be sufficient for the CRA to characterize the taxpayer's trading activities as a business, a number of these factors in combination may be sufficient to do so. In every instance, the particular circumstances of the sale would need to be evaluated before a determination can be made.

Taxpayers may elect that *all* gains and losses on the sale of Canadian securities be treated as capital gains or losses during their lifetime, provided they are neither a trader nor a dealer in securities nor a non-resident. CRA interprets a *dealer* or *trader* in securities to be a taxpayer who participates in the promotion or underwriting of a particular issue of shares or who, to the public, is a dealer in shares. In general, an employee of a corporation engaged in these activities is not a dealer. If, however, as a result of employment, an employee engages in insider trading to realize a quick gain, the taxpayer will be considered to be a *trader* of those particular shares.

Disposition of Shares

The general rule of determining capital gains involves subtracting the adjusted cost base plus any costs of selling the shares from the proceeds of the sale.

Example: An investor buys 100 ABC common shares at $6, and sells the 100 shares at $10 two years later. In the year of sale, the investor's taxable capital gain would be as follows:

Gross proceeds from sale (100 × $10)		$ 1,000.00
Less:	Adjusted cost base – Cost of shares (100 × $6) including a $17 commission	$ 617.00
		$ 383.00
Less:	Commission on Sale	25.00
	Capital Gain	$ 358.00
	Taxable Capital Gain (50% of $358)	$ 179.00

Investors who receive stock dividends or who subscribe to dividend reinvestment plans must declare these as income in the year the dividend is paid. Investors should keep a record of stock dividends and reinvestments as they increase the adjusted cost base of the investment. When the stock is sold, the higher adjusted cost base will reduce any capital gain and increase any capital loss.

ADJUSTED COST BASE – IDENTICAL SHARES

The adjusted cost base of shares sold is generally composed of the purchase price plus commission expense. However, investors often own a number of the same class of shares that were bought at different prices. When a taxpayer owns identical shares in a company, the method used to calculate the adjusted cost base of such shares is known as the *average cost method*. An average cost per share is calculated by adding together the cost base of all such stock and dividing by the number of shares held.

> **Example:** An investor buys 200 ABC common at $6 in January Year I, and 100 ABC common at $9 in June of Year II. Thus, when the investor sells any of these ABC common shares, the cost base used will be the average cost, or $7 per share, calculated as follows:
>
> | | | | |
> |---|---|---|---|
> | 200 × $6 | = | $ | 1,200.00 |
> | 100 × $9 | = | $ | 900.00 |
> | Total cost | = | $ | 2,100.00 |
> | $2,100 ÷ 300 | = | | $7.00 per share |

ADJUSTED COST BASE OF CONVERTIBLE SECURITIES

When an investor exercises the conversion right attached to a security, the conversion is deemed not to be a disposition of property, and therefore no capital gain or loss arises at the time of the conversion. Instead, the adjusted cost base of the new shares acquired will be deemed to be that of the original convertible securities.

> **Example:** An investor buys 100 ABC preferred shares at a total cost of $6,000. Each preferred share is convertible into 5 ABC common shares. These securities are later converted into the common and the investor now holds 500 ABC common shares. For tax purposes, the adjusted cost base of each ABC common share is $12, calculated as follows:
>
> | | |
> |---|---|
> | Adjusted cost base of each preferred share (composed of original cost plus commission) : | $60 |
> | Number of common shares acquired through conversion of one preferred share : | 5 shares |
> | Adjusted cost base of one common share ($60 ÷ 5): | $12 per share |

ADJUSTED COST BASE OF SHARES WITH WARRANTS OR RIGHTS

Investors acquire warrants and rights in one of three ways:

- Through direct purchase in the market

- By owning shares on which a rights offering is made

- By purchasing a unit of securities (e.g., a bond with warrants attached)

The method by which warrants and rights are acquired is important because there is a different tax treatment for the shares acquired when the warrants or rights are exercised.

Direct purchase of warrants and rights: In this case, the tax treatment is the same as that discussed above under convertible securities.

Rights received from direct share ownership: The cost base of the original shares purchased must be adjusted in this case.

When the warrants or rights are not exercised: Warrants and rights are not always exercised. Instead, the investor may sell them in the open market or allow them to expire. If the warrants and rights were directly purchased, the capital loss would equal the purchase cost plus commission. If the warrants and rights were acquired at zero cost, there is neither a capital gain nor loss.

If the warrants and rights were received at zero cost and then sold in the open market, their cost would be considered to be zero and all the profits realized would be taxed as capital gains.

Disposition of Debt Securities

For tax purposes, *debt securities* include bonds, debentures, bills, notes, mortgages, hypothec and similar obligations. (A Canada Savings Bond or a provincial savings bond cannot generate a capital gain or loss because such bonds do not fluctuate in value and either mature or are redeemed at par.)

If the seller of a debt security is in the business of trading securities, proceeds from the sale must be included in business income, which is taxed as income. However, the sale or redemption of a debt security by an ordinary taxpayer often produces a capital gain or capital loss.

Capital gains and losses on debt securities are determined in the usual manner (i.e. proceeds of sale less adjusted cost base and expenses of the sale). At the time of disposition, a debt security may have accrued interest owing. Accrued interest is not included in the capital gains calculation. Rather, interest at the date of sale is income to the vendor and may be deducted from interest subsequently received by the purchaser when reporting income on an income tax return.

Example: An investor buys $1,000 principal amount of a 10% bond at par and has to pay accrued interest of $80 at the time of purchase.

$1,000 principal amount of 10% bonds @ $100	$ 1,000
Plus: Accrued interest	80
Total cost	$ 1,080

The buyer includes, as investment income for the year of purchase, net interest income of $20 from the bond ($100 interest for the year less $80 accrued interest paid to the seller). When the buyer later sells the bond, the adjusted cost base is $1,000 – not $1,080.

The seller of the bond includes for the year of sale investment income of $80 accrued interest that was received from the sale and any other interest received from owning the bond during the year. On the same return, the proceeds of disposition of $1,000 are used to calculate a capital gain or loss.

Capital Losses

A **capital loss** is the result of selling a security for less than its purchase price. Capital losses are calculated in the same manner as capital gains. They can only be deducted from capital gains in most circumstances. However, two additional factors involved in capital losses are important.

WORTHLESS SECURITIES

When a security becomes worthless, the security holder must fill out a form (from the CRA) electing to declare the security worthless, so that a capital loss can be realized for tax purposes. Of course, the tax rule does not apply to instruments that have an expiry date such as warrants, rights or options. Capital losses for such securities, which have expired, may be claimed without any declaration being signed.

One exception to the rule above occurs when a security becomes worthless due to bankrupcy (or under certain conditions, insolvency) of the underlying company. In this situation the *Income Tax Act* deems the taxpayer to have disposed of the security for nil proceeds and reacquired it at a cost of nil.

SUPERFICIAL LOSSES

A **superficial loss** occurs when securities sold at a loss are repurchased within 30 calendar days before or after the sale and are still held at the end of 30 days after the sale. Superficial losses are *not* tax deductible as a capital loss. The tax advantage may not be totally lost but, in most cases, is simply deferred.

The superficial loss rules are intended to make it more difficult for taxpayers to sell and re-purchase assets solely for the purpose of creating deductible capital losses. The rules are designed to avoid situations where taxpayers do not have the full intent of selling a stock and are only doing so temporarily to obtain a capital loss.

Example: An investor buys 100 XYZ shares at $30 in mid April and later sells the shares at $25 on May 1. He incurs a $500 capital loss ($3,000 - $2,500). Normally an allowable capital loss of $250 (50% of $500) would be deductible against taxable capital gains. However, the superficial loss rules would apply in the following two scenarios:

• On May 15, the investor decides to repurchase 100 XYZ shares at a price close to the $25 sale price and hold the shares until July. Because the transaction takes place within 30 days after the sale on May 1 and the shares are held 30 days after the original sale, the loss is considered a superficial loss, not a capital loss and is not deductible against taxable capital gains.

• On April 29, the investor decides to purchase an additional 100 shares of XYZ near the initial $30 purchase price and hold the shares until July. He then carries out the sale of the 100 XYZ shares on May 1 at $25. Since the same shares were purchased less than 30 days before the sale on May 1 and owned for at least 30 days after the original sale, this loss is also considered a superficial loss.

Tax rules for superficial losses apply not only to trades made by the investor but also a person affiliated with the investor including:

- The investor's spouse or common-law spouse; or

- Corporations controlled by the investor and/or spouse.

- Trust in which the investor is a majority interest beneficiary

Although superficial losses are non-deductible for tax purposes, in most cases the taxpayer eventually receives the tax benefit of the superficial loss when the investment is sold. The amount of the superficial loss is added to the cost of the repurchased shares, thereby reducing the ultimate capital gain.

> **Example:** (using the previous example) If the investor's $500 capital loss had been a superficial loss and the shares were repurchased at $25 before May 31, the loss of $5 per share would be added to the cost of each XYZ share (100 in this example) owned on May 31. By so doing, the potential future amount of the capital gain is reduced.

If, later, 100 XYZ is sold at $40 per share, the capital gain is calculated as follows:

Proceeds from disposition (100 × $40)			$ 4,000.00
Less:	Cost of repurchasing shares (100 × $25)	$ 2,500.00	
	Commission on purchases	45.00	
	Superficial loss (100 × $5)	500.00	3,045.00
			$ 955.00
Less:	Commission on sale		60.00
	Capital gain		$ 895.00
	Taxable capital gain (50% of $895)		$ 447.50

Superficial losses do not apply, however, to losses which result from leaving Canada (emigration), death of a taxpayer, the expiry of an option, or a deemed disposition of securities by a trust or a sale of securities to a controlled corporation (A deemed disposition is a disposition assumed to have occurred even though an actual sale did not take place).

Tax Loss Selling

A decision to hold or sell a security should be based on the investor's expectations for that security. However, in some circumstances, taxes may also be a consideration. For example, an investor may own shares whose market price has declined and the forecast is limited with no potential for appreciation in the immediate future. By selling the shares at this time, the investor creates a capital loss which can be used to reduce capital gains from other securities. Proceeds from the sale can then be re-invested in more attractive securities.

When a tax loss sale looks advantageous without breaching investment principles, a taxpayer should consider the following factors:

- If subsequent repurchase is planned, the timing of the sale and repurchase must be carefully scheduled to avoid a superficial loss.

- For tax purposes, the settlement date (usually three business days after the transaction date) is the date on which transfer of ownership takes place. This is an important tax rule for investors to remember when making securities sales near the end of a calendar year. For example, an investor who sells a stock on the last day of December does not incur a capital loss for the taxation year in which the sale occurred. The loss would apply to the next taxation year, since the settlement date would be in early January.

Complete the following Online Learning Activities

Calculating Investment Gains and Losses

To determine the tax treatment of capital gains and losses, investors first need to understand how the Canada Revenue Agency calculates the gain or loss. In this activity, you will review the calculations required to determine the taxable portion of a gain (or loss) and then apply the calculations in various scenarios.

 Complete the **Calculating Investment Gains and Losses** activity.

 Complete the **Calculating Investment Gains and Losses** quiz.

WHAT ARE TAX DEFERRAL PLANS?

The principle of tax deferral plans is to encourage Canadians to save for retirement by enabling them to reduce taxes paid during high earning (and high taxpaying) years. Tax payment is deferred until retirement years when income and tax rates are normally lower.

The most common tax deferral vehicles are explained below.

Registered Pension Plans (RPPs)

A **registered pension plan** (**RPP**) is a trust, registered with CRA or the appropriate provincial agency, which is established by a company to provide pension benefits for its employees when they retire. Both employer and employee contributions to the plan are tax-deductible.

Tax-assisted retirement savings plans, regardless of the timing of the contributions, or the contributor (employee or employer), use a uniform contribution level of 18% of earned income as the amount that can be contributed towards retirement to a maximum dollar amount per year, depending on the type of plan. It is necessary for the taxpayer to determine the contributions made to, or the value of the benefit accruing to an employee from registered pension plans.

The amount determined is called the **Pension Adjustment** (**PA**). The PA reduces the amount an individual can contribute to a registered retirement savings plan (RRSP) so that the annual contribution limit, on all plans combined, is not exceeded. Employers, or administrators of pension plans, report a plan member's PA on the employee's T4.

Employers may upgrade employee pension plans within certain limits by making changes to existing pension plans or by introducing new plans. When an upgrade occurs, an employer may make additional contributions to an employee plan due to the increased benefits. This amount, calculated as the difference between the old plan PA and the new plan PA, is called the **Past Service Pension Adjustment** (**PSPA**). The PSPA also reduces the amount an employee can contribute to an RRSP.

Investors do not have to contribute the maximum contribution allowed on all plans combined in any given year. If an investor does not contribute the maximum allowed carry-forward provisions will permit the individual to make up the deficient contributions, called "RRSP Carry Forward Room", in future years.

In general terms, there are two types of RPPs – **money purchase plans** (**MPP**) and **defined benefit plans** (**DBP**). In a MPP (also known as a **defined contribution plan** (**DCP**)) the contributions to the plan are predetermined and the benefits, at retirement, will depend on how the contributions were invested. In a DBP the benefits are predetermined based on a formula including years of service, income level and other variables, and the contributions will be those necessary to fund the predetermined plan benefits.

The maximum tax-deductible employee and employer contributions are as follows:

MONEY PURCHASE PLANS

The combined employer/employee contributions cannot exceed the lesser of:

*   18% of the employee's current year compensation; and

*   The MPP contribution limit (which is indexed annually to inflation).

DEFINED BENEFIT PLANS

The combined employer/employee contributions will be deductible up to the amount recommended by a qualified actuary so that the plan is adequately funded. The current DBP limits are designed to provide an employee a maximum pension of 2% of pre-retirement earnings per year of service. The current limit is indexed to inflation. The actual benefits an employee receives depends on the terms of the pension plan.

In addition, the employee current service contributions are restricted to the lesser of:

*   9% of the employee's compensation for the year; and

* $1,000 plus 70% of the employee's PA for the year.

Registered Retirement Savings Plans (RRSPs)

Registered Retirement Savings Plans (**RRSPs**) are available to individuals to defer tax and save for retirement years. Annual contributions are tax-deductible up to allowable limits. Income earned in the plan accumulates tax-free as long as it remains in the plan.

Essentially there are two types of RRSPs: Single Vendor RRSPs and Self-Directed RRSPs. There are no limits as to the number of plans a person can hold. Funds can be transferred tax-free from plan to plan if the taxpayer/investor so desires. This is accomplished by completing a transfer document with the trustee of the new plan. The documents are then forwarded to the original plan's trustee.

Single Vendor Plans: In these plans, the holder invests in one or more of a variety of GICs, segregated pooled funds or mutual funds. The investments are held in trust under the plan by a particular issuer, bank, insurance company, credit union or trust company. To qualify as acceptable investments for an RRSP (either Single Vendor or Self-Directed), pooled funds must be registered with the CRA. In Single Vendor RRSPs, no day-to-day investment decisions are required to be made by the holder. There may be a trustee fee charged for this type of plan in addition to any costs incurred for purchasing the investments themselves.

Self-Directed Plans: In these, holders invest funds or contribute certain acceptable assets such as securities directly into a registered plan. The plans are usually administered for a fee by a Canadian financial services company. One advantage of Self-Directed RRSPs is that investors can make all investment decisions. Another advantage is that, while there are rules with respect to allowable content, a full range of securities may be held in these plans, including GICs, money market instruments, bonds, equities and mutual funds. Investors may also hold direct foreign investments in these RRSPs.

There are special features that the investor should understand about an RRSP account. First, an RRSP is a trust account designed to benefit the owner at retirement. Withdrawals from an RRSP are subject to a graduated withholding tax and such withdrawals must be included in income in the year withdrawn. More tax may be payable at year-end, depending on the income level of the taxpayer. Second, an RRSP cannot be used as collateral for loan purposes.

CONTRIBUTIONS TO AN RRSP

There is no limit to the number of RRSPs an individual may own. However, there is a restriction on the amount that may be contributed to RRSPs on a per-year basis. The maximum annual tax deductible contributions to RRSPs an individual can make is the lesser of:

- 18% of the previous year's earned income; and

- The RRSP dollar limit for the year.

From the lesser of the above two amounts:

- Deduct the previous year's PA and the current year's PSPA.

- Add the taxpayer's unused RRSP contribution room at the end of the immediately preceding taxation year.

The RRSP dollar contribution limit is $22,970 in 2012. The limit is indexed to inflation each year. The contributions must be made in the taxation year or within 60 days after the end of that year to be deductible in that year.

Individuals can carry forward unused contribution limits indefinitely.

Earned income for the purpose of RRSP contributions may be simply defined as the total of:

- Total employment income (less any union or professional dues)

- Net rental income and net income from self-employment

- Royalties from a published work or invention and research grants

- Some alimony or maintenance payments ordered by a court

- Disability payments from CPP or QPP

- Supplementary Employment Insurance Benefits (SEIB), such as top-up payments made by the employer to an employee who is temporarily unable to work (for parental or adoption leave, for example), but not the Employment Insurance (EI) benefits paid by Human Resources and Social Development Canada

Planholders who make contributions to RRSPs in excess of the amount permitted by legislation may be subject to a penalty tax. Over-contributions of up to $2,000 may be made without penalty. A penalty tax of 1% per month is imposed on any portion of over-contribution that exceeds $2,000.

A planholder may contribute securities already owned to an RRSP. According to the CRA, this contribution is considered to be a **deemed disposition** at the time the contribution is made. Consequently, in order to calculate the capital gain or loss, the planholder must use the fair market value of the securities (The fair market value is the price at which the property would sell for on the open market) at the time of contribution as the proceeds from disposition. Any resulting capital gain is included in income tax for the year of contribution. Any capital loss is deemed to be nil for tax purposes. This type of contribution is called a **contribution in kind**.

> *Example:* Mr. Wu bought 100 shares of Grow Stock Inc. shares at a price of $10 for a total value of $1,000. Two years later, the shares have increased in value to $20 per share.
>
> Mr. Wu decides to contribute the shares to his self-directed RRSP when the fair market value of the shares is $20.
>
> - The contribution to the RRSP would be the fair market value of the securities. So the contribution would be $2,000 to his RRSP. His RRSP would now hold the shares.
>
> - Because Mr. Wu had an accrued capital gain of $1,000 ($2,000 fair market value - $1,000 cost =$1,000 gain), he must include that capital gain in his taxes for the year, even though he still owns the shares.

SPOUSAL RRSPs

A taxpayer may contribute to an RRSP registered in the name of a spouse or common-law spouse and still claim a tax deduction. If the taxpayer is also a planholder, he or she may contribute to the spouse's plan only to the extent that the contributor does not use the maximum contribution available for his or her own plan.

Example: Sofie and Nigel are married and contribute to RRSPs. Sofie has a maximum contribution limit of $11,500 for her own RRSP, but contributes only $10,000, she may contribute $1,500 to Nigel's spousal RRSP. Nigel's RRSP contribution limits are not affected by the spousal RRSP, which is a separate plan. (Therefore, Nigel, in this example, would have two plans: one for personal contributions and one for contributions made by Sofie *on his behalf.*)

Unless converted to a Registered Retirement Income Fund (RRIF) or used to purchase certain acceptable annuities, the withdrawal from a spousal plan is taxable income to the spouse – not the contributor – since the spousal RRSP belongs to the spouse in whose name it is registered. However, any withdrawals of contributions to a spousal plan claimed as a tax deduction by a contributing spouse made:

• In the year the contribution is made, or

• In the two calendar years prior to the year of withdrawal,

  are taxable to the contributor in the year of withdrawal rather than to the planholder.

Example: In each of six consecutive years, a husband contributes $1,000 to his wife's RRSP, which he claims as tax deductions. In the seventh year there are no contributions, and the wife de-registers the plan. Thus, for the seventh taxation year:

• The husband includes as taxable income in his tax return the sum of $2,000 (contributions: 7th year – nil; 6th year – $1,000; 5th year – $1,000); and

• The wife includes as taxable income in her tax return the sum of $4,000 (i.e., contributions to the plan made in years 1, 2, 3 and 4) plus all earnings that accumulated on the total contributions of $6,000 in the plan.

OTHER TYPES OF CONTRIBUTIONS

Some pension income can be transferred directly to RRSPs. The following transfers can be contributed without affecting the regular tax-deductible contribution limits outlined elsewhere:

• Lump sum transfers from RPPs and other RRSPs, if transferred to the individual's RRSP on a direct basis, are not included in income and no deduction arises.

• Allowances for long service upon retirement often known as retiring allowances, for each year of service, under very specific guidelines.

TERMINATION OF RRSPs

An RRSP holder may make withdrawals or de-register the plan at any time but mandatory de-registration of an RRSP is required *during the calendar year when an RRSP plan holder reaches age 71.*

The following maturity options are available to the plan holder in the year he or she turns 71:

• Withdraw the proceeds as a lump sum payment which is fully taxable in the year of receipt;

• Use the proceeds to purchase a life annuity.

• Use the proceeds to purchase a fixed term annuity which provides benefits to a specified age;

- Transfer the proceeds to a Registered Retirement Income Fund (RRIF) which provides an annual income; or

- A combination of the above.

RRIFs, fixed-term annuities and life annuities, available from financial institutions which offer RRSPs, permit the taxpayer to defer taxation of the proceeds from de-registered RRSPs. Tax is paid only on the annual income received each year.

Should the annuitant die, benefits can be transferred to the annuitant's spouse. Otherwise, the value of any remaining benefits must be included in the deceased's income in the year of death. Under certain conditions, the remaining benefits may be taxed in the hands of a financially dependent child or grandchild, if named as beneficiary. The child or grandchild may be entitled to transfer the benefits received to an eligible annuity, an RRSP or an RRIF.

If a person dies before de-registration of an RRSP, the surviving spouse may transfer the plan proceeds tax-free into his or her own RRSP as long as the spouse is the beneficiary of the plan. If there is no surviving spouse or dependent child, the proceeds from the plan are taxed in the deceased's income in the year of death.

ADVANTAGES OF RRSPs

The following are some of the advantages provided by RRSPs:

- A reduction in annual taxable income during high taxation years through annual tax-deductible contributions;

- Shelter of certain lump sum types of income from taxation through tax-free transfer into an RRSP;

- Accumulation of funds for retirement, or some future time, with the funds compounding earnings on a tax-free basis until withdrawal;

- Deferral of income taxes until later years when the holder is presumably in a lower tax bracket;

- Opportunity to split retirement income (using spousal RRSPs) which could result in a lower taxation of the combined income and the opportunity to claim two, $2,000 pension tax credits.

DISADVANTAGES OF RRSPs

The following are some of the disadvantages provided by RRSPs:

- If funds are withdrawn from an RRSP, the planholder pays income tax (not capital gains tax) on the proceeds withdrawn;

- The RRSP holder cannot take advantage of the dividend tax credit on eligible shares that are part of an RRSP;

- If the plan holder dies, all payments out of the RRSP to the planholder's estate are subject to tax as income of the deceased, unless they are to be received by the spouse or, under certain circumstances, a dependent child or grandchild;

- The assets of an RRSP cannot be used as collateral for a loan.

Registered Retirement Income Funds (RRIFs)

As explained previously, a RRIF is one of the tax deferral vehicles available to RRSP holders who wish to continue the tax sheltering of their plans. The planholder transfers the RRSP funds into a RRIF. Each year (beginning with the year following acquisition of the RRIF) the planholder must withdraw and pay income tax on a fraction of the total assets in the fund, the "annual minimum amount". The assets are composed of capital plus accumulated earnings. The annual amount is determined by a table designed to provide benefits to the holder until death. The term of the RRIF may be based on the age of the holder's spouse (if younger) instead of the planholder's own age to extend the term, and reduce the amount of the required withdrawal.

While there is a minimum amount that must be withdrawn each year, there is no maximum amount.

A taxpayer can own more than one RRIF. Like a RRSP, a RRIF may be self-directed by the holder through instructions to the financial institution holding the RRIF, or it may be managed. A wide variety of qualified investment vehicles within the Canadian content framework are available for self-directed plans including stocks, bonds, investment certificates, mutual funds and mortgages.

RRIFs started prior to 1993 are paid out according to a prescribed schedule, which differs from the schedule for those started after 1992. Contact the Canada Revenue Agency for further information.

Deferred Annuities

An **annuity** is an investment contract through which the holder deposits money to be invested in an interest-bearing vehicle that will return not only interest but also a portion of the capital originally invested. With **immediate annuities**, payments to the holder start immediately. With **deferred annuities**, payments start at a date specified by the investor in the contract. Both types of annuities can be paid for in full at the beginning of the contract. The deferred annuity can also be paid for in monthly instalments until the date the annuity will begin payment.

Contributions to a deferred annuity, unlike those to an RRSP, do not reduce current taxable income since contributions are not tax deductible.

The annuitant is taxed only on the interest element of the annuity payments and not on the capital portion. This is because the annuity is purchased with after-tax income. This contrasts with annuities bought with money from RRSPs. In this case, the full annuity payment is taxable because the principal cost of the annuity was not taxed when deposited to the RRSP.

However, some deferred annuities may be registered as RRSPs. Investments in such annuities, within RRSP contribution limits, are deductible from income for tax purposes in the year deposited. The proceeds are fully taxable.

Since the interest earned during the accumulation phase is taxable on an annual basis outside a registered plan, deferred annuities are usually purchased with registered funds.

Deferred annuities are available only through life insurance companies.

Tax-Free Savings Accounts (TFSA)

The **Tax-Free Savings Account** (**TFSA**) is an entirely new kind of savings vehicle. Since coming into existence at the start of 2009, TFSAs have been welcomed by commentators as the most exciting financial planning and wealth management tool for individual Canadians since RRSPs were introduced in 1957. That's primarily because income earned within a TFSA will not be taxed in any way throughout an individual's lifetime. In addition, there are no restrictions on the timing or amount of withdrawals from a TFSA, and the money withdrawn can be used for any purpose.

BASIC RULES

Any resident of Canada who is at least 18 years of age can open a TFSA. You don't have to have earned any income in the preceding or current year to be able to contribute to a TFSA. The money you contribute can come from a tax refund, a bequest, savings, a gift, or earnings from employment or business. The TFSA contribution was limited to $5,000 a year starting in 2009. After 2009, the contribution amount is indexed to inflation and rounded to the nearest $500. The annual 2013 TFSA contribution limit is $5,500. Whenever you don't make the full annual contribution, you can carry forward that "contribution room" and use it any time in the future.

TAXES

While the money contributed to a TFSA is not tax-deductible, there is no tax payable on the income earned in the TFSA – whether it be interest, dividends or capital gains.

QUALIFIED INVESTMENTS

Individuals can invest the amounts in a TFSA in a wide variety of products such as GICs, savings accounts, stocks, bonds or mutual funds. The kinds of investments you can put in a TFSA are basically the same as the ones you can put in an RRSP. These are called "qualified investments."

CONTRIBUTIONS

Your contribution room every year consists of the TFSA dollar limit for that year ($5,000 in 2009) plus any withdrawals you made in the preceding year, along with any unused contribution room. Based on information provided by the issuer, the Canada Revenue Agency (CRA) will determine the TFSA contribution room for each eligible individual. Your annual contribution room will be indicated on your notice of assessment. If you contribute more than your contribution room allows, you will be taxed at the rate of 1% of the excess contribution every month.

WITHDRAWALS

Withdrawals can be made from a TFSA at any time. There is no limit to how much may be withdrawn and there is no penalty or tax on withdrawals. If you wish, you can later replace/re-contribute the money you have withdrawn, but you don't have to. If you have unused TFSA contribution room, you could replace/re-contribute the amount you withdrew in the same calendar year (up to the amount of unused TFSA contribution room available). If you do not have unused TFSA contribution room then you must wait until the next calendar year to replace/re-contribute the amount you withdrew. If you do want to replace/re-contribute the money you withdrew, there's no deadline for doing so.

A TFSA is a versatile and user-friendly type of account that makes it appealing to save, because the income earned in the account is never taxed, there is a lot of flexibility in making contributions and withdrawals and all residents over the age of 18 can set one up.

Because the rules let you withdraw money and then replace/re-contribute it (in a future calendar year if you currently do not have unused TFSA contribution room) without being taxed, a TFSA is a good way to save for a variety of expenditures at different stages of a person's life: tuition fees, repayment of student loans, a wedding, a holiday, a new car, a house, or even increasing the value of the estate you leave to your heirs. Basically, a TFSA can benefit you through your entire adult life cycle. Also, you could put aside the maximum yearly contribution as an emergency fund.

Registered Education Savings Plans (RESPs)

Registered Education Savings Plans (RESPs) are tax-deferred savings plans intended to help pay for the post-secondary education of a beneficiary. Although contributions to a plan are not tax-deductible, there is a tax-deferral opportunity since the income accumulates tax-deferred within the plan. On withdrawal, the portion of the payments that were not original capital will be taxable in the hands of the beneficiary or beneficiaries, provided that they are enrolled in qualifying or specified educational programs. The assumption is that, at the time of withdrawal, the beneficiaries or beneficiary would be in a lower tax bracket than the contributor. Consequently, withdrawals from the plan should be taxed at a lower rate.

There is no maximum amount that can be contributed in a single calendar year for each beneficiary. However, there is a lifetime maximum contribution of $50,000 per beneficiary. Contributions can be made for up to 31 years but the plan must be collapsed within 35 years of its starting date. This time limitation requires contributors to decide when would be the best time to start the plan.

There are two types of RESPs, pooled plans and self-directed plans. As their name suggests, pooled or group plans are plans to which a number of subscribers make contributions for their beneficiaries. The pooled funds are managed, usually conservatively, by the plan administrators. Annual contributions are generally pre-set. Under group plans, the administrator determines the amount paid out to beneficiaries.

Self-directed plans are administered by a number of institutions including banks, mutual fund companies, and investment brokers. Contributions tend to be more flexible and contributors can participate in both the investment and distribution decisions.

More than one beneficiary can be named in any particular plan. These "family" plans are often used by families with more than one child. If one of the named beneficiaries does not pursue post-secondary education, all of the income can be directed to the beneficiaries who do attend.

The contributor (versus the beneficiary) can withdraw the income from an RESP provided that the plan has been in existence more than 10 years and that none of the named beneficiaries has started qualified post-secondary programs by age 21 or all of the named beneficiaries have died.

If the beneficiaries do not attend qualifying programs, contributors are allowed to transfer a maximum of $50,000 of RESP income to their RRSPs. This is dependent on there being sufficient contribution room remaining in the RRSP. No taxes are charged on contributions that were made to the RESP when they are withdrawn, but revenues earned on the contributions made to the plan will be taxed at the contributor's regular income tax level, plus an additional penalty tax of 20%.

If the contributor (as opposed to the beneficiary) starts to withdraw income from the RESP, the plan must be terminated by the end of February of the following year.

CANADA EDUCATION SAVINGS GRANTS (CESGs)

Canada Education Savings Grants (**CESGs**) provide further incentive to invest in RESPs. Under this program, the federal government makes a matching grant of 20% of the first $2,500 contributed each year to the RESP of a child under 18. Depending on family income, an additional CESG is available over and above the basic CESG amount.

Worth between $500 and $600 per year (enhancements have been made to the program— see below), this grant is forwarded directly to the RESP firm and does not count towards the contributor's lifetime contribution limit. The lifetime grant a beneficiary can receive is $7,200. However, CESGs must be repaid if the child does not go on to a qualifying post-secondary institution.

Table 25.4 provides an example of the CESG program.

TABLE 25.4	CANADA EDUCATION SAVINGS GRANTS PROGRAM			
	Basic CESG			**Total CESG**
	Contribution	**%**	**$**	
All families	$2,500	20%	$500	$500
	Additional CESG			**Total CESG**
Families earning*:	**On the First:**	**%**	**$**	
Under $42,708	$500	20%	$100	$600
Between $42,708 and $85,414	$500	10%	$50	$550

* For 2012.
Source: Adapted from Human Resources and Skill Development Canada website

Thus, a family earning under $42,708 that contributes $2,500 per beneficiary in a year will receive a CESG of $600 a year per beneficiary — 20% on the $2,500 from the basic CESG and an additional 20% on the first $500 invested in the program ($2,500 × 20% + $500 × 20%).

Pooled Registered Pension Plans (PRPPs)

Pooled Registered Pension Plans (**PRPPs**) are a new type of retirement savings plan *proposed* by the federal government. PRPPs are designed to address the gap in employer pension plan coverage by providing Canadians with an accessible, large-scale and low-cost pension plan. PRPPs will hold assets pooled together from multiple participating employers, allowing workers to take advantage of lower investment management costs that result from membership in a large pooled pension plan. PRPPs will be administered by eligible financial institutions such as banks and insurance companies. This design reduces the risk and cost that employers would normally bare when offering a retirement plan for employees.

Participation in a PRPP would include employees of an employer (with as few as two employees) that offers a PRPP, individuals who work for an employer that does not offer a PRPP, and self-employed individuals.

A PRPP can be designed to permit members to make their own investment decisions, or to select from investment options, provided by the plan administrator, that include varying levels of risk and reward based on investor profiles.

Much like an RRSP, contributions to a PRPP would be limited to available contribution room based on earned income, and contributions would be tax deductible.

> The federal government is currently in the final stages of bringing the *Pooled Registered Pension Plans Act* into force (as of the time of writing in late fall 2012). The *Act* will apply to federally regulated companies. The federal government intends for the plan to be available to Canadians sometime in 2013 as soon as the provinces and territories pass their respective legislation to allow provincially regulated employers to participate in the plan alongside federally regulated companies.

Complete the following Online Learning Activities

Tax-Deferral Plans

Canadians can lower their tax burden and defer tax payments in a number of different ways including: registered pension plans (RPPs), registered retirement savings plans (RRSPs), registered retirement income funds (RRIFs), tax-free savings account (TFSA), and registered education savings plans (RESPs). In this exercise, you will review the various tax-deferral plans and the advantages of using such plans to reduce taxes and increase wealth.

 Complete the **Tax-Deferral Plans** activity.

 Complete the **Tax-Deferral Plans** quiz.

WHAT ARE TAX PLANNING STRATEGIES?

Income splitting is a tax savings strategy that involves transferring income from a family member in a higher tax bracket to a spouse, to children or to parents in a lower tax bracket so that the same income is taxed at a lower rate. However, as a result of tax law changes, the ability to split income in this manner now has limited applicability.

The use of spousal RRSPs is an effective method of income splitting. Other methods of income splitting include the use of family trusts, partnerships, small business corporations and investment holding companies. As there are many technicalities involved in establishing these structures, professional advice should be sought. These techniques are covered in more advanced courses offered by CSI, such as the *Wealth Management Essentials Course.*

The following strategies offer other planning opportunities in addition to income splitting.

Transferring income: Transferring income to family members can trigger what are called **attribution rules**. If property or income-producing assets are transferred from the taxpayer to other family members, the tax consequences may be passed back to the taxpayer. There is one exception to these rules and that occurs in the event of a marriage breakdown. If the married couple is living apart, the attribution rules relating to income and capital gains do not apply.

Both income and capital gains received by an individual from property transferred from or loaned by his or her spouse are attributed to the transferor unless the transfer is made for fair market value. If the transfer is made by way of a loan, the loan must bear interest. This rate cannot be less than the prescribed rates published by CRA. In addition, the interest must actually be paid within 30 days after the particular year to which the interest relates.

Paying expenses: When both spouses have earnings, non-deductible expenses are not always paid in a tax effective manner. Instead of using funds for investment purposes, the higher-income spouse should first pay all family expenses while the lower-income spouse invests as much of his/her income as practical. Thus the lower-income spouse should be able to maintain a larger investment portfolio for earning income. Presumably this income will be taxed at a lower rate than if earned by the other spouse.

Making loans: As discussed above, the attribution rules do not apply when money is loaned and interest is charged at a rate prescribed by CRA and paid within 30 days after the year-end. When an investment can be expected to generate earnings in excess of this interest, it is often worthwhile for the higher-income family member to loan funds, at the appropriate interest rate, to the lower-income family member. The lower-income individual would then purchase the investment. This would result in the excess of the investment earnings, over the interest charged, to be effectively transferred to the lower-income individual. The interest charged must, of course, be added to the income of the higher income family member.

Discharging debts: The attribution rules do not apply if a taxpayer discharges directly the debt of his or her spouse, a designated minor or non-arm's length individual. These persons would borrow money from another third party and the taxpayer would then repay the original debt directly to the third party. For example, a wife might borrow money to pay off her husband's car loan. The wife assumes the debt and pays it off from her income. The husband, who no longer has to make the loan payments can use this freed up income to invest.

Canada and Québec Pension Plan Sharing: The **Canada Pension Plan (CPP)** and the **Québec Pension Plan (QPP)** legislations permit spouses to share their CPP/QPP benefits. If both parties agree, the portion of the retirement pension being received can be split based on the ratio of time that the couple was living together to the period of time during which contributions were made. If both parties are eligible for a pension, both of these pensions must be shared.

Gifting to children or parents: It is possible for an individual to transfer investments to adult children or parents by way of a gift. Such a gift results in a deemed disposition at fair market value by the individual making the gift. Before making such a gift, it is important for the individual to consider the effect of any resulting capital gains or losses in the year the gift is made.

SUMMARY

After reading this chapter, you should be able to:

1. Describe the features of the Canadian income tax system, calculate income tax payable, and differentiate the tax treatment of interest, dividends, and capital gains (and losses).

    *   Canada taxes the world income of its residents (including companies incorporated in Canada and foreign companies with management and control in Canada) and the Canadian source income of non-residents.

    *   All taxpayers must calculate their taxable income on a yearly basis.

    *   Net income tax payable is calculated by taking the gross tax applied to all sources of income from employment, business, or investments less allowable deductions and exemptions, and then reducing the result by any permissible tax credits.

    *   There are four general types of income:
        *   Employment income (taxed on a gross receipt basis);

        *   Business income, including income from self-employment (the profit earned from producing and selling goods or rendering services);

        *   Capital property income (dividend and interest income);

        *   Capital gains and losses (profit or loss from disposition of property).

    *   Combining the provincial tax rate and the federal tax rate on the next dollar of income earned gives the taxpayer's combined marginal tax rate.

    *   Employers are required to withhold income tax on salaries and wages and remit this amount on their employees' behalf to the government. Some individuals, and all corporations, pay their taxes by instalments.

    *   Interest income is reported annually regardless of whether the cash is received (for all investment contracts acquired after 1989).

    *   Dividend income received from a taxable Canadian corporation is grossed up by a specified factor and then the taxpayer receives a tax credit.

    *   Foreign dividend income is generally taxed as regular income.

    *   Income earned on strip bonds and T-bills must be reported annually.

    *   Certain items related to the earning of investment income are eligible for deduction against investment income.

2.   Calculate capital gains and capital losses and assess strategies for minimizing tax liability.

- A capital gain arises from selling a capital property for more than the adjusted cost base plus any costs of disposing of the property.

- A capital loss arises from selling a capital property for less than the adjusted cost base plus any costs of disposing of the property.

- The effect on the adjusted cost base of warrants and rights, as well as shares acquired through the exercise of warrants and rights, differs depending on the method of acquisition.

- Disposition of worthless securities would result in an allowable capital loss.

- Superficial losses are not eligible as capital losses.

3.   Describe and differentiate the different tax deferral plans and their uses.

- Contributions to the plans are limited by legislation and are generally based on taxable income; taxpayers are usually able to carry forward unused contributions.

- A registered pension plan is a registered trust established by a company to provide pension benefits for its employees when they retire. Both employer and employee contributions to the plan are tax deductible.

- The two primary types of pension plans are defined benefit (benefits at retirement are based on a formula that is specific and defined) and defined contribution or money purchase (contributions to the plan are specified, and the eventual retirement benefit depends on money accumulated during the contribution period).

- Registered retirement savings plans are vehicles for individuals to save for retirement. Contributions are tax deductible up to allowable limits, and income accumulates tax deferred while it remains in the plan.

- RRSP contribution limits are based on earned income, which differs from taxable income.

- A variety of RRSPs (including single vendor, self-directed, and spousal) are available, allowing individuals to customize their plan to their specific circumstances.

- An RRSP holder may make withdrawals or de-register the plan at any time, but mandatory de-registration of an RRSP occurs during the calendar year when an RRSP plan holder reaches a specified age.

- Advantages of RRSPs include reduction in annual taxable income during high-taxation years as a result of tax-deductible contributions, the ability to shelter certain lump-sum types of income, accumulation of funds on a tax-deferred basis, deferral of income taxes to lower-taxed times, and the opportunity to split retirement income.

- Disadvantages of RRSPs include the inability to use the funds now, assets cannot be used as collateral for a loan, and foregoing the benefits of favoured tax treatment of investments that produce dividends and capital gains. All income is taxed as regular income when withdrawn.

- A registered retirement income fund (RRIF) is a tax-deferral vehicle available to RRSP holders who transfer some or all RRSP fund to a RRIF.

- A RRIF holder must make minimum, annual taxable withdrawals based on a formula related to age; there is no maximum withdrawal.

- An annuity is an investment contract in which a holder deposits money to be invested in an interest-bearing vehicle. Payments are composed of interest and a portion of original capital. Deferred annuities start payments at a date in the future chosen by the investor, while immediate annuities begin payments immediately.

- Income earned within a TFSA will not be taxed in any way throughout an individual's lifetime. There are no restrictions on the timing or amount of withdrawals from a TFSA, and the money withdrawn can be used for any purpose.

- Contributions to a TFSA are limited to $5,000 a year. After 2009, that amount will be indexed to inflation and rounded to the nearest $500. Withdrawals can be made from a TFSA at any time.

- Registered education savings plans (RESPs) are tax-deferred savings plans intended to help pay for the post-secondary education of a beneficiary. Contributions are not deductible but income accumulates in the plan on a tax-deferred basis.

- Contribution amounts to RESPs are subject to legislated maximums. The government matches a certain portion of eligible contributions (the Canada Education Savings Grant [CESG]).

- Pooled registered pension plans (PRPP) are tax-deferred savings plans that the government plans to implement sometime in 2013. PRPPs are designed to fill the gap that exists in employer-sponsored pension plans. Individuals that contribute to a PRPP will be limited by allowable contribution room, and contributions will be tax deductible.

4. Identify basic tax planning strategies and discuss their advantages.

- Income splitting involves transferring income from a highly taxed family member to a spouse, child, or parent who is in a lower tax bracket. Attribution rules may be triggered.

- Other tax-planning strategies include the higher-taxed spouse claiming tax-deductible investment expenses, making loans to family members, sharing government pension benefits, making gifts to children or parents, and spousal RRSPs.

Online Frequently Asked Questions

CSI has answered many frequently asked questions about this Chapter.
Read through online Module 25 FAQs.

Online Post-Module Assessment

Once you have completed the chapter, take the Module 25 Post-Test.

Chapter 26

Working with the Retail Client

26

Working with the Retail Client

CHAPTER OUTLINE

What is the Financial Planning Approach?

What are the Steps in Financial Planning Process?
- Establishing the Client-Advisor Relationship
- Collecting Data and Information
- Analyzing Data and Information
- Recommending Strategies to Meet Goals
- Implementing Recommendations
- Conducting a Periodic Review or Follow-Up

What is the Life Cycle Hypothesis?

What are Ethics and the Advisor's Standards of Conducts?
- The Code of Ethics
- Standards of Conduct

Summary

Appendix A

Appendix B – Client Scenarios

LEARNING OBJECTIVES

By the end of this chapter, you should be able to:

1. Evaluate the importance of and summarize the steps in the financial planning process.
2. Describe how life cycle hypothesis is used to understand a client's investment needs.
3. Summarize the five values on which the code of ethics is based and the five standards of conduct that advisors should apply in their relationships with clients.

ADVISING THE CLIENT

We have travelled a long road through this course, covering many topics. In this chapter, we move our focus to the role the advisor plays in dealing with retail clients. In providing financial advice through financial planning or wealth management services, clients and advisors move beyond looking narrowly at investing as buying, selling and trading securities, and focus on the purpose behind these activities.

Retail investing should be done with a reasoned approach to meeting needs, goals and objectives. Otherwise, clients will not likely succeed in achieving what they want, or simply not have realistic expectations of what they can expect to succeed. Financial planning provides a structure and framework that allows advisors to clearly understand their clients and formulate investment recommendations that fit a particular client today.

Tied into this approach is the important role ethics play in the process of making investment and financial planning decisions. When dealing with the public, advisors have a duty to act ethically, most importantly placing the needs and interests of the client above all else. Behaving ethically is the cornerstone of maintaining and enhancing the integrity of the capital markets.

This chapter brings together much of the learning in the course and looks at what else is necessary to help ensure that advisors are meeting the needs and reaching the goals of their clients.

WHAT IS THE FINANCIAL PLANNING APPROACH?

The financial planning approach means assessing clients' current financial and personal situation, constraints, goals and objectives and making recommendations through a financial plan to achieve these goals and objectives. The advisor may call on specialists in investment management, taxes, estate and financial planning and integrate the expert analysis, findings, and recommendations into a coherent plan to meet the client's needs. In fact, many large financial institutions have created internal teams of these specialists to support their advisors.

Financial planning involves analysis of clients' age, wealth, career, marital status, taxation status, estate considerations, risk tolerance, investment objectives, legal concerns and other matters. Accordingly, a very comprehensive view of present circumstances can be formed and future goals better defined. In addition, the very discipline and self-analysis required to flesh out a plan causes clients to have a clearer understanding of themselves and their goals, making success in achieving those objectives far more realistic and likely.

Before that plan is prepared, there are four objectives that must be considered. The plan to be created:

- Must be achievable

- Must accommodate changes in lifestyle and income level

- Should not be intimidating

- Should provide for not only the necessities but also some luxuries or rewards

Each person or family will have a unique financial plan with which to reach goals. However, there are some basic procedures that can be followed to begin a simple financial plan. These steps are common to all.

WHAT ARE THE STEPS IN FINANCIAL PLANNING PROCESS?

Typically, the financial planning process can be divided into the following steps:

1. Establishing the Client-Advisor relationship

2. Collecting data and information

3. Analyzing data and information

4. Recommending strategies to meet goals

5. Implementing recommendations

6. Conducting a periodic review or follow-up

Although financial planning involves the same set of steps for each client, an effective plan is a unique and specific plan that addresses the distinct needs of each client.

Establishing the Client-Advisor Relationship

Interviewing the client provides an opportunity to determine what issues and problems the client has identified and whether development of a financial plan will deal with them. It also helps both the advisor and the client to determine whether they feel that a long-term relationship can exist. During the interview, the advisor should discuss the financial planning approach and how it will help the client meet his or her objectives. The advisor should communicate to the client that there will be choices and decisions to be made regarding alternative strategies for dealing with planning issues. Likewise, there will be alternatives in choice of product which should be dealt with by specialists in each area. The advisor should also disclose any areas where a conflict of interest may arise.

If the initial interview is successful from both the advisor's and the client's viewpoint, the advisor should formalize the relationship with either a letter of engagement or a formal contract. This is to ensure that the client is fully aware of exactly what services the advisor will provide and what information the advisor will require in order to prepare a plan. The letter should also outline matters such as the method of compensation and the client's responsibility for the compensation of other professionals, such as lawyers and accountants.

Collecting Data and Information

An advisor contributes to a client's well being by understanding the difference between the client's current status and future requirements and goals, and by helping to resolve these differences. To do this effectively, information must be gathered about the client. To acquire this information, an advisor has to follow intuition and instinct while applying some sound techniques for gathering data and assessing the client's requirements.

Advisors are required to know the essential details about each of their clients including:

- The client's current financial and personal status

- The client's investment goals and preferences

- The client's risk tolerance

Successful advisors go beyond just knowing the essential details of a client's situation. They understand the client's unique personal needs and goals including:

- The process the client uses to make important decisions

- The way in which the client prefers to communicate with the advisor

- The psychological profile of the client

- The needs, goals, and aspirations of the client's family, if applicable

An advisor does far more than just manage the financial lives of clients and provide advice to help them achieve their financial goals. Clients must also be encouraged to assess and re-examine their goals in the context of their evolving business and personal lives. Clients' motivations must be understood. Sometimes the advisor has to dig deep to find them, because clients' motivations are not always readily apparent. The advisor must work with the clients to understand what makes them tick and how they can best build a financial strategy.

There are a number of methods to identify and define clients' motivations for pursuing a particular financial objective. Most of them involve actively listening to clients and interpreting their statements in the context of their unique personality, background, character and context. As this process continues, the advisor will most likely come face to face with a client's most intense emotions, for which money, itself, is merely a symbol.

It is the advisor's job to help the client articulate those emotions and build a financial strategy to keep them under control.

COMMUNICATING WITH AND EDUCATING THE CLIENT

The job of gathering information about the client is really just the start of the client communication process. This process also includes regular contact and education. Clients rely on an advisor for a number of reasons, but almost all of them share one characteristic. They all want someone to understand and attend to the details of their financial lives.

Clients want to know they have an advisor who is watching out for their interests, one who is thinking about them and is prepared to take the time and effort to call them, even when the news is not favourable.

The advisor's job will be easier if clients understand why specific decisions about the plan have been made. The advisor can explain in simple terms the technical nature of the plan's individual elements – "A global equity fund invests in stocks on markets around the world".

The greater challenge is to earn clients' full co-operation and trust in making these decisions. In fact, without a client's co-operation, advisors cannot do their job. To gain this trust, advisors have to explain how specific investments will help clients achieve their goals and what type of risks these investments carry.

OTHER INFORMATION REQUIRED

A great deal of information is necessary to prepare a plan, including:

Personal data: These include age, marital status, number of dependants, risk tolerance and health and employment status. An analysis of these factors may reveal special portfolio restrictions or investment objectives and thus help define an acceptable level of risk and appropriate investment goals.

Net worth and family budget: The advisor can obtain a precise financial profile by showing the client how to prepare a Statement of Net Worth and a Family Budget if the client does not already have these documents available. Appendix A of this chapter shows how this information may be presented. It is important to determine the exact composition of the client's assets and liabilities, the amount and nature of current income and the potential for future investable capital or savings. This information will be invaluable in determining the amount of income a portfolio will have to generate and the level of risk that may be assumed to achieve the client's financial goals.

Record keeping: Part of any financial plan includes advice or perhaps instructions for the client on keeping and maintaining adequate and complete records. It is important for family members to be aware of where records are kept so that they can access this information in an emergency. A document should be prepared which gives the location and details of wills, insurance policies, bank accounts, investment accounts as well as any other financial information. There should also be a list of the professional advisors used by the client, such as the name and contact information of any lawyers, accountants, financial planners, IAs or doctors consulted by the client.

Analyzing Data and Information

Setting personal investment objectives is a difficult task. The individual must objectively assess personal strengths and weaknesses as well as realistically review career potential and earnings potential. While to some, this in-depth review can be considered tedious and perhaps unnecessary, it should be noted that it is not possible to set realistic financial goals without one considering how to reach that goal. While many clients dream of striking it rich in the financial markets, those who actually reach that goal have done so by design, not by chance.

Since investments are selected to suit individual needs, it is essential to develop a clear client profile. Only by studying all factors that potentially affect a financial plan can suitable recommendations be made or an individual's investment strategy be designed.

EXAMPLE

Billy H. is a commissioned salesperson. His income is very high but it is very erratic. Billy is very risk tolerant and invests in more speculative vehicles. Ronnie W. is a geologist who works in the mining industry. Income is steady from the unionized plant. Ronnie is a risk-averse individual and invests mostly in GICs.

Despite the proclamations of both clients, the advisor must consider the personal circumstances of each individual. A person such as Billy H., whose income source is uncertain, may be better off having his money placed in relatively conservative investments, with a portion of the portfolio in liquid securities. The advisor may suggest that the client creates a small portion of the portfolio for speculative investments to address this need but should consider the broader picture – that income may be uncertain.

The other client, Ronnie W., is risk-averse by nature, but could be limiting investment choices because of an unrealistic fear. This fear should be addressed to ensure that it does not limit future decisions. Ronnie W. could invest in blue chip issues because of their relatively high quality and moderate risk.

Unless the advisor delves into personal circumstances such as job security, investment experience and possibly marital circumstances, important issues can be overlooked.

An individual's investment objectives are determined by a thorough analysis of his or her current financial position and future requirements. The New Account Application Form (NAAF) (see Appendix 26A.3) requires that investment objectives be clearly stated and that they govern investment actions. Investment objectives generally can be described as a desire for income, growth of capital, preservation of capital, tax minimization or liquidity. These investment objectives were described more fully in Chapter 15.

The client's tolerance for risk, investment knowledge and time horizon all impose constraints on the recommendations to be put forth in the financial plan. Constraints provide some discipline in the fulfilment of a client's objectives. Constraints, which may loosely be defined as those items that may hinder or prevent the advisor from satisfying the client's objectives, are often not given the importance they deserve in the policy formation process. This may result from the fact that objectives are a more comforting concept to dwell on than the discipline of constraints.

Recommending Strategies to Meet Goals

After collecting and analyzing the information, a plan of action must be developed for the client to follow. This plan of action may require the input of other professionals. If this is the case, the advisor should prepare a list of instructions for these professionals as well. Clearly defined goals and tasks, as well as a schedule for achievement can be of enormous benefit to the client. The financial plan should be simple, easy to implement and easy to maintain.

It is important to implement a financial plan in a timely manner. Once the preparatory work of collecting, analyzing, determining and calculating is finished, it is up to the client to decide to put all the carefully thought-out ideas and strategies in motion.

At this point the client should review the plan, the goals, the objectives and the risk tolerance levels. The client should be in agreement with them before any products are purchased or deals are struck. The investment advisor must ensure that the client understands each product chosen and is aware of the potential risks as well as the potential rewards.

Implementing Recommendations

At this stage, the advisor may help clients implement the recommendations. Some recommendations may be immediate, such as applying for insurance or paying down debt. Other recommendations will be implemented over a longer term, such as making periodic investments, contributing funds to an RRSP, etc.

If necessary, the advisor may refer clients to a business partner such as a lawyer, tax adviser, investment adviser, real estate broker, retirement specialist or insurance representative.

Conducting a Periodic Review or Follow-Up

The last step in this whole process is the review. A financial plan should never remain static. Just as investments rise and fall in market value, a person's financial situation can change. As well, economic changes, tax increases and health issues all can threaten even the "best-laid plans." While there is no set time frame for such a review, an annual review is the minimum required. Mini reviews may be necessary depending on the circumstances (i.e., changing tax, economic or employment status). In extreme circumstances, such as a job loss, it may be necessary to devise a completely new financial plan.

Revisions can include reviewing a will, changing beneficiaries and ensuring that the client is continuing to take advantage of all tax savings techniques. Recommendations can be simple – no changes are necessary – or could entail a great number of changes. It is important that the advisor follow up with the client to ensure that suggestions are carried out

This overview of the financial planning process provides the client with the structure of a basic financial plan but does not deal with specialized issues such as trusts, estate freezes, the need for insurance, etc. To complete a thorough analysis of needs and requirements, these areas must be addressed as well; however, it is beyond the scope of this text to do so. A more thorough discussion of these topics is provided in more advanced courses offered by CSI.

Complete the following Online Learning Activity

Gathering Information and Assessing Needs

This module focuses on assessing client objectives and goals. Apply your knowledge to answer the questions about how this advisor is handling her client.

 Complete the **Gathering Information** activity.

WHAT IS THE LIFE CYCLE HYPOTHESIS?

To add perspective to the process of setting objectives, it can be helpful to think in terms of the life cycle. **Life Cycle Hypothesis** states that the risk-return relationship of a portfolio changes because clients have different needs at different points in their lives. On this basis, it is assumed that younger clients can assume more risk in the pursuit of higher returns and that the risk-return relationship reverses itself as the client ages. In general, there are four definable stages in a person's adult life.

Early Earning Years – to age 35	At this time the client is starting a career, building net worth and assuming family and home ownership responsibilities. The most common priorities are to have a savings plan and near-cash investments for emergencies. However, when funds are available for investing, growth is usually the primary objective because of the magnitude and duration of expected future earnings.
Mid-Earning Years – age 35 to 55	In this stage an individual's expenses usually decline and income and savings usually increase. As a result, savings continue to be a very important factor in the growth of a client's investment capital. Because such clients have more discretionary income, investment objectives tend to focus on growth and tax minimization.
Peak Earning Years – age 55 to retirement	As a client approaches retirement, preservation of capital becomes an increasingly important objective. During this period, the average term of maturity of fixed-income investments should be shortened and the quantity of higher-risk common shares reduced.
Retirement Years	During this period clients most frequently have fixed incomes and only limited opportunities for employment. Therefore the primary investment objectives of retired clients are preservation of capital and income, with the relative importance of each being determined by comparing the level of retirement income to budget requirements. When income is adequate, preservation of capital is more important. There must be enough growth in the portfolio so that the client does not run out of money.

While convenient, the life cycle approach to financial planning is to be considered a mere guideline in developing any plan. It is true that some clients might easily conform to this life cycle model, but many individuals' financial or other circumstances simply do not fit into the convenient four-stage approach outlined here. Special circumstances require an individualized approach.

Although life cycle analysis can be helpful, it is far more important to consider the client's personal situation, financial position and responsibilities, tolerance for risk and investment knowledge. Only by assessing these factors in depth and relating them to the expressed needs of the client can the advisor help an individual develop specific investment objectives.

EXHIBIT 26.1 THE FINANCIAL PLANNING PYRAMID

One other tool to help the client and advisor to both clarify the client's current situation and identify planning needs is the **financial planning pyramid**. Although the financial planning pyramid may appear simplistic, it often helps for the advisor to use visual aids in dealing with clients. The financial planning pyramid helps the advisor and the client alike visualize goals and objectives and review investment strategy.

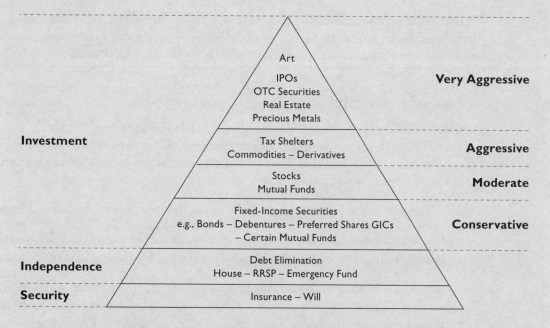

If the client is interested in IPOs for example, but lacks a Will and the proper insurance coverage, it is obvious that, by starting at the top with an IPO, the groundwork has not been done and the plan will be unstable. The client must have a good strong base from which to work to successfully reach the goals and objectives set.

Complete the following Online Learning Activity

Life Cycle Hypothesis

This theory states that investors have different needs at different stages in their lives. As needs change, risk-return objectives change. An advisor must be aware of these stages to make appropriate recommendations to clients.

 Complete **Life Cycle Hypothesis** activity to review your knowledge of the life stages.

WHAT ARE ETHICS AND THE ADVISOR'S STANDARDS OF CONDUCTS?

A critical element in building a solid trusting relationship with a client is behaving in an ethical manner. Ethics can be defined as a set of moral values that guide behaviour. Moral values are enduring beliefs that reflect standards of what is right and what is wrong.

The Code of Ethics

The securities industry has a Code of Ethics that establishes norms based upon the principles of trust, integrity, justice, fairness, honesty, responsibility and reliability. People registered to sell securities and mutual funds (registrants) must adhere to this code. The code encompasses the following five primary ethical values:

- Registrants must use proper care and exercise independent professional judgment.

- Registrants must conduct themselves with trustworthiness and integrity, and act in an honest and fair manner in all dealings with the public, clients, employers and colleagues.

- Registrants must, and should encourage others to, conduct business in a professional manner that will reflect positively on themselves, their firms and their profession. Registrants should also strive to maintain and improve their professional knowledge and that of others in the profession.

- Registrants must act in accordance with the securities act(s) of the province or provinces in which registration is held, and the requirements of all Self-Regulatory Organizations (SROs) of which the firm is a member must be observed.

- Registrants must hold client information in the strictest confidence.

It is important to understand the difference between ethical behaviour and compliance with rules. The rules set out standards. Some rules purely codify consensus practices. For example, stock trades settle three days after the trade date (T+3). Other rules approximate ethics by incorporating ethical behaviour, such as the law against stealing. However, compliance with rules only results in conformity with externally established standards.

While there are rules to deal with the most significant or common situations, rules cannot encompass every possible situation that may occur in day-to-day business. Following rules does not involve any judgment. People follow rules because they must, not necessarily because they believe it is morally correct. However, ethical behaviour requires internally established moral judgments. Ethical decision making is a system that can be applied to any situation.

The following short case illustrates an example of an action that would be compliant with rules but would violate ethical standards.

CASE #1   HANDLING AN ETHICAL ISSUE

An advisor, Betty Cho, is considering recommending that a client, Henry King, invest in a small but promising Internet company, NetTrack Enterprises. Betty's brother-in-law, Fred Wong, is NetTrack's main shareholder and CEO.

While there may not be a clear violation of industry rules or regulations, if Ms. Cho recommends NetTrack to her client, there is certainly an ethical issue that she is facing.

If she is acting in an ethically sound manner, Betty needs to:

1. Recognize that she faces a moral issue if she makes an investment recommendation in a situation in which she has a potential or actual conflict of interest.

2. Assess her options in terms of moral criteria and develop a morally appropriate strategy for managing conflict-of-interest situations. For instance, she should disclose to Henry that one of her relations has a major interest in NetTrack. She must consider whether her professional objectivity regarding NetTrack's promise might be compromised, or appear to be compromised, by her relationship to Fred.

3. Make a commitment to a morally appropriate strategy such as disclosure.

4. Have the courage to carry out the moral strategy by letting Henry know that Fred Wong is her brother-in-law.

This Code of Ethics establishes norms that incorporate, but are not limited to, strict compliance with "the letter of the law" but also foster compliance with the "spirit of the law." These norms are based upon ethical principles of trust, integrity, justice, fairness and honesty. The Code distills industry rules and regulations into five primary values.

Standards of Conduct

The securities industry has established Standards of Conduct, which expand on the Code of Ethics shown above and set out certain requirements for behaviour. These requirements are based in large part on the provincial securities acts and SRO rules. A brief summary of some of the key standards is discussed next.

EXHIBIT 26.2   CANADIAN SECURITIES INDUSTRY STANDARDS OF CONDUCT – *Summary*

Standard A – Duty of Care

- Know Your Client
- Due Diligence
- Unsolicited Orders

Standard B – Trustworthiness, Honesty and Fairness

- Priority of Client Interests
- Protection of Client Assets
- Complete and Accurate Information
- Disclosure

Standard C – Professionalism

- Client Business
- Client Orders
- Trades by Registered and Approved Individuals
- Approved Securities
- Personal Business
- Personal Financial Dealing with Clients
- Personal Trading Activity
- Other Personal Endeavours
- Continuous Education

Standard D – Conduct in Accordance with Securities Acts

- Compliance with Securities Acts and SRO Rules
- Inside Information

Standard E – Confidentiality

- Client Information
- Use of Confidential Information

STANDARD A – DUTY OF CARE

While duty of care encompasses a wide number of obligations towards parties, the obligation to know the client is of paramount importance in order to ensure the priority of clients' interests. Including this, the three major components of duty of care are:

- **Know Your Client**: The Know Your Client (KYC) rule is paramount for the industry. All registrants must make a diligent and business-like effort to learn the essential financial and personal circumstances and the investment objectives of each client. Client account documentation should reflect all material information about the client's current status, and should be updated to reflect any material changes to the client's status in order to assure suitability of investment recommendations.

- **Due Diligence**: Registrants must make all recommendations based on a careful analysis of both information about the client and information related to the particular transaction.

- **Unsolicited Orders**: Registrants who give advice to clients must provide appropriate cautionary advice with respect to unsolicited orders (an order entered by a client where there was no recommendation made by the client's IA or his/her dealer member) that appear unsuitable based on client information. The registrant must be aware of the objectives and strategies behind each order accepted on behalf of his or her clients, whether it is solicited or not. Registrants should take appropriate safeguarding measures when clients insist on proceeding with unsolicited, unsuitable orders.

As discussed earlier, an advisor must make a concerted effort to know the client – to understand the financial and personal status and aspirations of the client. Thus, the advisor will make recommendations for the client to invest funds in securities that reflect, to the best knowledge of the advisor, these considerations. The advisor, having provided sound advice, will therefore be above reproach for potentially unsuitable purchases and sales of securities for a client if the client does not heed the advisor's advice.

The advisor must make a diligent and business-like effort to learn the essential financial and personal circumstances and the investment objectives of each client. Client account documentation should reflect all material information about the client's current status, and should be updated to reflect any material changes to the client's status in order to assure suitability of investment recommendations.

According to IIROC, full-service brokers now have the opportunity to accept non-recommended trades (unsolicited orders) without a suitability obligation. To meet regulatory requirements in this matter, clients are required to sign a disclosure agreement document that gives their consent that non-recommended trades will not be subject to a suitability review.

STANDARD B – TRUSTWORTHINESS, HONESTY AND FAIRNESS

Registrants must display absolute trustworthiness since the client's interests must be the foremost consideration in all business dealings. This requires that registrants observe the following:

- **Priority of Client's Interest**: The client's interest must be the foremost consideration in all business dealings. In situations where the registrant may have an interest that competes with that of the client, the client's interest must be given priority.

- **Respect for Client's Assets**: The client's assets are solely the property of the client and are to be used only for the client's purposes. Registrants shall not utilize client's funds or securities in any way.

- **Complete and Accurate Information Relayed to Client**: Registrants must take reasonable steps to ensure that all information given to the client regarding his or her existing portfolio is complete and accurate. While the onus is on the investment firm to provide each client with written confirmations of all purchases and sales, as well as monthly account statements, the individual registrant must accurately represent the details of each client's investments to the client. The registrant must be familiar with the clients' investment holdings and must not misrepresent the facts to the client in order to create a more favourable view of the portfolio.

- **Disclosure**: Registrants must disclose all real and potential conflicts of interest in order to ensure fair, objective dealings with clients.

Advisors help clients think through their financial goals. In this role, clients need to know that the advisor is working to promote their best interests.

When clients trust their advisor, they do not personally have to verify everything that the advisor tells them. For example, they do not have to check the tax and estate implications of every investment recommendation or ask for details about its risk or volatility. They certainly do not waste time wondering if the advisor has made a recommendation that serves the advisor's interest rather than the client's own interest.

There are two parts to a trust relationship: trust in an advisor's *competence* and *integrity*. Both are essential. Competence, without integrity, leaves clients at the mercy of a self-serving professional. Integrity, without competence, puts clients in the hands of a well-meaning but inept professional.

In order to ensure that advisors and other registrants display absolute trustworthiness, the Standards of Conduct sets out that a client's interest must be the foremost consideration in all business dealings. In situations where the advisor may have an interest that competes with that of the client, the client's interest must be given priority. Furthermore, advisors must disclose all real and potential conflicts of interest in order to ensure fair, objective dealings with clients. This is why Betty Cho, in Case #1, should disclose her relationship with NetTrack's main shareholder, her brother-in-law.

In order to ensure that advisors are competent, they must meet proficiency requirements for their registration category. As well, the Canadian investment industry has a mandatory continuing education program, which helps ensure that investment industry professionals have the information and skills they need to serve their clients with the utmost professionalism.

CASE #2   GAINING A CLIENT'S TRUST

When Ottawa advisor Jo-Ann Carter assumed the account of 75-year-old Ena Beyer, she knew she had a challenge on her hands.

Mrs. Beyer, a widow, held more than $350,000 in a non-registered mutual fund account – and the entire amount was invested in a combination of GICs and a mortgage mutual fund. After the first meeting with her client, it was evident that her investment knowledge was very limited and that she relied almost entirely on her son for financial advice.

Therein lay the problem. Her son, a systems-services professional employed by a high-tech firm, had been generating great returns for his own portfolio by investing in various Canadian and U.S. technology stocks.

When Mrs. Beyer passed over a sheet of paper listing some of her son's recommendations, Carter immediately shook her head. The proposed list of holdings included an excessive amount in equities, especially aggressive high-growth situations, and not nearly enough in dividend-paying blue-chip names and fixed-income securities.

Convinced that the son's proposed strategy was overly aggressive for someone with Mrs. Beyer's client profile, Carter recommended to her a much more conservative approach. Mrs. Beyer balked at the suggestions for change, siding with her son over someone she was meeting only for the first time.

CASE #2   GAINING A CLIENT'S TRUST – *Cont'd*

The easy way out for Carter would have been to go along with what the son suggested and Mrs. Beyer wanted. Carter could easily have rationalized the choices, since one of Mrs. Beyer's objectives was to pass on an inheritance to her son. By questioning the son's judgment, Carter risked losing an attractive account, and one that would generate a good chunk of commission income right away.

But in good conscience, Carter could not go along with Mrs. Beyer's requests without making further inquiries to determine what in fact was in Mrs. Beyer's best interests. Carter asked her to set up a meeting with her son so that the three of them could discuss her situation together.

A few weeks later, the agreed-on meeting started poorly. Mrs. Beyer's son, Roy, seemed skeptical of Carter's abilities and was a little suspicious about her intentions. Undeterred, Carter patiently explained her responsibility as an advisor, her concerns about his mother's account and the reasons for her recommendations.

After the first meeting, Roy said he was not yet convinced, but would think about it. His mother concurred. "It took some time, but after a couple more meetings, her son was impressed with my recommendations," says Carter. "In the end, we had totally revamped the asset mix to ensure prudent allocation of his mother's investments."

With Mrs. Beyer more comfortable knowing her son was involved, Carter also felt more assured that she would be able to get better results for her client. "We now meet regularly and the trust that has developed between the three of us is very strong." More recently, this trust went even farther, and Mrs. Beyer's account became a discretionary managed account, since Roy has found himself increasingly too busy to oversee his mother's investments.

STANDARD C – PROFESSIONALISM

It is generally accepted that professionals, by having specialized knowledge, need to protect their clients, who usually do not have the same degree of specialized knowledge, and must continually strive to put the interests of their clients ahead of their own. Registrants must also make a continuous effort to maintain a high standard of professional knowledge.

- **Client business**: All methods of soliciting and conducting business must be such as to merit public respect and confidence.

- **Client Orders**: Every client order must be entered only at the client's direction unless the account has been properly constituted as a discretionary or managed account pursuant to the applicable regulatory requirements.

- **Trades by registered and approved individuals**: All trades and all acts in furtherance of trades, whether with existing or potential clients, must be effected only by individuals who are registered and approved in accordance with applicable legislation and the rules of the SROs.

- **Approved securities**: Only securities approved for distribution by the appropriate regulatory authority and partner, director or officer of the firm should be distributed, and all such transactions should be recorded in the normal way on the books and records of the firm.

- **Personal business**: All personal business affairs must be conducted in a professional and responsible manner, so as to reflect credit on the individual registrant, the securities firm and the profession.

- **Personal financial dealings with clients**: Registrants should avoid personal financial dealings with clients, including the lending of money to or the borrowing of money from them, paying clients' losses out of personal funds, and sharing a financial interest in an account with a client. Any personal financial or business dealings with any clients must be conducted in such a way as to avoid any real or apparent conflict of interest and be disclosed to the firm, in order that the firm may monitor the situation.

- **Personal trading activity**: Personal trading activity should be kept to reasonable levels. If a registrant is trading in his or her own account very actively on a daily basis, it is doubtful that the registrant will have enough time to properly service his or her clients. Excessive trading losses by a registrant will also present a negative image of the registrant as a responsible financial professional.

- **Other personal endeavours**: Each registrant must take care to ensure that any other publicly visible activity in which he or she participates (such as politics, social organizations or public speaking) is conducted responsibly and moderately so as not to present an unfavorable public image.

- **Continuous education**: It is the responsibility of each registrant to have an understanding of factors that influence the investment industry in order to maintain a level of competence in dealing with his or her clientele. A registrant must continually upgrade his or her levels of technical and general knowledge to ensure the accuracy and responsibility of his or her recommendations and advice.

When trust relationships are open-ended and involve "caring for" or "looking after" a client's interests, there is a *fiduciary relationship* between advisors and their clients. Fiduciary or trust relations in ethics and law are needed where there is an imbalance of knowledge or control between two morally related parties, such as a parent and a child, a physician and a patient, or a lawyer and a client. Fiduciary relationships are agent-principal relationships in which the principal has a certain vulnerability and the agent has greater expertise or authority.

In order to ensure that investment advisors and other registrants display the utmost in professionalism, the Standards of Conduct set a number of requirements. These requirements include that all methods of soliciting and conducting business must be such as to merit public respect and confidence, and that all personal business affairs be conducted in a professional and responsible manner.

CASE #3	BEING AWARE OF A CLIENT'S VULNERABILITY

There are times when Ron Springfield must advise a surviving spouse about what to do with inherited assets. But the time immediately following the death of a loved one is a time for grieving, not decision making, says Springfield, who over the years has guided many surviving spouses through this vulnerable period.

CASE #3   BEING AWARE OF A CLIENT'S VULNERABILITY – Cont'd

His widowed clients include Martina, whose retirement life in a peaceful small town in the B.C. interior was shattered by the sudden death, at age 67, of Ivan, her husband of 35 years. Amid the flurry of contacting friends and relatives and making funeral arrangements, Martina also worried about what she had to do about her deceased husband's RRSP and his other investment accounts. It was all overwhelming, particularly since it was Ivan, and not her, who had been the main overseer of the family's finances.

Martina felt some relief when she contacted Springfield by phone at the brokerage office. He assured her that no immediate action was required on her part. "The perception that most people in your situation have is, that things need to be done very quickly," Springfield told Martina. "The reality is that as long as you have enough cash on hand to pay the bills, there is really no great rush. When you're ready to sit down and talk, give me a call."

Though the timing of Ivan's passing was unexpected, such eventualities had been provided for in the financial plan crafted for the couple. Ivan's death triggered the payment of a life insurance policy that had been designed to cover any of his tax liabilities at death. The two largest tax payouts had to do with the deemed disposition of rental property owned by Ivan, and the deemed disposition of a portfolio of stocks, most of which had been held for at least ten years and had built up considerable capital gains.

Additionally, the life insurance policy had been over-funded so as to ensure that Martina, the beneficiary, would have a cash reserve to cover all of the one-time expenses associated with a death. For her, these included the costs of plane fare to enable her son and his young family to make the trip to the West Coast from their home in New Brunswick.

While mourners gathered to comfort the grieving widow, Springfield was quietly taking care of business. Shortly after the death, his assistant produced an estate-evaluation report listing the market value of Ivan's investment and RRSP assets as of the date of his death, and the maturity dates of his bond and GIC holdings.

The report laid out clearly the information needed by Martina's executor, lawyer or accountant in order to do their jobs. "This is a lot easier to do right after the death than several weeks later," says Springfield.

Meanwhile, Springfield reviewed Martina's own investment account, which he has been looking after for many years. He saw that a five-year GIC was just about to expire, and that some stocks and mutual funds had recently paid quarterly dividends into her account.

In the weeks and months to come, the probate process would play out, and Martina would seek advice from Springfield on how to invest her existing and inherited assets. But now was hardly the time for reinvestment decisions. Springfield knew from his conversation with Martina that she would need the money for short-term expenses like visitation, funeral, catering and other related expenses. After consulting with Martina, he transferred the available cash from Martina's investment account to her daily chequing account at her bank.

Less may be more, when it comes to helping clients who are bereaved or otherwise going through a period when they are feeling very vulnerable. "A death in the family immediately changes a client's profile," says Springfield. "People have a lot more need for liquidity. You try to get everything accumulated and make it easier for them."

STANDARD D – CONDUCT IN ACCORDANCE WITH SECURITIES ACTS

Registrants must ensure that their conduct is in accordance with the securities acts and the applicable SRO rules and regulations.

- **Compliance with securities acts and SRO rules**: Registrants must ensure that their conduct is in accordance with the securities acts of the province or provinces in which registration is held. The requirements of all SROs of which a registrant's firm is a member must be observed by the registrant. The registrant shall not knowingly participate in, nor assist in, any act in violation of any applicable law, rule or regulation of any government, governmental agency or regulatory organization governing his or her professional, financial or business activities, nor any act which would violate any provision of the industry Code of Ethics and Standards of Conduct.

- **Inside information**: If a registrant acquires non-public, material information, the information must neither be communicated (outside of the relationship) nor acted upon. Employees of a firm's trading, corporate finance or research departments must be aware of the need to safeguard non-public, confidential, material information received in the normal course of business.

STANDARD E – CONFIDENTIALITY

All information concerning the client's transactions and his or her accounts must be considered confidential and must not be disclosed except with the client's permission, for supervisory purposes or by order of the proper authority.

- **Client information**: Registrants must maintain the confidentiality of identities and the personal and financial circumstances of their clients. Registrants must refrain from discussing this information with anyone outside their firm, and must also ensure that the firm's client lists and other confidential records are not left out where they can be taken or observed by visitors to the office.

- **Use of confidential information**: Information regarding clients' personal and financial circumstances and trading activity must be kept confidential and may not be used in any way to effect trades in personal and/or proprietary accounts or in the accounts of other clients. Not only must registrants refrain from trading in their own accounts based on knowledge of clients' pending orders, but they must also refrain from using it as a basis for recommendations to other clients or passing this information along to any other parties.

In addition to being skilled in the areas of investment and financial management, advisors must be able to deal effectively with clients through the stages of data gathering, ongoing communication and education. As well, as the investment industry is built on trust and confidence, advisors must adhere to strict rules and regulations with respect to dealing with clients, and abide by the industry Code of Ethics that establishes trust, integrity, justice, fairness, honesty, responsibility and reliability.

In the Chapter Appendix B, two case studies are used to illustrate the integration of the portfolio management principles outlined earlier with the skill set required in building a relationship with the client. The situation in the first example – the Casuso family – contains many of the variables that an investment advisor has to assess in order to make suitable investment recommendations.

While the family is fictitious and the ultimate selections are only one person's view, the case study is a useful summary of the process. The second example - Johanna Von Rosen – presents a client that recently retired and highlights the important elements an advisor must take into consideration when recommending an asset mix given the client's unique situation.

Complete the following Online Learning Activity

The Five Values

The securities industry's code of ethics establishes norms based on the principles of trust, integrity, justice, fairness, honesty, responsibility, and reliability. The resulting five values are central to your role as advisor.

Complete the **Five Primary Ethical Values** activity to review your understanding of the five values.

SUMMARY

After reading this chapter, you should be able to:

1. Evaluate the importance of and summarize the steps in the financial planning process.

    • Gathering information properly fulfills legal requirements and allows an advisor to plan effectively for the client.

    • Effective communication establishes a relationship, builds trust, and allows an advisor to stay current with the client's situation.

    • Educating a client helps to establish clear objectives, expectations, and understanding of the client's investment situation and risk tolerance.

    • The six steps in the financial planning process are:
        – Establishing the Client-Advisor relationship
        – Collecting data and information
        – Analyzing data and information
        – Recommending strategies to meet goals
        – Implementing recommendations
        – Conducting a periodic review or follow-up

2. Describe how life cycle analysis and the financial planning pyramid are used to understand a client's investment needs.

    • Life Cycle Hypothesis states that the risk-return relationship of a portfolio changes because clients have different needs at different points in their lives.

    • It is assumed that younger clients can take on more risk in the pursuit of higher returns and that the risk-return relationship reverses as clients' age.

    • In general, there are four definable stages in a person's adult life: early earning years (to age 35); mid-earnings years (age 35 to 55); peak earning years (age 55 to retirement); and retirement years (after retirement from the work force).

3. Summarize the five values on which the code of ethics is based and the five standards of conduct that advisors should apply in their relationships with clients.

    • There are five primary ethical values on which the code of ethics is based:
        – Registrants must use proper care and exercise independent professional judgment;
        – Registrants must conduct themselves with trustworthiness and integrity, and act in an honest and fair manner in all dealings with the public, clients, employers and colleagues;
        – Registrants must, and should encourage others to, conduct business in a professional manner that will reflect positively on themselves, their firms and their profession, and registrants should strive to maintain and improve their professional knowledge and that of others in the profession;
        – Registrants must act in accordance with the securities act(s) of the province(s) in which registration is held and must observe the requirements of all self-regulatory organizations (SROs) of which the firm is a member;
        – Registrants must hold client information in the strictest confidence.

    • The standards of conduct build on the code of ethics:
        – Duty of care (know your client, due diligence, unsolicited orders);
        – Trustworthiness, honesty and fairness (priority of client interests, protection of client assets, complete and accurate information, disclosure);
        – Professionalism (client business, personal business, continuous education);
        – Conduct in accordance with securities acts (compliance with securities acts and SRO rules, inside information);
        – Confidentiality (client information, use of confidential information).

Online Frequently Asked Questions

CSI has answered many frequently asked questions about this Chapter. Read through online Module 26 FAQs.

Online Post-Module Assessment

Once you have completed the chapter, take the Module 26 Post-Test.

APPENDIX A

TABLE 26A.1   STATEMENT OF NET WORTH

ASSETS

Readily Marketable Assets

Cash (bank accounts, Canada Savings Bonds, etc.)	$ _____
Guaranteed investment certificates and term deposits	_____
Bonds – at market value	_____
Stocks – at market value	_____
Mutual funds – at redemption value	_____
Cash surrender value of life insurance	_____
Other	_____

Non-liquid Financial Assets

Pensions – at vested value	_____
RRSPs	_____
Tax shelters – at cost or estimated value	_____
Annuities	_____
Other	_____

Other Assets

Home – at market value	_____
Recreational properties – at market value	_____
Business interests – at market value	_____
Antiques, art, jewellery, collectibles, gold and silver	_____
Cars, boats, etc.	_____
Other real estate interests	_____
Other	_____
Total Assets	$ _____

LIABILITIES

Personal Debt

Mortgage on home	$ _____
Mortgage on recreational property	_____
Credit card balances	_____
Investment loans	_____
Consumer loans	_____
Other loans	_____
Other	_____

Business Debt

Investment loans	_____
Loans for other business-related debt	_____

Contingent Liabilities

Loan guarantees for others	_____
Total Liabilities	$ _____
ASSETS	_____
Minus LIABILITIES	_____
NET WORTH	$ _____

TABLE 26A.2   FAMILY BUDGET AND EARNINGS AVAILABLE FOR INVESTMENT

	Monthly	Total Monthly	Total Annual
NET EARNINGS			
Self	$ _____		
Spouse	$ _____		
Net Investment Income	$ _____	$ _____	$ _____
EXPENSES & SAVINGS			
Maintaining Your Home			
Rent or mortgage payments	$ _____		
Property taxes	$ _____		
Insurance	$ _____		
Light, water and heat	$ _____		
Telephone, cable	$ _____		
Maintenance and repairs	$ _____		
Other	$ _____		
Total Monthly		$ _____	
Total Annual			$ _____
Maintaining Your Family			
Food	$ _____		
Clothing	_____		
Laundry	_____		
Auto expenses	_____		
Education	_____		
Childcare	_____		
Medical, dental, drugs	_____		
Accident and sickness insurance	_____		
Other	_____		
Total Monthly		$ _____	
Total Annual			$ _____
Maintaining Your Lifestyle			
Religious, charitable donations	$ _____		
Membership fees	_____		
Sports and entertainment	_____		
Gifts and contributions	_____		
Vacations	_____		
Personal expenses	_____		
Total Monthly		$ _____	
Total Annual			$ _____
Maintaining Your Future			
Life insurance premiums	$ _____		
RRSP and pension plan contributions	_____		_____
Total Monthly Expenses and Savings		$ _____	
Total Annual Expenses and Savings		$ _____	
Available for Investment		$ _____	$ _____

EXHIBIT 26A.3   NEW ACCOUNT APPLICATION FORM

New Account Application Form
(to be completed by Advisor)

Account Supervision

Office _____   Account _____   I.A.

(1) (a) Name   Mr. _____   Phones: Home _____

Mrs. _____   Business_____

Miss _____   Other _____

(Please Print)

Home _____ (Street)   Fax_____

Address _____
(City)   (Province)   (Postal Code)

Date of Birth _____   Client's Social Insurance Number _____   Client's Citizenship _____

Type of Account Requested

(b) Is Advisor registered in the Province or   Yes _____   Cash _____   RRSP/RRI_____   U.S. Funds ___
Country in which the client resides?   No _____   Margin _____   Other _____

D.A.P _____   Pro_____   CDN Funds __

(2) Special Instructions:_____   Hold in Account __   Register and Deliver _____   DAP _____

Duplicate Confirmation _____   And/Or Statement

Name: _____   Name_____

Address _____   Address:_____

_____   _____

_____   Postal Code: _____   _____   Postal Code: _____

(3) Client's   Name_____   Type of Business _____
Employer: Address_____   Client's Occupation_____

(4) Family Information:

Spouse's Name _____   No. of Dependants _____

Occupation _____   Employer_____

Type of Business _____

(5) How long have you known client?   Advertising Lead __   Phone In _____   Have you met the client face to face?

Personal Contact__   Walk In _____   Yes _____   No _____

Referral by: _____   (name)   (if customer, give account no.) _____

EXHIBIT 26A.3 NEW ACCOUNT APPLICATION FORM – Cont'd

(6) If yes for Questions 1, 2, or 3, provide details in (11).

1. Will any other person or persons:

(a) Have trading authorization in this account?   No___ Yes___

(b) Guarantee this account?   No___ Yes___

(c) Have a financial interest in such accounts?   No___ Yes___

2.. Do any of the signatories have any other accounts or control the trading in such accounts?   No___ Yes___

3. Does client have accounts with other brokerage firms? (Type_____)   No___ Yes___

4. Is this account   (a) discretionary or (b) managed   (a) ___ (b) ___

Insider Information

5. Is client a senior officer or director of a company whose shares are traded on an exchange or in the OTC markets?   No___ Yes___

6. Does the client, as an individual or as part of a group, hold or control such a company? (_____)   No___ Yes___

(7)

(a) General Documents	Attached	Obtaining	(b) Trading Authorization Documents:	Attached	Obtaining
− Client's Agreement	_____		− For an Individual's Account	_____	_____
− Margin Agreement	_____		− For a Corporation, Partnership, Trust, etc.	_____	_____
− Cash Agreement	_____		− Discretionary Authority	_____	_____
− Guarantee	_____		− Managed Account Agreement	_____	_____
− Other	_____				

(8) **INVESTMENT KNOWLEDGE**

Sophisticated _____

Good _____

Limited _____

Poor/Nil _____

EST. NET LIQUID ASSETS

(Cash and securities less loans outstanding against securities)   A _____

ACCOUNT OBJECTIVES

Income _____ %

Capital Gains

   Short Term _____ %

   Medium Term _____ %

   Long Term _____ %

     100%

ACCOUNT RISK FACTORS

Low _____

Medium _____

High _____

     100%

EST. NET FIXED ASSETS

(Fixed assets less liabilities outstanding against fixed assets)   B _____

EST. TOTAL NET WORTH

(A + B = C)   C _____

APPROXIMATE ANNUAL INCOME FROM ALL SOURCES   D _____

EST. SPOUSE'S INCOME   E _____

(9) Bank Reference:

Name _____   Bank credit check acceptable?   Yes _____ No _____

Branch _____   Or Credit Bureau check acceptable?   Yes _____ No _____

Refer to _____   Above credit checks considered unnecessary

Accounts _____   Explain in (11)

(10) Deposit and/or Security Received _____

Initial _____   Buy _____   Solicited _____   Amount _____

Order _____   Sell _____   Unsolicited _____   Description _____

(11) Advisor's Signature _____   Designated Officer, Director or Branch Manager's Approval _____

Date _____   Date of Approval _____

Comments: _____

_____

Client Signature _____   Date _____

APPENDIX B – CLIENT SCENARIOS

Juan Casuso

Juan Casuso, 50, and his wife Emily, 44, have been married for 22 years. Their only child, Jim, who joined the armed forces plans a career as a naval officer.

Over the last nine years, Juan has been promoted three times as a manager at The National Retail Company. Juan enjoys his present responsibilities and plans to continue his career with his current employer. In addition to his $52,000 annual salary, Juan has company benefits that include both disability and life insurance and a limited coverage dental plan. However, he has not yet joined his company's money purchase pension plan. Emily is an executive secretary with a small engineering firm. She receives a $27,500 annual income and does not participate in a benefits package.

The Casusos have a fairly modest lifestyle, their home being the focal point of many of their social activities. As a result, they can live comfortably on $3,000 per month and could save approximately $20,000 per year if they choose to.

The Casusos' house is located in an older part of an Ontario city, and Juan believes it to be worth $260,000. In addition to the house they have two newer cars ($20,000 each), Emily's jewellery worth $7,000, and $5,000 each in savings accounts. Their liabilities are comprised of a $38,000 7% mortgage due on March 1st of next year, car loans of $7,000 and credit card debt of $1,800. Of great significance is the fact that Juan is the main beneficiary of his uncle's estate and has just received a bequest of approximately $270,000. This has caused him to decide to retire in 15 years' time.

PERSONAL EVALUATION

The Casusos are a two-income family with total annual earnings of $79,500. Their employment seems secure, their son is self-sufficient and there is no evidence of additional responsibilities that should be reflected in their portfolio. Their net worth and family budget indicate that their overall financial position is sound and that they could contribute $20,000 to their portfolio each year if they choose to.

Because Juan's income will be higher with the addition of the investment income, the tax consequences of different investments must be considered when making individual selections. His marginal tax bracket may potentially increase, depending on the amount and type of investment income he receives.

While the risk factor can only be assessed accurately in discussions with the Casusos, two factors indicate that risk should be kept low. First, their investment knowledge may be minimal because the majority of their assets are in deposits and the family home. Second, the Casusos wish to retire in 15 years but have only government pensions to generate retirement income. Therefore, they may have to rely heavily on their investments for income at retirement and cannot assume a high level of risk in their portfolio although equities are likely required. Finally, other than Juan's desire to retire in 15 years, there are no time constraints on their capital.

INVESTMENT OBJECTIVES

Juan Casuso's situation calls for a portfolio with a primary investment objective of growth and secondary objectives of tax minimization and safety. Growth is primary because of the need to generate capital to provide for retirement and because the family currently has excess income. Juan's potentially higher marginal tax rate suggests that investments that provide higher after-tax returns should be favoured in the portfolio. The importance of the portfolio to their retirement income suggests that speculative securities should be minimized although equity investments are still a very viable option.

TAX PLANNING FOR JUAN CASUSO

Tax planning can be an integral part of investment planning. Based on the tax-planning concepts outlined in Chapter 25, Juan Casuso should consider the following points.

- Juan must ensure that he is not overlooking allowable deductions such as investment counseling fees. If Juan is not confident that he can find all allowable deductions, he should have his tax return prepared by an expert.

- By postponing the receipt of income, Juan can delay income until he is in a lower tax bracket. In his current situation, he should seriously consider RRSP contributions and investing in growth securities. In the latter case, since Juan has the flexibility to take gains when he chooses, he can postpone some income indefinitely. Juan should also consider investing some of the portfolio into an RRSP, up to his contribution limit.

- Juan can utilize a tax-planning strategy that will ensure that some of his potential future income will be taxed in Emily's hands. Specifically, Juan can establish a spousal RRSP which, upon deregistration, will be taxed at a lower rate as part of Emily's income. In conjunction with a spousal RRSP, Juan may consider joining the company's pension plan so that both he and Emily will have independent pensions at retirement.

- Juan can select investments that will provide a better after-tax yield. For example, Juan can select discount bonds, if available instead of comparable bonds selling at par, dividend-paying preferred shares instead of bonds, and growth stocks instead of short-term fixed-income securities. In each case taxes will be minimized.

ASSET MIX

For the Casusos' situation, the asset mix could justifiably be cash 5%, fixed-income securities 15% and equities 80% (with a range of -5% +5% of the target in each asset class). Because Juan's primary investment objective is growth, it is appropriate to commit a high amount to equities; his income and other circumstances indicate a minimum need for liquidity of 5% in cash; and the balance of 15% to fixed-income securities for diversification.

RECOMMENDED PORTFOLIO

In constructing the portfolio, Juan's primary investment objectives determine the final asset weightings and the secondary objectives determine which specific types of securities should be selected within each group. Juan Casuso's secondary objectives of safety and tax minimization direct the portfolio manager into certain risk groups and specific securities within those groups.

Specifically, Juan's situation suggests that government Treasury bills would be most suitable in the cash component, that a 15-year average term to maturity be structured into the fixed-income section, and that equities be concentrated in the growth categories. Juan's tax minimization objective also helps to determine which specific securities would be appropriate. Here the portfolio manager would be directed to bonds trading at a discount and preferred shares in the fixed-income section, and common shares whose total return would be more the result of capital gains than dividends.

To facilitate the final step in the selection process, the portfolio manager can make percentage and dollar allocations to each of the basic risk groups. The results of this process are shown in Table 26B.1. Once completed, the portfolio manager would recommend those individual securities believed to be the most attractive in each area. When the choices have been made, a recommended portfolio is presented in the format shown in Table 26B.2 – Portfolio Valuation. This sample portfolio is only an example of what a real portfolio should look like and does not reflect actual market values.

TABLE 26B.1 RISK GROUP WEIGHTINGS		
Juan Casuso – $280,000 Portfolio	**% of Total**	**$ Amount**
Cash (5%):		
Government Quality	5%	$14,000
Corporate Quality	–	–
Fixed-Income (15%):		
Short-Term	–	–
Mid-Term	5%	14,000
Long-Term	10%	28,000
Equities (80%):		
Conservative	25%	70,000
Growth	55%	154,000
Venture	–	–
Speculative	–	–
Total Portfolio	**100%**	**$280,000**

TABLE 26B.2 PORTFOLIO VALUATION

Holdings	Security	Current Price $	Approx. Market Value $	Per Cent of Total Value %	Indicated Int. Rate or Div. % or $	Indicated Annual Income $	Current Yield %
10,000	Gov. of Canada T-bill, 6 months	98.78	9,878.10	3.54	1.26	121.90	1.23
619	Cash		619.00	0.22	1.25	7.74	1.25
	TOTAL Cash Equivalents		**10,497.10**	**3.76**		**129.64**	**1.24**
Bonds and Debentures							
10,000	Prov. of Ontario, 4.20%, June 2, 10 years to maturity	106.30	10,630.00	3.81	4.20	420.00	3.95
10,000	Royal Bank, 4.93%, July 16, 15 years to maturity	106.10	10,610.00	3.80	4.93	493.00	4.65
10,000	Gov of Canada, 3.75%, June 1, 19 years to maturity	108.90	10,890.00	3.90	3.75	375.00	3.44
	TOTAL Bonds & Debentures		**32,130.00**	**11.51**		**1,288.00**	**4.01**
Preferred Shares							
600	Bank of Nova Scotia	27.98	16,788.00	6.01	1.56	936.00	5.58
	TOTAL Preferred Shares		**16,788.00**	**6.01**		**936.00**	**5.58**
Common Shares							
1,000	Bombardier	5.02	5,020.00	1.80	0.10	100	1.99
1,500	Telus	46.68	70,020.00	25.08	2.00	3,000.00	4.28
1,500	BCE	34.47	51,705.00	18.52	1.83	2,745.00	5.31
1,000	Royal Bank	56.40	56,400.00	20.20	2.00	2,000.00	3.55
2,000	iShares S&P/TSX 60	18.29	36,580.00	13.10	0.44	880.00	2.41
	Total Common Shares		**219,725.00**	**78.72**		**8,725.00**	**3.97**
	TOTAL Portfolio		**279,140.10**	**100.00**		**11,078.64**	**3.97**

Johanna Von Rosen

Johanna Von Rosen has just retired at age 65. She had been a bookkeeper with a large number of small companies in her career and was unemployed for long periods of time on several occasions. In 1981, Johanna started her own bookkeeping service, but the venture did not succeed and left her with debts that took three years to pay off.

Johanna is a quiet, independent person who is single. In addition, she never joined a pension plan and did not seem to have excess cash or adequate qualifying income on those few occasions when she considered an RRSP. Her financial situation includes the house that she purchased in 1975 and the $30,000 she has in a savings account. Johanna currently has no debts.

Johanna plans to sell her house (market value $120,000) and use the proceeds and her savings to generate income. Because she did not make maximum contributions to the Canada Pension Plan, she will only receive about $700 per month in Old Age Security and Canada Pension Plan benefits. Fortunately, these amounts will increase with inflation. Johanna has already found an apartment and feels that she requires $2,000 per month to live comfortably.

PERSONAL EVALUATION

In retirement, Johanna has only a modest lifestyle to maintain and no dependants to provide for. However, her position is complicated by the fact that she has a very small guaranteed income and a fixed amount of investment capital. Because her annual income will barely satisfy her needs, minimizing risk becomes a very important factor in her portfolio and tax minimization only a minor consideration.

INVESTMENT OBJECTIVES

Because approximately two-thirds of Johanna's income will be derived from her portfolio, her primary investment objective is income and her secondary objective is safety. To meet these objectives, Johanna requires a portfolio that is heavily invested in fixed-income securities.

THE RECOMMENDED PORTFOLIO

Johanna Von Rosen's dependence on the portfolio for income demands that the portfolio manager weight the fixed-income section heavily. The average term to maturity within the class would be shorter than the average term indicated by the outlook for interest rates. In addition, individual selections should be concentrated in government issues to further reduce risk. Since Johanna is only 65 years old, a small allocation to conservative equities may be considered.

Table 26B.3 indicates weightings that would be appropriate for Johanna Von Rosen and Table 26B.4 a recommended portfolio.

TABLE 26B.3   RISK GROUP WEIGHTINGS

Johanna Von Rosen – $150,000 Portfolio	% of Total	$ Amount
Cash (10%):		
Government Quality	10%	$15,000
Corporate Quality	–	–
Fixed-Income (80%):		
Short-Term	53%	80,000
Mid-Term	17%	25,000
Long-Term	10%	15,000
Equities (10%):		
Conservative	10%	15,000
Growth	–	–
Venture	–	–
Speculative	–	–
Total Portfolio	**100%**	**$150,000**

TABLE 26B.4   PORTFOLIO VALUATION

Holdings	Security	Current Price $	Approx. Market Value $	Per Cent of Total Value %	Indicated Int. Rate or Div. % or $	Indicated Annual Income $	Current Yield %
15,000	GOC T-bill, 9 months	98.78	14,817.00	9.68	1.26	183.00	1.24
754	Cash		754.00	0.49	1.25	9.43	1.25
	TOTAL Cash Equivalents		**15,571.00**	**10.18**		**192.43**	**1.24**
Bonds and Debentures							
20,000	Prov.of B.C. 9.50% January 23, 7 years to maturity	132.34	26,468.00	17.30	9.50	1,900.00	7.18
15,000	Bell Canada 6.15% June 15, 4 years to maturity	94.03	14,104.50	9.22	6.15	922.50	6.54
15,000	Prov.of Ontario 7.75% July 24, 1 year to maturity	105.48	15,822.00	10.34	7.75	1,162.50	7.35
20,000	Gov of Canada 7.25% June 1, 2 years to maturity	108.20	21,640.00	14.14	7.25	1,450.00	6.70
15,000	Prov of Nfld 6.15% April 17, 23 years to maturity	91.17	13,675.50	8.94	6.15	922.50	6.75
20,000	Gov of Canada 10% June 1, 3 years to maturity	122.06	24,412.00	15.96	10.00	2,000.00	8.19
	TOTAL Bonds & Debentures		**116,122.00**	**75.90**		**8,357.50**	**7.20**
Preferred Shares							
200	Bank of Nova Scotia	27.98	5,596.00	3.66	1.56	312.00	5.58
	TOTAL Preferred Shares		**5,596.00**	**3.66**		**312.00**	**5.58**
Common Shares							
200	Bank of Montreal	61.32	12,264.00	8.02	2.80	560.00	4.57
100	BCE Inc.	34.47	3,447.00	2.25	1.83	183.00	5.31
	Total Common Shares		**15,711.00**	**10.27**		**743.00**	**4.73**
	TOTAL Portfolio		**153,000.00**	**100.00**		**9,604.93**	**6.28**

Chapter 27

Working With the Institutional Client

27

Working With the Institutional Client

LEARNING OBJECTIVES

By the end of this chapter, you should be able to:

1. Define the term institutional client.
2. Differentiate between retail client suitability requirements and institutional information requirements.
3. Describe the roles and responsibilities of the participants in the institutional marketplace.

THE INSTITUTIONAL MARKET

Brokerage firms serve two types of clients: retail and institutional. Although outnumbered by retail clients, institutional clients hold power and influence in financial markets that belie their ranks. The market value of the average institutional account would dwarf the market value of the average retail account. The average institutional client is also far more experienced and knowledgeable than the average retail client.

In this chapter, we examine the process of working with the institutional client. We start with an overview of the institutional marketplace and provide the exact definition of an institutional client. We then compare the institutional client with the retail client, and outline the responsibilities for maintaining an account for each of the two. Finally, we examine the roles and responsibilities of six broker dealer employees who play a key role in working with institutional clients.

KEY TERMS

Accredited investor

Agency trader

Analyst

Broker dealer

Institutional salesperson

Institutional trader

Investment banker

Liability trader

Research associate

WHO ARE INSTITUTIONAL CLIENTS?

An institutional client is a legal entity that represents the collective financial interests of a large group. A mutual fund, insurance company, pension fund and corporate treasury are just a few examples. We will discuss these groups in more detail below.

The group's financial interests are the objectives that serve their members' goals. Group members can be shareholders, pensioners or employees. Goals can be diverse, ranging from hedging out currency exposure in a $100 million bond fund portfolio, to growing pension assets faster than inflation over a particular period. A group's goal might also be to raise $400 million in a stock offering for a corporation, for example, or to minimize tracking error in an exchange-traded fund.

Institutional clients are also distinguished by the size of their accounts. At a minimum, institutional clients have a fiduciary responsibility for the millions of dollars of their members' assets. A massive account size also accords institutional clients lower fees and commissions, compared to the average fees paid by the retail client.

Due to their size, institutions dominate the financial landscape. Institutional clients consist of the following groups:

Corporate Treasuries	A corporate treasury department is responsible for managing the firm's financial assets in support of the company's business activities. Duties range from general management of company finances to decisions on funding and risk management. A corporate treasury department engages in activities that may require the services of a **broker dealer**. These may include hedging the currency risk of a foreign subsidiary or accessing the most inexpensive capital possible by selling equity or debt in a domestic or foreign market.
	A broker dealer is a firm that trades securities for its own account or on behalf of its customers. When buying or selling on behalf of a customer, the firm is said to be acting as a broker. When buying or selling for its own account, the institution is said to be acting as a dealer. In Canada, they are primarily subsidiaries of a commercial bank.
Insurance Companies	Insurance companies accept premiums from policyholders to fund potential payoffs in the event of a contingent loss suffered by a policyholder. Examples of contingent loss include physical damage to property or possessions, personal injury or loss of life, or legal claims made by others against the customer. The process by which the insurance company chooses the risks to insure and the suitable amount of premium to be paid is called underwriting. The premiums are then reinvested into the insurance company's own portfolio of financial and real assets. Investment horizons tend to be long term.
	Some insurance company activities require the help of a broker dealer. These activities include buying and selling equities and bonds, providing a supply of newly issued securities, supplying the market research to support trading activity, and hedging the interest rate risks of its bond portfolios.

Pension Funds

A pension fund is a pool of assets managed with the goal to supply its beneficiaries income during their retirement years. A pension fund could represent the interests of either public or private sector employees (For example, the Ontario Teachers' Pension Plan (OTPP)).

Pension funds, like insurance companies, have a long investment horizon. If the pension fund is managed directly by the public or private sector employees, broker dealers help pension plans by buying and selling equities and bonds and supplying the market research to support that activity. Otherwise, broker dealers aid indirectly by supporting the investment managers hired by the pension funds to manage their assets.

Mutual Funds

A mutual fund is a pool of assets managed for the benefit of its unitholders, who own the assets. The fund can assume any number of objectives, or operate in any number of markets. For example, a mutual fund could invest in bonds or equities, operate in domestic or foreign markets, or follow an active investing philosophy or an indexing philosophy.

Broker dealers help mutual funds by buying and selling equities and bonds on their behalf, providing a supply of newly issued securities, supplying the market research to support trading activity, or hedging out currency or pricing risks in their portfolios.

Hedge Funds

A hedge fund is a pool of assets managed for the benefit of its unitholders. Unlike a mutual fund, a hedge fund is not regulated at all in terms of investment activity, and is free to utilize whatever investment strategies in any market the fund management feel best suited to its strength (including the use of leverage). However, not everyone is free to invest in a hedge fund. Investors must be accredited by certain income and asset standards before being allowed to invest in a hedge fund.

A hedge fund may have a long or short investment horizon, depending on the strategy of the fund. Broker dealers assist hedge funds by buying and selling equities, bonds or derivatives on their behalf; supplying the market research to support that activity; or hedging out pricing risks in their portfolios.

Endowments

An endowment is a pool of assets created from gifts and donations for the purpose of creating income to help an organization achieve its specific goals. An organization may include a charity or university, and its aims are not for profit. For example, the goal might be to fund annual scholarships, buy medical supplies for foreign relief workers or finance the creation of educational media. The endowment owns the assets. Typically, an endowment requires the principle to remain intact in perpetuity.

Endowments, especially in the case of larger funds, are free to use whatever investment strategy the custodians of the fund see fit. Broker dealers assist endowments similar to hedge funds, by assisting the managers in charge of their portfolios to buy and sell equities, bonds or derivatives on their behalf; supplying the market research to support trading activity; providing a supply of newly issued securities; or hedging out pricing risks.

Trusts	Like an endowment, a trust is also a pool of assets. Unlike an endowment, however, a trust is created by a settlor (a person or organization) for the good of another party, known as the beneficiary. The trust terms can spell out specific aims for the use of the assets, although none are required. A trustee manages the trust's assets. The trustee has fiduciary duty to the beneficiaries.
	There are various reasons for creating a trust, including tax planning, asset protection and estate planning. Trusts that are big enough to be considered an institutional account are usually managed as charitable or family trusts of high net worth individuals.
	The investment horizon of a trust is long, typically the life span of the beneficiary. Broker dealers help trusts by buying and selling equities and bonds on their behalf, providing a supply of newly issued securities, supplying the market research to support trading activity or hedging out pricing risks in their portfolios.

WHAT ARE THE SUITABILITY REQUIREMENTS FOR INSTITUTIONAL CLIENTS?

An institutional client is bigger than the retail client in every way. The institutional client has greater net worth, larger accounts, more market knowledge and more experience than the retail client, and has more sophisticated needs. These differences also stand out in the way regulations are set for the opening, operation and supervision of institutional client accounts versus those for retail accounts.

For example, when it comes to client suitability tests, standards for retail clients are far stricter than for institutional clients. As discussed earlier, the Know-Your-Client (KYC) rule requires every registered dealer and salesperson to obtain a client's essential financial and personal circumstances, investment objectives and risk tolerance, in a diligent and comprehensive manner.

An institutional client deemed sophisticated or large enough is considered an **accredited investor** under current regulations. An accredited investor may include a Canadian bank, a trust company, a person or company registered as an adviser or dealer (subject to a few exceptions), a pension fund, any level of government (federal, provincial or municipal), or an investment fund advised by a registered portfolio manager.

Institutional clients, as accredited investors, are not scrutinized to the same degree as retail clients. The difference in level of scrutiny is based on the premise that an institutional client's objectives, risk tolerance and financial situation are not the dealer's concern. The institutional client has auditors, internal compliance staff, shareholders and regulatory bodies that take care of that. These clients are exempt from certain suitability requirements that apply to retail clients.

Individuals may also be considered accredited investors provided they meet certain conditions:

- Net income before taxes must exceed $200,000 (or $300,000 with a spouse, if married) in each of the past two years; or,
- Must own, either alone or together with a spouse, at least $1 million in net financial assets; or,
- Must own, either alone or together with a spouse, net assets of at least $5 million.

Suitability Standards for Institutional Clients

According to IIROC Rule 2700, a dealer member need only determine if the institutional client is sophisticated and capable enough of making its own investment decisions. If the dealer has reasonable grounds to conclude that the institutional client is capable, the dealer's suitability obligation is fulfilled. If no grounds exist, the dealer must determine the appropriate level of suitability owed to that customer so that the institutional client fully understands the potential risks and rewards.

The rule also outlines the relevant points dealers should consider when making that initial determination, as follows:

- Any written or oral understanding that exists between a dealer member and its client regarding the client's reliance on the dealer member

- The presence or absence of a pattern of acceptance of the dealer member's recommendations

- The use by a client of ideas, suggestions, market views and information obtained from other dealer members, market professionals or issuers, particularly those relating to the same type of securities

- The use of one or more investment dealers, portfolio managers, investment counsel or other third party advisors

- The general level of the client's experience in financial markets

- The specific client experience with the type of instrument(s) under consideration, including the client's ability to independently evaluate how market developments would affect the security and ancillary risks, such as currency rate risk

- The complexity of the securities involved

If suitability is not determined, dealer members can still be exempt from this suitability obligation. This occurs when the dealer executes a trade on the instructions of another dealer member, portfolio manager, investment counsel, bank, trust company or insurer. IIROC also provides Product Due Diligence guidelines for dealer members. Most importantly, for dealers to meet their suitability obligations, they must know the products that they sell to clients.

WHAT ARE THE ROLES AND RESPONSIBILITIES IN THE INSTITUTIONAL MARKET?

As mentioned earlier, the needs of institutional clients vary from trading services to security issuance to market research. Member dealers have organized themselves to fill those needs. Whether involved with equities, fixed income or derivatives, a number of professionals commonly deal with institutional clients. The following lists some key positions in the institutional market:

Research Associate	Also known as the associate analyst, the research associate is the entry-level position for other jobs in the equity and fixed income markets. The research associate reports to a senior analyst, mainly builds financial or pricing models, conducts industry or company research and helps write reports and commentary. Associate analysts basically free up the senior analysts' time to attend to more value added tasks.
	Typically, education requirements are, at minimum, an MBA, CFA, or CA designation. It is possible to be hired without these qualifications, but only in the more technical fields, such as chemistry or mining, where a master's degree in the field is more appropriate. For those dealing in derivatives, the Derivatives Fundamentals Course offered by CSI, provides an excellent knowledge base of the various derivatives instruments.
Analyst	Also known as the sell side or research analyst, the analyst is considered an expert in respect to a specific company or sector, and provides other front office staff with ongoing coverage in their area of specialty. For example, investment bankers look to the equity analyst for a financial forecast on companies they cover. Institutional clients may look to the derivatives analyst for market knowledge and trading ideas. Analyst ranks are often filled from within, usually from the trading desk or associate ranks.
	Education requirements are similar to those for associate analysts but relevant work experience also counts a great deal.
Institutional Sales	The institutional salesperson's main job is to be a relationship manager, serving as the liaison between the dealer and the client.
	Education requirements for those in the equity and fixed income arenas are typically less rigid compared to the research associate role, mostly because salespeople tend to be generalists: they speak to all types of clients about a wide range of products and subjects, and to a wide range of analysts. However, an MBA or CFA designation is typical for institutional salespersons.
Institutional Trader	A trader can execute orders on behalf of clients (agency traders) or on behalf of the dealer member (liability traders).

Investment Banker	An investment banker is responsible for building the following three areas of the dealer's business: 1. **Corporate Finance**: Raising debt and equity capital for corporations 2. **Public Finance**: Raising capital for governments and their agencies 3. **Mergers & Acquisitions**: Providing advice on mergers, buy-outs, asset sales and corporate restructurings, valuations and fairness opinions Positions in the investment banking department are stratified over the following three basic responsibilities: 1. **Analysts and associates**: Responsible for the analytical work 2. **Vice-presidents or associate directors**: Responsible for day-to-day management 3. **Managing directors**: Responsible for the strategic direction of the business The senior investment banking staff also takes more responsibility for maintaining corporate relationships and has more client interaction. An undergraduate economics or business degree may be sufficient to get new staff into the associate ranks. To gain responsibility, associates would need an MBA or LLB following their second year. Those who are more advanced can be fast tracked into an associate role by their fourth year.

Let's now discuss in detail the two positions that serve the most important roles within dealer members, working with institutional clients, salespersons and traders:

- Institutional Salesperson

- Institutional Trader

The Role of the Institutional Salesperson

As mentioned earlier, the institutional salesperson is the client relationship manager, the conduit between the customer's needs and the dealer. It's a dynamic job. The salesperson markets the dealer's analysts, takes management teams for presentations to clients, takes clients to site visits or entertains clients.

A good salesperson is an effective pipeline in managing the flow of information and products to clients. The dealer member's research ideas and analysts are highlighted to clients interested in the sectors the dealer covers or specializes in.

To perform the job well, a salesperson needs to do the following three things well:

1. **Build and maintain strong relationships with clients**. Salespeople need to apply the Know Your Client rules to the utmost degree because institutional clients can and will demand the highest level of service and professionalism. Those salespersons that do so will gain the client's trust and respect (and business).

2. **Work at a dealer with good research and/or investment banking services**. Salespeople need to be backed by good research and/or investment banking services to sell. The dealer should have a well-regarded team of analysts that institutional clients consider near or at the top of their specialty. A good research group will give their sales team plenty of ideas to talk about and plenty of opportunities to build relationships. The dealer should also have a good investment banking group that can procure product to sell.

3. **Develop deep knowledge about the dealer member's products and the market factors that affect their pricing**. Salespeople must gain a certain level of expertise about the products they sell and of the companies/businesses/sectors that affect the market for those products. For example, a salesperson who sells credit derivatives should be intimately familiar with credit market spreads, monetary conditions and business condition risks. Familiarity breeds confidence. The salesperson's confidence will show when speaking to clients about their investment needs.

Accounts among salespeople are typically divided as follows:

• **Geographically**: Dealers segregate accounts by geographical area to make it logistically simpler for their salespeople to visit clients.

• **By account type**: Dealers categorize accounts into two types: fundamental and hedge/arbitrage. Fundamental accounts belong to long-only money managers. To get the managers' business, the salesperson has to emphasize the dealer's intellectual resources and ability to generate money-making ideas that will help the manager's overall business. Hedge/arbitrage accounts are more like trading accounts and tend to be more interested in money-making ideas.

• **By relationships**: Some dealers allocate accounts to those salespersons with whom the client has the best relationship.

EXHIBIT 27.1	A DAY IN THE LIFE OF AN INSTITUTIONAL EQUITY SALESPERSON – *For information only*
6:00 A.M.	Have a quick breakfast, scan the newspapers, check the pager and Bloomberg for any new events.
7:00 A.M.	Once at the office, I check emails, read the morning research notes and prepare for the morning Sales/Trading/Research meeting.
7:30 A.M.	During the meeting, I ask traders about market flows and analysts about any developments that might impact their recommendations. The sales group is updated on the current status of corporate finance deals and highlights from company visits.
8:15 A.M.	I'm at my desk making morning calls to clients and sending out notes via email to clients with trading and morning meeting comments. I try to be as succinct as possible because our clients also tend to be inundated with information.
8:30 A.M.	Call portfolio manager Smith with a follow up on the consumer products stock he has been analyzing.
8:40 A.M.	Call a Montreal based account to give some feedback on a management visit to technology company Z that he couldn't attend. I tie the visit back to my firm's recommendation on Z and the view on the sector. I mention the firm is a buyer of company Z stock on the trading desk.
9:05 A.M.	Call portfolio manager Jones with comments from our copper mining analyst regarding his interpretation of recent drill results.
9:30 A.M.	Call the senior resource analyst at my hedge fund client to discuss some earnings estimates made by our energy analyst. Although the estimates were on the morning email, I want to highlight the companies they didn't already own that look interesting.
9:50 A.M.	Meet the senior management team of an auto parts company whose IPO we are leading. I take them to visit one of our institutional clients.
11:15 A.M.	I head to a meeting at another dealer's office to get information on an income trust IPO they are leading.
11:55 A.M.	Finish off the morning calls.
12:00 P.M.	I co-host a client luncheon with management of a senior mining company in the boardroom.
2:15 P.M.	Attend a sales/trading/research conference call to review flows in the market, and to update news from the morning and stocks to watch for in the afternoon.
2:30 P.M.	I take our bank analyst to visit portfolio manager B.
3:30 P.M.	I book company and analyst meetings for the next day. I check emails, return phone calls and sort through some research.
4:00 P.M.	Stock market closes.
4:15 P.M.	The entire sales desk attends a meeting where analysts focus on a specific trading idea or new technology, or revisit a prior recommendation.
5:15 P.M.	Read a recent research report from our real estate analyst. I return a few more phone calls and recheck my schedule for the next day.
5:45 P.M.	Head out to a dinner hosted by an out of town client.

The Role of the Institutional Trader

Firms have the following two types of traders serving institutional accounts:

• Agency Traders

• Liability Traders

AGENCY TRADERS

Agency traders manage trades for institutional clients. They do not trade the dealer member's capital, and they trade only when acting on behalf of clients. Agency traders do not merely take orders; they must manage institutional orders with minimal market impact and act as the client's eyes and ears for relevant market intelligence.

Agency traders need to pay attention to a myriad of information sources. They need to be aware of client intentions at all times, watch for news or events that might affect client orders, and come up with trading ideas to generate commissions.

Information overwhelms agency traders from all directions, arriving from print media, internet sources, blogs and real time news services. In addition, agency traders have industry contacts with whom they share information. All of the information is necessary to get a sense of the whole picture and to instantly analyze unexpected events that could move markets.

Filling orders with minimal market impact means that the agency trader makes the transaction with the lowest possible cost to the institutional client. Institutional orders, if improperly executed, could cost the client tens of thousands of dollars extra, or much more. For example, an agency equity trader could choose to completely fill an order in one swoop, or break up the order into pieces, if the market for the stock is too small at the moment or if prices might be more favourable later in the day. For an agency derivatives trader, getting a good fill means finding a counterparty that is both credit worthy and willing to price the derivative favourably for the client.

Agency traders also need to develop and maintain good relationships with their clients. Although they do not have as much contact with clients as salespeople, agency traders need to establish a comfort level with clients so that their clients know their assets are being well served on the frontlines of the markets.

Part of establishing a comfort level is coming up with the occasional trading idea. Each institutional client has a commission allocation by which business is divided among dealers. Other than the regular business allocated to a specific dealer, each institution has some leeway to pay out extra commissions to each dealer. It is part of the agency trader's responsibility to capture some of this discretionary business for his dealer.

LIABILITY TRADERS

Liability traders have the responsibility to manage the dealer's trading capital to encourage market flows and facilitate the client orders that go into the market, while aiming to lose as little of that capital as possible. Liability traders can be considered those who set the direction for agency traders. Whereas agency traders have formal client responsibilities, liability traders have lighter responsibilities or none at all.

Liability traders are assigned specific sectors of the market. On an equity desk, one trader could be covering gold stocks, while another covers telecom stocks. On a fixed income desk, one trader could be covering asset backed securities, while another covers high yield issues. On a derivatives desk, one trader could be covering fixed-to-floating interest rate swaps, while a counterpart trades floating-to-fixed swaps.

The liability trader walks a fine line daily between market share and profitability. Establishing the dealer as a market leader in a sector will help raise the dealer's reputation as the preferred dealer when issuing or trading those securities. But that will likely tie up a large proportion of trading capital. Liability traders still need to be intimately familiar with their sectors; how clients are exposed, or will be exposed, to those sectors; and how fundamentals are driving the ebb and flow of the market.

Liability traders can use the dealer's trading capital either reactively or proactively. Reactive trading refers to making trades based on a reaction to some event or request that has occurred. Proactive trading refers to taking the initiative to enter a trade in the absence of a triggering event or request. The following is an example of using capital reactively:

> The dealer has a client who wants to sell 100,000 shares of XYZ stock. The market on XYZ stock is $10 bid, $10.10 ask. The dealer's liability desk makes a market and buys the 100,000 shares at $10.10. Because it is not in the business of holding stocks long term, the liability desk tries to offload the stock that day. Hopefully, market conditions will improve for the liability trader to sell into. If conditions do not improve and the trader sells into the market at $10 bid and $10.10 ask, the dealer will lose $10,000 on the sale of XYZ at $10.

Another example of a reactive trade occurs when a derivatives dealer is approached to be the counterparty on a contract. The trade will occur at an agreeable price if the liability trader can find a second counterparty or make another trade to offset his exposure.

Using capital proactively for example, the liability trader could make a market in a security that is deemed favourable by one of the dealer's analysts. By accumulating inventory and accentuating demand via analyst reports, the dealer is ready to fill orders by the time institutional accounts are solicited by the dealer's salespeople.

Another proactive example occurs when the dealer becomes active in a particular stock or sector in order to create underwriting or investment banking deals. Underwriting and investment banking is a high margin business. If the dealer is seen to be the top market maker in that space, the dealer can more effectively pitch to be a leading underwriter on the next new issue.

Complete the following Online Learning Activity

Roles and Responsibilities

In this activity you will learn more about the different roles and responsibilities of participants in the institutional marketplace.

 Complete the **Roles and Responsibilities** activity.

SUMMARY

By the end of this chapter, you should be able to:

1. Define the term institutional client.

    - An institutional client is a legal entity that represents the collective financial interests of a large group. A mutual fund, insurance company, pension fund and corporate treasury are examples.

    - The group's financial interests are the objectives that serve their members' goals.

    - In contrast, retail clients are typically individuals with much smaller sums to invest.

2. Differentiate between retail client suitability requirements and institutional information requirements.

    - When it comes to client suitability tests, standards for retail clients are far stricter than for institutional clients.

    - The difference in level of scrutiny is based on the premise that an institutional client's objectives, risk tolerance and financial situation are not the dealer's concern.

    - An accredited investor is an entity sophisticated or large enough that the suitability requirements applicable to this type of client are different than those for retail clients. Individuals may also be considered accredited investors, provided that certain conditions are met.

    - According to IIROC Rule 2700, a dealer member need only determine if the institutional client is sophisticated and capable enough of making its own investment decisions.

3. Describe the roles and responsibilities of the participants in the institutional marketplace.

    - The institutional salesperson is the client relationship manager, the conduit between the customer's needs and the dealer. The salesperson markets the dealer's analysts, takes management teams for presentations to clients, takes clients to site visits or entertains clients.

    - Agency traders manage trades for institutional clients. They do not trade the dealer member's capital, and they trade only when acting on behalf of clients. Agency traders must manage institutional orders with minimal market impact and act as the client's eyes and ears for relevant market intelligence.

    - Liability traders have the responsibility to manage the dealer's trading capital to encourage market flows and facilitate the client orders that go into the market, while aiming to lose as little of that capital as possible. Liability traders can be considered those who set the direction for agency traders. Whereas agency traders have formal client responsibilities, liability traders have lighter responsibilities or none at all.

Online Frequently Asked Questions

CSI has answered many frequently asked questions about this Chapter.
Read through online Module 27 FAQs.

Online Post-Module Assessment

Once you have completed the chapter, take the Module 27 Post-Test.

Summary for Volume 2

Congratulations on completing Volume 2 of the CSC!

You should take this opportunity to congratulate yourself on this significant accomplishment. By this point in your studies you have read over 600 pages of material, answered well over 200 post-assessment questions, completed activities, posted questions to our discussion boards—in other words, you've done a lot of work to get to this point. Although you have more work ahead of you as you prepare for the final exam, the finish line is in sight.

Volume 2 Focus

If you can think back to Volume 1 for a moment, you'll recall that our main focus for the first part of the course was understanding the different financial markets and financial instruments that help to facilitate the transfer of capital from savers to users through the various financial intermediaries.

Our focus shifted somewhat in Volume 2 towards applying what you learned to the various markets and financial instruments. The analysis was a little deeper and the real-world applicability a little more prevalent.

A quick recap:

- You learned about how to analyze the economy and public companies so that you better understand the role that market analysts play and the different types of financial reports they prepare.
- You learned about combining securities into a portfolio and the asset allocation process and studied mutual, segregated and hedge funds, and were given a very thorough overview of the many different types of managed, exchange-listed, and structured products available in the marketplace.
- And finally, you have a much better idea of the workings of fee based accounts, the Canadian taxation system and the differences between retail and institutional clients.

When Preparing for Your Exam

Now that you have completed Volume 2 of the course, are you able to answer the following?
- How does the approach technical analysts use to value a security differ from fundamental analysis?
- Can you calculate the intrinsic value of a stock using the dividend discount model?
- What impact does the increase in total debt outstanding have on the asset coverage ratio?
- Why is a high inventory turnover rate considered good for a company?
- If the beta on a stock is rising, what does that mean for the overall riskiness of the stock?
- What are the three primary investment objectives?
- What is the key different between the bottom-up and top-down investment approaches?
- What is the primary objective of a tactical asset allocation strategy?
- What are some of the key advantages of investing in mutual funds?
- How is the MER calculated?
- How do mutual funds generate taxable income?
- What is the right of withdrawal? The right of rescission?
- What are the key differentiating features of a segregated fund compared to a mutual fund?
- What are some of the tax consequences of investing in a segregated fund?
- What are some of the requirements to investing in a hedge fund?
- Under a merger hedge fund strategy, would you go long or short on the company being acquired?
- Can you list two disadvantages of investing in a closed-end fund?
- How does a leveraged ETF work?
- What are the features of a fee-based managed account?
- What are the three main types of PPNs?
- What is a risk associated with an index-linked GIC?
- What is a special purpose vehicle?
- How is a capital gain generated and calculated for tax purposes?

- How is a superficial loss created?
- What are the steps in the financial planning process?
- Can you list the five standards of conduct?
- Can you list the various types of institutional clients?

This is a random selection of topics and concepts and by no means an exhaustive list. However, it should give you a good idea of where your strengths and weaknesses are and may alert you to the need for additional review before attempting your Volume 2 exam.

We also encourage a thorough review of the glossary for the key terms you have come across in this second volume when preparing for the exam.

Glossary

The following is a glossary of investment terms that will help you study for the CSC examination and increase your overall knowledge of the investment industry. Some of the terms also have a general meaning, but only their specialized investment industry meaning is given here. Words in **bold face** type within definitions have their own glossary definitions. Note that this list is not complete: it should be used in conjunction with your own definitions of terms compiled during your studies and with the Index.

Accredited Investor

An individual or institutional investor who meets certain minimum requirement relating to income, net worth, or investment knowledge. Also referred to as a sophisticated investor.

Accrued Interest

Interest accumulated on a bond or debenture since the last interest payment date.

Adjusted Cost Base

The deemed cost of an asset representing the sum of the amount originally paid plus any additional costs, such as brokerage fees and commissions.

Advance-Decline Line

A tool used in technical analysis to measure the breadth of the market. The analyst takes difference between the number of stocks that increased in value each day less the number that have decreased.

After Acquired Clause

A protective clause found in a **bond's indenture** or **contract** that binds the **bond** issuer to pledging all subsequently purchased assets as part of the collateral for a bond issue.

After Market Stabilization

A type of arrangement where the dealer supports the offer price of a newly issued stock once it begins trading in the secondary market.

Agency Traders

Manage trades for institutional clients. They do not trade the dealer member's capital, and they trade only when acting on behalf of clients. Agency traders do not merely take orders; they must manage institutional orders with minimal market impact and act as the client's eyes and ears for relevant market intelligence.

Agent

An investment dealer operates as an agent when it acts on behalf of a buyer or a seller of a security and does not itself own title to the securities at any time during the transactions. See also **Principal**.

All or None Order (AON)

An order that must be executed in its entirety – partial fills will not be accepted.

Allocation

The administrative procedure by which income generated by the **segregated fund's** investment portfolio is flowed through to the individual contract holders of the fund.

Alpha

A statistical measure of the value a fund manager adds to the performance of the fund managed. If alpha is positive, the manager has added value to the portfolio. If the alpha is negative, the manager has underperformed the market.

Alternative Trading Systems (ATS)

Privately-owned computerized networks that match orders for securities outside of recognized exchange facilities. Also referred to as Proprietary Electronic Trading Systems (PETS).

American-Style Option

An option that can be exercised at any time during the option's lifetime. See also **European-Style Option**.

Amortization

Gradually writing off the value of an **intangible asset** over a period of time. Commonly applied to items such as **goodwill**, improvements to leased premises, or expenses of a new stock or bond issue. See also **Depreciation**.

Annual Information Form (AIF)

A document in which an issuer is required to disclose information about presently known trends, commitments, events or uncertainties that are reasonably expected to have a material impact on the issuer's business, financial condition or results of operations. Although investors are typically not provided with the AIF, the prospectus must state that it is available on request.

Annual Report

The formal financial statements and report on operations issued by a company to its shareholders after its fiscal year-end.

Annuitant

Person on whose life the **maturity** and **death benefit** guarantees are based. It can be the contract holder or someone else designated by the contract holder. In registered plans, the **annuitant** and contract holder must be the same person.

Annuity

A contract usually sold by life insurance companies that guarantees an income to the beneficiary or annuitant at some time in the future. The income stream can be very flexible. The original purchase price may be either a lump sum or a stream of payments. See **Deferred Annuity** and **Immediate Annuity**.

Any Part Order

A type of order in which the client will accept all stock in odd, broken or standard trading units up to the full amount of the order.

Arbitrage

The simultaneous purchase of a security on one stock exchange and the sale of the same security on another exchange at prices which yield a profit to the arbitrageur.

Arbitration

A method of dispute resolution in which an independent arbitrator is chosen to assist aggrieved parties recover damages.

Arrears

Interest or dividends that were not paid when due but are still owed. For example, **dividends** owed but not paid to **cumulative preferred** shareholders accumulate in a separate account (arrears). When payments resume, dividends in arrears must be paid to the preferred shareholders before the **common** shareholders.

Ask

The lowest price a seller will accept for the financial instrument being quoted. See also **Bid**.

Asset

Everything a company or a person owns or has owed to it. A statement of financial position category.

Asset Allocation

Apportioning investment funds among different categories of assets, such as cash, fixed income securities and equities. The allocation of assets is built around an investor's risk tolerance.

Asset-backed commercial paper (ABCP)

A type of security that has a maturity date of less than one year, typically in the range of 90 to 180 days, with a legal and design structure of an asset-backed security.

Asset Mix

The percentage distribution of assets in a portfolio among the three major asset classes: cash and equivalents, fixed income and equities.

Assuris

A not for profit company whose member firms are issuers of life-insurance contracts and whose mandate is to provide protection to contract holders against the insolvency of a member company.

At-the-Money

An **option** with a strike price equal to (or almost equal to) the market price of the underlying security. See also **Out-of-the-money** and **In-the-money.**

Attribution Rules

A Canada Revenue Agency rule stating that an investor cannot avoid paying taxes at their marginal rate by transferring assets to other family members who have lower personal tax rates.

Auction Market

Market in which securities are bought and sold by brokers acting as **agents** for their clients, in contrast to a **dealer** market where trades are conducted **over-the-counter.** For example, the Toronto Stock Exchange is an auction market.

Audit

A professional review and examination of a company's financial statements required under corporate law for the purpose of ensuring that the statements are fair, consistent and conform with **International Financial Reporting Standards (IFRS).**

Authorized Shares

The maximum number of **common** (or **preferred**) shares that a corporation may issue under the terms of its charter.

Autorité des marchés financiers (Financial Services Authority) (AMF)

The body that administers the regulatory framework surrounding Québec's financial sector: securities sector, the distribution of financial products and services sector, the financial institutions sector and the compensation sector.

Averages

A statistical tool used to measure the direction of the market. The most common average is the **Dow Jones Industrial Average**.

Back-End Load

A sales charge applied on the redemption of a **mutual fund**.

Balance of Payments

Canada's interactions with the rest of the world which are captured here in the current account and capital account.

Bank of Canada

Canada's central bank which exercises its influence on the economy by raising and lowering short-term interest rates.

Bank Rate

The minimum rate at which the Bank of Canada makes short-term advances to the chartered banks, other members of the **Canadian Payments Association** and investment dealers who trade in the money market.

Bankers' Acceptance

A commercial draft (i.e., a written instruction to make payment) drawn by a borrower for payment on a specified date. A BA is guaranteed at maturity by the borrower's bank. As with T-bills, BAs are sold at a discount and mature at their face value, with the difference representing the return to the investor. BAs may be sold before maturity at prevailing market rates, generally offering a higher yield than Canada T-bills.

Banking Group

A group of investment firms, each of which individually assumes financial responsibility for part of an **underwriting.**

Bankrupt

The legal status of an individual or company that is unable to pay its creditors and whose **assets** are therefore administered for its creditors by a Trustee in Bankruptcy.

Basis Point

One-hundredth of a percentage point of bond yields. Thus, 1% represents 100 basis points.

Bear

One who expects that the market generally, or the market price of a particular security, will decline. See also **Bull.**

Bear Market

A sustained decline in equity prices. Bear markets are usually associated with a downturn (recession or contraction) in the business cycle.

Bearer Security

A security (stock or bond) which does not have the owner's name recorded in the books of the issuing company nor on the security itself and which is payable to the holder, i.e., the holder is the deemed owner of the security. See also **Registered Security.**

Beneficial Owner

The real (underlying) owner of an account, securities or other assets. An investor may own shares which are registered in the name of an investment dealer, trustee or bank to facilitate transfer or to preserve anonymity, but the investor would be the beneficial owner.

Beneficiary

The individual or individuals who have been designated to receive the **death benefit**. Beneficiaries may be either revocable or irrevocable.

Best Efforts Underwriting

The attempt by an investment dealer (underwriter) to sell an issue of securities, to the best of their abilities, but does not guarantee that any or all of the issue will be sold. The investment dealer is not held liable to fulfill the order or to sell all of the securities. The underwriter acts as an **agent** for the issuer in distributing the issue.

Beta

A measure of the sensitivity (i.e., volatility) of a stock or a mutual fund to movements in the overall stock market. The beta for the market is considered to be 1. A fund that mirrors the market, such as an index fund, would also have a beta of 1. Funds or stocks with a beta greater than 1 are more volatile than the market and are therefore riskier. A beta less than 1 is not as volatile and can be expected to rise and fall by less than the overall market.

Bid

The highest price a buyer is willing to pay for the financial instrument being quoted. See also **Ask.**

Blue Chip

An active, leading, nationally known common stock with a record of continuous dividend payments and other strong investment qualities. The implication is that the company is of "good" investment value.

Blue Sky

A slang term for laws that various Canadian provinces and American states have enacted to protect the public against securities frauds. The term blue skyed is used to indicate that a new issue has been cleared by a securities commission and may be distributed.

Bond

A certificate evidencing a **debt** on which the issuer promises to pay the holder a specified amount of interest based on the **coupon** rate, for a specified length of time, and to repay the loan on its maturity. Strictly speaking, assets are pledged as security for a bond issue, except in the case of government "bonds", but the term is often loosely used to describe any funded debt issue.

Bond Contract

The actual legal agreement between the issuer and the bondholder. The contract outlines the terms and conditions – the **coupon** rate, timing of coupon payments, **maturity** date and any other terms. The bond contract is usually administered by a trust company on behalf of all the bondholders. Also called a **Bond Indenture** or **Trust Deed**.

Bond Indenture

See **Bond Contract**.

Book Value

The amount of net assets belonging to the owners of a business (or shareholders of a company) based on **statement of financial position** values. It represents the total value of the company's assets that shareholders would theoretically receive if a company were liquidated. Also represents the original cost of the units allocated to a **segregated fund** contract.

Bottom-Up Analysis

An investment approach that seeks out undervalued companies. A fund manager may find companies whose low share prices are not justified. They would buy these securities and when the market finally realizes that they are undervalued, the share price rises giving the astute bottom up manager a profit. See also **Top-Down Analysis**.

Bought Deal

A new issue of stocks or bonds bought from the issuer by an investment dealer, frequently acting alone, for resale to its clients, usually by way of a **private placement** or short form prospectus. The dealer risks its own capital in the bought deal. In the event that the price has to be lowered to sell out the issue, the dealer absorbs the loss.

Bourse de Montréal

A stock exchange (also referred to as the Montréal Exchange) that deals exclusively with non-agricultural options and futures in Canada, including all options that previously traded on the **Toronto Stock Exchange** and all futures products that previously traded on the Toronto Futures Exchange.

Broker

An investment dealer or a duly registered individual that is registered to trade in securities in the capacity of an agent or principal and is a member of a **Self-Regulatory Organization**.

Broker of Record

The broker named as the official advisor to a corporation on financial matters; has the right of first refusal on any new issues.

Bucketing

Confirming a transaction where no trade has been executed.

Budget Deficit

Occurs when total spending by the government for the year is higher than revenue collected.

Budget Surplus

Occurs when government revenue for the year exceeds expenditures.

Bull

One who expects that the market generally or the market price of a particular security will rise. See also **Bear**.

Bull Market

A general and prolonged rising trend in security prices. Bull markets are usually associated with an expansionary phase of the **business cycle**. As a memory aid, it is said that a bull walks with his head up while a **bear** walks with his head down.

Business Cycle

The recurrence of periods of **expansion** and **recession** in economic activity. Each cycle is expected to move through five phases – the **trough, recovery, expansion, peak, contraction (recession)**. Given an understanding of the relationship between the business cycle and security prices an investor or fund manager would select an **asset mix** to maximize returns.

Business Risk

The risk inherent in a company's operations, reflected in the variability in earnings. A weakening in consumer interest or technological obsolescence usually causes the decline. Examples include manufacturers of vinyl records, eight track recording tapes and beta video machines.

Buy-Back

A company's purchase of its common shares either by tender or in the open market for cancellation, subsequent resale or for **dividend reinvestment plans**.

Buy-Ins

The obligation to buy back the stock after selling it short if adequate margin cannot be maintained by the client and/or if the originally borrowed stock is called by its owner and no other stock can be borrowed to replace it.

Call Feature

A clause in a bond or preferred share agreement that allows the issuer the right to "call back" the securities prior to maturity. The company would usually do this if they could refinance the **debt** at a lower rate (similar to refinancing a mortgage at a lower rate). Calling back a security prior to maturity may involve the payment of a penalty known as a **call premium**.

Call Option

The right to buy a specific number of shares at a specified price (the **strike price**) by a fixed date. The buyer pays a **premium** to the seller of the call option contract. An investor would buy a call option if the underlying stock's price is expected to rise. See also **Put Option**.

Call Price

The price at which a bond or preferred share with a **call feature** is redeemed by the issuer. This is the amount the holder of the security would receive if the security was redeemed prior to maturity. The call price is equal to par (or a stated value for preferred shares) plus any **call premium**. See also **Redemption Price**.

Call Protection Period

For callable bonds, the period before the first possible call date.

Callable

May be redeemed (called in) upon due notice by the security's issuer.

Canada Deposit Insurance Corporation (CDIC)

A federal Crown Corporation providing deposit insurance against loss (up to $100,000 per depositor) when a member institution fails.

Canada Education Savings Grant (CESG)

An incentive program for those investing in a **Registered Education Savings Plan (RESP)** whereby the federal government will make a matching grant of a maximum of $500 to $600 per year of the first $2,500 contributed each year to the RESP of a child under age 18.

Canada Pension Plan (CPP)

A mandatory contributory pension plan designed to provide monthly retirement, disability and survivor benefits for all Canadians. Employers and employees make equal contributions. Québec has its own parallel pension plan Québec Pension Plan (QPP).

Canada Premium Bonds (CPBs)

A relatively new type of savings product that offers a higher interest rate compared to the Canada Savings Bond and is redeemable once a year on the anniversary of the issue date or during the 30 days thereafter without penalty.

Canada Savings Bonds (CSBs)

A type of savings product that pays a competitive rate of interest and that is guaranteed for one or more years. They may be cashed at any time and, after the first three months, pay interest up to the end of the month prior to being cashed.

Canada Yield Call

A callable bond with a call price based on the greater of (a) par or (b) the price based on the yield of an equivalent-term Government of Canada bond plus a specified yield spread. Also known as a Doomsday call. See also **Call Price** and **Callable Bond**.

Canadian Derivatives Clearing Corporation (CDCC)

The CDCC is a service organization that clears, issues, settles, and guarantees options, futures, and futures options traded on the Bourse de Montréal (the Bourse).

Canadian Investor Protection Fund (CIPF)

A fund that protects eligible customers in the event of the insolvency of an IIROC dealer member. It is sponsored solely by IIROC and funded by quarterly assessments on dealer members.

Canadian Life and Health Insurance Association Inc. (CLHIA)

The national trade group of the life insurance industry, which is actively involved in overseeing applications and setting industry standards.

Canadian National Stock Exchange (CNSX)

Launched in 2003 as an alternative marketplace for trading equity securities and emerging companies.

Canadian Originated Preferred Securities (COPrS)

Introduced to the Canadian market in March 1999, as long-term junior subordinated debt instruments. This type of security offers features that resemble both long-term corporate bonds and preferred shares.

Canadian Payments Association (CPA)

Established in the 1980 revision of the *Bank Act*, this association operates a highly automated national clearing system for interbank payments. Members include chartered banks, trust and loan companies and some credit unions and caisses.

Canadian Securities Administrators (CSA)

The CSA is a forum for the 13 securities regulators of Canada's provinces and territories to co-ordinate and harmonize the regulation of the Canadian capital markets.

Canadian Unlisted Board (CUB)

An Internet web-based system for investment dealers to report completed trades in unlisted and unquoted equity securities in Ontario.

CanDeal

Provides institutional investors with electronic access to federal bond bid and offer prices and yields from its six bank-owned dealers.

CanPx

A joint venture of several IIROC member firms and operates as an electronic trading system for fixed income securities providing investors with real-time bid and offer prices and hourly trade data.

Capital

Has two distinct but related meanings. To an economist, it means machinery, factories and inventory required to produce other products. To an investor, it may mean the total of financial **assets** invested in securities, a home and other fixed assets, plus cash.

Capital and Financial Account

Account which reflects the transactions occurring between Canada and foreign countries with respect to the acquisition of assets, such as land or currency. Along with the **current account** a component of the **balance of payments**.

Capital Gain

Selling a security for more than its purchase price. For non-registered securities, 50% of the gain would be added to income and taxed at the investor's marginal rate.

Capital Loss

Selling a security for less than its purchase price. Capital losses can only be applied against capital gains. Surplus losses can be carried forward indefinitely and used against future capital gains. Only 50% of the loss can be used to offset any taxable capital loss.

Capital Market

Financial markets where **debt** and **equity** securities trade. Capital markets include organized exchanges as well as private placement sources of debt and equity.

Capital Stock

All shares representing ownership of a company, including preferred as well as common. Also referred to as **equity capital**.

Capitalization or Capital Structure

Total dollar amount of all **debt**, **preferred** and **common** stock, and **retained earnings** of a company. Can also be expressed in percentage terms.

Capitalizing

Recording an expenditure initially as an **asset** on the **statement of financial position** rather than as an expense on the **statement of comprehensive income**, and then writing it off or **amortizing** it (as an expense on the **statement of comprehensive income**) over a period of years. Examples include interest, and research and development.

Carry Forward

The amount of RRSP contributions that can be carried forward from previous years. For example, if a client was entitled to place $13,500 in an RRSP and only contributed $10,000, the difference of $3,500 would be the unused contribution room and can be carried forward indefinitely.

Cash Account

A type of brokerage account where the investor is expected to have either cash in the account to cover their purchases or where an investor will deliver the required amount of cash before the settlement date of the purchase.

Cash Flow

A company's profit for a stated period plus any deductions that are not paid out in actual cash, such as **depreciation**. For an investor, any source of income from an investment including **dividends**, interest income, rental income, etc.

Cash-Secured Put Write

Involves writing a **put option** and setting aside an amount of cash equal to the strike price. If the cash-secured put writer is assigned, the cash is used to buy the stock from the exercising put buyer.

Cash Value

The current market value of a **segregated fund** contract, less any applicable deferred sales charges or other withdrawal fees

CBID

An electronic trading system for fixed-income securities operating in both retail and institutional markets.

CDS Clearing and Depository Services Inc. (CDS)

CDS provides customers with physical and electronic facilities to deposit and withdraw depository-eligible securities and manage their related ledger positions (securities accounts). CDS also provides electronic clearing services both domestically and internationally, allowing customers to report, confirm and settle securities trade transactions.

Central Bank

A body established by a national Government to regulate currency and **monetary policy** on a national/international level. In Canada, it is the Bank of Canada; in the United States, the Federal Reserve Board; in the U.K., the Bank of England.

Chart Analysis

The use of charts and patterns to forecast buy and sell decisions. See also **Technical Analysis**.

Chinese Walls

Policies implemented to separate and isolate persons within a firm who make investment decisions from persons within a firm who are privy to undisclosed material information which may influence those decisions. For example, there should be separate fax machines for research departments and sales departments.

Class A and B Stock

Shares that have different classes sometimes have different rights. Some may have superior claims over other classes or may have different voting rights. Class A stock is often similar to a participating preferred share with a prior claim over Class B for a stated amount of dividends or assets or both, but without voting rights; the Class B may have voting rights but no priority as to dividends or assets. Note that these distinctions do not always apply.

Clearing Corporations

A not-for-profit service organization owned by the exchanges and their members for the clearance, settlement and issuance of **options** and **futures**. A clearing corporation provides a guarantee for all options and futures contracts it clears, by becoming the buyer to every seller and the seller to every buyer.

Closed-End Fund

Shares in closed-end investment companies are readily transferable in the open market and are bought and sold like other shares. Capitalization is fixed. See also **Investment Company**.

Closet Indexing

A portfolio strategy whereby the fund manager does not replicate the market exactly but sticks fairly close to the market weightings by industry sector, country or region or by the average market capitalization.

Coincident Indicators

Statistical data that, on average, change at approximately the same time and in the same direction as the economy as a whole.

Collateral Trust Bond

A bond secured by stocks or bonds of companies controlled by the issuing company, or other securities, which are deposited with a **trustee**.

Commercial Paper

An unsecured promissory note issued by a corporation or an asset-backed security backed by a pool of underlying financial assets. Issue terms range from less than three months to one year. Most corporate paper trades in $1,000 multiples, with a minimum initial investment of $25,000. Commercial paper may be bought and sold in a secondary market before maturity at prevailing market rates.

Commission

The fee charged by a stockbroker for buying or selling securities as agent on behalf of a client.

Commodity

A product used for commerce that is traded on an organized exchange. A commodity could be an agricultural product such as canola or wheat, or a natural resource such as oil or gold. A commodity can be the basis for a **futures** contract.

Common Stock

Securities representing ownership in a company. They carry voting privileges and are entitled to the receipt of dividends, if declared. Also called common shares.

Competitive Tender

A distribution method used in particular by the Bank of Canada in distributing new issues of government marketable bonds. Bids are requested from primary **distributors** and the higher bids are awarded the securities for distribution. See also **Non-Competitive Tender**.

Compound Interest

Interest earned on an investment at periodic intervals and added to the amount of the investment; future interest payments are then calculated and paid at the original rate but on the increased total of the investment. In simple terms, interest paid on interest.

Confirmation

A printed acknowledgement giving details of a purchase or sale of a security which is normally mailed to a client by the broker or investment dealer within 24 hours of an order being executed. Also called a contract.

Consolidated Financial Statements

A combination of the financial statements of a parent company and its subsidiaries, presenting the financial position of the group as a whole.

Consolidation

See **Reverse Split**.

Consumer Price Index (CPI)

Price index which measures the cost of living by measuring the prices of a given basket of goods. The CPI is often used as an indicator of **inflation**.

Continuation Pattern

A chart formation indicating that the current trend will continue.

Continuous Disclosure

In Ontario, a reporting issuer must issue a press release as soon as a material change occurs in its affairs and, in any event, within ten days. See also **Timely Disclosure**.

Contract Holder

The owner of a **segregated fund** contract.

Contraction

Represents a downturn in the economy and can lead to a recession if prolonged.

Contributions in Kind

Transferring securities into an **RRSP**. The general rules are that when an asset is transferred there is a **deemed disposition**. Any **capital gain** would be reported and taxes paid. Any **capital losses** that result cannot be claimed.

Conversion Price

The dollar value at which a **convertible** bond or security can be converted into common stock.

Conversion Privilege

The right to exchange a bond for common shares on specifically determined terms.

Convertible

A **bond**, **debenture** or **preferred** share which may be exchanged by the owner, usually for the **common stock** of the same company, in accordance with the terms of the conversion privilege. A company can force conversion by calling in such shares for redemption if the **redemption price** is below the market price.

Convertible Arbitrage

A strategy that looks for mispricing between a convertible security and the underlying stock. A typical convertible arbitrage position is to be long the convertible bond and short the common stock of the same company.

Convexity

A measure of the rate of change in duration over changes in yields. Typically, a bond will rise in price more if the yield change is negative than it will fall in price if the yield change is positive.

Corporate Note

An unsecured promise made by the borrower to pay interest and repay the principal at a specific date.

Corporation or Company

A form of business organization created under provincial or federal statutes which has a legal identity separate from its owners. The corporation's owners (shareholders) have no personal liability for its debts. See also **Limited Liability**.

Correction

A price reversal that typically occurs when a security has been overbought or oversold in the market.

Correlation

A measure of the relationship between two or more securities. If two securities mirror each other's movements perfectly, they are said to have a positive one (+1) correlation. Combining securities with high positive correlations does not reduce the risk of a portfolio. Combining securities that move in the exact opposite direction from each other are said to have perfect negative one (-1) correlation. Combining two securities with perfect negative correlation reduces risk. Very few, if any, securities have a perfect negative correlation. However, risk in a portfolio can be reduced if the combined securities have low positive correlations.

Cost Accounting Method

Used when a company owns less than 20% of a subsidiary.

Cost of Sales

A **statement of comprehensive income** account representing the cost of buying raw materials that go directly into producing finished goods.

Cost-Push Inflation

A type of inflation that develops due to an increase in the costs of production. For example, an increase in the price of oil may contribute to higher input costs for a company and could lead to higher inflation.

Coupon Rate

The rate of interest that appears on the certificate of a **bond**. Multiplying the coupon rate times the **principal** tells the holder the dollar amount of interest to be paid by the issuer until **maturity**. For example, a bond with a **principal** of $1,000 and a coupon of 10% would pay $100 in interest each year. Coupon rates remain fixed throughout the term of the bond. See also **Yield**.

Covenant

A pledge in a **bond indenture** indicating the fulfilment of a promise or agreement by the company issuing the debt. An example of a covenant may include the promise not to issue any more debt.

Cover

Buying a security previously sold short. See also **Short Sale**.

Covered Writer

The writer of an option who also holds a position that is equivalent to, but on the opposite side of the market from the short option position. In some circumstances, the equivalent position may be in cash, a convertible security or the underlying security itself. See also **Naked Writer**.

CUB

Canadian Unlisted Board – a web-based trade reporting system for unlisted securities.

Cum Dividend

With **dividend**. If you buy shares quoted cum dividend, i.e., before the ex dividend date, you will receive an upcoming already-declared dividend. If shares are quoted **ex-dividend** (without dividend) you are not entitled to the declared dividend.

Cum Rights

With rights. Buyers of shares quoted cum rights, i.e., before the **ex-rights** date, are entitled to forthcoming already-declared rights. If shares are quoted ex rights (without rights) the buyer is not entitled to receive the declared rights.

Cumulative Preferred

A **preferred** stock having a provision that if one or more of its **dividends** are not paid, the unpaid dividends accumulate in **arrears** and must be paid before any dividends may be paid on the company's **common shares**.

Current Account

Account that reflects all payments between Canadians and foreigners for goods, services, interest and dividends. Along with the **capital and financial account** it is a component of the **balance of payments**.

Current Assets

Cash and assets which in the normal course of business would be converted into cash, usually within a year, e.g. accounts receivable, inventories. A **statement of financial position** category.

Current Liabilities

Money owed and due to be paid within a year, e.g. accounts payable. A **statement of financial position** category.

Current Ratio

A **liquidity ratio** that shows a company's ability to pay its current obligations from **current assets**. A current ratio of 2:1 is the generally accepted standard. See also **Quick Ratio**.

Current Yield

The annual income from an investment expressed as a percentage of the investment's current value. On stock, calculated by dividing yearly **dividend** by market price; on bonds, by dividing the **coupon** by market price. See also **Yield**.

Custodian

A firm that holds the securities belonging to a **mutual fund** or a **segregated fund** for safekeeping. The custodian can be either the insurance company itself, or a qualified outside firm based in Canada.

Cyclical Stock

A stock in an industry that is particularly sensitive to swings in economic conditions. Cyclical Stocks tend to rise quickly when the economy does well and fall quickly when the economy contracts. In this way, cyclicals move in conjunction with the **business cycle**. For example, during periods of **expansion** auto stocks do well as individuals replace their older vehicles. During **recessions**, auto sales and auto company share values decline.

Cyclical Unemployment

The amount of unemployment that rises when the economy softens, firms' demand for labour moderates, and some firms lay off workers in response to lower sales. It drops when the economy strengthens again.

Day Order

A buy or sell order that automatically expires if it is not executed on the day it is entered. All orders are day orders unless otherwise specified.

Dealer Market

A market in which securities are bought and sold **over-the-counter** in which dealers acts as **principals** when buying and selling securities for clients. Also referred to as the **unlisted market**.

Dealer Member

A stock brokerage firm or investment dealer which is a member of a stock exchange or the **Investment Industry Regulatory Organization of Canada**.

Dealer's Spread

The difference between the **bid** and **ask** prices on a security.

Death Benefit

The amount that a segregated fund policy pays to the beneficiary or the estate when the market value of the segregated fund is lower than the guaranteed amount on the death of the **annuitant**.

Debenture

A certificate of indebtedness of a government or company backed only by the general credit of the issuer and unsecured by mortgage or lien on any specific asset. In other words, no specific assets have been pledged as collateral.

Debt

Money borrowed from lenders for a variety of purposes. The borrower typically pays interest for the use of the money and is obligated to repay it at a set date.

Debt/Equity Ratio

A **ratio** that shows whether a company's borrowing is excessive. The higher the ratio, the higher the **financial risk**.

Declining Industry

An industry moving from the **maturity** stage. It tends to grow at rates slower than the overall economy, or the growth rate actually begins to decline.

Deemed Disposition

Under certain circumstances, taxation rules state that a transfer of property has occurred, even without a purchase or sale, e.g., there is a deemed disposition on death or emigration from Canada.

Default

A **bond** is in default when the borrower has failed to live up to its obligations under the **trust deed** with regard to interest, **sinking fund** payments or has failed to redeem the bonds at maturity.

Default Risk

The risk that a debt security issuer will be unable to pay interest on the prescribed date or the **principal** at **maturity**. Default risk applies to debt securities not equities since equity **dividend** payments are not contractual.

Defensive Stock

A stock of a company with a record of stable earnings and continuous **dividend** payments and which has demonstrated relative stability in poor economic conditions. For example, utility stock values do not usually change from periods of **expansion** to periods of **recession** since most individuals use a constant amount of electricity.

Deferred Annuity

This type of contract, usually sold by life insurance companies, pays a regular stream of income to the **beneficiary** or annuitant at some agreed-upon start date in the future. The original payment is usually a stream of payments made over time, ending prior to the beginning of the annuity payments. See also **Annuity**.

Deferred Preferred Shares

A type of preferred share that pays no dividend until a future maturity date.

Deferred Sales Charge

The fee charged by a **mutual fund** or insurance company for redeeming units. It is otherwise known as a **redemption fee** or **back-end load**. These fees decline over time and are eventually reduced to zero if the fund is held long enough.

Deferred Tax Liabilities

The income tax payable in future periods. These liabilities commonly result from temporary differences between the book value of assets and liabilities as reported on the statement of financial position and the amount attributed to that asset or liability for income tax purposes.

Defined Benefit Plan

A type of registered pension plan in which the annual payout is based on a formula. The plan pays a specific dollar amount at retirement using a predetermined formula.

Defined Contribution Plan

A type of registered pension plan where the amount contributed is known but the dollar amount of the pension to be received is unknown. Also known as a **money purchase plan**.

Delayed Floater

A type of **variable rate preferred share** that entitles the holder to a fixed dividend for a predetermined period of time after which the dividend becomes variable. Also known as a **fixed-reset** or **fixed floater**.

Delayed Opening

Postponement in the opening of trading of a security the result of a heavy influx of buy and/or sell orders.

Delisting

Removal of a security's listing on a **stock exchange**.

Demand Pull Inflation

A type of inflation that develops when continued consumer demand pushes prices higher.

Depletion

Refers to consumption of natural resources that are part of a company's assets. Producing oil, mining and gas companies deal in products that cannot be replenished and as such are known as wasting assets. The recording of depletion is a bookkeeping entry similar to **depreciation** and does not involve the expenditure of cash.

Depreciation

Systematic charges against earnings to write off the cost of an **asset** over its estimated useful life because of wear and tear through use, action of the elements, or obsolescence. It is a bookkeeping entry and does not involve the expenditure of cash.

Derivative

A type of financial instrument whose value is based on the performance of an underlying financial asset, commodity, or other investment. Derivatives are available on interest rates, currency, stock indexes. For example, a **call option** on IBM is a derivative because the value of the call varies in relation to the performance of IBM stock. See also **Options**.

Direct Bonds

This term is used to describe bonds issued by governments that are firsthand obligations of the government itself. See also **Guaranteed Bonds**.

Directional Hedge Funds

A type of **hedge fund** that places a bet on the anticipated movements in the market prices of equities, fixed-income securities, foreign currencies and commodities.

Director

Person elected by voting **common** shareholders at the annual meeting to direct company policies.

Directors' Circular

Information sent to shareholders by the **directors** of a company that are the target of a takeover bid. A recommendation to accept or reject the bid, and reasons for this recommendation, must be included.

Disclosure

One of the principles of securities regulation in Canada. This principle entails full, true and plain disclosure of all material facts necessary to make reasoned investment decisions.

Discount

The amount by which a **preferred** stock or **bond** sells below its **par value**.

Discount Brokers

Brokerage house that buys and sells securities for clients at a greater commission discount than full-service firms.

Discount Rate

In computing the value of a bond, the discount rate is the interest rate used in calculating the present value of future cash flows.

Discouraged Workers

Individuals that are available and willing to work but cannot find jobs and have not made specific efforts to find a job within the previous month.

Discretionary Account

A securities account where the client has given specific written authorization to a partner, director or qualified portfolio manager to select securities and execute trades for him. See also **Managed Account** and **Wrap Account**.

Disinflation

A decline in the rate at which prices rise – i.e., a decrease in the rate of inflation. Prices are still rising, but at a slower rate.

Disposable Income

Personal income minus income taxes and any other transfers to government.

Diversification

Spreading investment risk by buying different types of securities in different companies in different kinds of businesses and/or locations.

Dividend

An amount distributed out of a company's profits to its shareholders in proportion to the number of shares they hold. Over the years a **preferred** dividend will remain at a fixed annual amount. The amount of **common** dividends may fluctuate with the company's profits. A company is under no legal obligation to pay preferred or common dividends.

Dividend Discount Model

The relationship between a stock's current price and the present value of all future dividend payments. It is used to determine the price at which a stock should be selling based on projected future dividend payments.

Dividend Payout Ratio

A ratio that measures the amount or percentage of the company's profit that are paid out to shareholders in the form of dividends.

Dividend Reinvestment Plan

The automatic reinvestment of shareholder dividends in more shares of the company's stock.

Dividend Tax Credit

A procedure to encourage Canadians to invest in **preferred** and **common shares** of taxable, dividend-paying Canadian corporations. The taxpayer pays tax based on grossing up (i.e., adding 4 5% to the amount of dividends actually received) and obtains a credit against federal and provincial tax based on the grossed up amount in the amount of 19%.

Dividend Yield

A value ratio that shows the annual dividend rate expressed as a percentage of the current market price of a stock. Dividend yield represents the investor's percentage return on investment at its prevailing market price.

Dollar Cost Averaging

Investing a fixed amount of dollars in a specific security at regular set intervals over a period of time, thereby reducing the average cost paid per unit.

Domestic Bonds

Bonds issued in the currency and country of the issuer. For example, a Canadian dollar-denominated bond, issued by a Canadian company, in the Canadian market would be considered a domestic bond.

Dow Jones Industrial Average (DJIA)

A price-weighted **average** that uses 30 actively traded **blue chip** companies as a measure of the direction of the New York Stock Exchange.

Drawdown

A cash management open-market operation pursued by the Bank of Canada to influence interest rates. A drawdown refers to the transfer of deposits to the Bank of Canada from the direct clearers, effectively draining the supply of available cash balances. See also **Redeposit**.

Due Diligence Report

When negotiations for a new issue of securities begin between a dealer and corporate issuer, the dealer normally prepares a due diligence report examining the financial structure of the company.

Duration

A measure of bond price volatility. The approximate percentage change in the price or value of a bond or bond portfolio for a 1% point change in interest rates. The higher the duration of a bond the greater its risk.

Dynamic Asset Allocation

An **asset allocation** strategy that refers to the systematic rebalancing, either by time period or weight, of the securities in the portfolio, so that they match the long-term benchmark asset mix among the various asset classes.

Earned Income

Income that is designated by Canada Revenue Agency for **RRSP** calculations. Most types of revenues are included with the exception of any form of investment income and pension income.

Earnings Per Share (EPS)

A **value ratio** that shows the portion of net income for a period attributable to a single **common share** of a company. For example, a company with $100 million in earnings and with 100 million common shareholders would report an EPS of $1 per share.

Economic Indicators

Statistics or data series that are used to analyze business conditions and current economic activity. See also **leading, lagging**, and **coincident indicators**.

Economies of Scale

An economic principle whereby the per unit cost of producing each unit of output falls as the volume of production increases. Typically, a company that achieves economies of scale lowers the average cost per unit through increased production since fixed costs are shared over an increased number of goods.

Efficient Market Hypothesis

The theory that a stock's price reflects all available information and reflects its true value.

Election Period

When an investor purchases an **extendible** or **retractable bond**, they have a time period in which to notify the company if they want to exercise the option.

Elliot Wave Theory

A theory used in **technical analysis** based on the rhythms found in nature. The theory states that there are repetitive, predictable sequences of numbers and cycles found in nature similar to patterns of stock movements.

Emerging Industries

Brand new industries in the early stages of growth. Often considered as speculative because they are introducing new products that may or may not be accepted and may face strong competition from other new entrants.

Equilibrium Price

The price at which the quantity demanded equals the quantity supplied.

Equipment Trust Certificate

A type of debt security that was historically used to finance "rolling stock" or railway boxcars. The cars were the collateral behind the issue and when the issue was paid down the cars reverted to the issuer. In recent times, equipment trusts are used as a method of financing containers for the offshore industry. A security, more common in the U.S. than in Canada.

Equity

Ownership interest in a corporation's stock that represents a claim on its revenue and assets. See also **Stock**.

Equity Accounting Method

An accounting method used to determine income derived from a company's investment in another company over which it exerts significant influence.

Escrowed Shares

Outstanding shares of a company which, while entitled to vote and receive **dividends**, may not be bought or sold unless special approval is obtained. Mining and oil companies commonly use this technique when **treasury shares** are issued for new properties. Shares can be released from escrow (i.e., freed to be bought and sold) only with the permission of applicable authorities such as a stock exchange and/or securities commission.

Eurobonds

Bonds that are issued and sold outside a domestic market and typically denominated in a currency other than that of the domestic market. For example, a **bond** denominated in Canadian dollars and issued in Germany would be classified as a Eurobond.

European-Style Option

An **option** that can only be exercised on a specified date – normally the business day prior to expiration.

Event-Driven Hedge Funds

A type of **hedge fund** that seeks to profit from unique events such as mergers, acquisitions, stock splits or buybacks.

Ex-Ante

A projection of expected returns – what investors expect to realize as a return.

Exchange Fund Account

A special federal government account operated by the Bank of Canada to hold and conduct transactions in Canada's foreign exchange reserves on instructions from the Minister of Finance.

Exchange Rate

The price at which one currency exchanges for another.

Exchange-Traded Funds (ETFs)

Open-ended mutual fund trusts that hold the same stocks in the same proportion as those included in a specific stock index. Shares of an exchange-traded fund trade on major stock exchanges. Like index mutual funds, ETFs are designed to mimic the performance of a specified index by investing in the constituent companies included in that index. Like the stocks in which they invest, shares can be traded throughout the trading day.

Ex-Dividend

A term that denotes that when a person purchases a **common** or **preferred share**, they are not entitled to the **dividend** payment. Shares go ex-dividend two business days prior to the shareholder record date. See also **Cum Dividend**.

Exempt List

Large professional buyers of securities, mostly financial institutions, that are offered a portion of a new issue by one member of the banking group on behalf of the whole syndicate. The term exempt indicates that this group of investors is exempt from receiving a **prospectus** on a new issue as they are considered to be sophisticated and knowledgeable.

Exercise

The process of invoking the **rights** of the option or **warrant** contract. It is the holder of the option who exercises his or her rights. See also **Assignment**.

Exercise Price

The price at which a **derivative** can be exchanged for a share of the underlying security (also known as **subscription price**). For an **option**, it is the price at which the underlying security can be purchased, in the case of a **call**, or sold, in the case of a **put**, by the option holder. Synonymous with **strike price**.

Expansion

A phase of the **business cycle** characterized by increasing corporate profits and hence increasing share prices, an increase in the demand for capital for business expansion, and hence an increase in interest rates.

Expectations Theory

A theory stating that the **yield curve** is shaped by a market consensus about future interest rates.

Expiration Date

The date on which certain rights or option contracts cease to exist. For equity options, this date is usually the Saturday following the third Friday of the month listed in the contract. This term can also be used to describe the day on which warrants and rights cease to exist.

Ex-Post

The **rate of return** that was actually received. This historic data is used to measure actual performance.

Ex-Rights

A term that denotes that the purchaser of a **common share** would not be entitled to a rights offering. Common shares go ex-rights two business days prior to the shareholder of **record date**.

Extendible Bond or Debenture

A **bond** or **debenture** with terms granting the holder the option to extend the maturity date by a specified number of years.

Extension Date

For extendible bonds the maturity date of the bond can be extended so that the bond changes from a short-term bond to a long-term bond.

Face Value

The value of a bond or debenture that appears on the face of the certificate. Face value is ordinarily the amount the issuer will pay at maturity. Face value is no indication of market value.

Fee-Based Accounts

A type of account that bundles various services into a fee based on the client's assets under management, for example, 1% to 3% of client assets.

Fiduciary Responsibility

The responsibility of an investment advisor, mutual fund salesperson or financial planner to always put the client's interests first. The fiduciary is in a position of trust and must act accordingly.

Final Good

A finished product, one that is purchased by the ultimate end user.

Final Prospectus

The prospectus which supersedes the **preliminary prospectus** and is accepted for filing by applicable provincial securities commissions. The final prospectus shows all required information pertinent to the new issue and a copy must be given to each first-time buyer of the new issue.

Financial Intermediary

An institution such as a bank, life insurance company, credit union or mutual fund which receives cash, which it invests, from suppliers of capital.

Financial Risk

The additional risk placed on the common shareholders from a company's decision to use debt to finance its operations.

Financing

The purchase for resale of a security issue by one or more investment dealers. The formal agreement between the investment dealer and the corporation issuing the securities is called the **underwriting** agreement. A term synonymous with underwriting.

First-In-First-Out (FIFO)

Inventory items acquired earliest are sold first.

First Mortgage Bonds

The senior securities of a company as they constitute a first charge on the company's assets, earnings and undertakings before unsecured current liabilities are paid.

Fiscal Agent

An investment dealer appointed by a company or government to advise it in financial matters and to manage the underwriting of its securities.

Fiscal Policy

The policy pursued by the federal government to influence economic growth through the use of taxation and government spending to smooth out the fluctuations of the **business cycle**.

Fiscal Year

A company's accounting year. Due to the nature of particular businesses, some companies do not use the calendar year for their bookkeeping. A typical example is the department store that finds December 31 too early a date to close its books after the Christmas rush and so ends its fiscal year on January 31.

Fixed Asset

A tangible long-term asset such as land, building or machinery, held for use rather than for processing or resale. A **statement of financial position** category.

Fixed Exchange Rate Regime

A country whose central bank maintains the domestic currency at a fixed level against another currency or a composite of other currencies.

Fixed-Floater Preferred

See **Delayed Floater**.

Fixed-Income Securities
Securities that generate a predictable stream of interest or **dividend** income, such as **bonds**, **debentures** and **preferred shares**

Fixed-Reset Preferred
See **Delayed Floater.**

Flat
Means that the quoted market price of a **bond** or **debenture** is its total cost (as opposed to an accrued interest transaction). Bonds and debentures in default of interest trade flat.

Floating Exchange Rate
A country whose central bank allows market forces alone to determine the value of its currency, but will intervene if it thinks the move in the exchange rate is excessive or disorderly.

Floating Rate
A term used to describe the interest payments negotiated in a particular contract. In this case, a floating rate is one that is based on an administered rate, such as the **Prime Rate**. For example, the rate for a particular note may be 2% over Prime. See also **Fixed Rate.**

Floating-Rate Debentures
A type of **debenture** that offers protection to investors during periods of very volatile interest rates. For example, when interest rates are rising, the interest paid on floating rate debentures is adjusted upwards every six months.

Floor Trader
Employee of a member of a stock exchange, who executes buy and sell orders on the floor (trading area) of the exchange for the firm and its clients.

Forced Conversion
When a company's stock rises in value above the **conversion price** a company may force the **convertible** security holder to exchange the security for stock by calling back the security. Faced with receiving a lower **call price** (par plus a call premium) or higher valued shares the investor is forced to convert into **common shares.**

Foreign Bonds
If a Canadian company issues **debt** securities in another country, denominated in that foreign country's currency, the bond is known as a foreign **bond**. A bond issued in

the U.S. payable in U.S. dollars is known as a foreign bond or a "Yankee Bond." See also **Eurobond.**

Foreign Exchange Rate Risk
The risk associated with an investment in a foreign security or any investment that pays in a denomination other than Canadian dollars, the investor is subject to the risk that the foreign currency may depreciate in value.

Foreign Pay
A Canadian debt security issued in Canada but pays interest and principle in a foreign currency is known as a foreign pay **bond**. This type of security allows Canadians to take advantage of possible shifts in currency values.

Forward
A forward contract is similar to a **futures** contract but trades on an OTC basis. The seller agrees to deliver a specified commodity or financial instrument at a specified price sometime in the future. The terms of a forward contract are not standardized but are negotiated at the time of the trade. There may be no secondary market.

Frictional Unemployment
Unemployment that results from normal labour turnover, from people entering and leaving the workforce and from the ongoing creation and destruction of jobs.

Front-End Load
A sales charge applied to the purchase price of a **mutual fund** when the fund is originally purchased.

Front Running
Making a practice, directly or indirectly, of taking the opposite side of the market to clients, or effecting a trade for the advisor's own account prior to effecting a trade for a client.

Full Employment
The level of unemployment due solely to both frictional and structural factors, or when cyclical unemployment is zero.

Fully Diluted Earnings Per Share
Earnings per common share calculated on the assumption that all **convertible** securities are converted into **common** shares and all outstanding **rights**, **warrants**, **options** and contingent issues are exercised.

Fundamental Analysis
Security analysis based on fundamental facts about a company as revealed through its financial statements and an analysis of economic conditions that affect the company's business. See also **Technical Analysis.**

Funded Debt
All outstanding bonds, debentures, notes and similar debt instruments of a company not due for at least one year.

Futures
A contract in which the seller agrees to deliver a specified commodity or financial instrument at a specified price sometime in the future. A futures contract is traded on a recognized exchange. Unlike a forward contract, the terms of the futures contract are standardized by the exchange and there is a **secondary market**. See also **Forwards.**

Good Delivery Form
When a security is sold it must be delivered to the broker properly endorsed, not mutilated and with (if any) coupons attached. To avoid these difficulties and as a general practice most securities are held in street form with the broker.

Good Faith Deposit
A deposit of money by the buyer or seller of a futures product which acts as a financial guarantee as to the fulfilment of the contractual obligations of the futures contract. Also called a performance bond or **margin.**

Good Through Order
An order to buy or sell that is good for a specified number of days and then is automatically cancelled if it has not been filled.

Good Till Cancelled Order
An order that is valid from the date entered until the close of business on the date specified in the order. If the order has not been filled by the close of the market on that date, it is cancelled. This type of order can be cancelled or changed at any time.

Goodwill
Generally understood to represent the value of a well-respected business – its name, customer relations, employee relations, among others. Considered an **intangible asset** on the **statement of financial position.**

Government Securities Distributors

Typically an investment dealer or bank that is authorized to bid at Government of Canada debt auctions.

Greensheet

Highlights for the firm's sales representatives the salient features of a new issue, both pro and con in order to successfully solicit interest to the general public. Dealers prepare this information circular for in-house use only.

Gross Domestic Product (GDP)

The value of all goods and services produced in a country in a year.

Gross Profit Margin

A **profitability ratio** that shows the company's rate of profit after allowing for cost of sales.

Growth Stock

Common stock of a company with excellent prospects for above-average growth; a company which over a period of time seems destined for above-average expansion.

Guaranteed Amount

The minimum amount payable under **death benefits** or **maturity guarantees** provided for under the terms of the **segregate fund** contract.

Guaranteed Bonds

Bonds issued by a crown corporation but guaranteed by the applicable government as to interest and principal payments.

Guaranteed Income Supplement (GIS)

A pension payable to **OAS** recipients with no other or limited income.

Guaranteed Investment Certificate (GIC)

A deposit instrument most commonly available from trust companies, requiring a minimum investment at a predetermined rate of **interest** for a stated term. Generally nonredeemable prior to maturity but there can be exceptions.

Guaranteed Minimum Withdrawal Benefit Plans (GMWB)

A GMWB plan is similar to a variable annuity. With a GMWB, the client purchases the plan, and the GMWB option gives the planholder the right to withdraw a certain fixed percentage (7% is typical) of the initial deposit every year until the entire principal is returned, no matter how the fund performs.

Halt in Trading

A temporary halt in the trading of a security to allow significant news to be reported and widely disseminated. Usually the result of a pending merger or a substantial change in dividends or earnings.

Hedge Funds

Lightly regulated pools of capital in which the hedge fund manager invests a significant amount of his or her own capital into the fund and whose offering memorandum allows for the fund to execute aggressive strategies that are unavailable to mutual funds such as short selling.

Hedging

A protective manoeuvre; a transaction intended to reduce the risk of loss from price fluctuations.

High Water Mark

Used in the context of how a hedge fund manager is compensated. The high water mark sets the bar above which the fund manager is paid a portion of the profits earned for the fund.

Holding Period Return

A transactional **rate of return** measure that takes into account all **cash flows** and increases or decreases in a security's value for any time frame. Time frames can be greater or less than a year.

Hypothecate

To pledge securities as collateral for a loan. Referred to as collateral assignment or hypotec in Québec for **segregated funds**.

ICE Futures Canada (formerly the Winnipeg Commodity Exchange)

An exchange that trades agricultural futures and options exclusively.

Income Splitting

A tax planning strategy whereby the higher-earning spouse transfers income to the lower-earning spouse to reduce taxable income.

Income Tax Act (ITA)

The legislation dictating the process and collection of federal tax in Canada, administered by Canada Revenue Agency.

Income Trusts

A type of **investment trust** that holds investments in the operating assets of a company. Income from these operating assets flows through to the trust, which in turn passes on the income to the trust unitholders.

Index

A measure of the market as measured by a basket of securities. An example would be the S&P/TSX Composite Index or the S&P 500. Fund managers and investors use a stock index to measure the overall direction and performance of the market.

Index-Linked GICs

A hybrid investment product that combines the safety of a deposit instrument with some of the growth potential of an equity investment. They have grown in popularity, particularly among conservative investors who are concerned with safety of capital but want yields greater than the interest on standard interest bearing GICs or other term deposits.

Indexing

A portfolio management style that involves buying and holding a portfolio of securities that matches, closely or exactly, the composition of a benchmark **index**.

Individual variable insurance contract (IVIC)

The term used in the IVIC Guidelines to describe a **segregated fund** contract.

Inflation

A generalized, sustained trend of rising prices.

Inflation Rate

The rate of change in prices. See also **Consumer Price Index**.

Inflation Rate Risk

The risk that the value of financial assets and the purchasing power of income will decline due to the impact of **inflation** on the real returns produced by those financial assets.

Information Circular

Document sent to shareholders with a **proxy**, providing details of matters to come before a shareholders' meeting.

Initial Public Offering (IPO)
A new issue of securities offered to the public for investment for the very first time. IPOs must adhere to strict government regulations as to how the investments are sold to the public.

Initial Sales Charge
A commission paid to the financial adviser at the time that the policy is purchased. This type of sales charge is also known as an acquisition fee or a **front-end load**.

Insider
All directors and senior officers of a corporation and those who may also be presumed to have access to nonpublic or inside information concerning the company; also anyone owning more than 10% of the voting shares in a corporation. Insiders are prohibited from trading on this information.

Insider Report
A report of all transactions in the shares of a company by those considered to be insiders of the company and submitted each month to securities commissions.

Instalment Debentures
A bond or **debenture** issue in which a predetermined amount of principal matures each year.

Instalment Receipts
A new issue of stock sold with the obligation that buyers will pay the issue price in a specified series of instalment payments instead of one lump sum payment. Also known as Partially Paid Shares.

Institutional Client
A legal entity that represents the collective financial interests of a large group. A mutual fund, insurance company, pension fund and corporate treasury are just a few examples.

Intangible Asset
An **asset** having no physical substance (e.g., **goodwill**, patents, franchises, copyrights).

Integrated Asset Allocation
An **asset allocation** strategy that refers to an all-encompassing strategy that includes consideration of capital market expectations and client risk tolerance.

Interest
Money charged by a lender to a borrower for the use of his or her money.

Interest Coverage Ratio
A **debt ratio** that tests the ability of a company to pay the interest charges on its debt and indicates how many times these charges are covered based upon earnings available to pay them.

Interest Rate Risk
The risk that changes in interest rates will adversely affect the value of an investor's portfolio. For example, a portfolio with a large holding of long-term bonds is vulnerable to significant loss from changes in interest rates.

International Financial Reporting Standards (IFRS)
A globally accepted high-quality accounting standard already used by public companies in over 100 countries around the world.

Interval Funds
A type of **mutual fund** that has the flexibility to buy back its outstanding shares periodically. Also known as closed-end discretionary funds.

In-the-Money
A call option is in-the-money if its strike price is below the current market price of the underlying security. A **put option** is in-the-money if its strike price is above the current market price of the underlying security. The in-the-money amount is the option's **intrinsic value**.

Intrinsic Value
That portion of a **warrant** or **call** option's price that represents the amount by which the market price of a security exceeds the price at which the warrant or call option may be exercised (exercise price). Considered the theoretical value of a security (i.e., what a security should be worth or priced at in the market).

Inventory
The goods and supplies that a company keeps in stock. A **statement of financial position** item.

Inventory Turnover Ratio
Cost of sales divided by **inventory**. The ratio may also be expressed as the number of days required to sell current inventory by dividing the ratio into 365.

Investment
The use of money to make more money, to gain income or increase capital or both.

Investment Advisor (IA)
An individual licensed to transact in the full range of securities. IAs must be registered in by the securities commission of the province in which he or she works. The term refers to employees of **SRO** member firms only. Also known as a Registrant or Registered Representative (RR).

Investment Company, or Fund
A company which uses its capital to invest in other companies. There are two principal types: **closed-end** and **open-end** or **mutual fund**. Shares in closed-end investment companies are readily transferable in the open market and are bought and sold like other shares. Capitalization is fixed. Open-end funds sell their own new shares to investors, buy back their old shares, and are not listed. Open-end funds are so-called because their capitalization is not fixed; they normally issue more shares or units as people want them.

Investment Counsellor
A professional engaged to give investment advice on securities for a fee.

Investment Dealer
A person or company that engages in the business of trading in securities in the capacity of an agent or principal and is a member of IIROC.

Investment Industry Association of Canada (IIAC)
A member-based professional association that represents the interests of market participants.

Investment Industry Regulatory Organization of Canada (IIROC)
The Canadian investment industry's national self-regulatory organization. IIROC carries out its regulatory responsibilities through setting and enforcing rules regarding the proficiency, business and financial conduct of dealer firms and their registered employees and through setting and enforcing market integrity rules regarding trading activity on Canadian equity marketplaces.

Investment Policy Statement
The agreement between a portfolio manager and a client that provides the guidelines for the manager.

Investments in Associates
The ownership a company has in another company. As a general rule, significant influence is presumed to exist when a company owns 20% or more of the voting rights of the other company.

Investor
One whose principal concern is the minimization of risk, in contrast to the **speculator**, who is prepared to accept calculated risk in the hope of making better-than-average profits, or the gambler, who is prepared to take even greater risks.

Irrevocable Beneficiary
A beneficiary whose entitlements under the **segregated fund** contract cannot be terminated or changed without his or her consent.

Issue
Any of a company's securities; the act of distributing such securities.

Issued Shares
That part of **authorized shares** that have been sold by the corporation and held by the shareholders of the company.

Junior Bond Issue
A corporate bond issue, the collateral for which has been pledged as security for other more senior debt issues and is therefore subject to these prior claims.

Junior Debt
One or more **junior bond issues**.

Keynesian Economics
Economic policy developed by British economist John Maynard Keynes who proposed that active government intervention in the market was the only method of ensuring economic growth and prosperity. See also **Monetarism**.

Know Your Client Rule (KYC)
The cardinal rule in making investment recommendations. All relevant information about a client must be known in order to ensure that the registrant's recommendations are suitable.

Labour Force
The sum of the population aged 15 years and over who are either employed or unemployed.

Labour Sponsored Venture Capital Corporations (LSVCC)
LSVCCs are investment funds, sponsored by labour organizations, that have a specific mandate to invest in small to medium-sized businesses. To encourage this mandate, governments offer generous tax credits to investors in LSVCCs.

Lagging Indicators
A selection of statistical data, that on average, indicate highs and lows in the business cycle behind the economy as a whole. These relate to business expenditures for new plant and equipment, consumers' instalment credit, short-term business loans, the overall value of manufacturing and trade inventories.

Large Value Transfer System (LVTS)
A Canadian Payments Association electronic system for the transfer of large value payments between participating financial institution.

Leading Indicators
A selection of statistical data that, on average, indicate highs and lows in the business cycle ahead of the economy as a whole. These relate to employment, capital investment, business starts and failures, profits, stock prices, inventory adjustment, housing starts and certain commodity prices.

LEAPS
Long Term Equity Anticipation Securities are long-term (2-3 year) option contracts.

Leverage
The effect of fixed charges (i.e., debt interest or preferred dividends, or both) on per-share earnings of **common** stock. Increases or decreases in income before fixed charges result in magnified percentage increases or decreases in **earnings per common share**. Leverage also refers to seeking magnified percentage returns on an investment by using borrowed funds, **margin accounts** or securities which require payment of only a fraction of the underlying security's value (such as rights, warrants or options).

Liabilities
Debts or obligations of a company, usually divided into **current liabilities**—those due and payable within one year—and long-term liabilities—those payable after one year. A **statement of financial position** category.

Liability Traders
Have the responsibility to manage a dealer's trading capital to encourage market flows and facilitate the client orders that go into the market, while aiming to lose as little of that capital as possible. Liability traders can be considered those who set the direction for **agency traders**. Whereas agency traders have formal client responsibilities, liability traders have lighter responsibilities or none at all.

Life Cycle
A model used in financial planning that tries to link age with investing. The underlying theory is that an individual's asset mix will change, as they grow older. However the life cycle is not a substitute for the "know your client rule".

Limit Order
A client's order to buy or sell securities at a specific price or better. The order will only be executed if the market reaches or betters that price.

Limited Liability
The word limited at the end of a Canadian company's name implies that liability of the company's shareholders is limited to the money they paid to buy the shares. By contrast, ownership by a **sole proprietor** or **partnership** carries unlimited personal legal responsibility for debts incurred by the business.

Limited Partnership
A type of partnership whereby a limited partner cannot participate in the daily business activity and liability is limited to the partner's investment.

Liquidity
1. The ability of the market in a particular security to absorb a reasonable amount of buying or selling at reasonable price changes. 2. A corporation's current assets relative to its current liabilities; its cash position.

Liquidity Preference Theory
A theory that tries to explain the shape of the **yield curve**. It postulates that investors want to invest for the short-term because they are risk averse. Borrowers, however, want long-term money. In order to entice investors to invest long-term, borrowers must offer higher rates for longer-term money. This being the case, the yield curve should slope upwards reflecting the higher rates for longer borrowing periods.

Liquidity Ratios
Financial ratios that are used to judge the company's ability to meet its short-term commitments. See **Current Ratio**.

Liquidity Risk
The risk that an investor will not be able to buy or sell a security quickly enough because buying or selling opportunities are limited.

Listed Stock
The stock of a company which is traded on a stock exchange.

Listing Agreement
A stock exchange document published when a company's shares are accepted for listing. It provides basic information on the company, its business, management, assets, capitalization and financial status.

Load
The portion of the offering price of shares of most open-end investment companies (**mutual funds**) which covers sales commissions and all other costs of distribution.

London InterBank Offered Rate (LIBOR)
The rate of interest charged by large international banks dealing in Eurodollars to other large international banks.

Long Position
Signifies ownership of securities. "I am long 100 BCE common" means that the speaker owns 100 **common shares** of BCE Inc.

Long-Term Bond
A bond with greater than 10 years remaining to maturity.

Macroeconomics
Macroeconomics focuses on the performance of the economy as a whole. It looks at the broader picture and to the challenges facing society as a result of the limited amounts of natural resources, human effort and skills, and technology.

Major Trend
Underlying price trend prevailing in a market despite temporary declines or rallies.

Managed Account
An account whereby a licensed portfolio manager has the discretion to decide and execute suitable investment decisions on behalf of clients.

Managed Product
A pool of capital gathered to buy securities according to a specific investment mandate. The pool seeds a fund managed by an investment professional that is paid a management fee to carry out the mandate.

Management Expense Ratio
The total expense of operating a **mutual fund** expressed as a percentage of the fund's **net asset value**. It includes the **management fee** as well as other expenses charged directly to the fund such as administrative, audit, legal fees etc., but excludes brokerage fees. Published rates of return are calculated after the management expense ratio has been deducted.

Management Fee
The fee that the manager of a **mutual fund** or a **segregated fund** charges the fund for managing the portfolio and operating the fund. The fee is usually set as fixed percentage of the fund's net asset value.

Managers' Discussion and Analysis (MD&A)
A document that requires management of an issuer to discuss the dynamics of its business and to analyze its financial statements with the focus being on information about the issuer's financial condition and operations with emphasis on liquidity and capital resources.

Margin
The amount of money paid by a client when he or she uses credit to buy a security. It is the difference between the market value of a security and the amount loaned by an investment dealer.

Margin Agreement
A contract that must be completed and signed by a client and approved by the firm in order to open a margin account. This sets out the terms and conditions of the account.

Margin Call
When an investor purchases an account on margin in the expectation that the share value will rise, or shorts a security on the expectation that share price will decline, and share prices go against the investor, the brokerage firm will send out a margin call requiring that the investor add additional funds or marketable securities to the account to protect the broker's loan.

Marginal Tax Rate
The tax rate that would have to be paid on any additional dollars of taxable income earned

Market
Any arrangement whereby products and services are bought and sold, either directly or through intermediaries.

Market Capitalization
The dollar value of a company based on the market price of its issued and outstanding common shares. It is calculated by multiplying the number of outstanding shares by the current market price of a share.

Market Maker
A trader employed by a securities firm who is authorized and required, by applicable self-regulatory organizations (SROs), to maintain reasonable liquidity in securities markets by making firm bids or offers for one or more designated securities.

Market Order
An order placed to buy or sell a security immediately at the best current price.

Market Risk
The non-controllable or systematic risk associated with equities.

Market Segmentation Theory
A theory on the structure of the **yield** curve. It is believed that large institutions shape the yield curve. The banks prefer to borrow short term while the insurance industry, with a longer horizon, prefers long-term money. The supply and demand of the large institutions shapes the curve.

Marketability
A measure of the ability to buy and sell a security. A security has good marketability if there is an active secondary market in which it can be easily bought and sold at a fair price.

Marketable Bonds
Bonds for which there is a ready market (i.e., clients will buy them because the prices and features are attractive).

Marking-to-Market
The process in the futures market in which the daily price changes are paid by the parties incurring losses to the parties earning profits.

Married Put or a Put Hedge
The purchase of an underlying asset and the purchase of a put option on that underlying asset.

Material Change
A change in the affairs of a company that is expected to have a significant effect on the market value of its securities.

Mature Industry

An industry that experiences slower, more stable growth rates in profit and revenue than growth or emerging industries, for example.

Maturity

The date on which a loan or a **bond** or **debenture** comes due and is to be paid off.

Maturity Date

The date at which the contract expires, and the time at which any **maturity guarantees** are based. Segregated fund contracts normally mature in 10 years, although companies are allowed to set longer periods. Maturities of less than 10 years are permitted only for funds such as protected mutual funds, which are regulated as securities and are not segregated funds.

Maturity Guarantee

The minimum dollar value of the contract after the guarantee period, usually 10 years. This amount is also known as the annuity benefit.

Medium-Term Bond

A bond with 5 to 10 years remaining to maturity.

Microeconomics

Analyzes the market behaviour of individual consumers and firms, how prices are determined, and how prices determine the production, distribution, and use of goods and services.

Monetarists

School of economic theory which states that the level of prices as well as economic output is determined by an economy's money supply. This school of thought believes that control of the money supply is more vital to economic prosperity than the level of government spending, for example. See also **Keynesian Policy**.

Monetary Aggregates

An aggregate that measures the quantity of money held by a country's households, firms and governments. It includes various forms of money or payment instruments grouped according to their degree of liquidity, such as M1, M2 or M3.

Monetary Policy

Economic policy designed to improve the performance of the economy by regulating money supply and credit. The Bank of Canada achieves this through its influence over short-term interest rates.

Money Market

That part of the **capital** market in which short-term financial obligations are bought and sold. These include **treasury bills** and other federal government securities, and **commercial paper**, and **bankers' acceptances** and other instruments with one year or less left to maturity. Longer term securities, when their term shortens to the limits mentioned, are also traded in the money market.

Money Purchase Plan (MPP)

A type of **Registered Pension Plan**; also called a **Defined Contribution Plan**. In this type of plan, the annual payout is based on the contributions to the plan and the amounts those contributions have earned over the years preceding retirement. In other words, the benefits are not known but the contributions are.

Montréal Exchange (ME)

See **Bourse de Montréal**.

Mortgage

A contract specifying that certain property is pledged as security for a loan.

Mortgage-Backed Securities

Bonds that claim ownership to a portion of the cash flows from a group or pool of mortgages. They are also known as mortgage pass-through securities. A servicing intermediary collects the monthly payments from the issuers and, after deducting a fee, passes them through (i.e., remits them) to the holders of the security. The MBS provides liquidity in an otherwise illiquid market. Every month, holders receive a proportional share of the interest and principal payments associated with those mortgages.

Mortgage Bond

A bond issue secured by a **mortgage** on the issuer's property.

Moving Average

The average of security or commodity prices calculated by adding the closing prices for the underlying security over a pre-determined period and dividing the total by the time period selected.

Moving Average Convergence-Divergence (MACD)

A technical analysis tool that takes the difference between two moving averages and then generates a smoothed **moving average** on the difference (the divergence) between the two moving averages.

Multi-Disciplinary Accounts

Fee-based accounts that are an evolution of separately managed accounts. With multi-disciplinary accounts, separate models are combined into one overall portfolio model in a single account.

Multi-Manager Accounts

A type of fee-based account that offers clients and their advisors more choice in terms of product and services. Often, clients are aligned with two or more portfolio models and each portfolio model is a component of the client's greater diversified holdings.

Multiple

A colloquial term for the **Price/Earnings** ratio of a company's common shares.

Mutual Fund

An **investment fund** operated by a company that uses the proceeds from shares and units sold to investors to invest in stocks, bonds, derivatives and other financial securities. Mutual funds offer investors the advantages of diversification and professional management and are sold on a load or no load basis. Mutual fund shares/units are redeemable on demand at the fund's current **net asset value per share** (NAVPS).

Mutual Fund Dealers Association (MFDA)

The Self-Regulatory Organization (SRO) that regulates the distribution (dealer) side of the mutual fund industry in Canada.

Mutual Fund Wraps

Are established with a selection of individual funds managed within a client's account. Mutual fund wraps differ from funds of funds. The client holds the actual funds within their account, as opposed to a fund that simply invests in other funds. In most cases, a separate account is established for the client and the selected funds are held inside that dedicated account.

Naked Writer

A seller of an **option** contract who does not own an offsetting position in the underlying security or a suitable alternative.

NASDAQ

An acronym for the National Association of Securities Dealers Automated Quotation System. NASDAQ is a computerized system that provides brokers and dealers with price quotations for securities traded OTC.

National Debt
The accumulation of total government borrowing over time .It is the sum of past deficits minus the sum of past surpluses.

National Policies
The Canadian Securities Administrators have developed a number of policies that are applicable across Canada. These coordinated efforts by the CSA are an attempt to create a national securities regulatory framework. Copies of policies are available from each provincial regulator.

National Do Not Call List (DNCL)
The Canadian Radio-television and Telecommunications Commission (CRTC) has established Rules that telemarketers and organizations that hire telemarketers must follow. The DNCL Rules prohibit telemarketers and clients of telemarketers from calling telephone numbers that have been registered on the DNCL for more than 31 days.

National Registration Database (NRD)
A web-based system that permits mutual fund salespersons and investment advisors to file applications for registration electronically.

Natural Unemployment Rate
Also called the full employment unemployment rate. At this level of unemployment, the economy is thought to be operating at close to its full potential or capacity.

Negative Pledge Provision
A protective provision written into the trust indenture of a company's debenture issue providing that no subsequent mortgage bond issue may be secured by all or part of the company's assets, unless at the same time the company's debentures are similarly secured.

Negotiable
A certificate that is transferable by delivery and which, in the case of a registered certificate, has been duly endorsed and guaranteed.

Negotiated Offer
A term describing a particular type of financing in which the investment dealer negotiates with the corporation on the issuance of securities. The details would include the type of security to be issued, the price, coupon or dividend rate, special features and protective provisions.

Net Asset Value
For a **mutual fund**, net asset value represents the market value of the fund's share and is calculated as total assets of a corporation less its liabilities. Net asset value is typically calculated at the close of each trading day. Also referred to as the **book value** of a company's different classes of securities.

Net Change
The change in the price of a security from the closing price on one day to the closing price on the following trading day. In the case of a stock which is entitled to a **dividend** one day, but is traded ex-dividend the next, the dividend is not considered in computing the change. The same applies to **stock splits**. A stock selling at $100 the day before a two-for-one split and trading the next day at $50 would be considered unchanged. The net change is ordinarily the last figure in a stock price list. The mark +1.10 means up $1.10 a share from the last sale on the previous day the stock traded.

Net Profit Margin
A **profitability ratio** that indicates how efficiently the company is managed after taking into account both expenses and taxes.

New Account Application Form (NAAF)
A form that is filled out by the client and the IA at the opening of an account. It gives relevant information to make suitable investment recommendations. The NAAF must be completed and approved before any trades are put through on an account.

New Issue
An offering of stocks or bonds sold by a company for the first time. Proceeds may be used to retire outstanding securities of the company, to purchase fixed assets or for additional working capital. New debt issues are also offered by government bodies.

New York Stock Exchange (NYSE)
Oldest and largest stock exchange in North America with more than 1,600 companies listed on the exchange.

NEX
A new and separate board of the TSX Venture Exchange that provides a trading forum for companies that have fallen below the Venture Exchange's listing standards. Companies that have low levels of business activity or who do not carry on active business will trade on the NEX board, while companies that are actively carrying on business will remain with the main TSX Venture Exchange stock list.

No Par Value (n.p.v.)
Indicates a common stock has no stated face value.

Nominal GDP
Gross domestic product based on prices prevailing in the same year not corrected for inflation. Also referred to as current dollar or chained dollar GDP.

Nominal Rate
The quoted or stated rate on an investment or a loan. This rate allows for comparisons but does not take into account the effects of inflation.

Nominee
A person or firm (bank, investment dealer, CDS) in whose name securities are registered. The shareholder, however, retains the true ownership of the securities.

Non-Client and Professional Orders
A type of order for the account of partners, directors, officers, major shareholders, IAs and employees of member firms that must be marked "PRO" , "N-C" or "Emp", in order to ensure that client orders are given priority for the same securities.

Non-Competitive Tender
A method of distribution used in particular by the Bank of Canada for Government of Canada marketable bonds. **Primary** distributors are allowed to request **bonds** at the average price of the accepted **competitive tenders**. There is no guarantee as to the amount, if any, received in response to this request.

Non-Controlling Interest
1. The equity of the shareholders who do not hold controlling interest in a controlled company; 2. In **consolidated financial statements** (i) the item in the **statement of financial position** of the parent company representing that portion of the **assets** of a consolidated subsidiary considered as accruing to the shares of the subsidiary not owned by the parent; and (ii) the item deducted in the **statement of comprehensive income** of the parent and representing that portion of the subsidiary's earnings considered as accruing to the subsidiary's shares not owned by the parent.

Non-Cumulative
A preferred dividend that does not accrue or accumulate if unpaid.

Odd Lot
A number of shares which is less than a **standard trading unit**. Usually refers to a securities trade for less than 100 shares, sometimes called a broken lot. Trading in less than 100 shares typically incurs a higher per share commission.

Of Record
On the company's books or records. If, for example, a company announces that it will pay a **dividend** on January 15 to shareholders of record, every shareholder whose name appears on the company's books on that date will be sent a dividend cheque from the company.

Offer
The lowest price at which a person is willing to sell; as opposed to bid which is the highest price at which one is willing to buy.

Offering Memorandum
This document is prepared by the dealer involved in a new issue outlining some of the salient features of the new issue, but not the price or other issue-specific details. It is used as a pre-marketing tool in assessing the market for the issue as well as for obtaining expressions of interest.

Offering Price
The price that an investor pays to purchase shares in a **mutual fund**. The offering price includes the charge or load that is levied when the purchase is made.

Offsetting Transaction
A futures or option transaction that is the exact opposite of a previously established long or short position.

Office of the Superintendent of Financial Institutions (OSFI)
The federal regulatory agency whose main responsibilities regarding insurance companies and **segregated funds** are to ensure that the companies issuing the funds are financially solvent.

Officers
Corporate employees responsible for the day-to-day operation of the business.

Old Age Security (OAS)
A government pension plan payable at age 65 to all Canadian citizens and legal residents.

Ombudsman for Banking Services and Investments (OBSI)
An independent organization that investigates customer complaints against financial services providers.

Open-End Fund
See **Mutual Fund**.

Open Interest
The total number of outstanding option contracts for a particular **option** series. An opening transaction would increase open interest, while a closing transaction would decrease open interest. It is used as one measure of an option class's liquidity.

Open Market Operations
Method through which the Bank of Canada influences interest rates by trading securities with participants in the money market.

Opening Transaction
An option transaction that is considered the initial or primary transaction. An opening transaction creates new rights for the buyer of an **option**, or new obligations for a seller. See also **Closing Transaction**.

Operating Band
The Bank of Canada's 50-basis-point range for the overnight lending rate. The top of the band, the **Bank Rate**, is the rate charged by the Bank on **LVTS** advances to financial institutions. The bottom of the band is the rate paid by the Bank on any **LVTS** balances held overnight by those institutions. The middle of the operating band is the target for the overnight rate.

Operating Income
The income that a company records from its main ongoing operations.

Operating Performance Ratios
A type of ratio that illustrates how well management is making use of company resources.

Option
A right to buy or sell specific securities or properties at a specified price within a specified time. See **Put Options** and **Call Options**.

Option Premium
The amount paid to enter into an option contract, paid by the buyer to the seller or writer of the contract.

Option Writer
The seller of the option who may be obligated to buy (put writer) or sell (call writer) the underlying interest if assigned by the option buyer.

Oscillator
A **technical analysis** indicator used when a stock's chart is not showing a definite trend in either direction. When the oscillator reading reaches an extreme value in either the upper or lower band, this suggest that the current price move has gone too far. This may indicate that the price move is overextended and vulnerable.

Out-of-the-Money
A **call option** is out-of-the-money if the market price of the underlying security is below its **strike price**. A **put option** is out-of-the-money if the market price of the underlying security is above the strike price.

Output Gap
The difference between the actual level of output and the potential level of output when the economy is using all available resources of capital and labour.

Outstanding Shares
That part of **issued shares** which remains outstanding in the hands of investors.

Over-Allotment Option
An activity used to stabilize the aftermarket price of a recently issued security. If the price increases above the offer price, dealers can cover their short position by exercising an overallotment option (also referred to as a **green shoe** option) by either increasing demand in the case of covering a short position or increasing supply in the case of over-allotment option exercise.

Overcontribution
An amount made in excess to the annual limit made to an **RRSP**. An overcontribution in excess of $2,000 is penalized at a rate of 1% per month.

Overlay Manager
The overlay manager works with advisors in servicing clients. This is not a referral but a partnership, in which the advisor retains the client's assets. The service incorporates the existing trusted relationship of the advisor,

whom the client has become comfortable dealing with.

Override

In an **underwriting**, the additional payment the **Financing Group** receives over and above their original entitlement for their services as financial advisors and syndicate managers or leads.

Over-the-Counter (OTC)

A market for securities made up of securities dealers who may or may not be members of a recognized stock exchange. Over-the-counter is mainly a market conducted over the telephone. Also called the **unlisted**, inter-dealer or street market. NASDAQ is an example of an over-the-counter market.

Paper Profit

An unrealized profit on a security still held. Paper profits become realized profits only when the security is sold. A paper loss is the opposite to this.

Par Value

The stated **face value** of a **bond** or stock (as assigned by the company's charter) expressed as a dollar amount per share. Par value of a common stock usually has little relationship to the current market value and so no par value stock is now more common. Par value of a **preferred** stock is significant as it indicates the dollar amount of assets each preferred share would be entitled to should the company be liquidated.

Pari Passu

A legal term meaning that all securities within a series have equal rank or claim on earnings and assets. Usually refers to equally ranking issues of a company's **preferred** shares.

Participating Preferred

Preferred shares which, in addition to their fixed rate of prior dividend, share with the **common** in further **dividend** distributions and in capital distributions above their par value in liquidation.

Participation Rate

The share of the working-age population (15 and older) that is in the labour market, either working or looking for work.

Partnership

A form of business organization that involves two or more people contributing to the business and legislated under the federal Partnership Act.

Past Service Pension Adjusted (PSPA)

An employer may increase a member's pension by the granting of additional past service benefits to an employee in a **defined benefit plan**. Plan members who incur a PSPA will have their **RRSP** contribution room reduced by the amount of this adjustment.

Payback Period

The time that it takes for a convertible security to recoup its premium through its higher yield, compared with the dividend that is paid on the stock.

Peer Group

A group of managed products (particularly mutual funds) with a similar investment mandate.

Pension Adjustment (PA)

The amount of contributions made or the value of benefits accrued to a member of an employer-sponsored retirement plan for a calendar year. The PA enables the individual to determine the amount that may be contributed to an **RRSP** that would be in addition to contributions into a **Registered Pension Plan**.

Performance Bonds

What is often required upon entry into a futures contract giving the parties to a contract a higher level of assurance that the terms of the contract will eventually be honoured. The performance bond is often referred to as margin.

Personal Disposable Income

The amount of personal income an individual has after taxes. The income that can be spent on necessities, nonessential goods and services, or that can be saved.

Phillips Curve

A graph showing the relationship between inflation and unemployment. The theory states that unemployment can be reduced in the short run by increasing the price level (inflation) at a faster rate. Conversely, inflation can be lowered at the cost of possibly increased unemployment and slower economic growth.

Point

Refers to security prices. In the case of shares, it means $1 per share. In the case of **bonds** and **debentures**, it means 1% of the issue's **par value**, which is almost universally

100. On a $1,000 bond, one point represents 1% of the face value of the bond or $10. See **Basic point**

Political Risk

The risk associated with a government introducing unfavourable policies making investment in the country less attractive. Political risk also refers to the general instability associated with investing in a particular country.

Pooled Account

A type of managed product structure whereby by investors' funds are gathered into a legal structure, usually a trust or corporation. An investor's claim to the pool's returns is proportional to the number of shares or units the investor owns. The pools are often open-ended, which means units are issued when there are net cash inflows to the fund, or units are redeemed when there are net cash outflows.

Portfolio

Holdings of securities by an individual or institution. A portfolio may contain debt securities, preferred and common stocks of various types of enterprises and other types of securities.

Potential Output

The maximum amount of output the economy is capable of producing during a given period when all of its available resources are employed to their most efficient use.

Preferred Dividend Coverage Ratio

A type of profitability ratio that measures the amount of money a firm has available to pay dividends to their preferred shareholders.

Preferred Shares

A class of share capital that entitles the owners to a fixed **dividend** ahead of the company's common shares and to a stated dollar value per share in the event of liquidation. Usually do not have **voting rights** unless a stated number of dividends have been omitted. Also referred to as preference shares.

Preliminary Prospectus

The initial document released by an underwriter of a new securities issue to prospective investors.

Premium

The amount by which a **preferred** stock or **debt** security may sell above its **par value**. In the case of a new issue of **bonds** or stocks, the amount the market price rises over the original selling price. Also refers to that part of the **redemption** price of a bond or preferred share in excess of face value, par value or market price. In the case of **options**, the price paid by the buyer of an option contract to the seller.

Prepaid Expenses

Payments made by the company for services to be received in the near future. For example, rents, insurance premiums and taxes are sometimes paid in advance. A **statement of financial position** item.

Prepayment Risk

The risk that the issuer of a bond might prepay or redeem early some or all principal outstanding on the loan or mortgage.

Prescribed Rate

A quarterly interest rate set out, or prescribed by Canada Revenue Agency under **attribution** rules. The rate is based on the Bank of Canada rate.

Present Value

The current worth of a sum of money that will be received sometime in the future.

Price-Earnings (P/E) Ratio

A **value ratio** that gives investors an idea of how much they are paying for a company's earnings. Calculated as the current price of the stock divided current **earnings per share**.

Primary Distribution or Primary Offering of a New Issue

The original sale of any issue of a company's securities.

Primary Market

The market for new issues of securities. The proceeds of the sale of securities in a primary market go directly to the company issuing the securities. See also **Secondary Market**.

Prime Rate

The interest rate chartered banks charge to their most credit-worthy borrowers.

Principal

The person for whom a broker executes an order, or a **dealer** buying or selling for its own account. The term may also refer to a person's capital or to the face amount of a **bond**.

Principal Protected Note

A debt-like instrument with a maturity date whereby the issuer agrees to repay investors the amount originally invested (the principal) plus interest. The interest rate is tied to the performance of an underlying asset, such as a portfolio of mutual funds or common stocks, a market index, a hedge fund or a portfolio of hedge funds. PPNs guarantee only the return of the principal.

Private Equity

The financing of firms unwilling or unable to find capital using public means—for example, via the stock or bond markets.

Private Family Office

An extension of the advisor's client servicing approach. In this approach, instead of having only one advisor, a team of professionals handles all of an affluent client's financial affairs within one central location.

Private Placement

The underwriting of a security and its sale to a few buyers, usually institutional, in large amounts.

Pro Rata

In proportion to. For example, a **dividend** is a pro rata payment because the amount of dividend each shareholder receives is in proportion to the number of shares he or she owns.

Probate

A provincial fee charged for authenticating a **will**. The fee charged is usually based on the value of the assets in an estate rather than the effort to process the will.

Productivity

The amount of output per worker used as a measure of efficiency with which people and capital are combined in the output of the economy. Productivity gains lead to improvements in the standard of living, because as labour, capital, etc. produce more, they generate greater income.

Profit

That part of a company's revenue remaining after all expenses and taxes have been paid and out of which dividends may be paid.

Profitability Ratios

Financial ratios that illustrate how well management has made use of the company's resources.

Program Trading

A sophisticated computerized trading strategy whereby a portfolio manager attempts to earn a profit from the price spreads between a portfolio of equities similar or identical to those underlying a designated stock index, e.g., the Standard & Poor 500 Index, and the price at which **futures** contracts (or their options) on the index trade in financial futures markets. Also refers to switching or trading blocks of securities in order to change the asset mix of a portfolio.

Prospectus

A legal document that describes securities being offered for sale to the public. Must be prepared in conformity with requirements of applicable securities commissions. See also **Red Herring** and **Final Prospectus**.

Proxy

Written authorization given by a shareholder to someone else, who need not be a shareholder, to represent him or her and vote his or her shares at a shareholders' meeting.

Prudent Portfolio Approach

An investment standard. In some provinces, the law requires that a fiduciary, such as a trustee, may invest funds only in a list of securities designated by the province or the federal government. In other provinces, the trustee may invest in a security if it is one that an ordinary prudent person would buy if he were investing for the benefit of other people for whom he felt morally bound to provide. Most provinces apply the two standards.

Public Float

That part of the issued shares that are outstanding and available for trading by the public, and not held by company officers, directors, or investors who hold a controlling interest in the company. A company's public float is different from its **outstanding shares** as it also excludes those shares owned in large blocks by institutions.

Purchase Fund

A fund set up by a company to retire through purchases in the market a specified amount of its outstanding **preferred** shares or debt if purchases can be made at or below a stipulated price. See also **Sinking Fund**.

Put Option

A right to sell the stock at a stated price within a given time period. Those who think a stock may go down generally purchase puts. See also **Call Option**.

Quick Ratio

A more stringent measure of liquidity compared with the **current ratio**. Calculated as **current assets** less inventory divided by **current liabilities**. By excluding inventory, the ratio focuses on the company's more liquid assets.

Quotation or Quote

The highest bid to buy and the lowest offer to sell a security at a given time. Example: A quote of 45.40–45.50 means that 45.40 is the highest price a buyer will pay and 45.50 the lowest price a seller will accept.

Quotation and Trade Reporting Systems (QTRS)

Recognized stock markets that operate in a similar manner to exchanges and provide facilities to users to post quotations and report trades.

Rally

A brisk rise in the general price level of the market or in an individual stock.

Random Walk Theory

The theory that stock price movements are random and bear no relationship to past movements.

Rate of Return

See **Yield**.

Rational Expectations

School of economic theory which argues that investors are rational thinkers and can make intelligent economic decisions after evaluating all available information.

Real Estate Investment Trust (REIT)

An investment trust that specializes in real estate related investments including mortgages, construction loans, land and real estate securities in varying combinations. A REIT invests in and manages a diversified portfolio of real estate.

Real GDP

Gross Domestic Product adjusted for changes in the price level. Also referred to as constant dollar GDP.

Real Interest Rate

The **nominal rate** of interest minus the percentage change in the **Consumer Price Index** (i.e., the rate of inflation).

Record Date

The date on which a shareholder must officially own shares in a company to be entitled to a declared **dividend**. Also referred to as the date of record.

Red Herring Prospectus

A preliminary **prospectus** so called because certain information is printed in red ink around the border of the front page. It does not contain all the information found in the **final prospectus**. Its purpose: to ascertain the extent of public interest in an issue while it is being reviewed by a securities commission.

Redemption

The purchase of securities by the issuer at a time and price stipulated in the terms of the securities. See also **Call Feature**.

Redemption Price

The price at which **debt** securities or **preferred** shares may be redeemed, at the option of the issuing company.

Redeposit

An open-market cash management policy pursued by the Bank of Canada. A redeposit refers to the transfer of funds from the Bank to the direct clearers (an injection of balances) that will increase available funds. See also **Drawdown**.

Registered Education Savings Plans (RESPs)

A type of government sponsored savings plan used to finance a child's post-secondary education.

Registered Pension Plan (RPP)

A trust registered with Canada Revenue Agency and established by an employer to provide pension benefits for employees when they retire. Both employer and employee may contribute to the plan and contributions are tax-deductible. See also **Defined Contribution Plan** and **Defined Benefit Plan**.

Registered Retirement Income Fund (RRIF)

A tax deferral vehicle available to **RRSP** holders. The planholder invests the funds in the RRIF and must withdraw a certain amount each year. Income tax would be due on the funds when withdrawn.

Registered Retirement Savings Plan (RRSP)

An investment vehicle available to individuals to defer tax on a specified amount of money to be used for retirement. The holder invests money in one or more of a variety of investment vehicles which are held in trust under the plan. Income tax on contributions and earnings within the plan is deferred until the money is withdrawn at retirement. RRSPs can be transferred into Registered **Retirement Income Funds** upon retirement.

Registered Security

A security recorded on the books of a company in the name of the owner. It can be transferred only when the certificate is endorsed by the registered owner. Registered debt securities may be registered as to principal only or fully registered. In the latter case, interest is paid by cheque rather than by coupons attached to the certificate. See also **Bearer Security**.

Registrar

Usually a trust company appointed by a company to monitor the issuing of **common** or **preferred** shares. When a transaction occurs, the registrar receives both the old cancelled certificate and the new certificate from the transfer agent and records and signs the new certificate. The registrar is, in effect, an auditor checking on the accuracy of the work of the transfer agent, although in most cases the registrar and transfer agent are the same trust company.

Regular Delivery

The date a securities trade settles – i.e., the date the seller must deliver the securities. See also **Settlement Date**.

Regular Dividends

A term that indicates the amount a company usually pays on an annual basis.

Reinvestment Risk

The risk that interest rates will fall causing the cash flows on an investment, assuming that the **cash flows** are reinvested, to earn less than the original investment. For example, **yield to maturity** assumes that all interest payments received can be reinvested at the yield to maturity rate. This is not necessarily true. If interest rates in the market fall the interest would be reinvested at a lower rate. Reinvestment risk recognizes this risk.

Relative Value Hedge Funds

A type of hedge fund that attempts to profit by exploiting irregularities or discrepancies in the pricing of related stocks, bonds or derivatives.

Reporting Issuer

Usually, a corporation that has issued or has outstanding securities that are held by the public and is subject to continuous disclosure requirements of securities administrators.

Reset

A contract provision which allows the **segregated fund** contract holder to lock in the current market value of the fund and set a new maturity date 10 years after the reset date. Depending on the contract, the reset dates may be chosen by the contract holder or be triggered automatically.

Resistance Level

The opposite of a **support level**. A price level at which the security begins to fall as the number of sellers exceeds the number of buyers of the security.

Restricted Shares

Shares that participate in a company's earnings and assets (in liquidation), as **common** shares do, but generally have restrictions on **voting rights** or else no voting rights.

Retail Investor

Individual investors who buy and sell securities for their own personal accounts, and not for another company or organization. They generally buy in smaller quantities than larger **institutional investors**.

Retained Earnings

The cumulative total of annual earnings retained by a company after payment of all expenses and **dividends**. The earnings retained each year are reinvested in the business.

Retractable

A feature which can be included in a new **debt** or **preferred** issue, granting the holder the option under specified conditions to redeem the **security** on a stated date – prior to maturity in the case of a bond.

Return on Equity

A **profitability ratio** expressed as a percentage representing the amount earned on a company's **common shares**. Return on equity tells the investor how effectively their money is being put to use.

Reversal Patterns

Formations that usually precede a sizeable advance or decline in stock prices.

Reverse Split

A process of retiring old shares with fewer shares. For example, an investor owns 1,000 shares of ABC Inc. pre split. A 10 for 1 reverse split or **consolidation** reduces the number held to 100. Results in a higher share price and fewer shares outstanding.

Revocable Beneficiary

A beneficiary whose entitlements under the **segregated fund** contract can be terminated or changed without his or her consent.

Right

A short-term privilege granted to a company's **common** shareholders to purchase additional common shares, usually at a discount, from the company itself, at a stated price and within a specified time period. Rights of listed companies trade on stock exchanges from the **ex-rights** date until their expiry.

Right of Action for Damages

Most securities legislation provides that those who sign a prospectus may be liable for damages if the prospectus contains a misrepresentation. This right extends to experts e.g., lawyers, auditors, geologists, etc., who report or give opinions within the text of the document.

Right of Redemption

A mutual fund's shareholders have a continuing right to withdraw their investment in the fund simply by submitting their shares to the fund itself and receiving in return the dollar amount of their **net asset value**. This characteristic is the hallmark of mutual funds. Payment for the securities that have been redeemed must be made by the fund within three business days from the determination of the net asset value.

Right of Rescission

The right of a purchaser of a new issue to rescind the purchase contract within the applicable time limits if the **prospectus** contained an untrue statement or omitted a material fact.

Right of Withdrawal

The right of a purchaser of a new issue to withdraw from the purchase agreement within two business days after receiving the prospectus.

Risk Analysis Ratios

Financial ratios that show how well the company can deal with its debt obligations.

Risk-Averse

Descriptive term used for an investor unable or unwilling to accept the probability or chance of losing capital. See also **Risk-Tolerant**.

Risk-Free Rate

The rate of return an investor would receive if he or she invested in a risk free investment, such as a **treasury bill**.

Risk Premium

A rate that has to be paid in addition to the **risk free rate** (T-bill rate) to compensate investors for choosing securities that have more risk than T-Bills.

Risk-Tolerant

Descriptive term used for an investor willing and able to accept the probability of losing capital. See also **Risk-Averse**.

Sacrifice Ratio

Describes the extent to which **Gross Domestic Product** must be reduced with increased unemployment to achieve a 1% decrease in the inflation rate.

Sale and Repurchase Agreements (SRAs)

An open-market operation by the Bank of Canada to offset undesired downward pressure on overnight financing costs.

SEC

The Securities and Exchange Commission, a federal body established by the United States Congress, to protect investors in the U.S. In Canada there is no national regulatory authority; instead, securities legislation is provincially administered.

Secondary Issue

Refers to the redistribution or resale of previously issued securities to the public by a dealer or investment dealer syndicate. Usually a large block of shares is involved (e.g., from the settlement of an estate) and these are offered to the public at a fixed price, set in relationship to the stock's market price.

Secondary Market

The market where securities are traded through an exchange or **over-the-counter** subsequent to a **primary offering**. The proceeds from trades in a secondary market go to the selling dealers and investors, rather than to the companies that originally issued the shares in the **primary market**.

Securities

Paper certificates or electronic records that evidence ownership of **equity** (**stocks**) or debt obligations (**bonds**).

Securities Acts

Provincial Acts administered by the securities commission in each province, which set down the rules under which securities may be issued and traded.

Securities Administrator

A general term referring to the provincial regulatory authority (e.g., Securities Commission or Provincial Registrar) responsible for administering a provincial Securities Act.

Securities Eligible for Reduced Margin

Securities which demonstrate sufficiently high liquidity and low price volatility based on meeting specific price risk and liquidity risk measures.

Securitization

Refers in a narrow sense to the process of converting loans of various sorts into marketable securities by packaging the loans into pools. In a broader sense, refers to the development of markets for a variety of **debt** instruments that permit the ultimate borrower to bypass the banks and other deposit-taking institutions and to borrow directly from lenders.

Segregated Funds

Insurance companies sell these funds as an alternative to conventional **mutual funds**. Like mutual funds, segregated funds offer a range of investment objectives and categories of securities e.g. equity funds, bond funds, balanced funds etc. These funds have the unique feature of guaranteeing that, regardless of how poorly the fund performs, at least a minimum percentage (usually 75% or more) of the investor's payments into the fund will be returned when the fund matures.

Self-Directed RRSP

A type of RRSP whereby the holder invests funds or contributes certain acceptable assets such as securities directly into a registered plan which is usually administered for a fee by a Canadian financial services company.

Self-Regulatory Organization (SRO)

An organization recognized by the Securities Administrators as having powers to establish and enforce industry regulations to protect investors and to maintain fair, equitable, and ethical practices in the industry and ensure conformity with securities legislation. Canadian SROs include the **Investment Industry Regulatory Organization of Canada** and, the **Mutual Fund Dealers Association**.

Selling Group

Investment dealers or others who assist a **banking group** in marketing a new issue of securities without assuming financial liability if the issue is not entirely sold. The use of a selling group widens the distribution of a new issue.

Sentiment Indicators

Measure investor expectations or the mood of the market. These indicators measure how bullish or bearish investors are.

Separately Managed Account

A managed product structure whereby individual accounts are created for each investor. In either case, an investment manager is guided by an investment mandate.

Serial Bond or Debenture

See **Instalment Debenture**.

Settlement Date

The date on which a securities buyer must pay for a purchase or a seller must deliver the securities sold. For most securities, settlement must be made on or before the third business day following the transaction date.

Share of Profit of Associates

A company's share of an unconsolidated subsidiary's revenue. The equity accounting method is used when a company owns 20% to 50% of a subsidiary.

Short-Form Prospectus Distribution System

This system allows reporting issuers to issue a short-form **prospectus** that contains only information not previously disclosed to regulators. The short form prospectus contains by reference the material filed by the corporation in the **Annual Information Form**.

Short Position

Created when an investor sells a security that he or she does not own. See also **short sale**.

Short Sale

The sale of a security which the seller does not own. This is a speculative practice done in the belief that the price of a stock is going to fall and the seller will then be able to cover the sale by buying it back later at a lower price, thereby making a profit on the transactions. It is illegal for a seller not to declare a short sale at the time of placing the order. See also **Margin**.

Short-Term Bond

A bond with greater than one year but less than five years to maturity.

Short-Term Debt

Company borrowings repayable within one year that appear in the current liabilities section of the **statement of financial position**. The most common short-term debt items are: bank advances or loans, notes payable and the portion of funded debt due within one year.

Single-Manager Account

A type of fee-based account that is directed by a single portfolio manager who focuses considerable time and attention on the selection of securities, the sectors to invest in and the optimal asset allocation.

Simplified Prospectus

A condensed prospectus distributed by mutual fund companies to purchasers and potential purchasers of fund units or shares.

Sinking Fund

A fund set up to retire most or all of a debt or preferred share issue over a period of time. See also **Purchase Fund**.

Small Cap

Reference to smaller growth companies. Small cap refers to the size of the **capitalization** or investments made in the company. A small cap company has been defined as a company with an outstanding stock value of under $500 million. Small cap companies are considered more volatile than large cap companies.

Soft Landing

Describes a business cycle phase when economic growth slows sharply but does not turn negative, while inflation falls or remains low.

Soft Retractable Preferred Shares

A type of retractable preferred share where the redemption value may be paid in cash or in common shares, generally at the election of the issuer.

Sole Proprietorship

A form of business organization that involves one person running a business whereby the individual is taxed on earnings at their personal income tax rate.

SPDRs

An acronym for the Standard & Poor Depository Receipts (a type of derivative). These mirror the S&P 500 Index. They are referred to as "Spiders".

Special Purchase and Resale Agreements (SPRAs)

An open-market operation used by the Bank of Canada to relieve undesired upward pressure on overnight financing rates.

Speculator

One who is prepared to accept calculated risks in the marketplace. Objectives are usually short to medium-term capital gain, as opposed to regular income and safety of principal, the prime objectives of the conservative investor.

S&P/TSX Composite Index

A benchmark used to measure the performance of the broad Canadian equity market.

Split Shares

A security that has been created to divide (or split) the investment attributes of an underlying portfolio of common shares into separate components that satisfy different investment objectives. The preferred shares receive the majority of the dividends from the common shares held by the split share corporation. The capital shares receive the majority of any capital gains on the common shares.

Spot Price

The market price of a commodity or financial instrument that is available for immediate delivery.

Spousal RRSP

A special type of RRSP to which one spouse contributes to a plan registered in the beneficiary spouse's name. The contributed funds belong to the beneficiary but the contributor receives the tax deduction. If the beneficiary removes funds from the spousal plan in the year of the contribution or in the subsequent two calendar years, the contributor must pay taxes on the withdrawn amount.

Spread

The gap between **bid** and **ask** prices in the quotation for a security. Also a term used in option trading.

SRO

Short for self-regulatory organization such as the **Investment Industry Regulatory Organization of Canada**.

Standard Deviation

A statistical measure of risk. The larger the standard deviation, the greater the volatility of returns and therefore the greater the risk.

Standard Trading Unit

A regular trading unit which has uniformly been decided upon by the stock exchanges, in most cases it is 100 shares, but this can vary depending on the price of the stock.

Statement of Cash Flow

A financial statement which provides information as to how a company generated and spent its cash during the year. Assists users of financial statements in evaluating the company's ability to generate cash internally, repay debts, reinvest and pay dividends to shareholders.

Statement of Changes in Equity

A financial statement that shows the total comprehensive income kept in the business year after year.

Statement of Comprehensive Income

A financial statement which shows a company's revenues and expenditures resulting in either a profit or a loss during a financial period.

Statement of Financial Position

A financial statement showing a company's **assets**, **liabilities** and **equity** on a given date.

Statement of Material Facts

A document presenting the relevant facts about a company and compiled in connection with an underwriting or secondary distribution of its shares. It is used only when the shares underwritten or distributed are listed on a recognized stock exchange and takes the place of a prospectus in such cases.

Stock

Ownership interest in a corporation's that represents a claim on its earnings and assets.

Stock Dividend

A pro rata payment to common shareholders of additional common stock. Such payment increases the number of shares each holder owns but does not alter a shareholder's proportional ownership of the company.

Stock Exchange

A marketplace where buyers and sellers of securities meet to trade with each other and where prices are established according to laws of supply and demand.

Stock Savings Plan

Some provinces allow individual residents of the particular province a deduction or tax credit for provincial income tax purposes on investments made in certain prescribed vehicles. The credit or deduction is a percentage figure based on the value of investment.

Stock Split

An increase in a corporation's number of shares outstanding without any change in the shareholders' equity or market value. When a stock reaches a high price making it illiquid or difficult to trade, management may split the stock to get the price into a more marketable trading range. For example, an investor owns one **standard trading unit** of a stock that now trades at $70 each (portfolio value is $7,000). Management splits the stock 2:1. The investor would now own 200 new shares at a market value, all things being equal, of $35 each, for a portfolio value of $7,000.

Stop Buy Orders

An order to buy a security only after it has reached a certain price. This may be used to protect a short position or to ensure that a stock is purchased while its price is rising. According to TSX rules these orders become **market orders** when the stop price is reached.

Stop Loss Orders

The opposite of a **stop buy order**. An order to sell a security after its price falls to a certain amount, thus limiting the loss or protecting a paper profit. According to TSX rules these orders become **market orders** when the stop price is reached.

Stop Orders

Orders that are used to buy or sell after a stock has reached a certain price. See **Stop Buy Orders**, **Stop Loss Orders**.

Strategic Asset Allocation

An asset allocation strategy that rebalances investment portfolios regularly to maintain a consistent long-term mix.

Street Name

Securities registered in the name of an investment dealer or its nominee, instead of the name of the real or beneficial owner, are said to be "in street name." Certificates so registered are known as street certificates.

Strike Price

The price, as specified in an option contract, at which the underlying security will be purchased in the case of a **call** or sold in the case of a **put**. See also **Exercise Price**.

Strip Bonds or Zero Coupon Bonds

Usually high quality federal or provincial government bonds originally issued in **bearer** form, where some or all of the interest **coupons** have been detached. The bond principal and any remaining coupons (the residue) then trade separately from the strip of detached coupons, both at substantial discounts from par.

Structural Unemployment

Amount of unemployment that remains in an economy even when the economy is strong. Also known as the natural **unemployment rate**, the full employment unemployment rate.

Structured Preferreds

See **Equity Dividend Shares**.

Structured Product

A passive investment vehicle financially engineered to provide a specific risk and return characteristic. The value of a structured product tracks the returns of reference security known as an underlying asset. Underlying assets can consist of a single security, a basket of securities, foreign currencies, commodities or an index.

Subordinated Debenture

A type of junior **debenture**. Subordinate indicates that another debenture ranks ahead in terms of a claim on assets and profits.

Subscription or Exercise Price

The price at which a right or **warrant** holder would pay for a new share from the company. With options the equivalent would be the **strike** price.

Subsidiary

Company which is controlled by another company usually through its ownership of the majority of shares.

Suitability

A registrant's major concern in making investment recommendations. All information about a client and a security must be analyzed to determine if an investment is suitable for the client in accounts where a suitability exemption does not apply.

Superficial Losses

Occur when an investment is sold and then repurchased at any time in a period that is 30 days before or after the sale.

Supply-Side Economics

An economic theory whereby changes in tax rates exert important effects over supply and spending decisions in the economy. According to this theory, reducing both government spending and taxes provides the stimulus for economic expansion.

Support Level

A price level at which a security stops falling because the number of investors willing to buy the security is greater than the number of investors wishing to sell the security.

Surrender Value

The cash value of an insurance contract as of the date that the policy is being redeemed. This amount is equal to the market value of the **segregated fund**, less any applicable sales charges or administrative fees.

Suspension in Trading

An interruption in trading imposed on a company if their financial condition does not meet an exchange's requirements for continued trading or if the company fails to comply with the terms of its listing agreement.

Swap

An over-the-counter forward agreement involving a series of cash flows exchanged between two parties on specified future dates.

Sweetener

A feature included in the terms of a new issue of **debt** or **preferred** shares to make the issue more attractive to initial investors. Examples include **warrants** and/or **common** shares sold with the issue as a unit or a **convertible** or **extendible** or **retractable** feature.

Syndicate

A group of investment dealers who together underwrite and distribute a new issue of securities or a large block of an outstanding issue.

System for Electronic Document Analysis and Retrieval (SEDAR)

SEDAR facilitates the electronic filing of securities information as required by the securities regulatory agencies in Canada and allows for the public dissemination of information collected in the filing process

Systematic Risk

A non-controllable, non-diversifiable risk that is common to all investments within a given asset class. With equities it is called **market** risk, with fixed income securities it would be **interest rate** risk.

Systematic Withdrawal Plan

A plan that enables set amounts to be withdrawn from a **mutual fund** or a segregated fund on a regular basis.

T3 Form

Referred to as a Statement of Trust Income Allocations and Designations. When a mutual fund is held outside a registered plan, unitholders of an unincorporated fund is sent a T3 form by the respective fund.

T4 Form

Referred to as a Statement of Remuneration Paid. A T4 form is issued annually by employers to employees reporting total compensation for the calendar year. Employers have until the end of February to submit T4 forms to employees for the previous calendar year.

T5 Form

Referred to as a Statement of Investment Income. When a mutual fund is held outside a registered plan, shareholders are sent a T3 form by the respective fund.

Tactical Asset Allocation

An **asset allocation** strategy that involves adjusting a portfolio to take advantage of perceived inefficiencies in the prices of securities in different asset classes or within sectors.

Takeover Bid

An offer made to security holders of a company to purchase voting securities of the company which, with the offeror's already owned securities, will in total exceed 20% of the outstanding voting securities of the company. For federally incorporated companies, the equivalent requirement is more than 10% of the outstanding voting shares of the target company.

Tax Free Savings Account (TFSA)

A savings vehicle whereby income earned within a TFSA will not be taxed in any way throughout an individual's lifetime. In addition, there are no restrictions on the timing or amount of withdrawals from a TFSA, and the money withdrawn can be used for any purpose.

Tax Loss Selling

Selling a security for the sole purpose of generating a loss for tax purposes. There may be times when this strategy is advantageous but investment principles should not be ignored.

T-Bills

See **Treasury bills**.

Technical Analysis

A method of market and security analysis that studies investor attitudes and psychology as revealed in charts of stock price movements and trading volumes to predict future price action.

Term to Maturity

The length of time that a **segregated fund** policy must be held in order to be eligible for the **maturity guarantee**. Normally, except in the event of the death of the **annuitant**, the term to maturity of a segregated-fund policy is 10 years.

Thin Market

A market in which there are comparatively few bids to buy or offers to sell or both. The phrase may apply to a single security or to the entire stock market. In a thin market, price fluctuations between transactions are usually larger than when the market is liquid. A thin market in a particular stock may reflect lack of interest in that issue, or a limited supply of the stock.

Tilting of the Yield Curve

The yield curve that results from a decline in long-term bond yields while short-term rates are rising.

Time to Expiry

The number of days or months or years until expiry of an option or other derivative instrument.

Time Value

The amount, if any, by which the current market price of a **right**, **warrant** or **option** exceeds its **intrinsic value**.

Time-Weighted Rate of Return (TWRR)

A measure of return calculated by averaging the return for each subperiod in which a cash flow occurs into a return for a reporting period.

Timely Disclosure

An obligation imposed by securities administrators on companies, their officers and directors to release promptly to the news media any favourable or unfavourable corporate information which is of a material nature. Broad dissemination of this news allows non-insiders to trade the company's securities with the same knowledge about the company as insiders themselves. See also **Continuous Disclosure**.

Tombstone Advertisements

A written advertisement placed by the investment bankers in a public offering of securities as a matter of record once the deal has been completed.

Top-Down Approach

A type of fundamental analysis. First, general trends in the economy are analyzed. This information is then combined with industries and companies within those industries that should benefit from the general trends identified.

Toronto Stock Exchange (TSX)

The largest stock exchange in Canada with over 1,700 companies listed on the exchange.

Trade Payables

Money owed by a company for goods or services purchased, payable within one year. A current liability on the statement of financial position.

Trade Receivables

Money owed to a company for goods or services it has sold, for which payment is expected within one year. A current asset on the statement of financial position.

Trading Unit

Describes the size or the amount of the underlying asset represented by one option contract. In North America, all exchange-traded options have a trading unit of 100 shares.

Trailer Fee

Fee that a **mutual fund** manager may pay to the individual or organization that sold the fund for providing services such as investment advice, tax guidance and financial statements to investors. The fee is paid annually and continues for as long as the investor holds shares in the fund.

Transaction Date

The date on which the purchase or sale of a security takes place.

Transfer Agent

An agent, usually a trust company, appointed by a corporation to maintain shareholder records, including purchases, sales, and account balances. The transfer agent may also be responsible for distributing dividend cheques.

Treasury Bills

Short-term government debt issued in denominations ranging from $1,000 to $1,000,000. Treasury bills do not pay interest, but are sold at a discount and mature at par (100% of **face value**). The difference between the purchase price and par at maturity represents the lender's (purchaser's) income in lieu of interest. In Canada, such gain is taxed as interest income in the purchaser's hands.

Treasury Shares

Authorized but unissued stock of a company or previously issued shares that have been re-acquired by the corporation. The amount still represents part of those issued but is not included in the number of shares outstanding. These shares may be resold or used as part of the option package for management. Treasury shares do not have voting rights nor are they entitled to dividends.

Trend

Shows the general movement or direction of securities prices. The long-term price or trading volume of a particular security is either up, down or sideways.

Trust Deed (Bond Contract)

This is the formal document that outlines the agreement between the **bond** issuer and the bondholders. It outlines such things as the **coupon** rate, if interest is paid semi-annually and when, and any other terms and conditions between both parties.

Trustee

For bondholders, usually a trust company appointed by the company to protect the security behind the bonds and to make certain that all covenants of the trust deed relating to the bonds are honoured. For a **segregated fund**, the trustee administers the assets of a **mutual fund** on behalf of the investors.

TSX Venture Exchange

Canada's public venture marketplace, the result of the merger of the Vancouver and Alberta Stock Exchanges in 1999.

Two-Way Security

A security, usually a **debenture** or **preferred** share, which is **convertible** into or exchangeable for another security (usually common shares) of the same company. Also indirectly refers to the possibility of profiting in the future from upward movements in the underlying common shares as well as receiving in the interim interest or dividend payments.

Underlying Security

The security upon which a derivative contract, such as an option, is based. For example, the ABC June 35 call options are based on the underlying security ABC.

Underwriting

The purchase for resale of a security issue by one or more investment dealers or underwriters. The formal agreements pertaining to such a transaction are called underwriting agreements.

Unemployment Rate

The percentage of the work force that is looking for work but unable to find jobs.

Unified Managed Account

A type of fee-based account that includes the same benefits as **multi-disciplinary accounts**. Enhancements include performance reports from the respective sub-advisors, outlining distinct models contained within the single custody account.

Unit

Two or more corporate securities (such as **preferred** shares and **warrants**) offered for sale to the public at a single, combined price.

Unit Value

The value of one unit of a **segregated fund**. The units have no legal status, and are simply an administrative convenience used to determine the income attributable to contract holders and the level of benefits payable to beneficiaries.

Universal Market Integrity Rules (UMIR)

A common set of trading rules that are applied in all markets in Canada. UMIR are designed to promote fair and orderly markets.

Unlisted

A security not listed on a stock exchange but traded on the **over-the-counter** market.

Unlisted Market

See also **dealer market**.

Valuation Day

The day on which the assets of a **segregated fund** are valued, based on its total assets less liabilities. Most funds are valued at the end of every business day.

Value Manager

A manager that takes a research intensive approach to finding undervalued securities.

Value Ratios

Financial ratios that show the investor the worth of the company's shares or the return on owning them.

Variable Rate Preferreds

A type of preferred share that pays dividends in amounts that fluctuate to reflect changes in interest rates. If interest rates rise, so will dividend payments, and vice versa.

Variance

Another measure of **risk** often used interchangeably with volatility. The greater the variance of possible outcomes the greater the risk.

Vested

The employee's right to the employer contributions made on his or her behalf during the employee's period of enrollment.

Volatility

A measure of the amount of change in the daily price of a security over a specified period of time. Usually given as the standard deviation of the daily price changes of that security on an annual basis.

Voting Right

The stockholder's right to vote in the affairs of the company. Most **common** shares have one vote each. **Preferred** stock usually has the right to vote only when its **dividends** are in **arrears**. The right to vote may be delegated by the shareholder to another person. See also **Proxy**.

Voting Trust

An arrangement to place the control of a company in the hands of certain managers for a given period of time, or until certain results have been achieved, by shareholders surrendering their voting rights to a trustee for a specified period of time.

Waiting Period

The period of time between the issuance of a receipt for a preliminary prospectus and receipt for a final prospectus from the securities administrators.

Warrant

A certificate giving the holder the right to purchase securities at a stipulated price within a specified time limit. Warrants are usually issued with a new issue of securities as an inducement or sweetener to investors to buy the new issue.

Working Capital

Current assets minus **current liabilities**. This figure is an indication of the company's ability to meet its short-term debts.

Working Capital Ratio

Current assets of a company divided by its **current liabilities**.

Wrap Account

Also known as a wrap fee program. A type of fully discretionary account where a single annual fee, based on the account's total assets, is charged, instead of commissions and advice and service charges being levied separately for each transaction. The account is then managed separately from all other wrap accounts, but is kept consistent with a model portfolio suitable to clients with similar objectives.

Writer

The seller of either a **call** or **put option**. The option writer receives payment, called a premium. The writer in then obligated to buy (in the case of a put) or sell (in the case of a call) the underlying security at a specified price, within a certain period of time, if called upon to do so.

Yield – Bond & Stock

Return on an investment. A stock yield is calculated by expressing the annual dividend as a percentage of the stock's current market price. A bond yield is more complicated, involving annual interest payments plus amortizing the difference between its current market price and par value over the bond's life. See also **Current Yield**.

Yield Curve

A graph showing the relationship between yields of bonds of the same quality but different **maturities**. A normal yield curve is upward sloping depicting the fact that short-term money usually has a lower yield than longer-term funds. When short-term funds are more expensive than longer term funds the yield curve is said to be inverted.

Yield to Maturity

The rate of return investors would receive if they purchased a **bond** today and held it to **maturity**. Yield to maturity is considered a long term bond yield expressed as an annual rate.

Yield Spread

The difference between the yields on two debt securities, normally expressed in basis points. In general, the greater the difference in the risk of the two securities, the larger the spread.

Zero Coupon Bonds

See **Strip Bonds**.

Selected Web Sites

If you are connected to the Internet, you have access to all kinds of financial information. This list is far from complete. Many of these sites will have links to other related sites. Remember to type the site "address" exactly as listed. Some sites track usage by asking you for a password. Do not confuse the need to register and provide a password with the necessity to become a subscriber. Some sites offer a limited amount of information for free and require you to register and pay a fee before you can access more detailed information.

BANKING

Canadian Bankers Association: *www.cba.ca*

GOVERNMENT SOURCES

Bank of Canada: *www.bankofcanada.ca* or *www.banqueducanada.ca*

Canada Revenue Agency: *www.cra-arc.gc.ca*

Financial Industry Regulatory Authority: *www.finra.org*

Industry Canada: *www.ic.gc.ca*

Office of the Superintendent of Financial Institutions: *www.osfi-bsif.gc.ca*

Statistics Canada: *www.statcan.gc.ca*

U.S. Securities and Exchange Commission: *www.sec.gov*

HEDGE FUNDS

Canadian Hedge Fund Watch: *www.canadianhedgewatch.com*

Dow Jones Credit Suisse Hedge Fund Index: *www.hedgeindex.com*

Greenwich Alternative Investments: *www.greenwichai.com*

Hedge Fund Association: *www.thehfa.org*

Hedge Fund Centre: *www.hedgefundcenter.com*

HedgeFund Intelligence: *www.hedgefundintelligence.com*

INSURANCE

Financial Advisors Association of Canada (ADVOCIS): *www.advocis.ca*

Insurance Canada: *www.insurance-canada.ca*

INVESTMENT ORGANIZATIONS

Canadian Deposit Insurance Corporation: *www.cdic.ca*

Canadian Derivatives Clearing Corporation: *www.cdcc.ca*

Canadian Investor Protection Fund (CIPF): *www.cipf.ca*

Canadian Securities Institute: *www.csi.ca*

Canadian Society of Technical Analysts: *www.csta.org*

CDS Clearing and Depository Services Inc: *www.cds.ca*

EDGAR: *www.edgr.com*

International Organization of Securities Commissions: *www.iosco.org*

Investment Industry Regulatory Organization of Canada: *www.iiroc.ca*

Mutual Fund Dealers Association of Canada: *www.mfda.ca*

North American Securities Administrators Association: *www.nasaa.org*

System for Electronic Document Analysis and Retrieval: *www.sedar.com*

World Federation of Exchanges: *www.world-exchanges.org*

INVESTOR SERVICES

Advice for Investors: *www.adviceforinvestors.com*

BigCharts: *www.bigcharts.com*

Globeinvestor: *www.theglobeandmail.com/globe-investor*

Investorwords: *www.investorwords.com*

Investopedia: *www.investopedia.com*

iShares: *http://ca.ishares.com/home.htm*

Quicken Financial Network: *www.quicken.ca*

Stockhouse: *www.stockhouse.ca*

Yahoo Finance: *http://ca.finance.yahoo.com/*

MUTUAL FUNDS

Fund Library: *www.fundlibrary.com*

Globe Investor - Funds: *www.globefund.com*

Investment Funds Institute of Canada: *www.ific.ca*

NEWS ORGANIZATIONS AND PUBLICATIONS

Canada Newswire: *www.newswire.ca*

Canoe (Canadian Online Explorer): *www.canoe.ca*

Financial Post: *www.financialpost.com*

Globe and Mail: *www.theglobeandmail.com*

Moneysense: *www.moneysense.ca*

PROVINCIAL SECURITIES ADMINISTRATORS

Alberta: *www.albertasecurities.com*

British Columbia: *www.bcsc.bc.ca*

Manitoba: *www.msc.gov.mb.ca*

Ontario: *www.osc.gov.on.ca*

Québec: *www.lautorite.qc.ca*

New Brunswick: *www.nbsc-cvmnb.ca/nbsc*

Newfoundland and Labrador: *www.gs.gov.nl.ca*

Northwest Territories: *www.justice.gov.nt.ca/securitiesregistry*

Nova Scotia: *www.gov.ns.ca/nssc*

Prince Edward Island: *www.gov.pe.ca/securities*

Saskatchewan: *www.sfsc.gov.sk.ca*

Territory of Nunavut: *www.gov.nu.ca*

Yukon: *www.community.gov.yk.ca/corp/securities_about.html*

STOCK EXCHANGES

CBOE: *www.cboe.com*

CNSX: *www.cnsx.ca*

Bourse de Montréal: *www.m-x.ca*

Ice Futures Canada: *www.theice.com/futures_canada.jhtml*

Nasdaq: *www.nasdaq.com*

New York Stock Exchange: *www.nyse.com*

NYSE Euronext: *http://usequities.nyx.com/*

Toronto Stock Exchange: *www.tmx.com*

TSX Venture Exchange: *www.tmx.com*

TAXATION

Canada Revenue Agency: *www.cra-arc.gc.ca*

Canadian Tax Foundation: *www.ctf.ca*

Ernst & Young (Canada): *www.ey.com*

KPMG: *www.kpmg.ca*

PricewaterhouseCoopers: *www.pwc.com*

Index

Index

Income trusts, 22•6 to 22•7
  business trusts, 22•5, 22•8 to 22•9
  real estate investment trusts (REITs), 22•7
  taxation, 22•8 to 22•9
  two primary categories, 22•7
Incorporation, 11•6 to 11•10
  advantages and disadvantages, 11•7 to 11•8
  jurisdiction, 11•8
  procedure, 11•6 to 11•10
Index funds, 19•9 to 19•10
  hedge funds, 21•8
  mutual fund management style, 19•12
  portfolio management style, 16•12
Index-linked GICs, 24•10 to 24•12
Index-linked notes, 6•8
Indirect investment, 1•5
Individual variable insurance contract (IVIC), 20•5
Industry analysis, 13•11 to 13•16
  competitive forces, 13•14
  product or service, 13•11 to 13•12
  stage of growth, 13•13 to 13•14
  stock characteristics, 13•14 to 13•16
Industry rotation, 16•14 to 16•15
Inflation, 4•25 to 4•28, 13•7 to 13•9, 13•10 to 13•11, 13•17
  causes, 4•28
  costs, 4•27 to 4•28
  differentials, 4•33
  impact, 13•10 to 13•11
  real interest rate, and, 4•25
  real rate of return, and, 7•15 to 7•16
  risk, 15•10
Information circular, 11•10
Initial public offering (IPO), 11•13, 11•21, 11•27 to 11•28
Insider reporting, 3•25
Insider trading, 3•24 to 3•25
Insiders, defined, 3•24
Instalment debentures, 1•8, 6•20
  corporate treasuries, 27•4
  definition, 1•8
  endowments, 27•5
  hedge funds, 27•5
  insurance companies, 27•4
  mutual funds, 27•5
  pension funds, 27•5
  suitability standards, 27•7
  trusts, 27•6
Institutional salesperson, 27•8

Institutional securities firms, 2•7 to 2•8
Institutional traders, 27•8
Insurance Companies Act (Canada), 2•15
Insurance industry, 2•14 to 2•16
  life insurance companies, 2•14 to 2•15
  products and services, 2•15
  property and casualty insurance, 2•14 to 2•15
  regulation, 2•15 to 2•16
Intangible assets, 12•8 to 12•9
Integrated asset allocation, 16•22
Integrated firms, 2•7
Interest coverage ratios, 14•17 to 14•18
Interest rate, 4•23 to 4•25
  bond prices and, 7•19 to 7•20
  differentials, 4•33
  effect on economy, 4•24
  expectations, 4•24 to 4•25
  factors, 4•23 to 4•24
  nominal and real, 4•24 to 4•25
  term structure, 7•15 to 7•16
Interest rate anticipation, 16•16
Interest rate risk, 15•10
International Financial Reporting Standards (IFRS), 12•8, 12•11, 12•19
Interval funds, 22•5
In-the-money, 10•18
  of options, 10•18
  of rights, 10•37 to 10•38
  of warrants, 10•39 to 10•40
Inventories, 12•9
Inventory turnover ratio, 14•20 to 14•21
Investigations, 3•21
Investment advisors (IAs), 1•11, 3•14
  registration and training, 3•14 to 3•15
Investment banker, 27•9
Investment constraints, 15•22 to 15•23
  legal, 15•23
  liquidity, 15•22
  tax requirements, 15•22
  time horizon, 15•22
  unique circumstances, 15•23
Investment dealers, 2•7
Investment funds, 1•9,
Investment Funds Standards Committee (IFSC), 19•5
Investment Industry Association of Canada (IIAC), 3•9

Investment Industry Regulatory Organization of Canada (IIROC), 1•17, 13•8 to 3•9, 3•15
Investment objectives, 15•20 to 15•22
  growth of capital, 15•21
  income, 15•20 to 15•21
  marketability, 15•21
  overview of portfolio management, 15•17
  portfolio risk and return, 15•18 to 15•23
  safety of principal, 15•20
  tax minimization, 15•20
Investment policy statement, 15•23
Investment representatives (IRs), 3•15
Investments in associates, 12•9, 12•23
Investors' rights, 3•21 to 3•22
Irrevocable designation of beneficiary, 20•6
Issued shares, 11•17

J

Jones, Alfred, 21•7

K

Keynes, John Maynard, 5•5
Keynesian economics, 5•5
Know your client, 3•16
Krugman, Paul, 26•14

L

Labour force, 4•20
Labour Force Survey, 4•20
Labour market in Canada, 4•22
  participation rate, 4•20
  unemployment rate, 4•20 to 4•23
Labour-sponsored venture capital corporation (LSVCC), 18•17 to 18•18
  advantages, 18•17 to 18•18
  disadvantages, 18•18
Laddering, 16•6
Lagging indicators, 4•18
Large Value Transfer System (LVTS), 5•16
Laws of Demand and Supply, 4•7